THE NETHERLANDS

THE NETHERLANDS

Negotiating Sovereignty in an Interdependent World

THOMAS R. ROCHON

School of Politics and Economics
Claremont Graduate University

Westview Press
A Member of the Perseus Books Group

Map 8.1:
Oostindie and Passman, Dutch Attitudes Toward Colonial Empires, Indigenous Cultures, and Slaves. *Eighteenth Century Studies*, volume 31, Spring 1998. © American Society for Eighteenth-Century Studies. Reprinted by permission of the Johns Hopkins University Press.

Nations of the Modern World: Europe

Copyright © 1999 by Westview Press, A Member of the Perseus Books Group

Find us on the World Wide Web at www.westviewpress.com

Published in 1999 in the United States of America by Westview Press, 5500 Central Avenue, Boulder, Colorado 80301-2877, and in the United Kingdom by Westview Press, 12 Hid's Copse Road, Cumnor Hill, Oxford OX2 9JJ

Library of Congress Cataloging-in-Publication Data
Rochon, Thomas R., 1952–
  The Netherlands: negotiating sovereignty in an interdependent
world / Thomas R. Rochon.
     p.   cm.—(Nations of the modern world.   Europe)
  Includes bibliographical references and index.
  ISBN 0-8133-2880-2 (hc)
  1. State. The.   2. Sovereignty.   3. Netherlands—Politics and
government—1945-   4. Netherlands—Foreign relations—1948-
5. Democracy—Netherlands.   6. Political culture—Netherland.
I. Title.   II. Series.
JC259.R63   1999
320.1'5'09492—dc21   99-21633
                                                                                          CIP

The paper used in this publication meets the requirements of the American National Standard for Permanence of Paper for Printed Library Materials Z39.48-1984.

10   9   8   7   6   5   4   3   2

For Rudy Andeweg, Cees van der Eijk, Galen Irwin,
André Mommen, and Patrice Visser:
Models of academic colleagueship

Contents

4   POLITICAL PARTIES
AND ELECTORAL CHANGE   68

5   THE INSTITUTIONS OF
DUTCH DEMOCRACY   109

6   THE POLICY PROCESS   155

7   THE WELFARE STATE   189

**8   SMALL COUNTRY IN
           A WORLD MARKET   231**

**9   NEGOTIATING SOVEREIGNTY IN AN
          INTERDEPENDENT WORLD   272**

Tables and Figures

Tables

Figures

The Kingdom of the Netherlands

Holland, ge biedt geen ruimte als aan den geest
Holland, the only room you offer is for the spirit
—Henriette Roland Holst

Acknowledgments

I thought that I knew a lot about Dutch politics and society when I began this project. But I soon learned that there is a world of difference between competence in a specific area of research and being able to write a wide-ranging text on the evolution of political institutions and processes. As a work of synthesis, this book owes even more than the usual intellectual debt to those whose patient sifting of documents and analysis of data have generated the body of research on which I have relied. I want to thank first and foremost those scholars whose research is cited in the notes and reference list. This book is possible only because of their work.

I would like to single out for special thanks the compilers of the *InterNetKrant* (e-mail address: ink@splinter.moffitt.usf.edu), a daily Dutch news summary that is put together by six volunteers (one for each day newspapers are published in the Netherlands) and e-mailed to subscribing readers around the world. The Internet has transformed the extent to which one can keep up with events in a given country without ever leaving one's office or home. It is easy to lose sight of the fact, though, that the utility of the Internet relies in no small degree on the compilers of *InterNetKrant:* Jack Spaapen, Huib Zeegers, Ale de Boer, Sjaak Paridaens, Jack Raats, and Theo Vroon.

The most moving words in this book are not mine, but rather those of the poets and printers whose clandestine work during World War II is cited in Chapter 3. I owe a special debt of gratitude to Sigrid Perry and the Special Collections staff of the Northwestern University Library for bringing this work to my attention.

I benefited enormously from careful readings of the manuscript in draft form by Bob Cox, Paulette Kurzer, Arend Lijphart, and Dietlind Stolle, all of whom made suggestions that proved to be valuable in preparing the final version. André Mommen was a particularly rigorous reader who saved me from a number of errors of fact and interpretation. If André ever tired of arriving at work to find yet another question from me in his e-mail, he never showed it.

Cees van der Eijk gave me key insights into elections and the party system at the moments when it counted most: just as I was starting the project and just as I was finishing it. Cees and his colleagues on the 1998 Dutch Parliamentary

Election Study were also extraordinarily generous in allowing me early access to the most recent Dutch Parliamentary Election Study.

Portions of Chapters 3 and 4 were previously published as a chapter in *Parties and Party Systems: Essays in Honor of Samuel J. Eldersveld* (Ann Arbor: University of Michigan Press, 1999), edited by Birol Yeşilada. I thank both Birol and Sam Eldersveld for their comments on that earlier incarnation of my analysis of change in the Dutch party system.

This is the third preface in which I have had the privilege of thanking a remarkable research assistant, Jason Abbott. For this book even more than for the others, our collaboration became a contest between my ability to ask for obscure information and Jason's ability to find it. Jason always won. Thanks, Jason, for sticking with me.

I first learned of the openness and generosity of the Dutch political science community as an apprehensive graduate student preparing to do dissertation research in a country I had never before visited. In the twenty years since then, I have relied extensively on friends in the country whose attention to Dutch politics has been more consistent than my own. These scholars have been particularly generous in sharing with me their knowledge and their hospitality. I dedicate this book to them.

Data Sources

The data presented in various parts of this book draw upon twelve studies of the Dutch electorate in election years between 1956 and 1998, as well as upon the Eurobarometer series of twice-yearly studies. See Cees van der Eijk and Kees Niemöller (1994) for an account of the history and content of studies of the Dutch electorate.

Data for 1956 are from a survey executed by the Nederlandse Instituut voor Publieke Opinie (NIPO) and reported in their book *De Nederlandse kiezer.* 1967 data come from a survey by the Sociaal-Wetenschappelijk Instituut of the Free University of Amsterdam. Data for 1968 are reported in Lijphart (1974). Data for 1970, 1971, and 1972–1973 are from the Dutch Election Study, 1970–1973, for which the principal investigators are Felix Heunks, M. Kent Jennings, Warren Miller, Philip Stouthard, and Jacques Thomassen. Additional 1971 data come from the 1971 Dutch Parliamentary Election Study, with principal investigators Robert Mokken and Frans Roschar. The 1977 Dutch Parliamentary Election Study was conducted by Galen Irwin, Jan Verhoef, and Caspar Wiebrens; the 1981 Dutch Parliamentary Election Study by C. van der Eijk, B. Niemöller, and A.Th.J. Eggen; the 1982 Dutch Parliamentary Election Study by C. van der Eijk, M. J. Koopman, and B. Niemöller; the 1986 Dutch Parliamentary Election Study by C. van der Eijk, G. A. Irwin, and B. Niemöller; the 1989 Dutch Parliamentary Election Study by H. Anker and E. V. Oppenhuis; the 1994 Dutch Parliamentary Election Study by H. Anker and E. V. Oppenhuis; and the 1998 Dutch Parliamentary Election Study by Kees Aarts and Henk van der Kolk.

Beginning in 1970, each of the Dutch Parliamentary Election Studies was carried out by means of personal interviews, and all were based on multistage probability samples. Data from these studies are available from the Steinmetz Archive in Amsterdam and the Inter-University Consortium for Political and Social Research (ICPSR) in Ann Arbor, except for the 1977 Dutch Parliamentary Election Study, which is available only from the Steinmetz Archive.

Figure 4.6 is based on the Eurobarometer survey series from 1973 to 1992. The Eurobarometers are sponsored by the Commission of the European Union, and are available through the ICPSR.

The principal investigators, the ICPSR, and the Steinmetz Archive bear no responsibility for the use of the data in this book.

1

THE NETHERLANDS IN AN INTERDEPENDENT WORLD

"God made the earth, but the Dutch made the Netherlands." So goes the phrase that captures as well as any one phrase can the Dutch attitude toward their country. This saying summarizes not only the status of a coastal lowland on the front lines of the giant forces of nature, but also the Dutch sense of being wedged between the larger, more powerful states of Europe. The crest of the province Zeeland depicts a lion rampant standing above the waves. It bears the motto "I fight and emerge." Notice that the motto is not "I emerge and fight." The Netherlands had to fight to emerge as an independent and prosperous nation.

The Dutch struggle for existence has been a two-front war. One front in the war is the battle to hold the sea out of a country much of whose land area consists of the delta plains of three large rivers: the Rhine, the Maas, and the Schelde. More than half the country lies below sea level, necessitating the system of dikes and pumps (traditionally powered by windmills) for which the country is famous.

It was not a promising place to have settled a nation. Apart from its fisheries, some coal deposits, and natural gas fields that were not discovered until the 1950s, the country is virtually without ores and other natural resources. Despite the fame of agricultural exports such as cheeses, meats, beer, and flowers, the natural quality of the soil is uneven. Thomas Jefferson took a tour through the Netherlands in March 1788 on his way to serve as U.S. ambassador to France. As Jefferson (1984: 633) noted in his journal:

1

The lower parts of the low countries seem partly to have been gained from the sea, and partly to be made up of the plains of the Yssel, the Rhine, the Maese [Maas], and the Schelde [Rivers] united. [Until you reach the city of] Utrecht nothing but plains are seen, a rich black mould, wet, lower than the level of the waters which intersect it; almost entirely in grass; few or no farm-houses, as the business of grazing requires few laborers. . . . The plains, after passing Utrecht, become more sandy; the hills are very poor and sandy, generally waste in broom, sometimes a little corn.

If the American character has been shaped by the occupancy of a sparsely settled continent with seemingly limitless expanses of fertile land and other natural resources, the Dutch character has been formed by the experience of a large population crowded into a limited space, whose best soil lies at the bottom of marshes and lake beds, and which is always subject to threat of flooding from the sea. When prosperity came to the Netherlands in the seventeenth century, foreign observers and the Dutch themselves were amazed. "That beats the Dutch" became a standard expression in England when someone saw an unlikely event.

The second front in the Dutch struggle for survival has been its rivalry with larger European neighbors. For much of the country's existence since its rebellion from the Burgundian-Hapsburg Empire in 1568, the Netherlands has had to defend itself against Spain, England, and France. The country's wealth and domination of important trade routes, its espousal of republican government on a continent of monarchs, and anti-Catholic views of the Dutch Reformed Church set the Dutch provinces against the larger European powers in the seventeenth century. At the same time, the Dutch were developing a trade network that linked the European economies to each other and brought to these countries rare and precious goods from the rest of the world. Rivalry and partnership went hand in hand in Dutch relations with the larger European states.

As a founding member of the European Union, the Netherlands continues to develop ever closer economic and political ties with its larger neighbors, while seeking also to maintain a distinctive social and cultural presence. The issues and institutions of interstate relations have changed since the founding of the country over four hundred years ago, but the underlying dilemmas facing the Netherlands have not. Andries Hoogerwerf (1993: 21), in an introduction to Dutch politics written for a Dutch audience, states matter-of-factly, "We are strongly dependent on developments with our trading partners and on the world market. We experience the political and economic influences of the United States, East Europe, Japan and the Third World. We feel the influence of policies determined in the European Community, NATO, the United Nations and multi-national corporations." In short, we may take it as a point of departure that prosperity and security in the Netherlands are dependent on developments in other countries and in international organizations. The Dutch themselves are acutely aware of this fact.

The specific tribulations of any country are a unique product of its location, characteristics, and history. But Dutch struggles for sovereignty and prosperity are of increasing relevance elsewhere. For much of its history, the Netherlands faced distinctive problems as a small nation. In today's world, however, there is a real sense in which all countries are small.

National leaders and ordinary citizens everywhere face the problems and opportunities created by a shrinking world. In the economy, the most important issues are preservation of national industries and jobs despite increased capital mobility and international economic competition. Culturally, the challenge is to maintain national traditions in the face of powerful homogenizing forces. Politically, the challenge is to maintain the autonomy of choice that has traditionally been associated with national sovereignty. The ability to elect one's leaders democratically means nothing if key decisions are being made in Brussels, Berlin, or Washington, D.C.

The Netherlands faces these issues just as other European countries do. It is perhaps true that the Netherlands faces these issues more intensively than the larger European countries, because its smallness makes it more vulnerable to international forces. It is important not to exaggerate how small the Netherlands is, for its population is easily the largest of the eleven smaller West European democracies.[1] And yet, the concentration of economic, cultural, and political power in the contemporary world is such that the differences between large and small European countries are becoming less and less relevant. The important difference between the Netherlands and larger countries is that the Netherlands has been trying for more than four hundred years to maneuver in an international system it has not been able to control. The Dutch have spent four centuries testing the winds and trimming their sails in response to international currents. These are skills that larger countries have just in the last generation been forced to develop. What lessons have the Dutch learned along the way that might be applied elsewhere in Europe, not to mention in the United States? The Dutch national experience offers in concentrated form a kind of laboratory for strategies of adaptation to a world of interdependence and rapid change, in which no one country has the resources to control its environment by brute force. An examination of three aspects of the Dutch experience yields notable insights.

First, the Netherlands is a trading society that was the preeminent commercial empire of the seventeenth century, creating what Simon Schama (1988) has called "an embarrassment of riches." Its wealth made it a rival of the other European powers, France and Britain. But a small population and land area ultimately left the country unable to compete with these larger European powers. The question that the Britons and the French were forced to ask themselves in the middle of the twentieth century, and the question that many Americans ask themselves today, is: "What is the role of my country in a world of numerous powers, when the expense of a global military reach is too great for any one country to bear?" The Dutch response to this question has been to adopt a policy of internationalism and multilateralism.

Second, the Netherlands has been from its inception a divided society. Its political institutions were created to help mediate between religious communities and economic classes whose mutual antagonisms seemed at times to make internal strife a possibility.[2] More recently, the post–World War II experience of decolonization has forced the country to absorb unprecedented numbers of immigrants, and has made the Netherlands into a multiethnic society. These experiences have taught Dutch leaders the benefits of policymaking by inclusive bargaining, a process that Arend Lijphart (1975) calls "the politics of accommodation."

The third aspect of the Dutch experience that illuminates more general societal and political issues concerns the country's response to increasing prosperity in the decades after World War II. As the country became wealthy beyond anything dreamed of in the "Golden Century" (1620 to 1720), the Dutch developed a plan for a new kind of society in which poverty would be eliminated and all citizens would have an opportunity to develop fully their skills and interests. Although the welfare state has been a general phenomenon of the last half of the twentieth century, in the Netherlands the concept was advanced to a degree found elsewhere only in Scandinavia. The Dutch welfare state was famed for such innovations as the concept of not only providing all citizens with the necessities of life, but also making full participation in society a right of citizenship. This translated into such programs as theater tickets for the unemployed and the public support of artists.

On this front too the Netherlands—like other countries—has been forced to adjust to an era of slower growth and intense international economic competition. The taxes and labor costs associated with the welfare state have been increasingly questioned. High rates of unemployment and an aging population made social assistance more expensive than its founders ever imagined. Benefits paid to the unemployed, the sick, and the aged were scaled back, and some programs (like the artist support program) were eliminated. This experience has brought home once again a central lesson of Dutch history: Pragmatism and flexibility are requisite for survival in a changing environment.

Internationalism, multilateralism, inclusive bargaining, pragmatism, and flexibility are perspectives that the Dutch have applied over and over to problems including protecting their land from the sea, integrating new groups into the polity, and surviving and prospering as a small country wedged between larger neighbors. This survey of contemporary society and politics in the Netherlands will focus on areas in which the Dutch experience is illustrative of issues and dilemmas facing all advanced industrial democracies. The three aspects of the Dutch experience discussed above translate into challenges that are particularly emblematic of those facing modern states generally: the maintenance of prosperity in an increasingly integrated and competitive world economy; the maintenance of domestic peace in the face of religious, class, and ethnic divisions; and the achievement of justice in a society without material want. As we shall see, the Dutch have developed distinctive responses to each of these challenges. In this book, we will examine three centuries of Dutch efforts to cope with interdependence, keeping in mind always the lessons that the Dutch laboratory holds for the rulers and the peoples of other advanced industrial democracies.

NOTES

1. These include the five Nordic countries along with Austria, Belgium, Ireland, Luxembourg, and Switzerland.

2. See Chapter 3 on the religious and class cleavages that have long split the Dutch and that at times put the nation seemingly on the verge of violence.

2

THE SETTING OF DUTCH POLITICS: PHYSICAL AND POLITICAL ORIGINS

In a book called *The Dutch and Their Dikes* published by the Ministry of Water Affairs in 1956, the history of Dutch water control is referred to as the "eighth day of creation," in which humans take over the job begun by God. There is no disrespect intended toward the Lord's work, but it does appear that the job of making the plains, deltas, and estuaries of the Low Countries fit for human habitation was left unfinished. Arriving around the time of the birth of Christ, Roman legions found a terrain of coastal sand dunes bordering the North Sea. Inland lay the swamps, lakes, and lowlands that were susceptible to periodic flooding. The soil was sandy and vegetation was sparse, suitable for grazing sheep and cows but not for raising crops. In documenting life in this remote outpost of the Roman Empire, the historian Pliny observed that

> the Ocean pours out over a vast stretch of land, at two intervals by day and by night, in a tidal wave so enormous that their eternal struggle in the course of nature makes one doubt whether the soil belongs to the land or to the sea. A miserable people lives there on high hills or on elevations, which they throw up with their own hands to a height which they know from experience to be that of the highest tide, and on these

6

spots they have built their huts. They are like seafarers when the water covers the surrounding land, like shipwrecked people when the waves have retreated.[1]

With the entire countryside lying at or barely above sea level, the first permanent inhabitants of the region built earthen mounds, known as *terpen,* on which they could live and to which their animals could retreat when the floodwaters came. Through the centuries these mounds grew in size, achieving up to forty acres in area and as much as twenty to thirty feet in height, as the people endeavored to withstand flood conditions (Rijkswaterstaat 1956: 25).

As intent as the Romans were on extending their empire, they found the Netherlands a bit intimidating. Bernard Vlekke (1943: 18) notes that "the dreary, damp land north of the rivers seemed wholly unsuitable for settlements even to the hardened veterans of the Roman legions." Although the Romans built fortifications along the Rhine and IJssel Rivers from which to launch expeditions into the Germanic territories, they abandoned the area toward the end of the third century when a flood broke through the coastal dunes and inundated the region. The Dutch themselves have proven, of necessity, to be more resilient.

There are actually two sources of threat from the water. To the west, storms in the North Sea may pound over the coastal dunes and overrun the estuaries created by the mouths of the major Dutch rivers. The threat of flooding from the east is hardly less grave, for these same rivers sometimes carry floodwaters from central Europe toward the sea. When high tides, swollen rivers, and onshore winds of hurricane force happen to coincide, the result is disaster.

To any Dutch person, the dates December 14, 1287, November 18, 1421, November 1, 1570, and February 1, 1953, are immediately recognizable as four in the long series of dates recording disastrous floods. Flooding in the northern part of the country in 1287 killed an estimated 50,000 people while transforming the northern marsh area into an open sea, the *Zuyderzee,* some of whose area was reclaimed as dry land only in the twentieth century. The most recent of the devastating floods, in 1953, was caused by a North Sea storm that inundated 360,000 acres in the southwestern part of the country, drowning 1,835 people and leaving 300,000 homeless. A generally sober history of dike-building by the Ministry of Water Affairs wrote of February 1, "In that horrible night, the dikes burst everywhere, everywhere, everywhere" (Rijkswaterstaat 1956: 140).

Although the system of defenses from floods is today substantially more sophisticated than the mounds built by the Frisians, the open sea and the rivers that flow through the Netherlands continue to represent both threat and opportunity. Foreigners have bucolic images of the Dutch landscape, with its canals, dikes, and windmills, but these intrinsic features are all means of protecting the population from flooding, of reclaiming rich pastureland from the lake beds that lie below sea level, of constructing waterways that connect major Dutch ports to the open sea and to the great rivers that flow from central Europe. The Dutch survive by holding back the sea, but they also prosper by living alongside it.

Although the institutions and character of a nation can never be explained solely in terms of its physical features, the main traits of the Dutch polity, including internationalism and cooperation, have indeed been more or less forced upon the country by its location and geophysical traits. The small area of the country and the lack of natural resources meant that economic development could proceed only by intensive trading with others. Proximity to the ocean and to inland rivers made that trade possible. The very origins of social and political organization in the Netherlands can be found in the history of building dikes, dams, and canals. During a period of no central authority in the area, between the fifth and eleventh centuries, dikes were built piecemeal. When threatened by flooding, inlanders were more likely to construct their own dikes than to help shore up more distant sea dikes. Efforts to channel water away from one area would often create new problems for those living in other areas. This lack of regional cooperation could be costly. When the sea wall in southwestern Friesland disappeared beneath the waves of a fourteenth-century storm, taking the town of Westbierum with it, inhabitants of inland towns suddenly found themselves on the new coastline and were forced to raise their own sea defenses.

The habit of cooperation in fighting the sea was learned over a long period of time, and sometimes painfully. One of the most bitter experiences occurred in the South Holland area known as the *Grote Waard*. Settlement began there in the eleventh century, initially on the highest patches of ground. Over the next two hundred years these first villages were connected by dikes, and by the year 1300 the entire 123,500-acre area (50,000 hectares) had been enclosed by dikes (Lambert 1971: 120). The protection of an area that not only faced the North Sea but also drained the Maas and Waal Rivers was at that time the greatest triumph of Dutch water engineering. But maintenance of the dikes was left to the owners of adjacent fields. This system was not only unfair (everyone in the region benefited, whether or not their land bordered the rivers), but it also created a pattern of uneven maintenance. If even one segment of a long dike was allowed to deteriorate, its failure to withstand a storm could open a breach that would flood the entire region.

Adding to the risk of flooding in the *Grote Waard* was the fact that an important part of the local economy depended on the manufacture of salt, obtained by digging water-soaked peat from the ground, burning it, and refining salt from its ashes. The easiest place to find peat was in the swampy areas just outside the dikes, and over time the extraction of peat adjacent to the dikes tended to undermine the ground on which they stood. Residents of the *Grote Waard* paid the price in the St. Elizabeth's Day flood of 1421, which swept away twenty villages and claimed 10,000 lives. So extensive was the flooding that much of the region remained underwater for centuries.

It took the development of more centralized authorities, such as the counts of Holland and the bishops of Utrecht, to coordinate efforts by consolidating local water control boards (known as *waterschappen*) into larger units. By the year 1300 these boards were assigning responsibility for upkeep of the dikes not simply to whoever owned the adjoining land, but proportionately to all landowners within the area protected by the dike. Dikes were thus declared a matter of the public interest and a tax system was put into place to maintain them. Beginning in the Middle Ages and continuing through all the vicissitudes of invasion and rule by Germanic tribes, Norsemen, and the Burgundians, the one constant in the political life of the Netherlands was continuity of the water control boards, whose task was the maintenance of the system of dikes and pumps. Members of the water control boards are still today elected by property owners, and their executive committees are appointed by the Crown. This ensures a mix of central direction and local control.

The technology, finances, and political authority necessary to undertake large projects of land reclamation came together beginning in the seventeenth century, enabling the conversion of swamps and shallow lakes into livable space. The great innovator in this field was Jan Adriaanszoon (1575–1650), who developed the system of creating polders, areas of dry land enclosed by a dike. By erecting a dike around a marsh or lake, water from within the dike could be pumped to a series of canals outside the dike. Adriaanszoon, known to his contemporaries by the nickname "Water Drainer" *("Leeghwater"),* traveled to France, England, Denmark, Prussia, and Flanders to demonstrate his techniques of land reclamation.

As steam pumps replaced windmills, and then later as electric pumps replaced steam engines, ever greater feats of moving water from one place to another became possible. Adriaanszoon had developed a plan in 1620 for draining the great inland lake known as the Haarlem Lake *(Haarlemmermeer),* but pumps powerful enough to accomplish his dream were not developed until 1852. In the greatest feat of all, the *Zuyderzee* was divided from the North Sea in 1932 by a nineteen-mile-long Barrier Dam *(Afsluitdijk).* This turned the *Zuyderzee* into a freshwater body, renamed Lake IJssel *(IJsselmeer).* Beginning in the late 1920s and continuing for the rest of the century, polders on Lake IJssel were enclosed and then drained. Former fishing ports have now become inland towns; on the Wieringer polder, cows wander among the remnants of shipwrecks as they graze on reclaimed meadow. Harry Mulisch, in his 1973 novel *Last Call,* writes of a storm sweeping across the landscape of a Lake IJssel polder:

> Where fifteen years ago fishes swam and the wrecks of ships stuck out of the sea bed, a youth now whisks past [on a motorcycle]. . . . At roof level, it would now have been rough weather on the Zuyder Zee, fishermen would have struck the mainsail and battened down the hatches, while in the villages along the shore their wives in fluttering black skirts would have stood at quayside in silence, a mumbled prayer on their lips. (Mulisch [1973] 1989: 13–14)

Even the largest Dutch cities, Amsterdam and Rotterdam, exist by virtue of Dutch water engineering. Rotterdam, the world's busiest cargo port, would not even have access to the North Sea were it not for the Rotterdam Waterway.[2]

Amsterdam, once called "the Venice of the North," is built on marshland. The city's buildings are supported by wooden piles driven thirteen to sixty feet into the ground. Amsterdam City Hall (now Royal Palace), completed in 1655, rests on 13,659 piles having an average length of forty feet. As Constantijn Huygens wrote:

> *Oh golden swamp with heaven's plenitude replete,*
> *Storehouse of East and West—all water and all street.*[3]

The significance of these projects in land reclamation and water control can hardly be overstated in a country where 60 percent of the population lives on land that would be submerged during high tides (not to mention seasonal flooding) were nature allowed to rule. From the year 1200 to the present, the Dutch have added 20 percent to the area of their country (7,000 square kilometers), just over one-third of which was created in the Lake IJssel project. The priority the Dutch attached to winning land from the sea is suggested by the fact that they spent more money draining land during the seventeenth century than the East India and West India Companies spent developing a global trade network.[4] God did make most of the Netherlands, but the Dutch have lent substantial assistance.

Development of a Political Identity

The local and regional traditions created by the need to cooperate in building sea defenses predate the development of a united political authority. Although the struggle against the sea is quite old, the Netherlands has existed within its present borders as a sovereign state for less than two hundred years. Prior to that time, the terms "Netherlands" or "Low Countries" were used to refer to the areas now encompassed by the Netherlands, Belgium, and Luxembourg. Politically, the region was not united under a single ruler until the late fourteenth century, when Philip the Fair, Duke of Burgundy, acquired the provinces of Holland, Zeeland, Brabant, and Limburg, as well as much of Belgium, through his marriage to Margaret of Male. Philip's successors on the Burgundian throne steadily added to their holdings, so that by the time of Charles V (1500–1555) the entire region was united under Burgundian rule with its capital in Brussels.

Unification under the Burgundians, however, did not end the importance of regional traditions, identities, and freedoms. Compared to much of feudal Europe, the Low Countries were marked by decentralized rule and a great dispersion of landownership. To induce peasants to undertake the work of constructing dikes, dams, and canals, landowners had to offer title to a portion of the land. With neither the Catholic Church nor the nobility able to accumulate large landholdings, the pattern of feudalism so prevalent elsewhere in Europe did not take root in the Low Countries. As Audrey Lambert (1971: 114) observes, "The distinction between servile and free, which long persisted as a feature of society elsewhere in Europe, disappeared in the marshes of the Netherlands at an early date."

The extent of feudal authority in the region was also reduced by the early growth of towns, whose middle-class residents did not accept rule by the Catholic bishops (Lucas 1929: 13–28). Painstaking study by Jan de Vries (1984) has demonstrated that the Low Countries were far more urbanized in the sixteenth and seventeenth centuries than their European neighbors. This was due primarily to the growth of manufacturing in the southern regions (present-day Belgium) and the growth of trade in the northern areas (present-day Netherlands).[5] By creating a basis of wealth independent of landownership, inhabitants of the towns were able to resist control by the Church and the rural nobility. Their wealth put them in a relatively strong bargaining position with any sovereign who sought to tax them. In contrast to the absolutist monarchs of France and England, the "Seventeen Provinces" of the Low Countries retained a great deal of autonomy from the dukes of Burgundy and from each other. Their wealth was made available for Burgundian wars of conquest in exchange for continued rights of consultation and for affirmation of the town and provincial charters in which local rights were spelled out. The "Privileges of 1477," for example, contained a clause permitting disobedience against a prince who would encroach upon the rights of a town. And the tradition of the "Joyous Entry" reserved for the towns the right of accepting a new prince only after he swore acceptance of the local charters. Strictly speaking, then, the Seventeen Provinces were not ruled by a hereditary monarch, but by a prince who earned his place through adherence to rules that the towns shaped and defended.

It was precisely this characteristic of Burgundian rule over the Low Countries that led to its demise. The Burgundian Empire reached the apex of its influence when Charles V was elected Holy Roman Emperor in 1519. This linked the Burgundian Empire to the Hapsburg Empire, a development of special importance to the Low Countries because it opened up trade with peoples of the Iberian peninsula and the lands bordering the Mediterranean (Lambert 1971: 181). But it also inaugurated a period of increasing tensions between the Seventeen Provinces and Burgundian rulers who sought to centralize their growing empire.

These tensions grew to the breaking point after the 1555 abdication of Charles V in favor of his son, Philip II. Desirous of emulating the kings of France and England, Philip moved his court to Madrid and ruled the Hapsburg Empire in the fashion of an absolute monarch. Integrating the Seventeen Provinces into the Spanish Hapsburg Empire would require a substantial reduction of the autonomy of the towns, and particularly the introduction of a system of regular taxation that would yield an income independent of the political demands of the town leaders. As the wealthiest part of the empire, the Seventeen Provinces already contributed large amounts to the royal treasury. Customs duties and fees from Dutch shipping brought four times as much revenue to the Spanish treasury as the annual plunder of silver brought from the New World (Lambert 1971: 187). But centralization and expansion of the state as envisaged by Philip II would require still greater sums.

The wealthy merchants (known as regents) who controlled the leading Dutch towns were not favorably inclined to absolutist rule by a king who spoke no Dutch and was surrounded by Spanish advisers. The issue was not only taxation but also political and religious autonomy. There was growing Calvinist sentiment in the northern Netherlands, and it was increasingly clear that religious pluralism was not part of Philip's design for a Catholic kingdom.

The conflict between Catholic forces of centralization and Protestant forces of local autonomy did not take long to boil over into open revolt. Philip's representatives in the Seventeen Provinces were the stadholders, whom he named to govern in cooperation with the regents of the leading towns. The charge given to each stadholder was to guard the rights and lordship of Philip II, to seek the welfare of the territories, to appoint officers to the judiciary and to enforce the sentences of the courts, to appoint mayors and members of town councils, and when needed to call together representatives of the towns and the nobility in a Council of State (Rowen 1988: 4). Because of their length of tenure in office, and because of the power of the local regents, stadholders generally became less the agents of central control than brokers searching for consensus between the interests of the Crown and those of the towns and provinces.

Determined to assert greater control over the region, Philip II in 1559 appointed his half sister, Margaret of Parma, to the new post of governor-general over the whole of the Seventeen Provinces. Believing further that the provinces could be molded into a great kingdom only if united in faith, Philip also appointed Cardinal Granvelle to be Margaret's chief adviser on political and religious affairs. Their first act was to reorganize the Catholic Church in the provinces in a way that would put more resources under control of the bishops and less under control of the local nobles and merchants. This resulted in 1564 in a "nobles' strike," led by William of Orange, Philip's stadholder for the provinces of Holland, Zeeland, and Utrecht. The provincial nobility refused to attend meetings of the Council of State until Granvelle was recalled to Spain.

This first act of disobedience, though intended for limited aims and never linked to claims for independence, nonetheless played an important part in developing among the provincial nobles an awareness of being united by common interests against the demands of a distant sovereign. Success in getting Granvelle recalled to Madrid only furthered the sense that the towns should cooperate to advance their common interests. The nobles' strike, however, also heightened Philip's determination to assert greater control over the region. As pressure for conformity to the Catholic faith increased, the Dutch public took matters in their own hands in 1566 by starting a wave of attacks on Catholic churches. Provincial officials stood by as mobs destroyed stained glass, statues, paintings, and church treasures. Margaret of Parma ordered the stadholders to restore order by force. The stadholders, with William of Orange again in the lead, chose instead to negotiate with leading Calvinist preachers, ultimately reaching a compromise under which Calvinists would be allowed to continue their open-air preaching in exchange for an end to violence in the Catholic churches. Although the compromise left the Catholic Church in its dominant position, it also opened up the opportunity for Calvinism to expand its influence through the development of "hedge preaching."

This compromise was unacceptable to Philip II's vision of a religiously unified kingdom. Repudiating the agreement reached by his stadholders, Philip sent the Duke of Alva in August 1567 to reassert by military means both Catholic orthodoxy and his own authority. Several thousand people were executed in the following year for participation in the iconoclastic riots. Moreover, Alva determined to assert supremacy of the central government by introducing new taxes without the customary consultation and consent of the Council of State.[6] The challenge to the traditional autonomy of the provinces was clear.

Forceful repression of Calvinism and unilateral imposition of new taxes led ultimately to the break between the Netherlands and King Philip. William of Orange again took the lead by leaving his stadholdership to return to his ancestral domain in Nassau, then a county in present-day Germany, where he hired an army to fight the Duke of Alva. The wealthy merchants of the towns also united behind the desire to reassert local control. The popularity of Calvinist belief among the general public gave a mass base to what would otherwise have been a squabble among central and local rulers. William of Orange may have been the only person who could lead such a coalition of city and countryside, elites and masses. Of the nobility himself, William had always been solicitous of the interests of the urban regent class when he was stadholder of Holland, Zeeland, and Utrecht. William's conversion from Catholicism to Calvinism cemented his unique standing within the coalition of rebels.[7]

The nobles, merchants, and Calvinists among the common people did not have many interests in common, but their shared antipathy to Spanish rule gave the revolt its program. The central demands of the coalition were that Philip II respect existing town charters and privileges and that religious practice be a matter of local choice.[8] As William of Orange put it in 1568, when the war against Spain was just beginning, "The privileges [of the towns and estates] are not free grants of the sovereign to his subjects, but form contracts binding both prince and people."[9] These words articulated a new and radical creed in a Europe dominated by absolutist monarchs. They anticipate by nearly a century the social contract theory of Jean-Jacques Rousseau, in which the powers of government are seen as rooted in a voluntary and revocable grant from the people. Although no leaders of the Dutch revolt advocated anything like the mass democracy we know today, they were nonetheless in the forefront of the thinking of their day on the responsibility of government to seek consent for its policies.

The Eighty Years War

Opponents of King Philip II had little reason to be optimistic about their chances of success in war against Spain. Not only were his military forces far superior both on land and at sea, but the Seventeen Provinces were at odds with each other. Only seven of the seventeen joined the revolt, largely in the northern regions that today comprise the Netherlands. Traditions of local autonomy ran so deep that there was dissension even within provinces. Most of the major towns in the province of Holland joined the revolt, but Amsterdam did not. The Catholicism of Amsterdam merchants and their desire to maintain the Mediterranean trade kept the city loyal to Spain until 1578, when the toll taken by the rebels on Amsterdam shipping became too great to bear and the city switched sides.

The rebel provinces in the north were united in their war aims, but that spirit of unity did not supplant their determination to control their individual destinies. Each province insisted on maintenance of its own army, and each retained some measure of control over how its soldiers would be used (Rowen 1988: 84). Troops of one province could not be stationed in another without explicit agreement on cost sharing and on their orders ('t Hart 1993: 35). Five provinces maintained their own navies, and these too operated independently. All lawmaking powers were reserved to the provinces, and their union was limited to the purposes of winning the war against Spain. Astounded observers from orderly, absolutist England wrote, "Every Province is absolute in itself onely, sometimes they consult together, but can do nothing untill their Consultations are approved of by every Province" (Johnson and Marsh 1664: 28). Although representatives of the rebel provinces met regularly in a body called the States General, this assembly "was more a conference of ambassadors from separate countries than a parliament."[10]

Frustrated by the need to obtain authorization for every undertaking from the provinces—and even from the individual towns of Holland—William of Orange was forced on several occasions to obtain affirmations by the States General of his authority over the conduct of the war. William remained preoccupied with the war effort, and left the provinces to run themselves. This proved to be the formula that worked best, allowing room for central control where necessary and for regional autonomy in all other matters.

Spain had a great military advantage, and the early results of battle were uniformly negative for the rebels. The manufacturing city of Haarlem fell to a Spanish siege in 1573, as did Middelburg, the chief port of Zeeland. The defeat of Haarlem was followed by execution of the entire garrison of 2,000 troops, after they had laid down their arms. This brutality proved to be a turning point that stiffened the resolve of other Dutch towns. Months into the siege of Leiden, after the townspeople had been driven to eat their pets to avoid starvation, the besieging forces called on the town to surrender. "Not yet," came the reply. Not as long as "we have every one of us a left arm to eat, and reserve the right arm to beat the tyrant and the rest of you which are his bloody ministers from our walles."[11]

From then on, extraordinary measures were taken to break the sieges of Holland's towns. The siege of Alkmaar was defeated when the townspeople breached their dikes and flooded the area surrounding the town. The siege of

Leiden lasted from March to October 1574, driving the population to the edge of starvation. Again the siege was broken only when the main dikes of southern Holland were opened up to flood the plain and allow rebel ships to sail to the rescue. Breaking the siege of Leiden was the occasion of a major celebration in rebel territories, but it was also obvious that some means other than submersion would have to be found to keep territory out of Spanish hands.

The first rebel military successes had already come from the "Sea Beggars" *(Geuzen),* Dutch privateers operating out of England who preyed both on Spanish shipping and on Dutch merchant ships from cities not active in the rebel cause. Unfortunately for the rebellion, however, the Sea Beggars were not above helping themselves to English cargoes as well, and after several such incidents Queen Elizabeth ordered them from her shores. Forced to find a new home port, the Sea Beggars crossed the North Sea to Den Briel, a small port in southern Holland. They found (to their surprise) that the Spanish garrison there had recently evacuated to fight against a small army mobilized by one of William's brothers. The Sea Beggars took control of the port on April 1, 1572, a date that is still marked as the first victory of the revolution. From Den Briel, the Sea Beggars were able to capture other small ports up and down the coast. Four years into the fighting, the Dutch rebels had finally gained their first territorial base in the Low Countries.

Philip's response to these defeats was to consolidate his control over the southern provinces. These efforts culminated in January 1579 in the Union of Arras, a separate peace between King Philip and what is now Belgium. The northern provinces replied in kind that same year with their Union of Utrecht, a compact between sovereign provinces that made clear their continued autonomy from each other by referring to themselves as "the allies."

Although the Union of Utrecht is today seen as the founding document of the Dutch Republic, it makes clear that the rebel provinces were fighting to reestablish their former rights under Philip's rule—a remarkable testimony to the holding power of traditional authority. Formal break with Philip was decreed by the States General only in 1581, after Philip pronounced William an outlaw and offered a reward and a grant of nobility to anyone who could assassinate him. The Act of Abjuration was couched in a logic that anticipated the American Declaration of Independence by nearly two hundred years. It declared that a prince must rule for the benefit of the people, "even as a shepherd keeps his sheep. . . . If, then, the shepherd proves a tyrant, the subjects have a natural right to depose him."[12] The basis of the revolt was "an aristocratic republic," to use a phrase of the time. Leading citizens of the United Provinces (those provinces united under the Union of Utrecht) were expected to govern for the general prosperity and freedom.

The war with Spain lasted eighty years, from 1568 to 1648. The last seventy years of the conflict, however, only had the effect of confirming the boundaries of the two blocs created in 1579 by the Unions of Arras and Utrecht. Efforts by troops of the northern provinces to take control of the south always stumbled on the unwillingness of the local populations to assist the rebels, who were unlikely to grant the southerners freedom to continue practicing as Catholics.

The Dutch revolt against Philip II of Spain was an assertion of regional autonomy against a ruler who was increasingly seen as foreign and whose policies were viewed as inimical to Dutch interests. The traditions of local autonomy that so nearly wrecked the military chances of the rebels would persist into the nineteenth century. Even so, by the end of the war against Spain, residents of the United Provinces had no doubt that they were Dutch, that they should govern themselves, and that they should be governed together. It is fruitless to debate whether the economic interests of city merchants or the religious interests of the growing Calvinist movement were paramount in the rebellion, for both were intertwined in a developing regional identity. The experience of the Eighty Years War for independence thus cemented the idea of a merchant-dominated Calvinist republic, suspicious both of Catholicism and of strong central government. The cleavage between Protestant and Catholic was to ripen into a structural feature of Dutch governance in the twentieth century, as we shall see in Chapter 3.

The experience of struggle against Spain united the provinces in a way that mere geographic proximity had never done. It was in this period that the Dutch were moved to invent their history, putting together patriotic chronicles from old stories to weave a tale of the Dutch in antiquity, stressing the energy and passion for liberty of "the Batavian people" as they struggled against Roman rule. An example of the new Dutch history is the tale of the Frisians, inhabitants of the north-central part of the country, who were responsible for one of the first recorded tax revolts. To pay their assessment to the Roman prefect Olennius, the Frisians were forced to sell their cattle and their lands. By A.D. 29, many Frisians were selling their wives and children into slavery to pay their tax bills, and even then their appeals for relief were not heard. In that year, the Frisians declared their independence from the Roman Empire and hanged the soldiers sent to collect the taxes. The prefect fled to a nearby fort, which the Frisians then besieged. Roman legionaries and auxiliaries sent to relieve the siege were defeated in battle. During their retreat, a unit of nine hundred soldiers was captured and slaughtered by the Frisians. Another unit, of four hundred soldiers, committed suicide rather than face the enraged locals. The end result was the withdrawal of Roman authority from the area.[13] Such tales created a sense of nationhood in an area previously protective of local autonomy. The battle for Dutch independence from Spain was, in this custom-crafted version of Dutch history, the extension of two millennia of struggle against foreign aggressors.

Governance of the United Provinces

Regents of the leading Dutch towns and provinces agreed that rule by an absolutist monarch would be arbitrary and unjust. They believed further that a government must respect local freedoms, both as a matter of principle and because local freedom would lead to a healthy and prosperous society. At the same time, the regents were not democrats in the modern sense. They certainly did not believe that the people were capable of governing themselves, and they would have reacted with horror to anything as radical as universal suffrage. The historian G. J. Schulte has aptly referred to the regents as "little local absolutists"—ruling like monarchs in their towns even while abhorring absolutism in the nation-state.[14]

Despite these reservations, the system of governance developed in the United Provinces was revolutionary because of its rejection of a strong monarchy. The basis of power in this system lay in the governing councils of the leading towns. Councillors were chosen for life from among the wealthiest individuals in the town on the theory that men of achievement were best able to govern in the interest of the town as a whole (Price 1994: 32ff.). Charles Wilson (1968: 55) aptly describes government by the regents as "a collective social dictatorship . . . but of a dispersed, disseminated kind, instinctively hostile to dynasticism, autocracy and theocracy alike."

The major towns in each province also participated in the Provincial States, a deliberative body that governed the province. The Provincial States were composed of one vote from each of the leading towns and one vote representing the nobility, who spoke for the countryside.[15] In Holland, whose size and wealth made it preeminent among the other provinces, many decisions required unanimity among its leading towns (Tracy 1990: 4). To a considerable extent, then, the United Provinces were really a confederation of city-states. Wijnand Mijnhardt (1998: 346) points out that "as many as 57 of the approximately one hundred towns with more than 2,500 inhabitants were directly involved in national decision-making through the sovereign assembly of the provincial states."

Although most areas of policymaking were reserved for the towns and the provinces, making foreign policy and administering justice were the responsibility of the United Provinces. This federal layer of authority was wielded by the States General, to which each province sent one delegate. The leader of the States General was the grand pensionary, whose role might be compared to that of a contemporary prime minister, except that he held office for life.

The other executive in the United Provinces was a diluted version of royalty: the stadholder. The stadholder, like the grand pensionary, was appointed for life. He was charged with the tasks that have classically belonged to the executive branch: justice (appointing magistrates and serving as the ultimate court of appeal) and defense (serving as the captain general of the armies and the admiral general of the navies). In practice, these powers were limited by the overall responsibility of the stadholder to the States General, and by the fact that military forces actually belonged to the provinces and were essentially on loan to the stadholder only in times of national emergency.

For much of the early history of the United Provinces, the power of the stadholder was even further limited by the fact that there were several of them. Each province had the right to elect its own stadholder, and the provinces did not always agree on the same incumbent. William of Orange was stadholder only of

Holland, Zeeland, and Utrecht, the most important provinces but by no means all of them. On his death, Groningen and Friesland chose William's nephew, Willem Lodewijk, to be stadholder, while Holland and the other four provinces chose William's son, Maurice.

The central tension in the Dutch system of government lay in the relationship between the grand pensionary and the stadholder. Both were responsible to the States General. But the practice of choosing a noble in the lineage of William of Orange gave the office of stadholder a monarchical cast. The practice of choosing the executive of the Provincial States of Holland to be grand pensionary, in turn, lent that post a greater affinity to the merchant class of the great coastal cities. The power of the grand pensionary was fortified by the fact that Holland supplied more than half the budget of the United Provinces. The power of the stadholder rested in the interior provinces, which were rural, relatively poor, and more orthodox in their Calvinism than the coastal provinces. Holland and the grand pensionary clung most tenaciously to the principle of decentralization of authority, while the stadholder and his provincial allies espoused stronger central control as a means of containing the power of Holland. When the trading interests of the merchant classes conflicted with the interests of the interior provinces, the result was conflict between the stadholder and the grand pensionary.

Such conflicts arose over a number of issues. The regents of Holland found the war against Spain burdensome due to the level of taxation needed to sustain the war effort and the effects of privateering on the safety of the merchant fleet. Grand Pensionary Oldenbarnevelt took the lead in concluding a twelve-year truce with Spain in 1609. This caused a deep estrangement with Stadholder Maurice, whose job was to prosecute the war (Rowen 1988: 42–53). Since the truce failed to obtain formal Spanish recognition of the independence of the United Provinces, followers of Maurice declared that Oldenbarnevelt had betrayed the nation. Maurice had Oldenbarnevelt arrested, tried for treason, and executed in 1619.

The same crisis was replayed in the middle of the century, when the 1648 Treaty of Münster finally ended what was soon dubbed the Eighty Years War.[16] The treaty was concluded at the behest of Dutch merchants whose trade dominance was now secured, and whose next goal was to lower taxation and the public debt by reducing the size of the military. Stadholder William II was opposed to the treaty, but he was unable to prevent its ratification. For the next two years he sought to minimize the effects of peace on his base of power by arguing for a continuation of military strength at the highest possible level. When agreement in the States General on the size of the army proved impossible to secure, William II ordered the representatives of six towns in Holland to be arrested. He also sent his army to the gates of Amsterdam, threatening military occupation of the province's leading city. A compromise was reached in which Holland backed down from its position. The resulting augmentation of William II's authority might have moved the United Provinces toward a monarchical system had he not contracted smallpox and died within months of his coup d'état against Amsterdam.

In the period of peace and prosperity that followed the death of William II, Grand Pensionary Johan de Witt and the merchant class that supported him ruled almost unchecked. De Witt was even able to persuade the States General to abolish the stadholderate in 1667. But the need for a stadholder was soon revived when the French army marched through the Southern Netherlands (Belgium) in 1672 and threatened invasion of the United Provinces themselves. The States General named Prince William III captain general. After a mob of William's supporters killed Grand Pensionary de Witt, the States General named William stadholder as well.

These conflicts between successive stadholders and grand pensionaries reflect the tensions inherent in any political system with two executives. Strong pensionaries and strong stadholders were never able to coexist, as proven by the deaths of Oldenbarnevelt and de Witt. But these were more than conflicts between strong personalities; they also reflected a fundamental cleavage within Dutch society. The issues separating supporters of the stadholder and supporters of the grand pensionary included the degree of orthodoxy of Calvinist thought,[17] the virulence of anti-Spanish feeling, and the desired degree of provincial autonomy. These issues created such stable divisions within the ruling elite that one can speak of factional conflict, a kind of precursor to modern party politics. The *Staatsgezind* (meaning "favoring the state") faction was aligned against the *Oranjegezind* ("favoring the House of Orange") faction. Tensions between these factions grew to such an extent that civil war seemed a real possibility during the seventeenth century (Rowen 1988: 205–229). Foreign observers, accustomed to the more orderly hierarchies of absolutism, wondered how the United Provinces were able to survive as a political entity. Such concerns understated the importance of everything that the two sides had in common: a fierce nationalism that would maintain independence at all costs, a desire to continue commercial expansion, and an aversion both to Catholicism and to strong monarchical government.

Despite these common elements of the Dutch political culture, the loosely confederal government of the United Provinces continued to struggle with its limited authority. The "Patriots movement" arose in the last part of the eighteenth century to champion a more centralized government that could modernize the country. Ultimately, they received their wish only when the French army marched into the United Provinces in 1795 to impose a new government more in accord with the centralizing principles of the French Revolution. The depth of division within the United Provinces is suggested by the fact that the invading French troops were accompanied by a Dutch legion, and the conquerors were greeted as liberators by urban dwellers who chafed against rule both by the stadholder and by the urban merchant class.[18]

Constitutionalization of a Monarchy

The French invasion brought an end to the United Provinces and substituted a new political order modeled on the French revolutionary government. Under the so-called Batavian Republic, power was centralized to a degree unimaginable even to the stoutest supporters of the stadholder. Guilds were abolished, local regulations were replaced by national legislation modeled on French law, the judiciary was reformed and centralized. The constitution of the Batavian Republic was modeled on the laws of France, and featured provision for a National Assembly elected by vote of all Christian males over the age of 20. Electoral districts were established based on population rather than town borders. Residents of the southern, Catholic provinces were given full political rights for the first time, as were Protestants outside the Dutch Reformed Church. The break from the past was made clear in the command that all members of the National Assembly swear, under alternative of imprisonment, their rejection of "Stadholder, Federalism, Aristocracy and Anarchy" (Andeweg 1989: 43).

As post-revolutionary France moved from egalitarian democracy to government by directorate to the crowning of Napoleon Bonaparte as emperor, so did the Dutch puppet regime also evolve. The Batavian Republic became the "Kingdom of Holland" in 1806, ruled by Napoleon's brother, King Louis Napoleon. Napoleon Bonaparte finally annexed the Netherlands to France in 1810, an arrangement that lasted until his defeat in 1813.

Although the French interlude in the governance of the Netherlands was brief, its effects on the Dutch polity in the form of a centralized state were permanent. A single legal code applicable to all the provinces was developed, and the powers of local and provincial authorities were reduced. Development of a national tax code gave the central state its own resources for the first time, and also shifted the tax burden more equally to all citizens by reducing the consumption taxes that had weighed heavily on the lower classes while leaving untouched the accumulated wealth of the privileged few.[19] A system of universal education was adopted and the state set general standards to be met by public and private schools alike. Less tangible but nonetheless considerable was the effect of centralization on the national consciousness: During this period of foreign occupation, feelings of nationalism were heightened. The cultural and historical ties that bind together all Dutch people became steadily stronger.

The advantages of these new institutional arrangements were obvious to the reconstituted Dutch government after Napoleon's downfall. As Adriaan Barnouw (1948: 177) put it:

> When the Prince of Orange returned to his own in 1813, he could do no better than take the French system over—lock, stock, and barrel. Justice was promptly administered without favoritism or graft, taxes were more evenly imposed and were less of a burden than before, the police system was severe but impartial, the military system a model of organization. The provinces, now called departments, and the municipalities had never before been governed with such efficiency and orderliness.

Having found agreeable the efficiencies of the French regime (if not its foreignness), the Dutch political class broke with their republican traditions and named

Frederick William, son of the last stadholder, William V, to be king of the Netherlands and Belgium, and grand duke of Luxembourg. Though he had expected to return to the Netherlands with the more limited powers of a stadholder, King William I quickly adopted an autocratic style of rule. Rather than engage in extensive consultation with the States General through the regular lawmaking process, William ruled whenever possible by royal decree. When he had to go to the States General at all, he relied heavily on the First Chamber, populated mainly by nobles whom he had named to life positions (much like the British House of Lords).

Histories of the period invariably describe William I as an enlightened autocrat, concerned above all to hasten industrialization of the country. But his penchant for centralization, including plans to make Dutch the standard language in the French-speaking part of Belgium and to reduce Catholic influence in education, recalled the hated centralizing policies of Philip II of Spain.[20] The Belgian portion of the kingdom was soon in revolt, and even in the northern Netherlands the regent class grew restive under their marginalization. Although there were as yet no political parties in the modern sense, delegates to the States General began to coalesce around the polarities of conservative (monarchical) versus liberal, and Protestant versus Catholic. The liberal tendency gradually became the strongest within the States General, not least because the Liberals managed to avoid religious division by adhering to their slogan *"vox populi, vox dei"*—the voice of the people is the voice of God.

In 1840 several leading Liberals organized a committee to develop proposals for constitutional revision. These included, most prominently, enlarged suffrage for the Second Chamber of the States General and a strengthening of the Second Chamber vis-à-vis the First Chamber and the cabinet. Although their proposals were at first rejected by the Crown, William II was not in principle hostile to the idea of greater democratization. His sympathies were strengthened by a period of popular unrest that began in 1845 when a failed potato crop raised food prices and left many hungry. This turmoil came to seem even more perilous in 1848 when revolution swept through many areas in Germany and France, toppling French king Louis Philippe. Believing that constitutional reform was the only way to save the monarchy, King William II promulgated the Liberal reforms and named Liberal leader Johan Rudolf Thorbecke as prime minister.

The new constitution divided the country into electoral districts, each of which would send two delegates to the Second Chamber, serving staggered two-year terms. The fact that each district elected one delegate every year was meant to enable the representative body to be closely reflective of changing currents in public opinion. The First Chamber, previously reserved for life appointments of the nobility, was now to be elected by representatives of the Provincial States (much as the U.S. Senate prior to 1913). Moreover, the Second Chamber was given powers that made it the preeminent legislative body. Under the earlier constitution, the Second Chamber could register disapproval of the government only by refusing to pass the annual budget. It was now also given the right to question individual ministers and to carry out its own investigations of policy problems. The First Chamber was limited to approving or disapproving measures passed by the Second Chamber; it thus lacked the proactive role given to the directly elected lower house.

Constitutional reforms of the mid–nineteenth century laid the groundwork for development of a modern democracy, but they did not in themselves create that democracy. For one thing, the suffrage remained highly restricted based on gender and tax-paying qualifications, so that even after the Liberal reforms only 11 percent of the adult male population had the right to vote. The franchise was gradually extended by 1910 to nearly two-thirds of adult males, primarily through the spread of economic prosperity rather than by reform of the electoral law. Universal suffrage for men was obtained in 1917, and for women in 1919, with consequences for Dutch political organization that we will examine in Chapters 4 and 5.

An equally significant restriction on the quality of democracy after the Liberal reforms of 1848 was the fact that in political practice clarification of the new relationship between the government and the Second Chamber took several decades. The constitution stated that the government was to be responsible to the parliament for its decisions. Did this mean that the government could not appoint a high-level official without parliamentary approval? That issue arose in 1866 when members of parliament disputed the government's right to appoint a governor-general in the colony of Java without the assent of the Second Chamber. A motion of censure against the government led King William III to dissolve the parliament and call for new elections. This election was fought essentially as a referendum on the respective powers of the Crown versus the parliament. Although the pro-monarchy forces gained slightly in this election, the new Second Chamber again refused to back the government. After a second parliamentary dissolution and election, deputies in the Second Chamber passed a resolution condemning the elections as unnecessary and then refused to pass the budget. Use of this ultimate weapon in the power struggle between the elected legislature and the monarch finally led the government to accept the principle of parliamentary assent to executive appointments, and the king to accept the principle of noninterference in political affairs. The primacy of the popularly elected Second Chamber was now established in practice as well as on paper.

Conclusion

In the relatively short span of three hundred years after the Union of Utrecht in 1579, the Dutch nation went from being a loosely organized federation of independent provinces to a unified state whose government was organized as a constitutional monarchy. At several crucial junctures the impulse for this transformation came from outside the country. Thus, for example, the territory of the Dutch state was established by the outcome of the war against Spain; French conquest of the Netherlands brought centralized government to the country; and the allies who ended Napoleon's reign permanently in 1815 made sure that the Dutch constitution written that year retained those centralizing features. The threat of popular revolution surfaced again in France and Germany in 1848, leading King William II to agree to significant reforms that put constitutional limits on the monarchy.

In each of these cases, though, it was up to Dutch leaders to seize upon these external circumstances and to use them to press for particular reforms. Thus, for example, Napoleon's military conquest of the Netherlands enabled the Dutch faction interested in political reform, a group known as the Patriots, to wrest power from both the urban regent class and the stadholder. Fifty years later the Liberal group in parliament took advantage of revolutionary turmoil elsewhere on the continent to press for constitutional reform.

Although there would be further constitutional revisions in the twentieth century, the institutions of contemporary governance were in place by the end of the nineteenth century. The Netherlands was on its way to becoming a democracy; it was now up to Dutch citizens to develop the social and political organizations that would represent them. We turn in the next chapter to the remarkable set of organizations that emerged.

NOTES

1. Cited in Rijkswaterstaat (1956: 23).

2. For details on the contemporary role of the port of Rotterdam in European trade, see Gaebe and Schamp (1994).

3. Cited in Barnouw (1943: 45).

4. Van Deursen (1991: 13). Not all water engineering projects add to the land area of the country. The Delta works project in the southwest closed off all southern river estuaries except the canal leading to the port of Rotterdam. In addition to protecting the south from killer storms like that of 1953, this project has created a chain of freshwater inland lakes where there was once open sea. For details, see Lambert (1971).

5. While just 4.4 percent of the German population lived in towns in 1650, as did 7.2 percent of the French population and 8.8 percent of the English/Welsh population, the corresponding percentages in the Low Countries were 20.8 percent for Belgium and 31.7 percent for the Netherlands. See de Vries (1984: 39).

6. These taxes were known as the "Twentieth Penny," a 5 percent tax on real estate, and the "Tenth Penny," a 10 percent excise tax on all transactions involving movable goods.

7. William is today known by the name "William the Silent," but in his own day his nickname was "William the Sly."

8. It would be misleading to call the demand to allow the provinces to regulate their own religious affairs a demand for religious freedom. It was the intention of several of the provincial governments to replace the established Catholic Church with an established Dutch Reformed Church that would be equally severe against dissenters.

9. As cited in Vlekke (1943: 37).

10. Price (1994: 212). Even monetary units, weights and measures, the legal code, and the calendar varied between provinces. See Haley (1972: 69).

11. As cited in Parker (1977: 160).

12. Cited in Barnouw (1948: 80). For an account of political thought on the revolt as a forerunner of the demand for liberty and rights in the American and French Revolutions, see van Gelderen (1992, 1993).

13. This account comes from Drummond and Nelson (1994: 82–83).

14. Cited in Rowen (1988: 151).

15. The representative of the nobility was also the chief executive of the Provincial States, known as the councillor pensionary. Tradition allowed this representative to speak first on any proposal placed before the Provincial States. This enabled a politically astute representative to set the tone for much of the subsequent debate, according to Rowen (1986: 36–37).

16. The treaty was a clear victory for the Netherlands, which obtained recognition of its sovereignty, the right to keep overseas territory taken from Spain during the war, unrestricted trade in the East and West Indies, and—perhaps most importantly—continued blockade of the Belgian port of Antwerp. Over the previous eighty years, Amsterdam's prosperity had been greatly advanced by the blockade of its rival to the south.

17. The importance of Calvinist religious belief in political life was such that theological differences on predestination came to play an important role in making and unmaking political coalitions.

18. Andeweg (1989: 43) reports that the Patriots have only recently been "rehabilitated from traitorous collaborators to nationalist modernizers" by writers of Dutch history.

19. Each province had its own tax system prior to the Batavian Republic. Friesland taxed horses and hearths, for example, while Holland taxed land, wine, beer, salt, soap, and cloth. The most innovative and productive tax may have been the tax on "unfounded lawsuits." See 't Hart (1993: 78, 125).

20. One difference, of course, is that William had a bias toward Calvinism, rather than the Catholicism of King Philip.

3

THE ORGANIZATION
OF DUTCH SOCIETY

Imagine a society in which the phrase "separate but equal" is not code for a system of racial inequality, but actually describes a consensually developed relationship between major social groups. Each group would have its own organizations that enable members to live separately from other parts of society. These organizations would be legally recognized and would receive public financial support on an equal footing. The society would be, in effect, a series of parallel subsocieties offering each group their own hospitals, schools, churches, hobby clubs, newspapers, labor unions, political parties, and radio and television broadcasts.

In the United States, such separation conjures up images of enforced racial segregation. In the Netherlands, this separation came about as a result of voluntary organizing by groups who defined themselves by their *levensbeschouwing,* or view of life. This is the social system of *zuilen,* or "pillars" of society.[1] The Dutch pillars are networks of organizations that create ideologically homogeneous subcultures within a larger, pluralistic society. The pillars have been disappearing over the last generation, but it is impossible even today to understand Dutch society and politics without a close examination of this social system.

Although the history of societal organizations with a political mission goes back at least to the medieval water control boards, we will focus in this chapter on three twentieth-century periods in which the institutions of modern Dutch society took shape. The first period is the development of popular organizations around the turn of the century. This was the period in which the pillars were formed. We will then look at the midcentury crisis caused by defeat in World War II and the brutal Nazi occupation that followed. This crisis reaffirmed the pillars but put them on a new cooperative footing with each other. The third turning point stems from secularization and the rise of new values over the last forty years, as well as from increasing ethnic pluralism. As we shall see, increased wealth, education, and cultural diversity have disrupted Dutch society in a way the German occupiers were unable to do. This third turning point has toppled the pillars and replaced them with a more fluid system of social organization and society-state relations.

We will begin this review of societal organization with a consideration of the waves of popular mobilization that occurred one hundred years ago. An understanding of the contemporary relationship between society and politics in the Netherlands begins with these patterns of mass mobilization, whose origins lie in the period of rapid industrialization of the country late in the nineteenth century.

Three Waves of Mobilization

In the year 1850 the Netherlands had 3 million inhabitants (compared to over 15 million today), most of whom lived in small towns and villages and worked in agriculture. Despite its early prominence as a center for international trade, the Netherlands had been largely bypassed by the industrial revolution, and during the nineteenth century its cities actually tended to decline in size. In 1850 the entire country had only one factory with 1,000 workers (Goudsblom 1967: 20). It was this era of Dutch history that inspired foreigners to make comments such as, "If the world is about to come to an end, I will move to Holland. There, everything happens fifty years later."[2]

This economic and social backwardness was reflected in the political system of the time. Government was still restricted to a small elite class. Even the Liberal reforms of 1848, though introducing a directly elected Second Chamber and making the government responsible to a parliamentary majority, kept voting rights restricted to a small fraction of the population. The Liberal leader J. R. Thorbecke referred to the post-reform parliament as "a freely elected general assembly, independent, deciding according to its own views and judgment, without any link with the voters."[3]

That was soon to change. Beginning in the 1870s, a series of issues affecting various social groups led to increasingly intensive popular mobilization. These were the issues of school subsidies, conflict over extension of the franchise, and the role of the state in regulating the relationship between capital and labor. Each of these issues led to the mobilization of social groups determined to press for their rights and to break the hold of the Liberals on government.

The Calvinist Réveil

For different reasons, leaders of the two largest denominations in the Netherlands—the Catholic Church and the Dutch Reformed Church—came to believe in the course of the nineteenth century that survival of their faith could only be guaranteed by development of a system of organizations reserved for members of the church. Their goals were to protect the faithful from secularizing influences and to develop a base of political power that would preserve group rights and resources.

The Dutch Reformed Church *(Nederlands Hervormd Kerk)* had long enjoyed a privileged position within society, due to its close association with the revolt against Spain and with the House of Orange (the stadholders and later the monarchy). Although the town-based regent class had a restrained view of the importance of Calvinist orthodoxy, they were nonetheless part of a ruling elite officially restricted to the Dutch Reformed Church. As Johan Goudsblom (1967: 17) put it, they "managed to take charge of the schools, to make membership in the Dutch Reformed Church a prerequisite for appointment to civic office, and to forbid by law all public religious worship outside this same church." A special pew was reserved for the regents in many towns, symbolizing the close if informal relationship between church and state (Price 1994: 71).

The growing strength of the liberal philosophy in the nineteenth century threatened the dominant position of the Dutch Reformed Church. "Liberalism," as the word is used in the Netherlands still today, refers to belief that the best society is one in which the role of the government is limited to guaranteeing equal rights and opportunities for all. In contemporary American terms, Dutch liberalism (and European liberalism more generally) is progressive in its approach to individual rights and liberties, though conservative in its belief in limited governmental regulation of corporations and other forms of economic activity.

To those who aspired to have the Dutch Reformed Church become the state church of the Netherlands, liberal doctrines of equal rights for Catholics and other Protestant denominations were highly threatening. The issue that served as a lightning rod for this discontent was the question of control over the elementary schools. One of the legacies of the French era of centralized government was the School Act of 1806, which placed all schools, regardless of denomination, under state control and subject to governmental standards. This was a tolerable situation for the Dutch Reformed Church as long as it had sufficient influence to ensure a close fit between "state education" and Dutch Reformed doctrine.[4] The determination of the Liberals to promote secularization of education, though, undermined this dominance. As Hans Daalder (1966: 200) points out, "Schools were vital to religion, culture, and political power. The issue touched not only the elites, moreover, but parents in all walks of life. It thus contributed to a thorough politicization of the still disenfranchised masses."

The dispute over control of the schools grew steadily in intensity. A government proposal in 1857 that would secularize the schools led to a fierce and famous parliamentary debate between the Liberal leader Johan Rudolf Thorbecke and Calvinist leader Guillaume Groen van Prinsterer on whether education by state-appointed lay people in a Christian nation could still be called Christian education. The Liberals succeeded in passing the Primary Education Act of 1857, which declared all elementary schools to be religiously neutral. This law, however, only crystallized the Calvinist opposition, whose leaders decided to organize their following and then reopen the issue from a stronger position.

The Protestant mobilization that followed was built upon a nineteenth-century religious awakening known as the *Réveil,* which sought "to rekindle the fervor and emotion of old-time Calvinism and bring religious experience back from the head to the heart" (Barnouw 1948: 186). This organizing drive was based on the central creed of Groen van Prinsterer: "In our isolation lies our strength." Groen van Prinsterer's ideas were translated into action by Abraham Kuyper, a brilliant political organizer who had been the motivating force behind a series of popular protests over the school issue, including both the Anti-School Law League (1872) and a petition movement against the Liberal School Bill of 1878 that obtained over 300,000 signatures—three times the size of the eligible electorate. Kuyper followed up this petition campaign by founding the Anti-Revolutionary Party (ARP) in 1879, a party whose name proclaimed its opposition to the secular spirit of the French Revolution. This was the first modern party in Dutch history, with a mass membership and a network of local organizations capable of acting in concert to press for a national political agenda.

Abraham Kuyper did not restrict his organizing efforts to the world of politics, seeking instead to reach directly to the *kleine luyden,* or "little people," most of whom did not have the right to vote. Kuyper was determined to inspire a renewal of the Calvinist fervor that had been a powerful force at several junctures of Dutch history, propelling the break with Spain and later supporting the stadholders against the wealthy merchants of the big cities. He established a Calvinist union movement in 1871, a daily Calvinist newspaper in 1872, and a Calvinist university (Amsterdam's Free University) in 1880.[5] Finding the Dutch Reformed Church to be insufficiently fundamentalist in its doctrines and insufficiently militant in its actions, Kuyper also established a new Calvinist denomination called the Reformed Churches *(Gereformeerde Kerken).*[6]

This schismatic tendency within Calvinism was not new. There was a protracted theological conflict in the 1630s over whether organ music in church was a means of giving greater glory to God or whether it was, in the words of one opponent, "a pagan novelty" (Schama 1988: 61). Eventually, the Synod of Delft adopted a classic Dutch solution, giving local churches each the right to decide the issue for themselves. Kuyper's establishment of the Reformed Churches in the late nineteenth century, then, followed a long tradition of local autonomy and differentiation within Dutch Calvinism. New, however, was Kuyper's emphasis on organizing the common people. Kuyper's view was that the only true sovereignty lay with God, and that the proper earthly expression of that sovereignty was not with the state but with the society, organized as a community of the faithful. As Kuyper put it:

> In the Calvinist sense we understand hereby, that the family, business, science, art and so forth are all social spheres, which do not owe their existence to the State, . . . but

which obey a high authority within their own bosom; an authority which rules by the grace of God. . . . [T]hese different developments of social life have nothing above themselves but God, and . . . the State cannot intrude here.[7]

Kuyper's inspiration helped Calvinist organizations develop into an unprecedentedly large social and political force. Supported by this network of popular organizations, the Anti-Revolutionary Party soon eclipsed the Conservatives as the primary opposition to the still-dominant Liberals.

Catholic Emancipation

Dutch Catholics quickly followed the Calvinist pattern of establishing an integrated set of organizations that would simultaneously protect Catholics from assimilation into Dutch society and develop a base for the projection of Catholic power into politics. Many of the issues of concern to Catholics were the same as those that inspired the mobilization of Calvinists. However, the Catholic movement was also directed at emancipation of a group that had long lived without full rights in the society. When the Eighty Years War for independence from Spain came to an end in 1648, Dutch Catholics were a minority in a nation whose self-identity had been forged in struggle against a Catholic king. Catholic churches had been seized and religious services forbidden during the early part of the revolt, in 1573. Catholics were barred from establishing schools, excluded from many professions, and banned from public office until the French conquest of 1795. The southern, Catholic provinces were never admitted as full partners in the United Provinces, being administered instead as semicolonial territories.

The Liberals championed a reversal of these conditions. Liberal reforms of 1848 permitted Catholics to worship publicly and to institute an ecclesiastical hierarchy in the Netherlands, leading to the establishment of five bishoprics by 1853. Catholics were content at first to be silent beneficiaries of the Liberal ideology; in fact, the Liberal leader J. R. Thorbecke was elected to parliament from the Catholic city of Maastricht. As Bishop Zwijsen put it in his report to Rome, "Holy Father, we can achieve a great deal in my land, so long as we do it quietly."[8]

But the Catholic-Liberal coalition was troubled by the Liberal drive for a national system of secular education. In 1868 the bishops officially condemned the Liberal education policy, thus breaking with their political patrons. Catholic leaders took advantage of their new rights to speak and organize publicly, and began building social organizations parallel to those of the Calvinist bloc. Groen van Prinsterer's principle of "sovereignty in one's own circle" found its parallel among Catholics in the idea of subsidiarity—a claim that the purpose of the social order is to enable its separate parts, the communities of faith, to reach their own goals within the wider society.[9] By about 1910, Catholics had established most of the elements of their own pillar alongside the Calvinist network of organizations. Like the Calvinists, Catholics crowned their pillar with a university of their own—the Catholic University at Nijmegen—in 1923. By then they had

> developed an almost autarkic Catholic community, within whose boundaries one not only supports a political party, but also subscribes to a Catholic newspaper, a Catholic fashion magazine, a Catholic illustrated weekly, and a Catholic youth magazine. The children enjoy Catholic education from nursery school to the university, and it is in a Catholic context that one listens to the radio, goes on a trip, buys life insurance, and enjoys art, science, and sport. It is . . . a system which to the ultimate degree has raised isolation to a style of life, even to the basic principle of life.[10]

Despite their history as second-class citizens, the Catholics, once united in a political party, quickly became a crucial pivot in governmental coalitions.[11] Liberal ascendancy had earlier been prolonged by Catholic support; now a Catholic coalition with the Anti-Revolutionary Party brought the Calvinists to power and made Abraham Kuyper prime minister in the early years of the twentieth century. The first Catholic prime minister took office in 1918—a development that was all but inconceivable even one generation earlier.

By the turn of the century, both Calvinists and Catholics were well on their way to having created separate communities rooted in networks of organizations among the faithful, and having the political muscle to guarantee protection from state authority. These networks of religious organizations, known as the confessional pillars, were created by the elites of each denomination to permit the long-term survival of their faiths. Both Catholics and Calvinists determined not to let the forces of industrialization and a growing state exert a homogenizing and controlling force over them.

Working-Class Mobilization

Industrialization in the Netherlands, though begun in earnest only in the last decades of the nineteenth century, was not spared the pattern of working-class poverty, insecurity, and degradation characteristic of the early phase of all industrial economies. Simultaneous industrial expansion and agricultural depression drove large numbers of people from the countryside to the major cities. Projects such as the Rotterdam port expansion of the 1870s brought tens of thousands of workers into the city, overrunning the housing supply and creating a pool of reserve labor that led to exploitation. Although the owners of Rotterdam's ship building, repair, and harbor facilities became wealthy, the men and women who came looking for work found an extraordinarily hard life waiting for them. Gerald Newton (1978: 86) explains that "slums were the working class way of life. Wages were low, 8 guilders being usual for a seven-day week of 73 and a half hours. Diet was still monotonous, bread was taxed to the hilt. . . . [W]orkers were lucky to have more than one day's holiday in two years. It can be no surprise, therefore, that the adults took to drinking gin, and the juveniles to crime and gang formation."

These were the people whom the socialists sought to reach. Associations of skilled workers had been formed as early as 1849, providing sickness benefits to members and trade schools for candidate-members. These proto-union organizations remained restricted to the skilled trades for several decades, because of the greater difficulties of organizing unskilled labor. A strike of railway tracklayers in 1869, for example, resulted in a two-year jail term for the leaders and a governmental ban on strikes.

Prior labor organizing by Catholic and Protestant leaders helped establish the legality of labor unions. By the time the late-industrializing Netherlands began to develop a working-class labor movement, the Calvinists had already created a model of how to organize a religious minority for the protection of group rights. Catholics, in turn, had demonstrated that this organizational model could be adopted by groups lower in social status and with less political power than the Dutch Reformed and Reformed Churches. This history of religious mobilization offered socialist organizers among the working class a useful template. At the same time, the success of religious mobilization meant that many members of the working class were already organized in groups antagonistic to socialism. The first Protestant labor union, called Patrimonium, was founded in 1877, just six years after formation of the first nationwide socialist union, the General Dutch Workers Union (ANWV). Catholics followed in 1888 with their own labor organization, the Roman Catholic People's League *(Roomsch-Katholieke Volksbond)*, dedicated to shielding Catholic workers from "the social errors of our time."[12] These confessional unions were highly successful in mobilizing workers behind the belief that there is a basic mutuality of interests between the classes. Coal miners in the southern province of Limburg, for example, were solidly organized in a Catholic union. In the early twentieth century, Limburg was perhaps the only place in all of Europe where a mining district was not a hotbed of socialism (Bakvis 1981: 42–43). Study of a small village at the center of the country from 1870 to 1920 shows that both Protestant and Catholic clergy assisted confessional unions by heightening the salience of moral issues, stressing the importance of church affiliation for eternal salvation, and condemning the class sentiments expressed by socialists (Verrips 1987).

The problem, from the socialist perspective, was to wean the working class away from these religious labor organizations. The religious loyalties of many in the working class led early socialist organizers to shape their appeals accordingly. The first prominent socialist leader was a former Lutheran minister, F. Domela Nieuwenhuis, who brought to socialism a chiliastic zeal familiar to all who had grown up with Calvinist or other forms of fundamentalist preaching.[13] Nieuwenhuis became the first socialist in parliament in 1887, but he ultimately migrated to anarchism and became marginal to the working-class movement. His place was taken by Pieter Jelles Troelstra and eleven other organizers of the Social Democratic Workers Party (SDAP, established 1894). Their founding program became known as *The Manifesto of the Twelve Apostles*. In 1902 Troelstra led the

SDAP in a fundamental break with marxist orthodoxy to declare that it would support the granting of subsidies to religious schools. This was, of course, a calculated effort to form a coalition with the religious parties against the business-oriented Liberals.[14]

By the time social democrats began to organize among the agricultural and industrial working classes, they had little choice other than to form their own network of organizations comparable to those of the Calvinists and Catholics. Anything less would have left their members dependent on confessional organizations for education, social services, newspapers, and recreation. Therefore, social democrats established not only labor unions (the Dutch Federation of Trade Unions, NVV, founded in 1906) and a political party (the SDAP), but also newspapers and broadcast associations, women's and youth organizations, and a variety of leisure groups.

These organizations turned the Dutch labor movement into a powerful force. In the first decades of the twentieth century, leaders of the Liberal and confessional parties tried to stem support for social democratic organizations by enacting the eight-hour workday; old-age, accident, and disability insurance; and public subsidies for low-cost housing. These reforms did not succeed in preventing the social democrats from creating their own pillar, duplicating the earlier organizational achievements of the Calvinists and the Catholics. But they did reinforce the SDAP strategy of following the path of parliamentary reform rather than the dream of proletarian revolution. In 1917 the social democrats achieved their single most important goal, universal male suffrage.[15] Although no social democrat participated in a governing coalition until 1939, much of the SDAP's early program was in place by the end of World War I.

A Society of Pillars

Calvinists, Catholics, and social democrats in the Netherlands created a society structured in religiously and ideologically homogeneous groups. To preserve each community of faith (including the socialist), pillar organizations provided for a full range of social services and activities carried out in the company of fellow members of the same pillar. Political parties cemented their associations with the pillars by appointing the chief editor of the main pillar newspaper to their executive committees, and by including in their parliamentary delegations representatives of the pillar's trade union, employers association, farmers association, and retailers organizations.

The pillar system was never fully developed, and it must always be remembered that the pillars were a metaphor for Dutch society rather than its reality. The metaphor fails to capture the fact that there were frequently divisions within the pillars, especially among the schism-prone Calvinists. It is also important to realize that not all pillars were equally comprehensive. The social democratic pillar never achieved the completeness of the confessional pillars, in that there is only one set of secular schools catering to students from all social class backgrounds. The liberal pillar was even more fragmentary. Liberalism came to power in the nineteenth century as an elite ideology rather than as a mass movement. Although the Liberals responded to the challenge of the other pillars by securing their own mass media outlets, their organizational network remained so incomplete that scholars generally refer to just three pillars—the Catholic, Calvinist, and social democratic—or to "three and a half."

Finally, the pillars could never completely insulate their adherents from contact outside the pillar, if only because members of the different faiths and social classes were geographically interspersed. Though the southern provinces of the Netherlands are predominantly Catholic and the rural east and north are predominantly Protestant, even these areas are not completely homogeneous in religion, and the coastal cities of North and South Holland are quite mixed.[16] Social democrats and liberals are found throughout the country. Despite this mingling of the population, though, adherents of the various *levensbeschouwingen* lived remarkably separate lives, and this element of separateness is captured by the pillar metaphor.

Growth and Extension of the Pillars

The pillars were not created all at once, but rather developed over several generations, from the last decades of the nineteenth century until after World War II. Wilbert van Vree (1994: 211) estimates that 200 associations were created each year in the mid-1880s; by 1915 there were 1,600 new associations being created each year. The era of pillar-building left the Netherlands with an extraordinarily dense network of social organizations. Even today, the Dutch have more organizational memberships than residents of other European countries.

As leaders of the pillars gained social and political influence, they were able to extend pillar organizations ever further within the society. Thus, for example, the principle of equal funding for all schools regardless of denomination or orientation was established in the historic 1917 compromise between pillar leaders known as the "Pacification." In 1889 only 20 percent of primary school students attended religious schools (Thurlings 1979: 84). By the 1930s, over 70 percent of primary school children were in Protestant or Catholic schools (Bax 1990: 131). This principle was later extended upward to the university level, and outward to such areas as hospitals and old-age homes.

The pillars were also effective in adapting to social changes during the first half of the twentieth century. As leisure time expanded, so did the importance of pillar-related clubs devoted to sports, educational enrichment, reading, and other such activities. In the years after World War II, the pillar networks were further extended to social welfare, mental health, and even research institutes. The pillars became more and more elaborate over time, increasing the extent to which people lived in a strictly pillarized subculture.

The most remarkable area of growth in pillar organizations was in the mass media. John Coleman (1978: 120) reports that in 1960 the Catholic population of 5 million was served by a Roman Catholic press service, twenty-two daily newspapers (two of them nationally distributed), another twenty-two weekly newspapers serving small towns, 270 weekly and monthly magazines, and forty-two scholarly journals.[17] Catholic and Protestant writers were trained in their own journalism schools (Bax 1990: 148–149). Pillarization of the newspapers made possible the classic Dutch story of the greengrocer who asks a customer if she prefers her vegetables wrapped in a Catholic, Protestant, or socialist newspaper.[18]

This tradition of pillar control of the print media was extended to other mass media as they developed. Radio airtime was divided between special associations created to broadcast Catholic, Calvinist, social democratic, and liberal (or "general") programming. After World War II, political leaders representing the pillars were able to squelch the demand for commercial television stations and instead extended the authority of the pillar radio associations to television as well. When a ship anchored in international waters broadcast commercial radio programming into the country, or when a television station located on an oil rig tried to do the same, the government sent the navy to shut down the station (Brants 1985: 108).

This determination to control education and the mass media reflects the fact that both were crucial to maintaining the pillar's *levensbeschouwing* among its adherents. Coleman (1978: 75) estimates that pillarized broadcast associations gave religious and church affairs close to four hours of weekly prime-time exposure on the country's only television station until the mid-1960s. This gave exceptional visibility to church doctrines and activities. If we can stretch the pillar metaphor a bit, the schools and media were the mortar that held the pillars together.

Assisted by governmental subsidies and protection from competition, the pillarized structure of Dutch society reached its peak in the decades just before and after World War II. Every observer of Dutch society has a favorite example to illustrate how far-reaching the pillar organizations came to be. The Catholic Goat-Breeders Association is often mentioned in this context (Gielen 1965; Bakvis 1981). My personal favorite is the Catholic Esperanto Society—an organization whose support for a universal language is belied by its own pillar-bound membership.

The pillarized society of the Netherlands looks exotic to American eyes because it stands in sharp contrast to the notion of a pluralist melting pot that figures so prominently in American democratic ideals. Pluralism recognizes that people have many interests, and that those interests are pursued in a variety of different organizations whose memberships do not overlap very much between one association and another. An American physician who is about to retire, enjoys the outdoors, and likes to hunt, might be a member of the American Medical Association, the American Association of Retired Persons, the Sierra Club, and the National Rifle Association. Each of these organizations is dedicated to particular interests of this hypothetical individual, but there is no overarching philosophy or conception of society that unites all of them. Nor would this outdoors-loving doctor expect to interact with the same people in all these organizations. The multiplicity of a person's interests is acknowledged in a pluralist system, but each interest is acted upon independently.

In the Dutch pillar system, by contrast, all the interests of an individual are seen through the prism of a *levensbeschouwing*. The encompassing ideology of each pillar meant that being part of a pillar involved more than just joining a series of organizations; it was also an expression of group solidarity. One does not "join" a pillar so much as one takes on its identity.

Although social divisions along the lines of religion and class go back to the origins of the Netherlands, development of the pillars accentuated consciousness of these bases of group identity and extended their significance to all areas of life. By noting small but telling signs of a Netherlander's origins—evinced in a regional accent, the number of initials before a surname, or the hand on which a wedding band is worn—an informed observer could fairly well guess which political party the person supports and predict with great accuracy which trade union federation, professional organization, and church the person belongs to. The observer may also be able to deduce what kind of school the person went to and where they are sending their children. It was possible to guess which newspaper they read and which radio/television association they belong to. Indeed, any one of these pieces of information was key to all the others. Any one piece could serve as a shorthand way of summarizing a whole host of values and opinions that the individual holds. In a society of subcultures, one need ask only the question "To which group do you belong?" The answer one receives will contain implicitly the answer to every other imaginable question about social identity and involvements.

Relations Between the Pillars

The existence of pillars within a society brings with it certain costs, one of which is the duplication of effort. Instead of a single health care organization in the Netherlands, there were three. There were 17,000 sports clubs and eighty-eight daily newspapers in the mid-1960s, all to service a population half the size of California's (Goudsblom 1967: 113, 117). The practice of giving state funding to both general and confessional schools can also lead to costly redundancy, particularly in small communities and in specialized areas of higher education. A small town might have Catholic, Protestant, and secular hospitals, clinics, and social service organizations, creating excess capacity and driving up costs (Baakman et al. 1989: 101; Kramer 1993: 78). In the larger cities, there were even separate "public" libraries for the different pillars. The town planners who organized settlement of newly reclaimed land on the Lake IJssel polders included provisions for a mixture of Catholic, Dutch Reformed, Reformed, and "unchurched" people, each with their own meeting halls, schools, health clinics, and so forth (Goudsblom 1967: 142–143).

Pillarization also imposes costs on social integration. The sense of distinctiveness that led to the desire to create separate organizations in the first place is only reinforced by the experience of living one's life among others of the same *levensbeschouwing*. When Ivan Gadourek (1961: 544–545) studied the schooling of young children during the 1940s and 1950s in the tulip bulb–growing town of Sassenheim, he found basic differences of historical interpretation between Catholic and Dutch Reformed school texts. The Catholic texts held that the sixteenth-century Inquisition was "a tribunal of the Church [whose members] were wise and pious bishops and priests." Martin Luther was said to have "rejected the Priesthood, the sacraments, and the Holy Mass." Dutch Reformed schoolbooks were very different, stating that "the Inquisition was merciless," and Luther's ninety-five Theses summed up "the shortcomings and lies of the Roman Church." Such divergent and mutually hostile interpretations of church history cannot but heighten the sense of estrangement between Catholics and Calvinists.

Even more troubling from the viewpoint of national identity are differences in interpretations of Dutch political history. William of Orange was the founding father of the Dutch state, and one's attitude toward William inevitably colors one's attitude toward the United Provinces and successor governments. The Catholic textbooks portrayed William of Orange as a capable politician whose conversion to Calvinism was a matter of opportunism rather than a profession of faith: "We must esteem Orange as the Founder of our independence but we cannot by far approve of all his deeds" (Gadourek 1961: 546–547). The Dutch Reformed history paints a far more enthusiastic picture and makes explicit the link between William of Orange, the Dutch Reformed Church, and the monarchy today:

> People gradually began to understand the love and the fidelity of the Prince. He was helping them. The people trusted him, both the Papist and the heretics. The nation should not be split up on account of religious differences! . . . And the love which we cherish for our Queen *now,* is still the same love for William of Orange *then,* the Founder of our Dynasty. (Gadourek 1961: 546–547)

This quotation from a Dutch Reformed history textbook gives an indication of the relationship between the pillars and the nation as a whole. True to Groen van Prinsterer's vision of "sovereignty in one's own circle," the basic unit of Dutch society is the community of faith. These affiliations represent one's primary loyalty, and it is the function of the state to make it possible for the pillar communities to live and work alongside each other. The Dutch people would cooperate in common endeavors where necessary but would otherwise remain within their own circle of co-believers.

To those leaders who founded the various pillar organizations, the purpose of this subcultural mobilization was not only to pursue group interests as effectively as possible, but also to preserve and heighten the sense of group distinctiveness. Conflicts between Catholics and Calvinists, even when rooted in ancient historical grievances, were kept alive in the pillar organizations. Thus Abraham Kuyper could in 1872 hold present-day Catholics responsible for the murder of Calvinists three hundred years earlier, during the revolt from Spain. God commands us, Kuyper thundered, "never to bridge the cleavage that separates the reformists from Rome."[19] These sentiments were echoed by ordinary people growing up within the pillars. As one Protestant put it, "I was brought up in fear of the Lord and in hatred of Rome" (Gielen 1965: 109). Catholics, in turn, were bombarded with messages that stressed the need to stick together to protect their rights, long past the time when any threat to group rights seemed plausible.[20] In all pillars, but especially the Catholic, people were encouraged to do their buying and hiring within the pillar whenever possible. It is little wonder, then, that interfaith marriages were rare in the Netherlands, compared to neighboring countries.[21] Ivan Gadourek's (1961: 112–113) study of the small town of Sassenheim showed that 82 percent of the population objected to interfaith marriages, and 41 percent objected to cross-denominational friendships.

These expressions of intergroup aloofness and hostility bring us to the question of how a society as thoroughly divided as the Netherlands can maintain domestic peace. The peak of revolutionary potential, often cited in Dutch histories of the twentieth century, was the statement by SDAP leader Troelstra in 1918 that revolutionary currents then sweeping through Germany would not stop at the Dutch border. Troelstra was roundly denounced for this by most of his fellow SDAP politicians, and his suggestion that the socialists seize power was met with a massive popular demonstration in support of the monarchy by people from all pillars. Troelstra spent the rest of his career trying to distance himself from his own outburst of revolutionary rhetoric, which cost him much of his influence within the SDAP. The civil wars of other countries with overlapping religious and class divisions, such as Northern Ireland, stand in tragic contrast to the domestic peace and national cohesion characteristic of the Netherlands.

How, then, do we explain coexistence of the pillars with attachment to a common set of national symbols and political institutions? As Arend Lijphart has explained in his books *The Politics of Accommodation* (1975) and *Democracy in Plural Societies* (1977), this is an issue of great importance to all divided societies where violence between linguistic, ethnic, or religious communities is either a reality or a possibility. Though they separate the population into isolated segments, the pillars of Dutch society actually make it easier to hold together a nation composed of diverse ideological and religious communities.

To see why this is so, consider Mancur Olson's (1969: 151) observation that "a society will, other things being equal, be more likely to cohere if people are socialized to have diverse wants with respect to private goods and similar wants with respect to public goods." Olson reasons that differences in taste on private goods foster cooperative behavior, since all parties will benefit from trade among themselves. For example, if I like to take evening classes and you like to earn money by teaching such classes, then our diverse tastes work out well for both of us. If others in society would rather play sports or watch television than take evening classes, that diversity is also good for me, since it increases my chances of being able to sign up for the classes I want.

Diversity in preferences for public goods is another matter altogether, because public goods cannot be varied to suit individual tastes. We must all consume the same governmental policies on the environment, education, and foreign affairs. There is bound to be an increased degree of social and political tension if highly organized groups differ on these matters.

The pillars help stabilize society under conditions of diverse demands for public goods by turning public goods into private goods. People who want Catholic education get Catholic education. Those who prefer Protestant or secular education are provided with goods to suit their taste, on the same publicly subsidized terms and with the same quality of instruction. Proportionality and equal treatment are applied to everything from broadcasting subsidies to the number of Catholics and Protestants hired to be city clerks.[22] The problem of conflicting demands for public goods is defused by meeting the varying demands of the pillars on an equal basis. As Hans Daalder (1955: 16) notes, "This would explain why the Netherlands can have party disputes that are almost theological in nature, and yet have sound administration, and why there can be such great disagreement over politics and yet, in some ways, alarmingly little over policy."

For this privatization of public policies and goods to work, it is important that each of the various religious and social groups accept the right of other groups to their separate institutions and preferences. In other words, there must be tolerance between groups. The Dutch were already in the seventeenth century internationally famous for their tolerance, though the extent of religious and personal freedom must be seen in the context of the period rather than compared to that which is normal today.[23] Immigrants to the Netherlands included Jews ousted from Spain, Portugal, Poland, and Lithuania, several waves of Protestant refugees from France, and even the Pilgrims from England.[24] In addition to the large Dutch Reformed and Catholic communities, there were also Lutherans, Remonstrants, Mennonites, and Jews, making tolerance a practical necessity. People such as René Descartes, John Locke, and Baruch Spinoza all came to the Netherlands to enjoy a freedom of thought so great compared to surrounding countries that half of all books published in Europe in the seventeenth century came off Dutch presses (Boxer 1990: 188–189).

This tolerance was not a celebration of diversity but rather a pragmatic acceptance of differences that one is powerless to eradicate. Immigrants brought shipbuilding skills, navigational techniques, legal training, banking expertise, and a hundred other capabilities to the fledgling republic. Moreover, the fact that all religious groups were in the minority meant that no group was sufficiently dominant to force its views on others. Catholics, Protestants, and people of no religious affiliation each constituted about a third of the population (the Catholics were somewhat larger as a group, the "unchurched" a bit smaller). The presence of multiple minorities forced each group to tolerate the others.

As a result, the Dutch Republic was semiofficially a Dutch Reformed state but was in practice a religiously diverse and tolerant nation. Although the laws of most seventeenth- and eighteenth-century towns forbade Catholics to hold mass in public, town councils made no effort to act against services held in private homes or even in specially constructed places of worship so long as they were not identifiable as churches from the outside. K.H.D. Haley (1972: 93) reports that the whereabouts of these places of Catholic worship were so widely known that Protestants were able to direct strangers to them.[25] Simon Schama (1988: 60) aptly captures the combination of Calvinist dominance and religious tolerance when he says that the Catholic minority "were obliged to worship in diplomatic privacy, but . . . were certainly not subjected to any systematic effort at repression." As long as the Netherlands remained a Calvinist nation in principle, the facts of the matter could be otherwise. This kind of acceptance continued to characterize relations between the pillars into the twentieth century.

A further pragmatic reason for the maintenance of peaceful relations between the pillars is the experience of shifting coalitions between them. Relations between leaders of the pillars changed over time with the prominence of different issues. Catholic leaders supported the Liberals for several decades in the nineteenth century, since the Liberal program promised equal rights for those not part of the Dutch Reformed or Reformed Churches. As emancipation was achieved, however, Dutch Catholics broke with the Liberals and forged an alliance with Protestant leaders on the issue of public support for denominational schools. And, as we have already seen, social democratic leaders supported religious schools in exchange for confessional support of universal suffrage. The fact that no group could form a majority, combined with the shifting nature of cross-pillar coalitions, created powerful incentives for cooperation. In this way, the pillars grew to maturity while maintaining an uneasy peace between them.

The Pillars After World War II

World War II posed a stern test of the pillar organization of Dutch society. The experience of German occupation between May 1940 and April 1945 was a devastating watershed in Dutch history, one that left many aspects of life in the Netherlands forever changed. The pillars were not, however, destroyed by the experience, and in fact came back after the war stronger than they had been before. Though pillar organizations were for the most part repressed during the occupation, they returned intact after liberation.

The war for the Netherlands was brief, as nine Dutch divisions were able to hold off eighteen German divisions, supported by paratroops and tanks, for just four days. Dutch Jews were immediately swept up in the Nazi policy of genocide against European Jewry. As early as the seventeenth century, Jews had settled in Amsterdam and were allowed to purchase citizenship for a nominal price. By the beginning of the nineteenth century, Amsterdam had the largest Jewish population of any city in the world.[26] This was no longer true in 1940, but there were still 140,000 Jews in Amsterdam at the beginning of World War II. The Nazis murdered 110,000 of them. Anne Frank's diary has made famous the fact that some Jews were able to hide in the closets and attics of neighbors' homes for the duration of the war.[27] But Ivo Schöffer (1973: 162) estimates that only 12,000 Dutch Jews were saved by hiding or by disguising their identity. Another 8,000 were spared by virtue of being married to gentiles. Only 6,000 of the over 100,000 Jews deported to the death camps ever returned. The Holocaust destroyed almost completely this small but vital segment of the pluralistic Dutch culture, and the Jewish population of the Netherlands today remains at just 30,000.

Although German racial beliefs caused the occupying government initially to adopt a relatively lenient policy toward Dutch Christians, the increasing labor and production demands of the war led to an ever more ruthless occupation. Three hundred thousand Christians were deported to labor camps as the Nazis steadily increased the intensity of their search for slave labor. About 23,000 of them died there. Several strikes and acts of sabotage organized during the war led to mass arrests and summary executions. The Germans retaliated for an attempt on the life of a local Gestapo chief by burning the village of Putten to the ground and deporting all 400 men of the town to the labor camps.

The most difficult phase of the war was the final six months. Broadcasting from London, Queen Wilhelmina ordered a general rail strike beginning in September 1944 to assist the Allied advance on the continent. The Dutch population anticipated that German troops would be driven out of the Netherlands within weeks, but the Allied effort to cross the Maas, Waal, and Rhine Rivers at a single stroke failed in the battle of Arnhem in late September. As a result, only the southern provinces of the country were liberated from Nazi occupation prior to the winter of 1944–1945, a season known still today as the "Hunger Winter." To conserve their own food supplies and in revenge for the continuing rail strike, German troops stopped all transport of food from the agricultural eastern part of the Netherlands to the coastal cities of the west. By April and May 1945, when Allied troops finally reached the northern provinces, everything that could be eaten— including tulip bulbs—had been consumed. Much of the population was on the verge of starvation. Simon Carmiggelt, a Dutch journalist who for thirty years wrote a daily column capturing the everyday words and actions of ordinary people, had this to say about the experience:

> How horrible everything was. The whole day it was eating, eating, always talking about eating. It began in the morning. Should we eat a piece of bread now or later? Usually Anna and he ate it all at the same time, but Fien preferred to keep hers. She began at eleven o'clock on her own. That irritated. Remarks were made. "So you've some left, have you? Well, we'll look on."[28]

These are the bare facts of a five-year trauma in a nation that had successfully maintained its neutrality during World War I and that falsely expected Germany to honor its neutrality in the Second World War. The terrible experience of defeat and occupation put the Dutch through trials of a magnitude that any society undergoes only rarely. Such hardships, experienced collectively and at the hands of a foreign enemy, naturally led to a reexamination of core values, reinforcing some of them and provoking a rejection of others. In Carmiggelt's column on the Hunger Winter, for example, Fien is a lodger of thirty years' standing suspected by the couple who own the house of hoarding food in her room. The old man creeps up the stairs and listens outside her room late at night for sounds of eating. She hears him and emerges to confess, tearfully, that she has been eating gingersnaps. The woman is ashamed that she has not shared the food with her friends; the man is ashamed that he has been reduced to listening outside her door. The column ends with the two sitting side by side on the stairs, dazed at what has become of them, suspecting that their old and familiar lives will never return.

By 1945, four themes had emerged as social consequences of the war. First, there was reinforcement of the religious beliefs that had throughout history played such a key part in Dutch society. Catholics and Calvinists alike turned to faith for strength and solace during the occupation. For example, when the first hostages were killed by the Nazis in reprisal for a general strike in Amsterdam in February 1941 (a strike called to protest the mass arrest of Jews in that city), the underground printer H. N. Werkman distributed an edition of Martin Luther's "Open Letter to the Christians of the Low Countries," written in 1523. Luther had written this letter after the burning of two Protestant monks by Catholic authorities in Brussels.

> Oh how contemptuously have those two souls been executed! But how wonderfully and with what joy shall they return and judge those by whom they have been unjustly convicted! It is such a little thing to be violated and killed by the world. . . . What is the world compared with God?[29]

A second consequence of the German occupation was to bring the Dutch Protestant and Catholic pillars together as never before. The sense of being part of a single community, united in opposition to a foreign oppressor, was a powerful one. Unlike the revolt from Spain, which pitted Protestant against Catholic, this was a common struggle of all Dutch people. Particularly as the war came to an end, there was a rejoicing and celebration of the Dutch spirit, a spirit identified not with the pillars but rather with the whole nation. A poem by Max Dendermonde, written in 1945 just after liberation of the northern city of Groningen, illustrates the sense of a common mission uniting both survivors and victims of the war:

> *A city is never just brick and stone*
> *with mortar and lead and wood and glass.*
> *The foundation is instead the spirit*
> *that survives in high tide and ebb*
>
> . . .

> *See, the stone and wood and glass and mortar*
> *are now reduced to ruin and dust.*
> *The spirit, still strong and undefiled*
> *will build itself a new house.*
> . . .
> *This we owe to those who fell:*
> *Their spirit and our hands are one . . .* [30]

The third effect of the war experience was to reinforce feelings of patriotism in general, and feelings of attachment to the royal family in particular. During the war the entire nation found in Queen Wilhelmina a symbol of their common plight. The fact that the Germans prohibited display of pictures of the royal family and purged textbooks of all reference to the House of Orange only increased the identification of Wilhelmina with resistance to the occupation (Eldersveld 1947). Many people risked their lives listening to her speeches broadcast from the other side of the English Channel. Socialists had long been ambivalent about the House of Orange, but during the war their underground newspaper *Het Parool* regularly printed the queen's speeches and pledged to support a continued monarchy after the war.

Wilhelmina spent the war years partly in Canada and mainly in London. She personified the government in exile, over which she—in the enforced absence of the voters—exerted great influence. When Crown princess Juliana gave birth to a baby girl in January 1943, she named her Margriet to honor the Dutch soldiers who fell to the German army in May 1940, while the blooms of the marguerite daisy were at their peak. Margriet's birth also inspired underground poetry in a population desperate for signs of hope.

> *The Hague is in ruins,*
> *There are no treasures for you here,*
> *But everyone will serve you*
> *When you come to us, Margriet!*[31]

In summary, the devastation of the war inspired among the Dutch a determination to work cooperatively to rebuild their country. Divisions between the pillars, expressed in daily antagonisms and irritations as well as in consistent exclusion of the social democrats from prewar governments, were outweighed in 1945 by belief in a common mission. Robert Cox (1993) observes that many political leaders who were unable to escape the country were interned in the former Abbey of San Michiel. Thrown together and with a great deal of time on their hands, they developed the view that "pillar-based conflict among political groups [was] a dysfunctional influence that had prevented effective governance of the country" (Cox 1993: 98).

The job of postwar reconstruction would be nothing less than daunting. An American report on conditions in the Netherlands noted this:

Liberation of the country in May 1945 found the Netherlands' economy in a state of widespread deterioration. . . . Hundreds of bridges had been blown up, the greater part of the rolling stock had disappeared, only 60 per cent of the inland merchant fleet was left, and the merchant marine had shrunk to about 50 per cent of its prewar tonnage. . . . About 10 per cent of the arable land was inundated [due to the destruction of dikes], the depletion of all stocks had crippled industry, nearly 100,000 houses had been completely destroyed and many more damaged, and hundreds of thousands of workers were still dispersed over Germany and other countries. The densely populated Western provinces faced catastrophe [due to famine]. (Bellquist 1948: 42)

The staggering tasks of postwar reconstruction were matched by an equally great determination of the population to work together. Never before had the ideas of the confessional labor unions about the dignity of manual labor and the reciprocal obligations of each social class to the others been as widely accepted. As we shall see in greater detail in Chapter 6, the Dutch inaugurated in the postwar years a system of centralized negotiation over labor conditions, social welfare, and macroeconomic policy. These central bargains, binding on all workers, were reached between leaders of the pillar-affiliated trade unions and employers associations, along with senior civil servants and leaders of the various political parties. Although the agreements held down wage levels so that firms could invest in reconstruction, workers in each of the pillar unions accepted these contracts without question. The Netherlands had a high strike rate between 1919 and 1932, but since World War II the country has had one of the lowest strike rates in the world (Koopmans 1996: 32).

The social democrats carried this new spirit the furthest in their determination to break through the pillar system and become a movement of the entire working class. The postwar social democratic party, the PvdA (*Partij van de Arbeid,* or Labor Party), set up Protestant and Catholic workgroups within its structure and succeeded in attracting a number of left-wing leaders and activists from the confessional pillars. But the response of the leaders of the other pillars was to tighten their own internal discipline. The Catholic bishops went so far as to publish in 1954 a letter, called the *Mandement,* in which they stated that membership in a socialist labor union or broadcast association would result in denial of the sacraments—in effect, excommunication. Even listening to radio programs sponsored by the socialist broadcast association was "strongly discouraged." The impact of this letter, and more generally of a renewed commitment to discipline within the pillars, led to a postwar restoration and even extension of the pillarized society.[32] Studies in the 1950s and 1960s show that about 90 percent of Catholics and Reformed Church members supported the political party, trade union, employers association, elementary school, broadcast association, and women's and youth clubs associated with their pillars. The percentages reading the "right" newspaper and joining the appropriate music or sports club were almost as high.[33] The pillars were, if anything, stronger after World War II than they had been before.

Postwar reestablishment of the pillar organizations, however, did not bring with it renewal of the pillar mentality as it had existed earlier in the century.

Indeed, the very word "pillars" came into wide currency only after World War II. To call the rival networks of religious and ideological organizations "pillars" was to view them as separate columns supporting the common roof of the Dutch state and nation. As Ivo Schöffer has pointed out, the central trait of the pillars is that they "implied mutual recognition, the conscious view that each separate ideological organization represented only a part which provided support to an overarching, larger whole."[34] The maintenance of organizational separatism was now combined with a cooperative spirit. The Netherlands had entered the heyday of what Arend Lijphart (1975) has called "the politics of accommodation" in his book of the same name.

Reinforcement of the Dutch pillars after World War II shows that these networks of organizations could adapt to changing social values and needs. However, the 1954 *Mandement* of the Catholic bishops proved to be the last determined effort by the leadership of a pillar to enforce unity within the organizational network. Two significant social changes were about to unravel the organizational pillars that had been built so systematically over the preceding eighty years. One of those changes has been a general trend throughout western Europe: the transformation of society caused by the long period of peace and economic growth in the postwar era. The other change, with which we shall begin, was more specific to the Netherlands. That was the revolution within Dutch Catholicism.

Crisis of Authority Within the Catholic Pillar

Beginning in the early years of the twentieth century, Dutch Catholics were the most tightly integrated of the three pillars. They also comprised perhaps the most traditional and loyal national body of Catholics anywhere on the globe. Faithfulness to the pillar and to the Catholic Church were both maintained through an unblinking assertion by the bishops that the spiritual and social health of the Catholic community required cohesion and isolation. As Cardinal de Jong declared in a 1953 radio broadcast to fellow Catholics, "Whatever we have accomplished, particularly in public life, we owe to our unity in our dealings with the outside world. But, as our emancipation progresses, that unity will be exposed to ever greater dangers. . . . Therefore, dear fellow believers of the Netherlands, stay one, one!"[35]

For decades the need to "stay one!" led the Catholic hierarchy to act as agents of social control. Herman Bakvis (1981: 37) observes that parish priests used home visits as an opportunity to check up on the reading and listening habits of a Catholic family, to be sure that the breadwinner had joined a Catholic union, to check for the regular spacing of children, and to remind adults to support the Catholic political party.

By the late 1950s, though, the bishops had begun to lose their conviction in the necessity of organizational unity. Declarations from the college of bishops indicated the need to distinguish between Catholicism as support for the pillar organizations and Catholicism as a community of faith. Beginning around 1960, the Catholic hierarchy chose to emphasize the latter. Eighty years earlier, Kuyper had built the Protestant pillar as a way of revitalizing Calvinism; now the bishops chose to de-emphasize their pillar in order to renew the spirit of Catholicism. In this the bishops anticipated many of the perspectives adopted in the mid-1960s as part of the Vatican II reforms. The desire was to reduce regulation of the daily lives of Catholics, placing greater responsibility on the individual to use the Church's teachings to make their own moral choices. As the Catholic comedian Frons Jansen put it, "In our church formerly everything was forbidden, except what was allowed—and you had to do that!"[36] In the 1960s, by contrast, noted Catholic sociologist J.M.G. Thurlings (1971: 134) observed that "Modern theology blurs the distinction between priest and layman and subjects the old ethics and doctrines to penetrating criticism, with the result that the traditional professional, the priest, has ceased to exercise his former authority."

This "deregulation" of Catholic life soon became a global phenomenon, but it hit the Dutch Catholic pillar like a bomb. In 1963 one of the bishops stated on television that the use of contraceptives should be left to the judgment of a married couple. In 1965 the bishops formally repealed the 1954 *Mandement* against membership in socialist organizations. The Catholic University at Nijmegen was soon appointing marxist professors to teach sociology, economics, and political science. The next year, the bishops published their *New Dutch Catechism,* a book that left open questions such as whether Mary gave virgin birth to Christ, cast doubt upon the concept of original sin, and suggested that the Last Supper was a symbolic myth (Coleman 1978: 247–251). In 1970 the Dutch bishops petitioned the Vatican to change the policy on priestly celibacy.

Most far-reaching of all was the redefinition of the relationship between bishops, priests, and laity, from a hierarchy to a community of faith. Following the Second Vatican Council, the Dutch established a National Pastoral Council consisting of the seven bishops along with elected representatives of the priesthood and laity. This council, and the Diocesan Councils that were formed shortly after, were soon debating the wisdom of Church doctrine on priestly celibacy and the use of contraceptives. John Coleman (1978: 114–115) estimates that 15 percent of the adult Catholic population took an active part in the Diocesan Councils between 1966 and 1976, debating theological issues in an entirely new way and creating what was referred to as "a church in movement."

The Dutch Catholic Church changed in the span of just a few years from being an ultra-traditional, hierarchical, and somewhat passive church to being an exuberant leader in the Vatican II spirit of reform. Cees Nooteboom's 1983 novel *Rituals* captured well the questioning spirit of the time when he had a character muse that "God sounds like an answer—that is what is most pernicious about the word. It has so often been used as an answer. He should have had a name that sounds like a question." Such attitudes often brought the Dutch Church into conflict with the Vatican in the retrenching atmosphere of the later 1960s and early

1970s, under Pope Paul VI. As Coleman (1978: 1) put it, "The Netherlands seemed the center for new theological, pastoral, liturgical, catechetical, and structural changes taking place within world Catholicism. . . . [The Dutch Church had become] a symbolic alternative to Rome."

These changes were not just matters of theological doctrine; they also affected the core relationships between pillar organizations. Speaking to a television audience just prior to the 1967 parliamentary election, one of the Dutch bishops said that it is not necessary to vote for the Catholic People's Party (KVP) to be a good Catholic. In that same year, the Dutch Catholic Union Federation (NKV) refused to endorse the KVP election list in retaliation for the party's role in bringing down a government that included the Labor Party (PvdA). In the early 1960s the Catholic broadcasting association, the KRO, had already decided to phase out the free airtime and uncritical public forum it had regularly given KVP leaders. The KRO began to dilute the specifically Catholic, and even generally religious, nature of much of its programming, concentrating instead on competing for viewers by offering secular entertainment.

Publicly visible cracks were proliferating within the Catholic pillar, and the Catholic population responded. There may have been a *réveil* of the spirit, but there was also an ebbing of adherence to the traditional expectations. Weekly attendance at mass, taking of the sacraments, and the number of people accepting a religious vocation all fell dramatically. Herman Bakvis (1981: 117) cites findings by the Catholic Social Research Institute that 64 percent of Catholics attended mass on an average week in January 1966. Six years later, in January 1972, the figure was down to 41 percent. And six years after that, in January 1978, only 28 percent of Catholics were attending mass. As late as the mid-1950s, the Dutch, just 1 percent of the world Catholic population, produced 10 percent of international missionaries (Coleman 1978: 2). By the end of the 1960s the number of priests in the Netherlands was in free fall, as resignations from the priesthood outnumbered ordinations by five to one (Coleman 1978: 302). The Dutch Catholic birthrate, always quite high because of faithful adherence to Church doctrine on the use of contraceptives, began rapidly to decline.

These changes in Catholic behavior did not mean that pillar organizations came to an end all at once. About 75 percent of Catholic families were still subscribing to a Catholic newspaper well into the 1970s, and nearly 100 percent of Catholic parents were sending their children to Catholic elementary schools (Bakvis 1981: 123). But while the organizational forms remained Catholic, their content became less so. The leading Catholic newspaper, the *Katholieke Volkskrant,* changed its name to the *Volkskrant* and became a national newspaper with a left-leaning editorial stance and only residual identification with the Catholic pillar. Although parents continued to send their children to Catholic schools, over a quarter of them thought that the need for specifically Catholic education was minimal (van Kemenade 1968: 117ff.). It is perhaps well that they did, for the proportion of nominally Catholic schools actually under the control of the clergy was declining, from over 80 percent in 1954 to under two-thirds in 1964. Other organizational foundations of the pillars have also been abandoned. There is now just a single organization for large employers, the VNO-NCW, compared to the three that existed before 1970 (Catholic, Protestant, and secular). There are still two national union federations descended from the pillar era, one Protestant (the CNV) and the other a coalition of the former Catholic and socialist union federations (the FNV). The core distinction between the CNV and FNV today is no longer religion, but rather their respective strategies of labor relations. Moderate unions with a Catholic background have without discomfort affiliated with what is still nominally a Protestant union federation.

By the 1970s, J.M.G. Thurlings (1978) could refer to the network of Catholic organizations as "the unstable pillar." The damage was partly self-inflicted by a Catholic hierarchy that no longer believed in the necessity of internal unity to preserve group strength. But the decay of Catholic orthodoxy was not only a consequence of having a liberal hierarchy, for the appointment of more conservative bishops beginning in 1970 did nothing to reverse the trend. Moreover, the Calvinist faithful also became substantially more independent of their own pillar during the 1960s and 1970s, even though the leadership of the Dutch Reformed and Reformed Churches did not embark on a deliberate change of direction.

One cause of the decline of the confessional pillars was secularization of the Dutch people. The proportion of Dutch identifying themselves as outside of any church doubled in just over twenty years, from 18 percent in 1960 to 37 percent in 1982 (Irwin and van Holsteyn 1989b: 34). Even those still claiming affiliation with a particular church became less faithful in their observance. Regular church attendance dropped from 44 percent of the Dutch population in 1967 to just 11 percent in 1994.[37]

A second reason for the end of the pillar system was change in the pillarized organizations themselves. Over time, pillar organizations found that common interests with their counterparts in the other pillars outweighed the remaining vestiges of historical rivalry and distrust. Hans Daalder (1991: 75) notes that these organizations were becoming "specialized, routinized and bureaucratized. This moved them further and further from the original ideological sources of their existence. They oriented themselves to their specific clienteles regardless of pillar, and began to develop new collaborations or mergers [with their counterpart organizations from other pillars]." In the mid-1960s, scholars had already begun to note an increasing amount of cooperation between professional organizations in different pillars, and some predicted that this would lead to a gradual decline of pillar cohesion.[38] Val Lorwin (1971: 166) captured this phenomenon succinctly when he wrote, "There is nothing so like a Socialist union's unemployment compensation office as a Catholic union's unemployment compensation office."

The revolution in telecommunications also contributed to deconfessionalization. Technical innovations in television transmission, such as cable and satellite dishes, made the former pillar monopoly of broadcast time infeasible. A law passed in 1966 allowed any association with 100,000 members access to television broadcast rights, hence breaking the pillar monopoly. European Union directives now mandate that commercial television broadcasting be allowed and that nations not try to protect their national television markets. These changes made it impossible to continue the previous insulation of the community of the faithful, or for that matter even to keep people watching Dutch television in preference to programming from other countries.[39] Television has become more purely a medium for entertainment, and "diversity [in broadcast fare] is no longer based on beliefs but merely on commercial considerations."[40] About 60 percent of the Dutch population belonged to a pillarized broadcast association in 1965; by 1985 the pillar broadcast associations accounted for just a third of memberships—and even those were substantially less pillar-oriented than they had been twenty years earlier (Bax 1990: 122).

This is precisely the kind of secularizing and homogenizing force that Guillaume Groen van Prinsterer, Abraham Kuyper, and the other pillar founders were trying to stave off. But the fall of the pillars was not due solely to a change of heart on the part of Catholic leaders, to the professionalization of organizational life, and to new television technologies. The public was changing too. In the late 1960s, new social values and new political demands were being expressed, and pillar authority was being challenged from below.

A Not-So-Silent Revolution

As we have already noted, a fundamental part of the postwar Dutch culture was acceptance by members of all social classes that reconstruction of the economy took priority over the issues of labor rights and income distribution that had dominated class relations in the early part of the century. As part of this far-reaching reconciliation of class conflict, the representatives of labor agreed to an extended period of moderate wage increases in exchange for a business commitment to investment in economic reconstruction and a governmental commitment to the development of a far-reaching welfare state. This cooperation between government and leading economic organizations helped produce almost three decades of rapid economic growth and full employment (1946–1974), accompanied by significant gains in the standard of living. Ironically, this material success also contributed to the downfall of the collaboration that made rapid reconstruction possible. A high level of affluence and security made the centralized bargaining system, which demanded enormous discipline within the labor movement, seem obsolete and unnecessary. There developed a widespread questioning of the pillar system and the political process that accompanied it, led by a vocal new generation that had not experienced the hardships of the Great Depression and World War II. The final chapter of the turbulent Dutch twentieth century was about to be written.

Agenda for a New Generation

In 1965 in the city of Amsterdam, a series of demonstrations brought together young people discontented with the materialistic orientation and bureaucratic organizations of postwar society. Composed of students and other youth born during or just after World War II, this protest marked a fundamental break with the existing political and economic consensus on reconstruction in the wake of the war's devastation. This youth movement came to be known as "Provo," and its followers were dubbed the "provotariat" by their most prominent leader, Roel van Duyn.

> PROVO has something against capitalism, fascism, bureaucracy, militarism, professionalism, dogmatism, and authoritarianism.
> PROVO calls for resistance wherever possible . . .
> PROVO regards anarchy as the inspirational source of resistance.
> PROVO wants to revive anarchy and teach it to the young.
> PROVO IS AN IMAGE.[41]

Within a year, Amsterdam's Provo leaders began to develop a series of "white" plans. The white bicycle plan, for example, would close the city center to automobiles, improve public transportation, and make available 20,000 white bicycles that people could pick up, ride to their destination, and leave for the next user. The white chimney plan would improve Amsterdam's air quality by monitoring smokestack emissions. The white chicken plan would put city police in white uniforms and replace their weapons with condoms and cooked chicken legs to be handed out to passersby as needed (de Vries 1966). The Kabouters (Gnomes), a successor group to Provo created in 1970, developed the outlines of an alternative society: alternative housing (created by breaking into empty houses and turning them into communal living spaces), alternative grocery stores with organic fruits and vegetables, volunteer services for the elderly, and tree-planting campaigns in the middle of cities.

These were extraordinarily innovative ideas at the time, and they contained in them the seeds of a new political agenda.[42] The concern about green spaces, organic foods, and smokestack emissions, for example, marked the beginning of the environmental movement. Efforts to reduce traffic congestion and the occupation of empty houses signaled the beginning of public involvement in urban planning.[43] Provo, in short, initiated a shift to a new political agenda that placed less stress on material affluence and more on the quality of life, less on political stability and more on direct participation in politics, less on decisionmaking by the leaders of pillar organizations and more on decentralization of power.

Provo and its successor groups were among the first of the new social movements to combine a political agenda with a social agenda. Many of their "Provocations" combined "artistic happenings" (they used the English phrase) with political demands, in the belief that art generates critical perspectives on authority. The first recognized leader of Provo, Robert Jasper Grootveld, was a magician who integrated political and social criticism into his act. Grootveld brought the Latin word *"ludiek"* to the Dutch language,[44] arguing that the only way to deal with authority (both governmental and in the private pillar organizations) was to poke fun at it.

The challenge to social and political authority represented by this new movement is best summarized in the 1970 "Proclamation of the Orange Free State" by the Kabouters:

> Out of the subculture of the existing order, an alternative society is growing. . . . [I]ndependent of the still ruling authorities, [this new culture seeks] to live its own life and to rule itself. This revolution takes place now. It is the end of the underground, of protest, of demonstrations; from this moment we spend our energy on the construction of an anti-authoritarian society.[45]

Although the language of revolution used by Provo and the Kabouters was a bit overblown, a new, more participatory society has indeed replaced the old patterns of hierarchical authority. One significant area of change has been within the family. Although research on authority patterns in the family has been confined largely to working-class families, there has clearly been an enormous growth of egalitarianism within the family, both between fathers and mothers and between parents and children. As Johan Goudsblom (1967: 136–137) observed in the mid-1960s:

> In the average Dutch family, the father is still the *head,* not merely de jure but also de facto. However, his authority is not as undivided and undisputed as it used to be. The old patriarchal system with the father ruling the extended family can still be found in some rural regions, but it is definitely on the wane. . . . Parent-child relations also seem to be altering toward greater egalitarianism.

The trend that Goudsblom was just beginning to see in the mid-1960s had accelerated ten years later. Results from questions in the 1977 Dutch Parliamentary Election Study showed that only 3 percent of respondents said that the father decides alone on such things as major purchases by the family or educational choices for the children. By contrast, when asked about the families they grew up in, 20 percent of respondents reported that their fathers had made major purchase decisions alone, and 27 percent said that their fathers made the decisions concerning the children's education. The same series of questions showed that not only had consultation of the mother on such decisions increased, but that consultation of the children had increased as well. Aided by laws creating employee councils in the workplace, authority patterns have become less hierarchical at work as well as in the family.

The greatest social revolution that occurred in the wake of the 1960s youth movements was in the area of relations between men and women. Calvinist and

Catholic religious traditions had long defined the role of women primarily in terms of motherhood and the home. Women were not allowed to own bank accounts until 1957, and a "year of grief" (during which one could not remarry) was legally mandatory for widows and divorced women until 1970 (Huggett 1971). As late as 1965, 85 percent of the public disapproved of working mothers of school-aged children. As late as 1981, only 38 percent of a sample of the Dutch public agreed that "a married woman has the same right to work as a man, even in a period of serious unemployment." Just over half the sample agreed that "A woman should not have a job outside the house if she has young children."[46] It is hardly surprising, then, that Dutch women long had the lowest rate of participation in the labor force of any advanced industrial democracy. Only 3 percent of married Dutch women worked in 1960, compared to percentages ranging from one-quarter to one-third of married women in Germany, France, Britain, and the United States at that time (Goudsblom 1967: 49).

But change has been rapid. By 1989 one-third of women with children under age 4 were in the labor force, and by 1996 the percentage of Dutch women in the labor force was higher than the average for other EU countries.[47] A similar change has occurred in higher education, where the proportion of women students increased from one-quarter in 1960 to more than half by 1990 (Kriesi 1993: 25). In politics, a state secretary (junior minister) was appointed in 1977 to help coordinate and promote what has become known in the Netherlands as "emancipation policy," and a parallel committee was established in the Second Chamber. The Anti-Revolutionary Party prohibited women from standing for election as late as 1956, but today about one-third of members of parliament are women and all major parties (including the ARP's successor party, the Christian Democratic Appeal [CDA]) have been aggressive in promoting women as candidates.[48] The proportion of women in the top civil service has increased only gradually, but more dramatic strides have been made in elective and appointive political offices ranging from mayor to minister.

These changes came about as a consequence of the women's movement that organized in the Netherlands during the 1960s and 1970s to demand more participation in the labor force and in politics. Dutch feminism has nineteenth-century roots in such women as Aletta Jacobs, who wrote to Prime Minister Thorbecke for permission to undertake university studies and then, having received a doctorate in medicine in 1879, devoted herself to work on family planning. Jacobs became president of the Association for Women's Voting Rights (VVVK) in 1903, and continued in that position until women's suffrage was won in 1919.[49]

Development of the pillars enabled women to organize early in the twentieth century, but the beginnings of an organization of women *as women* (as opposed to an organization of Catholic women or of socialist women) came only in the late 1960s. The breakthrough organization was *Man-Vrouw-Maatschappij* (MVM), or "Man-Woman-Society." Founded in 1968, MVM consisted primarily of professional women and men who pursued the goal of equal rights and career opportunities by working through the established political parties. A more radical organization of women arose about the same time, called the *Dolle Minas*. Oriented to consciousness-raising among women, the *Dolle Minas* helped start what is today an extensive network of women's discussion groups, theaters and art galleries, health centers, bookstores, publishing houses, cafés, adult education groups, and shelters for rape victims and victims of domestic violence. As Joni Lovenduski (1986: 86) put it, "In Holland in particular, considerable energy is put into creating agreeable and comfortable places where women meet, in the belief that there is no need to wait until after the revolution to learn that society might be different."

This burst of autonomous mobilization had a major impact on women in the more traditional pillarized organizations. In the 1960s, progressive Catholics were already challenging the approach of the *Mater Amabilis* (Loving Mother) and *Pater Fortis* (Strong Father) schools for young adults, which stressed stereotypical sex roles. By the end of the decade, psychology was replacing morality at the core of the curriculum in the Catholic schools, and a Catholic education no longer meant an education in Catholic beliefs about gender roles and the family (Vossen 1991).

Feminists also developed a strong presence in the women's groups within the various political parties and labor unions, and their influence can be seen in such changes as liberalization of the abortion law. Abortion had long been viewed in the Netherlands from a religious-ethical perspective. But under the influence of a movement campaign organized by a coalition of women's organizations called "We Women Demand," the debate came to be seen in terms of freedom of choice for women. The law regulating access to abortion was liberalized in 1981 to reflect exactly this perspective.[50] In 1970 women were on average more politically conservative than men, chiefly because of their religious beliefs. By 1985 women had become more liberal than men, having been transformed by secularization and the women's movement (Middendorp 1991: 198).

The spread of environmental consciousness is another area of changing social values whose origins can be traced to the Provo and Kabouter movements. With more than 15 million inhabitants in 42,000 square kilometers, the Netherlands is one of the most densely populated countries in the world.[51] The Dutch lifestyle is not a particularly polluting one; in fact, proximity of the major cities to each other results in less automobile dependence than is found in the United States or other large countries.[52] Even so, automobile ownership grew from less than 10 percent of households to almost 45 percent between 1959 and 1969, increasing the number of registered vehicles from less than a half million to 2.3 million (Schöffer 1973: 180; Jamison et al. 1990: 125). There is nothing unusual in that development, except that in the densely populated Netherlands this resulted in having fifty-five cars per square kilometer! Plans to restrict automobile usage were consequently among the first programs advocated by Provo and its successors.

Environmental consciousness may grow the most quickly when decay of the environment is rapid and tangibly apparent. In the case of the Netherlands, deterioration of the environment was quite rapid in the postwar decades: Edible salmon had been caught in the Hollandse IJssel near Rotterdam within living memory, but are no longer to be had. Smog made its first appearance in the urbanized western part of the country in the late 1960s (de Roos et al. 1980: 82–83). The galvanizing moment in the Dutch environmental movement was the 1979 discovery in the small town of Lekkerkerk that over 1,600 drums of industrial waste had been dumped in a residential neighborhood. Although the dumping had been done without a permit, local government officials later issued a retroactive permit without public hearings or other notice.

Knowledge that such a thing could happen created a turning point both for public organizing and for government action. In the wake of the Lekkerkerk cleanup the government identified 1,200 other hazardous waste sites around the country, adding to awareness of the fragility of the environment in a land-scarce country.[53] This has led to a growth of involvement in a wide variety of local groups organized for such causes as to protect a stretch of coastline or to save some piece of open ground from development. Such involvement is hardly new; Russell Dalton (1994: 25) gives the example of a group that formed in Amsterdam in 1904 to preserve a bird sanctuary threatened with becoming a landfill.[54] More recently, though, environmental consciousness has spread beyond the goals of creating nature preserves to touch more closely the environmental impacts of everyday patterns of behavior. The youth movements of the 1960s began this trend with their emphasis on eating organic foods and reducing automobile use.

By the mid-1970s, between six hundred and seven hundred local groups had been founded to champion environmental issues. These included groups oriented toward influencing governmental policy, groups seeking to force policy changes by mass mobilization, and groups concerned primarily with educating the public on strategies for environmentally sound living.[55] Since then, public campaigns have at times raised the visibility of environmental issues to uncommon heights: In the national elections of 1971 and 1972, a fifth of the electorate identified the environment as the most important issue facing the country. In 1989 an astounding 45 percent identified the environment as the most important issue, despite the simultaneous presence of double-digit unemployment.[56] Comparative research shows that the level of environmental concern is greater in the Netherlands than among other European publics, and that the Dutch public is more favorable to ecology groups than the public of any other country in the European Union (Heidenheimer et al. 1990: 317; Dalton 1994: 62). By the mid-1990s over 20 percent of the worldwide membership of Greenpeace was Dutch. Just how far the concern for environmental issues has spread may be judged from the recent decision of the five-star Kurhaus Hotel in Scheveningen to risk losing two of its five stars by providing guests with two hand towels instead of three, out of environmental considerations. Even Roel van Duyn, the early Provo leader, had by the 1980s become involved in an environmental organization that sought to connect environmental consciousness to each of the major ideological currents in Dutch society. As van Duyn put it, "Christianity represents the principle of stewardship of man on earth, liberalism a principle of responsible entrepreneurship, and socialism the principle of self-government."[57]

The appearance of Provo and the growth of the women's and environmental movements marked a shift from the era of postwar reconstruction to a new era of rethinking social and political priorities. This reorientation brought to politics an entirely new set of preoccupations including not only environmentalism and women's liberation, but also citizen participation and increased individual freedom to choose from a wider menu of lifestyles. Hanspeter Kriesi's (1993: 65) probing examination of changing values in the Netherlands shows that by the end of the 1980s two-thirds of the population wanted to live independently of church rules, and three-quarters preferred a society in which women have the same opportunities as men. Analysis of an advice column in a women's magazine over a forty-year period shows that the shift toward more libertarian, permissive values has been manifest in virtually every area of life.[58] By 1990, the Dutch population (together with the Danes) had become Europe's "most permissive nation with respect to moral issues such as divorce, homosexuality, prostitution, abortion, euthanasia and suicide."[59]

To those familiar with student politics of the late 1960s in other countries, the challenge to political authority by the Dutch new left will feel familiar. Ronald Inglehart (1990: 3) has demonstrated that throughout the advanced industrial democracies, "The incentives that motivate people to work, the issues that give rise to political conflict, people's religious beliefs, their attitudes concerning divorce, abortion, and homosexuality, the importance they attach to having children and raising families—all these have been changing." The fact that material security can be taken for granted, particularly in those advanced industrial societies that have also developed an extensive welfare state, has meant that people are instead turning their attention to the possibilities of self-expression in their social and political lives. Many of the changes in Dutch society over the last forty years, such as a decline in the strength of religious feeling and a turning away from hierarchical organizations, are part of a wider trend in which the individual has become much more self-assertive. Inglehart terms this phenomenon "postmaterialism," the spread of whose values has been a general phenomenon among advanced industrial societies. Postmaterialism has grown particularly rapidly in the Netherlands, and Inglehart's (1990: 93) extensive survey evidence shows that the Dutch public has the highest rate of adherence to postmaterialist values of any public in Europe or North America.

Postmaterialism has an added significance in the Netherlands, beyond that found elsewhere. For among the values most strongly associated with postmaterialism are a rejection of religion and of class differences as determining one's identity. These two dimensions of group identity were at the core of the system of pillar organizations, but they are not as significant to postmaterialists. Even the welfare state, a crowning achievement of the last fifty years, has come under attack by the postwar generation. Provo leaders argued that the welfare state was obsolete and had to be replaced by a "State of Well-Being" (de Vries 1966). As Roel van Duyn explains:

> While the growth of welfare and automation continue, the time is ripe for people to realize that the building up of material welfare is only a means to an end. What end? Life itself; [and] for humans that means creativity. . . . Economically useless creativity must no longer remain the privilege of the artist; only economically useless creativity can save us from boredom.[60]

This proclamation of the death of materialism and the shift to "economically useless creativity" as a central purpose in life has proven to be exaggeration. People are still deeply interested in economically useful activity. Stripped of their rhetorical excess, though, the ideas of Provo have been prophetic of a generational shift in political values and forms of political participation. These new values are found most strongly among the youngest age cohorts, to whom tales of discrimination against Catholics and of the Hunger Winter are just fragments of history.[61] Among the older generations, materialists outnumber postmaterialists by two to one, but among the youngest age cohorts, postmaterialists outnumber materialists by more than three to one. This generational shift mirrors exactly the decline in identification with the pillars, which is far more pronounced among younger citizens than among their elders (Dekker and Ester 1990).

The revolution in cultural values and social organization brought about by the maturation of postwar generations is part of a change in the social structure that will take several more generations to complete. The pillars have decayed in much the manner in which they were built: slowly, steadily, and in response to the forces of societal transformation.

Ethnic and Cultural Minorities

The decline of religious belief and practice, the rise of a postwar generation with new social and political values, and the decay of the pillars have each changed society from within. There has been one other social transformation of equal importance, namely the development of a multiethnic society as a consequence of immigration from without.

The population of the Netherlands has never been ethnically homogeneous. By A.D. 1000, migrations and invasions had brought Celtic, Roman, Saxon, Frankish, Viking, Jewish, and Slavic groups to the area (Newton 1978: 3). As the political borders of the Netherlands became firmer, these wholesale migrations ceased. But the country continued to receive large numbers of immigrants during the seventeenth century, particularly people with skills needed for the growing merchant economy. Shipbuilders, sailmakers, rope makers, lumber cutters, and those adept with pitch and tar were in special demand, as were people with experience in banking and finance.

The relative economic backwardness of the Netherlands made it less attractive for immigration from 1750 to 1950, resulting in a net emigration for that entire period. But two developments in the first decades after World War II, decolonization and the development of labor shortages, created a dramatic reversal of that pattern. Indonesian independence brought 250,000 refugees to the Netherlands between 1949 and 1958, most of whom had never before seen the country (Bagley 1973). Even so, immigrants from Indonesia came to the Netherlands as Dutch citizens, and many were fluent in the Dutch language and familiar with Dutch culture.[62] A similar migration of 150,000 people from Surinam (over one-third of the population) and 40,000 people from the Dutch Antilles occurred in the first half of the 1970s, in connection with the independence of Surinam in 1975.[63]

During the 1960s, between these two waves of immigration from the former colonies, a labor shortage developed in the Netherlands. To meet the need particularly for labor in unskilled and poorly paid jobs, 300,000 workers, mainly from Morocco and Turkey, were offered visas as guest workers between 1960 and 1974.[64] Although the increase in unemployment in the Netherlands after the first oil shock in 1974 brought a hasty end to this program, many of these immigrants remained in the country. Of the 780,000 non-Dutch people living in the country today, just over one-third are Moroccan or Turkish. Over half of that number were born in the Netherlands, and they are by now a permanent part of Dutch society.[65]

Unlike most immigrants from Indonesia, guest workers and their families came to the Netherlands without fluency in the Dutch language and without the cultural familiarity found among immigrants from the former colonies. Above all, they came as Moslems to a country where Christian traditions are deeply rooted. By the 1990s there were over 600,000 Moslems in the Netherlands, half of whom live in the country's four largest cities—Amsterdam, Rotterdam, The Hague, and Utrecht. Amsterdam alone has more than twenty-five mosques.

The entry of guest workers into the Netherlands has long since stopped, and the entry of Dutch citizens from colonial territories has greatly slowed. Today the largest sources of immigration are through marriage to a legal resident (which accounts for continued entry of Turks and Moroccans), and through agreement within the European Union for the free movement of people between member states. There is also significant immigration via requests for asylum, which numbered between 30,000 and 50,000 per year during the 1990s. Since the restrictions on asylum are now about as tight as the constitution and Dutch treaty obligations will permit, continued immigration has a self-sustaining character that places it beyond the control of public policy (van Amersfoort and Penninx 1994). Combined with the sharp decline in fertility among the native-born population since the late 1960s, continued immigration and higher fertility rates among immigrants will cause a natural increase in the percentage of the population that is either foreign born or first generation–descended of foreign born. The Central Statistical Bureau projects that 80 percent of population growth between now and 2015 will be among those with at least one foreign-born parent.

As a consequence of these developments, the Netherlands became an ethnically and culturally plural society in the last third of the twentieth century, to a degree unlike anything seen since the glory years of the United Provinces drew people from all over Europe.[66] This is not the result of any conscious policy. The extension of Dutch citizenship to inhabitants of the colonies after World War II was viewed as a gesture of solidarity to cement the colonial empire rather than as an invitation to move to the mother country. And guest workers were presumed to be just that—guests who would return home after several years of earning money in the Netherlands.

Without advance planning or preparation, then, the Dutch have in recent decades experienced for the first time large numbers of people who do not look like them and who do not share their culture in some important respects. Over 8 percent of the population of the Netherlands today was born abroad, and between 15 and 20 percent of the population has at least one parent born abroad. Because fully one-half of these immigrants have Dutch citizenship, they are not referred to as *buitenlanders* (foreigners), but rather as *allochtonen*.[67] The governmental definition of *allochtonen* includes "all those who have come from elsewhere to live in the Netherlands, and their descendants up to the third generation, in so far as the descendants wish to be viewed as *allochtonen*" (WRR 1989: 10). The key distinction being made, then, is not one of citizenship but rather of enculturation to the Dutch language and way of life. Those who immigrate are assumed to be "non-Dutch" in a cultural rather than legal sense. Children of immigrants may or may not still be *allochtonen*, depending on the degree to which they have broken out of the culture of their immigrant community. The *allochtonen*, then, should not be thought synonymous with non-Europeans or people of color. There are more *allochtonen* with German ancestry in the Netherlands (290,000) than with Indonesian ancestry (260,000).

The rapid increase in the number of *allochtonen* has created tensions and problems familiar to residents of plural societies elsewhere. Differences in educational attainment between Dutch and *allochtonen* have persisted despite special remedial programs (de Jong 1988). There are also differences in social status and economic achievement. During the unemployment crisis of the mid-1980s, Moroccans and Turks had an unemployment rate of 50 percent (Rath 1988: 631). Although unemployment generally has spiraled downward in the 1990s, lack of job skills and difficulties with the Dutch language have prevented *allochtonen* from benefiting fully from this trend (Entzinger 1994: 30–31). Urban concentration, high rates of unemployment, and the relative youth of *allochtonen* have, in turn, contributed to a relatively high crime rate among these populations. In 1997 there were more *allochtonen* in the prisons than (Dutch-born) *autochtonen*.[68]

These issues have caused a simmering resentment toward and among *allochtonen*. There were from the beginning tensions and occasional violence between guest workers and native Dutch youth. Rob Witte (1996: 116) notes dryly, "The management of the larger companies in the Netherlands seemed to be more enthusiastic about the arrival of a new labour force than the Dutch population in general." At the same time, the number and severity of antiforeigner incidents has been substantially lower in the Netherlands than in surrounding countries. An anti-immigrant political party called the Dutch People's Union was declared illegal and disbanded in 1978; a successor party called the Center Democrats won one parliamentary seat in 1989.[69] Anti-immigrant sentiment appears to have peaked in 1994 when minorities were considered the most important issue by voters. Liberal Party leaders then spoke of the need to limit immigration, and the Center Democrats came away with three seats in the parliamentary election held that year. The tide turned after 1994, though, as other political parties isolated the Center Democrats, which lost all of its seats in the 1998 election. Surveys of European publics have also showed the Dutch to be among those most tolerant of foreigners.[70]

Without minimizing the importance of violent incidents and of the support sometimes achieved by overtly racist political parties, the main question of interest from a comparative perspective is how the Netherlands has done as well as it has in the peaceful integration of new ethnic and cultural groups. One important factor is that the Dutch are fully accustomed to living in a society composed of minorities, and particularly of religious minorities. The pillars were an organizational means of keeping minority identities intact and making sure that each group would have its own voice and influence in politics. In some ways, then, Dutch traditions of social organization are particularly well suited to the incorporation of new ethnic and cultural communities.

Social organizing within new ethnic communities has indeed followed the path originally blazed by Calvinists and Catholics in the nineteenth century. Each ethnic minority has established its own social and cultural organizations, as well as tenant associations and social service organizations. Many of these organizations began as a means of linking ethnic communities in the Netherlands to developments in their home countries. Surinamese and Turkish organizations, for example, were sometimes formed as externally based support groups for particular political factions in their respective countries (Rath 1988: 636). The ongoing interest of foreign-born populations in developments in their home countries may account for the fact that over 40 percent of Turkish families in the Netherlands have a satellite dish![71]

As members of these groups decide that their future lies in the Netherlands, though, these organizations have gradually reoriented themselves to fostering participation and advancing group influence in Dutch society. A particularly striking example of this phenomenon is the South Moluccans, refugees from one of the islands in Indonesia who long resisted assimilation in the Netherlands and pressed instead for establishment of an independent Republic of South Molucca to which they could return. In the 1970s, South Moluccan activists hijacked several trains and took hostages at a school to pressure the Dutch government to lend diplomatic support to their cause. As a generation of Moluccans born in the

Netherlands has come of age, though, the dream of an independent Republic of South Molucca has gradually faded.[72]

Assimilation to the Dutch way of life means, among other things, creating organizations that express the needs of a minority community. Moslems in the Netherlands come mainly from Turkey and Morocco but also from Indonesia, Surinam, and Pakistan. Despite differences among these national communities, they collaborate in such pillar organizations as an Islamic broadcast association, which first received public subsidy in 1986. Since that time, there have been ninety minutes per week of radio programming and thirty minutes per week of television programming dedicated to religious instruction and news of Islamic communities and events in the Netherlands and elsewhere (Landman 1997). There are roughly twenty Islamic elementary schools in the Netherlands, established under the same law concerning state subsidies to education that was used by Calvinists and Catholics to build their schools in the first half of the century (Entzinger 1994: 27).

In addition to the "pillar privileges" of schools and broadcast time that can be enjoyed by any group, the Dutch government has also officially recognized some groups as ethnic minorities. Ethnic minorities are *allochtonen* with a low degree of social and cultural assimilation and a high degree of dependence on the welfare state.[73] Each ethnic minority group living in the Netherlands has created organizations that advise the government on policy.[74] Governmental policy on ethnic minorities stresses educational programs for children who do not speak Dutch at home, adult education with an emphasis on Dutch language and culture, and the development of apprenticeship programs and job skills to facilitate integration into the labor force (WRR 1989). A law passed in 1994 required all firms with more than thirty-five employees to develop a plan for having a proportionate number of ethnic minorities among their workers, though few employers have complied.[75] The grant of pillar-type privileges to ethnic minorities has been sufficiently striking that organizations of Chinese and Pakistani residents have petitioned to be recognized as ethnic minorities themselves (Rath 1988: 641).

In some respects, then, the extension of the pillar model to new ethnic and religious minorities has eased relations between longtime Dutch residents and the *allochtonen*. The pillar system has not been perfectly adapted to the new situation, if only because the new immigrant communities arrived just as the established pillars were collapsing. There are, for example, no trade union organizations established by or for *allochtonen;* they must instead choose from the alternatives originally developed for Protestants (the CNV) or for Catholics and socialists (now merged in the FNV). The established unions, though welcoming *allochtoon* members, have done relatively little to embrace their specific interests beyond general declarations of opposition to employment discrimination. Jan Rath (1988: 632) points out that unions stress the assimilation of new groups, urging that "the immigrants should, in their own interest, behave as 'ordinary' workers." The unions have not pressed for special training or employment programs for *allochtonen,* perhaps because these are not in the interest of the great bulk of their members. It is not surprising that workers from the new ethnic communities are less likely to join a union than are other Dutch workers.

The position of *allochtonen* in the Netherlands defies all easy generalization. This is due in part to the fact that such groups are themselves incredibly diverse, with different levels of education and of integration into Dutch society and culture. Sporadic local efforts to develop organizations that would champion the interests of "people of color" or of ethnic minorities in general have always failed because of the lack of solidarity between different ethnic communities.[76] Immigrants from Indonesia generally came to the Netherlands as largely enculturated citizens. Guest workers and their families, on the other hand, did not arrive with these advantages, though nearly 20 percent of residents with a Moroccan or Turkish background are now Dutch citizens. The extent of their assimilation is also suggested by the fact that about 50 percent of Moroccan and Turkish grooms in the mid-1990s married a woman of Dutch ancestry (Centraal Bureau voor de Statistiek 1996: 81).

The experience of immigrants from the former colonies has generally been that enculturation into Dutch society minimizes social tension and maximizes economic achievement. The legacy of the pillar system, though, is to enable a distinction to be made between enculturation and assimilation. Unlike the "melting pot" ideal in the United States, in which immigrant cultures are shed in favor of an American identity, the Dutch pillars have been a means of preserving minority identities while encouraging the acquisition of skills and values that enable one to prosper in the wider society. In some ways, the situation of ethnic minorities in the Netherlands today may be compared to that of Dutch Catholics in the eighteenth and nineteenth centuries. To the extent the comparison is valid, we may expect a long period in which ethnic minorities are enculturated without any significant degree of assimilation.

Although the Netherlands is not a country of immigrants in the same sense that may be said of the United States, Canada, or Australia, the country has never been so isolated as to give rise to a myth of common ancestral origins. The flow of people to and from the Netherlands has always been sufficiently great, and the preservation of group identities and customs has always been sufficiently strong, that the Dutch are highly conscious of being a country of minorities. "Dutchness" has therefore been defined as enculturation to the Dutch way of life. About 60 percent of Dutch people believe that foreigners should adapt to Dutch culture if they want to remain in the country, compared to only 20 percent who say that it is acceptable to maintain foreign culture and customs.[77] A law passed in 1997 mandated that all immigrants from outside the European Union must learn Dutch language and social customs, as well as being taught job skills when needed. A course of study involving up to six hundred hours of lessons was developed for this purpose.[78] This way of thinking can create harsh social judgments against those who are unable or unwilling to learn Dutch. But it has also enabled the

Netherlands to absorb several large waves of immigrants in the last forty years with substantially less tension than that found in neighboring countries.

Although it ended in deportation, the ideal case of enculturation may be found in the Gumus family, who came to the Netherlands from Turkey without a proper visa sometime in the early 1990s. Mr. and Mrs. Gumus proceeded to build a small but successful business making clothing, while their two sons did well in Amsterdam schools.[79] When it was discovered that they were living in the Netherlands without a proper visa, the public reaction was that a family that makes an honest living and assimilates to Dutch society should be permitted to stay regardless of the circumstances of their arrival. Dutch law says that anyone who can prove six consecutive years of legal (recorded) income on which tax has been paid in the Netherlands may receive a permit to remain; the Gumus family could demonstrate just five years. A motion introduced in parliament to make an exception for the Gumus family failed narrowly out of concern about setting an unmanageable precedent, and the family was sent back to Turkey in October 1997. Even so, the outpouring of sympathy for the Gumus family and the outrage in many quarters that they were deported illustrates the acceptance of immigrants who become enculturated and escape the welfare dependency syndrome.

Conclusion

During the course of the twentieth century, Dutch society witnessed first the creation and then the destruction of a remarkable set of institutions—the pillars. These ideologically integrated networks of social and political organizations were established in a competitive environment in which newly mobilized social groups sought to ensure their place in society and their rights in the polity. The pillars developed during three waves of social and political mobilization in the last decades of the nineteenth century and the first decades of the twentieth. The Calvinist pillar mobilized first as a means of revitalizing its tradition of doctrinal strictness and religious fervor, and to restore the central role of Protestant belief in the nation's governance. Catholic mobilization followed in a more defensive vein, drawing on a history of discrimination to persuade Catholics of the necessity of retreating to a collectively organized isolation. Socialist mobilization of the working class also took the pillar form, which by the early part of the twentieth century was the only means of stemming the loss of working-class loyalty to the religious pillars.

A second wave of social change in reaction to the trauma of World War II led to a reformulation of relations between the pillars. Although the pillars continued to isolate their respective populations with reasonable effectiveness, they developed a more cooperative relationship with each other as the task of rebuilding the country took precedence above group struggles over the distribution of rights and wealth. Defensive mobilization for the advancement of group rights receded into the category of historical struggles already won.

Finally, in the last third of the century, the pillars have been steadily dismantled. The distinguishing characteristics of each pillar—Protestant versus Catholic, Liberal versus Socialist, and confessional versus secular—lost their importance. The decay of the pillars was initiated by a crisis of unity within the Catholic pillar, and then exacerbated by the maturation of a postwar generation for whom the historical memories that fueled pillar unity were no longer relevant. Once the Catholic pillar began to tilt, the other pillars followed. For just as the building of the first (Protestant) pillar spurred development of the other pillars, so did the toppling of one pillar create the possibility for other pillars to realign themselves. As Val Lorwin (1971: 171–172) put it, "disarray within one ideological bloc tends . . . to encourage disarray within rival blocs. The hostility, or at least the perception of hostility, of other blocs is a source of intrabloc solidarity; the decline of another bloc diminishes the perception of hostility and threat." Today the pillars exist only as vestigial organizations, vehicles for the delivery of social services rather than a means of maintaining a coherent *levensbeschouwing* among some part of the population. The sociopolitical basis of the traditional pillars has been swept away.

Despite the dramatic decline of the pillars as the focus of group identity, the legacy of this social system remains significant. For one thing, ethnic minorities have taken steps to protect their identity and interests by following the time-honored tradition of constructing pillarized organizations. The Dutch answer to the American melting pot is to expect adherence to certain customs and institutions while permitting a minority group to otherwise control its own community life. This system worked as a means of maintaining peace between Calvinists, Catholics, and socialists in the early part of the twentieth century, and it is working to maintain peace with and between *allochtoon* communities at the turn of the twenty-first century.

As we shall see in coming chapters, the pillars also continue to shape the Dutch policy process. Major social and economic policies can be understood only as the outcome of bargaining between pillar leaders. Among the political consequences of the pillars is the fact that the political party system was created by pillar organizations. The decline of the pillars has therefore brought a revolution to the party system. This is the subject to which we turn in the next chapter.

NOTES

1. The Dutch word *levensbeschouwing* can refer either to a religious doctrine or to a secular ideology. It has no exact equivalent in English, but is an important concept in the Netherlands because agreement on a *levensbeschouwing* defines the boundaries of the pillars. See Kruijt (1957, 1959) for an early definition and analysis.

2. Heinrich Heine, cited in Goudsblom (1967: 21).

3. Cited in Daalder (1966: 198).

4. Until the French occupation, the Dutch Reformed Church was able in most parts of the country to determine both curriculum and licensing qualifications for teachers. In Utrecht in 1588 a schoolmaster "was required to teach the children the catechism and the

psalms. He had to take them along to the sermon, and warn them against the errors of the Papists, Anabaptists and other sectaries" (van Deursen 1991: 116).

5. The mass appeal of Kuyper's vision is demonstrated by his success in endowing the Free University with donations from people of modest means. According to Vlekke (1945: 317), "The money was collected in scores of thousands of small gifts, a few guilders, a few dimes, sometimes a few cents."

6. Note the plural "Churches," which denotes a high degree of local autonomy within the doctrinal confines of orthodox (Reformed) Calvinism.

7. Cited in Irving Hexham (1981: 114). Kuyper's ideas were later adapted by Dutch-descended Afrikaners in South Africa as a justification for racial apartheid. For a review of Calvinist thought in Africa, see Matreyek (1998).

8. Cited in Coleman (1978: 35). Concern about provoking a Calvinist backlash may also account for the fact that a national Catholic political party was not founded until 1926, well after the other major pillar groups had established their own political parties.

9. The principle of subsidiarity has in recent years been applied to the European Union (EU), where it describes an EU whose purpose is to coordinate activities that enable the member states to prosper. Thus, the Dutch pillars may be compared to the member states of the European Union today: They are the societal unit of ultimate value, and larger units exist to serve them. See Post (1989: 24–37) for further discussion of the principles of subsidiarity and sovereignty within circles.

10. L. J. Rogier (1956), cited in Kruijt and Goddijn (1972: 229).

11. From 1918 to World War II the Catholic party was known as the Roman Catholic State Party (RKSP). After World War II it became the Catholic People's Party (KVP). See Lipschits (1977: chapters 3 and 6) and Chapter 4 of this book.

12. The "errors" referred to here concern socialism. See Scholten (1980) and Kieve (1981) for an account of how the confessional pillars served to keep the working class away from socialism.

13. For example, Nieuwenhuis took to calling himself the "Messiah of the Coming New Order," according to Newton (1978: 88).

14. See Daalder (1966: 209) and Lipschits (1977: chapter 2).

15. It was agreed at the same time that women would be given voting rights, and universal suffrage was enacted in 1919.

16. Between 20 and 30 percent of the populations of Amsterdam, Rotterdam, and The Hague are Catholic, and cities in the southern provinces have about the same percentage of Protestants.

17. This listing of periodicals does not include the myriad newspapers and magazines sponsored by official Catholic organizations!

18. This story is cited in Kruijt (1959: 6). There is a great tradition of pillar humor in the Netherlands, as one might expect of so pervasive an institution. One true story from a religiously conservative town in the 1950s concerns a proposal before the city council to end the regulation prohibiting men and women from swimming together in the municipal pool. To everyone's astonishment, a Calvinist city council member voted for the proposal to allow mixed swimming, despite his party's vehement opposition to the practice. The council member later confessed that there had been a misunderstanding: He thought "mixed swimming" referred to allowing Calvinists and Catholics to swim together! Cited in Verboekend (1992: 46).

19. Cited in Post (1989: 36).

20. See for example Goddijn (1957).

21. See Coleman (1978: 77) and Post (1989: 180).

22. Ivan Gadourek (1961: 62) found that the number of positions in city hall and the total salaries paid were carefully apportioned between Protestants and Catholics according to their relative weights among the people of Sassenheim.

23. For example, the great Dutch jurist and philosopher Grotius was imprisoned for his support of religious pluralism within Calvinism. Sentenced to death, he survived only by escaping to Antwerp in a trunk.

24. Fearing linguistic and religious assimilation to Dutch culture—a fate that befell the French Huguenots—the Pilgrims later uprooted from the United Provinces and crossed the Atlantic to the New World.

25. See also Boxer (1990: 8–10, 137–140).

26. Hyma (1942: 28). In common with most other policies under the United Provinces, the acceptance of immigrants was a matter of local choice. Jews were welcomed in Amsterdam but not in some other Dutch cities; this led to a concentration of the Dutch Jewish community in Amsterdam. On the Dutch Jewish community between the seventeenth and nineteenth centuries, see also Boxer (1990: 144–146).

27. Anne Frank and her family were discovered and shipped to Bergen-Belsen, where Anne died at age 15 in March 1945.

28. From Simon Carmiggelt's "Hongerwinter, 1944," first published in *Het Parool,* then an underground newspaper, on January 9, 1945. The column is translated and reprinted in Carmiggelt (1966).

29. Luther (1941). *Sendbrief an die Christen im Niederland* was published by H. N. Werkman (in the original German!) in Heerenveen in 1941, and distributed by the underground publisher De Blauwe Schuit.

30. *Groningen Bevrijd* (1945) by Max Dendermonde.

31. Excerpted from Klaas Hanzen Heeroma (1943). *Margrieten* was written in May 1943, and published and distributed underground by the author in the same year.

32. According to J. P. Kruijt (1948), there was in one town a reassertion of pillar separation even in the celebrations marking German surrender. Catholics organized a separate gathering in a North Holland town because the Protestant girls gymnastics team was thought to be too daringly clad for the eyes of Catholic boys.

33. See Centraal Bureau voor de Statistiek (1966: 39), Coleman (1978: 68–77), and Houska (1985: 43).

34. Cited in Daalder (1984: 99–100).

35. Cited in Bakvis (1981: 33).

36. Cited in Coleman (1978: 144).

37. Centraal Bureau voor de Statistiek (1996). See also Zeegers et al. (1967), Kriesi (1993: 47), and Bryant (1981). The decline in observance was particularly sharp among Dutch Catholics. Eighty-seven percent of Catholics attended church services weekly in 1959, compare to only 42 percent in 1977 (Irwin and van Holsteyn 1989b: 36). Other measures of religious observance follow the same downward spiral. The proportion of marriages consecrated in a church rather than registered at city hall fell from over 60 percent in 1960 to just 40 percent in 1985 (Bax 1990: 164). The Dutch are still a religiously observant people compared to the French, British, or Germans, though they are substantially less reli-

gious than Americans and—more to the point—much less religious than their parents one generation ago.

38. See for example Gielen (1965: 132ff.).

39. Viewership of the three Dutch channels had sunk to 59 percent by 1992, according to 't Hart and Kok (1993: 132).

40. Brants (1985: 110). See also Brants and Kok (1978).

41. A self-description of Provo, from their first newsletter. Reprinted in de Jong (n.d.: 11–12).

42. Although the Dutch police never handed out condoms or chicken legs, the white bicycle plan was tried on a temporary basis in the 1960s and was reestablished in Amsterdam in 1998.

43. On the squatter movement's occupation of empty houses in Amsterdam, see Eckert and Willems (1986).

44. English cognate: ludicrous.

45. Cited in de Jong (n.d.: 16). For further discussions of the political and social program developed within Provo, see de Jongh (1966) and van der Staay (1966).

46. The 1965 opinion is reported in Sociaal en Cultureel Planbureau (1993: 332). The 1981 survey results are from the 1981 Dutch Parliamentary Election Study. A law passed in 1936 and valid until 1957 specified that women teachers and civil servants must retire upon marriage unless they are the sole source of income in their family.

47. See Moree (1994) and Visser and Hemerijck (1997: 25). As we shall see in Chapter 7, Dutch women are highly likely to work part-time. Even today they spend more time on domestic labor and less time on paid labor outside the home than the women of most other European countries (van der Lippe 1994; de Jong Gierfeld and Liefbroer 1995).

48. Leijenaar and Niemöller (1997: 132–133) point out that all parties except the relatively small State Reformed Party (SGP) take a proactive stance toward increasing the representation of women in politics. Not until 1995 did the SGP begin to alter its stance, and then only by accepting women as "special" members, meaning that women had neither a vote nor the right to take executive positions in the party structure.

49. In her pursuit of equality, Ms. Jacobs also attended the Amsterdam Theater unaccompanied by a man, tried to register to vote in 1883, and kept her maiden name after marriage (Bosch 1990: 9–12; see also Newton 1978: 98–103). There is relatively little in the agenda of the modern women's movement that she did not anticipate.

50. For discussion of the Dutch women's movement and abortion reform, see Outshoorn (1986), Lovenduski (1986: 276–277), Briët et al. (1987), and Becker and van Tiel (1990: 50–54). See also Hermsen and van Lenning (1991) for a selection of essays by Dutch feminist scholars exploring the issues of gender differences, women and education, sexuality, and social constructions of gender. For an overview of feminist writing on Dutch women in society and politics, see Outshoorn (1992).

51. At a comparable population density, there would be over 1.25 billion people living in the United States.

52. Heidenheimer et al. (1990: 312) show that per capita emissions of sulfur oxides, carbon monoxide, and particulate matter in the Netherlands are less than one-third of those in the United States. These emissions are primarily attributable to automobiles.

53. Jamison et al. (1990: 166). Perhaps for this reason, significant efforts have been made in the Netherlands to develop concepts and models that can be used to assess the costs of

environmental degradation. See for example Hueting and Bosch (1991) and Kuik et al. (1991).

54. The group, the Association for the Preservation of Natural Monuments, has today a quarter million members and a budget of more than US$12 million per year for purchases of land (Dalton 1994: 267).

55. Cramer (1989). See also Aalders et al.(1987: 75–110) for case studies of action groups concerned with environmental issues.

56. In between, fewer than 5 percent of the public mentioned the environment as the most important issue facing the country, according to Hoogerwerf (1993: 23). Environmental issues have in the Netherlands been subject to the same issue attention cycle that Downs (1972) has described for the United States.

57. Cited in Jamison et al. (1990: 175). To focus on the environment was a natural step for van Duyn; the more remarkable jump from the 1960s was his effort to connect his goals to the three established ideological currents in the Netherlands.

58. Brinkgreve and Korzec, cited in Thomassen and van Deth (1989: 67).

59. Kriesi (1993: 55). See also Inglehart and Andeweg (1993).

60. Cited in Buikhuisen (1966: 95–96).

61. One cultural legacy of the war years does remain: Germans are the least trusted of all European peoples, no less among Dutch youth than among their elders. Hitler's autobiography *Mein Kampf* was allowed to be printed in the Netherlands only in 1997, and even today it must carry a disclaimer from the publisher disavowing endorsement of the work and stating that it is offered only for purposes of historical research. *InterNetKrant*, October 29, 1997, page 1.

62. In the seventeenth century, the United East India Company had decreed that any of its employees who married native women must teach their wives and children Dutch and Christianity, according to Boxer (1990: 243).

63. Blakely (1993). In 1995 there were 175,000 Dutch citizens of Indonesian ancestry in the Netherlands, 159,000 citizens of Surinamese background, and 65,000 citizens originating from Aruba.

64. Work visas were extended to 156,000 Turks, 112,000 Moroccans, and 25,000 Spaniards under this program. See van Amersfoort and Penninx (1994) for details.

65. Although many guest workers stayed in the Netherlands a few years and then returned home, reverse emigration out of the Netherlands by Moroccans and Turks is today less than 5,000 per year.

66. Foreigners may have constituted as much as 10 percent of the population of the Dutch Republic during the seventeenth century, according to Ellemers (1984: 133).

67. *Allochtoon* (plural *allochtonen*) is a word constructed by analogy with the existing Dutch word *autochtoon,* which means "one who is born in his or her own country."

68. *InterNetKrant,* August 15, 1997, page 1. Sixty percent of those in youth detention facilities are *allochtonen.* Use of welfare benefits is also more intensive among *allochtonen,* according to Dörr and Faist (1997).

69. See Voerman and Lucardie (1992) and van Donselaar (1993) for accounts of the Dutch racist right.

70. An analysis of Dutch public opinion toward foreigners by Dekker (1993) shows less xenophobia in the Netherlands than in neighboring European countries, though the segment of the Dutch population most susceptible to nationalist and racist appeals is

the same as elsewhere: those who are older, less educated, and relatively uninterested in politics.

71. *InterNetKrant,* March 5, 1996, page 2.

72. This does not mean that Moluccan descendants in the Netherlands do not continue to follow with interest events in their homeland. Civil disorder in the Moluccan islands during 1999 led to several petition campaigns and protest marches among Dutch Moluccans, who blamed the Indonesian government for fomenting ethnic tensions in the region. It is striking, though, that this upsurge of Moluccan activism in the Netherlands contained no hint of the demand for independence and repatriation that was made in the 1970s.

73. WRR (1989: 10); Entzinger (1994: 31). The officially recognized ethnic minority groups are Surinamese, Antilleans, Arubans, Moluccans, Turks, Moroccans, Italians, Spaniards, Portuguese, Greeks, immigrants from the former Yugoslavia, Cape Verdians, gypsies, and tinkers. Note that Indonesians (other than Moluccans) are not on the list because of their high degree of social and cultural integration.

74. For discussion of the significance of external advisory organizations in Dutch politics, see Chapter 6.

75. *InterNetKrant,* June 4, 1996, pages 1–2. The law required businesses to register their existing *allochtoon* employees so that a baseline could be formed against which future gains in minority employment can be measured. Some associations of business owners have resisted this requirement, recalling that the registration of Jews by order of the Nazis in 1941 was the first step leading to their extermination (*Volkskrant,* January 6, 1996, page 3).

76. Indeed, a proposal by the minister of internal affairs in 1983 to establish a single "minorities council" that would advise the government on policy ran into opposition from minority-group representatives, each of whom preferred to keep their separate organizations and voices (Rath 1988: 638).

77. The remaining 20 percent took a position in between, according to Irwin and van Holsteyn (1997: 112).

78. *InterNetKrant,* November 7, 1997, page 2. The law specifically excludes immigrants from other European Union nations, since it is not legal to place restrictions on mobility within the EU. The law is of significance chiefly for asylum-seekers.

79. *InterNetKrant,* October 4, 1997, page 2. Clothing workshops in Amsterdam employ about 10,000 Turks, according to van Amersfoort and Penninx (1994).

4

POLITICAL PARTIES AND
ELECTORAL CHANGE

We have seen in Chapter 3 that Dutch society underwent extraordinarily rapid changes, beginning in the 1960s and continuing to the present. Until that time, religious and social class differences led to relatively rigid segmentation of the population into the pillars. Many pillarized organizations remain still today as a reminder of that past, but the significance of the issues that led to the creation of the pillars is now greatly reduced.

Since political parties were part of the pillar system, they were naturally swept up in this rapid reorientation of society. The Dutch electorate tended formerly to see voting as an extension of pillar loyalties; today there is a much more fluid and policy-based electoral competition between parties. The rise of new political issues, especially those championed by postwar generations, created a strategic problem for pillarized parties. Ideologically, they were vulnerable to new social values because they were so closely associated with the religious and class groupings whose relevance to politics began to wane in the late 1960s. The very system of linkages between political and social organizations, which served the parties so well for so long in the twentieth century, became a liability when those social organizations began to lose their relevance. Established political parties were thus torn between the desire to tap into these newly mobilizable constituencies and the need to continue representing the social groups that traditionally supported them.

Social change and the decline of the pillars, in short, created a new competitive environment for Dutch parties that has tested their capacity for strategic adaptation. The traditional parties have been highly effective in retaining their place in the party system, but they managed to do this only by abandoning much of their ideological and organizational heritage. As a consequence, the Dutch party system has been almost completely renewed since the 1960s, though much of that renewal has come through the adaptation of existing parties.

In this chapter, we will examine the traditional party system to see how the pillars were articulated in the realm of party politics. We will then look at the ways in which the party system was challenged by the breakdown of the pillars and the changes that followed. First, though, we will review the electoral system of the Netherlands, which sets the context for party competition.

The Electoral System

Political parties in all democracies must be responsive to the will of the voters, but they do not have to respond to the *same* voters in all types of electoral systems. In a district-based system such as that used in American or British elections, the objective of each party is to win a majority of the votes. To do that, a candidate must appeal to "the median voter," that voter (really a cluster of voters) whose opinions lie in the middle of the ideological distribution of the entire electorate.

The Dutch electoral system of proportional representation operates on very different principles. A political party can achieve success without winning a majority of the votes; it is sufficient to establish a much smaller following. Therefore, each party seeks to define for itself a particular niche in the electorate. A niche appealing to the median voter is one strategic alternative, but appeals to other portions of the spectrum of opinion are equally valid electoral strategies. The result is a proliferation of political parties, each with an ideological focus that is relatively narrow and coherent compared to parties in countries using the district system for elections.

Access to the ballot in Dutch elections is exceptionally easy. All that is required of a party is a list of candidates signed by twenty-five voters in each electoral region and submitted to the Election Commission by nomination day, along with a deposit of 25,000 guilders (just under US$15,000). The deposit is forfeit if the party does not gain three-quarters of the votes necessary to elect one representative. More than twenty parties have appeared on the ballot in recent national elections.

Campaigns are relatively inexpensive in the Netherlands, a fact that also makes it easy for small parties to compete. The official electoral campaign lasts just forty-three days, though parliamentary jockeying to establish campaign themes may go on for a year or more before the election. The actual campaign consists primarily of sending parliamentary candidates to contact voters in workplaces and shopping areas, while the party leader (*lijsttrekker,* or head of the party list)[1] makes one major appearance designed to produce a sound-bite for the evening news. Longtime pillarization of the mass media meant that each party had its own newspaper outlets, and each had privileged access to one of the broadcast associations that apportions airtime on radio and television. Though the media are no longer pillar-affiliated, there is still no tradition of paid campaign messages.

Instead, each party receives an hour of radio time per week and seven hours of television time per year, with more time given during a campaign (Lucardie 1993: 71). All parties receive the same amount of airtime, regardless of their size.

Campaign costs have recently accelerated in the Netherlands, as they have elsewhere, due to the hiring of permanent staff members for media relations and marketing. Total expenses in the 1989 national elections were 3.5 million guilders (about US$1.6 million) (Koole 1993), but in 1994 the Labor Party spent almost this much by itself. The Socialist Party purchased advertising time on a commercial television station during the 1998 election, beginning a practice that will surely spread. Even today, though, the entire national campaign of all major parties in the Netherlands costs less than the campaign for a large-state Senate seat in the United States. Membership dues account for the bulk of party funds spent on campaigns, and public funding provides the rest. Private and corporate contributions to political parties are virtually unknown in the Netherlands.[2]

Members of the Second Chamber are elected by proportional representation, using the quota system.[3] Parties submit lists of candidates and the voter selects one of those lists, with the option of designating a preferred candidate on the list.[4] The composition of the Second Chamber is then determined by counting down the party list and taking the number of nominees proportionate to the total number of votes received by the party.[5] In principle, a candidate further down on the party list could be elected over higher-ranked candidates by receiving a sufficiently large number of preference votes. In practice, more than 80 percent of Dutch citizens typically vote for the number-one candidate on the party list, choosing in effect not to exercise their preference vote option.[6] Since it requires only two-thirds of one percent of the vote to gain one of the 150 seats in the Second Chamber, the quota for entry of a new party is just under 60,000 votes nationwide.[7] The electoral system makes challenges by new political parties exceptionally easy to mount.

Ease of entry was not the intent of the parliamentary leaders who established the proportional representation system early in the twentieth century. Prior to 1917, the Second Chamber was elected from geographic districts, as is the U.S. Congress. In 1917, however, leaders of the various pillars reached a comprehensive agreement, the *Pacificatie,* which included adoption of proportional representation, the establishment of universal suffrage, and a legal requirement that all enfranchised citizens turn out to vote.

The logic of the leaders who established this electoral system was that they wanted elections to reflect as accurately as possible the relative strengths of the various pillars in the society. As Ken Gladdish (1991: 96) points out, the declining Liberals saw proportional representation as a means of survival, while the regionally concentrated Catholics expected PR to increase their representation by eliminating wasted votes. The interests of the growing Social Democratic Workers Party (SDAP) might better have been served by a district system, but the party was content to receive the benefits of universal suffrage, the other major electoral change introduced by the *Pacificatie*. The legal obligation to vote helped maintain high levels of turnout and reduced the possibility that some pillars would be advantaged by higher turnout rates.[8] The *Pacificatie* proved to be the "Big Bang" of the Dutch party system, replacing the dominance of local organizations and leaders with a new national party system whose components would endure with little change for fifty years.

The societal organizations that made up the pillars did their part as well to strengthen the link between pillar loyalty and party support. It was not uncommon for the faithful to be reminded from the pulpit of their obligation to vote for the "correct" party, and these reminders were particularly forceful in Catholic churches across the country. Herman Bakvis (1981: 81) notes that party memberships "were sold on a door-to-door basis or in blitzes in shopping areas. They were marketed much like other Catholic items, for example, calendars for missionary work."

The net effect of these arrangements was to make elections as similar as possible to a census of the population. Each pillar would support its associated political party, and each pillarized party would then be represented in the Second Chamber in proportion to its weight in the population. Party strengths varied only slightly between elections: The fastest growing party of the interwar period was the SDAP, which grew from twenty to twenty-four seats. Even the enfranchisement of women in 1919 did not change the working of this system, but simply extended it to the entire adult population. There was little competition between the pillarized parties, leading Arend Lijphart (1969) and others to refer to the Netherlands as a "cartel democracy."

Of course, these electoral practices were predicated on the assumption that each citizen would vote in accord with his or her pillar identity. And for a long time they did, until the rapid collapse of the confessional pillars beginning in the mid-1960s. This collapse caused a basic reorientation of the party system, a reorientation we shall explore later in this chapter.

The Traditional Dutch Party System

The Dutch are famous for the sheer number of parties that compete in elections, with somewhere between twenty and thirty parties usually presenting electoral lists and ten or more parties winning at least one seat in the Second Chamber. But this apparent complexity should not be allowed to obscure an underlying simplicity. The traditional party system had "only" five parties of real significance, each of which represented one of the organized religious and class groupings in Dutch society. Thus, it is common to refer to the four major currents in Dutch party politics: Protestant, Catholic, Socialist, and Liberal.[9] These currents are, of course, identical to the pillarized organization of Dutch society.[10] The Catholic People's Party (KVP); the two Protestant parties, the Anti-Revolutionary Party (ARP) and the Christian Historical Union (CHU); the social democratic Labor Party (PvdA);

and the secular conservative Liberal Party (VVD) represented the major religious and class groupings in the Netherlands.

For much of the twentieth century, the three major confessional parties could count on electoral support that closely and consistently reflected the relative strengths of each religious group in society. Despite the historic antagonisms between Protestants and Catholics in the Netherlands, the religious (or confessional) parties found common ground on the issue of public funding for religious schools. They cooperated to force a constitutional revision in 1887 that permitted subsidies to religious schools, and they first formed a joint government between 1888 and 1891. For most of the next hundred years, the religious parties had a majority in the parliament. Though divided on some issues, they have been consistent allies on the general proposition that the responsibility of the state is to foster the continued vitality of religious communities in the society. The kind of secular statism found in France, for example, is anathema to the major Protestant and Catholic parties. Indeed, the Anti-Revolutionary Party was so named for its opposition to the secular and centralizing principles of the French Revolution.

By the end of World War I the Socialists were also accepted as a mainstream parliamentary party. In 1917 they were able to achieve their primary objective of constitutional reform: universal male suffrage. Leaders of the other pillars hoped that this would encourage the SDAP to commit itself to parliamentary democracy rather than following the revolutionary example of the Bolsheviks in Russia. Those expectations were rewarded, as the SDAP consistently maintained a parliamentary focus of action. In most European countries, communists split from the socialist party over the issue of parliamentary versus revolutionary paths to power. In the Netherlands, the Communist Party (CPN) was created in 1909 when the SDAP *expelled* its revolutionary faction. When in the early 1930s some members of the SDAP left wing proposed mass encampments and demonstrations by the unemployed, they too were expelled from the party. Instead, SDAP leaders responded to the economic crisis by using parliamentary channels to propose a government works program.

In the late 1930s, the SDAP undertook a vigorous internal debate on the appropriateness of its marxist legacy, including the centrality of class struggle and whether marxists had to be absolutely opposed to cooperation with confessional parties. The traditional marxist belief that religion is the opiate of the masses posed a particular dilemma for Dutch socialists, if only because of the strength of that opiate in the Netherlands. Pragmatists in the SDAP realized that parliamentary influence required alliance with confessional parties. The Dutch social democrats consequently adopted a reformist viewpoint that eschewed marxist doctrines of secularism and class-based revolution long before their sister parties elsewhere in Europe. As Felix Rottenberg, chairman of the PvdA in 1995, put it, "We no longer sing the *Internationale*."[11] The PvdA, the postwar incarnation of the SDAP, has continued this reformist tradition despite (as we shall see) ideological firestorms in the late 1960s and 1970s.

The fourth and final major current in the party system is the oldest. The Liberal Party has historically represented the secular middle classes. The word "Liberal" in this context comes from the nineteenth-century position of the party as being in favor of greater power for the elected Second Chamber against the monarchy and the king's appointed ministers. The Liberals also championed a widening of the suffrage and legal equality between religious denominations. The mid–nineteenth-century Liberal leader Johan Rudolf Thorbecke led the drive for reform of the constitution, thereby securing Liberal Party dominance through the end of the century.[12]

Although they were democratic reformers, nineteenth-century leaders of the Liberal Party recognized that their support lay primarily in the middle and upper classes, and so the franchise was kept relatively restricted.[13] The Liberals had never been a united (or disciplined) political party, and after the *Pacificatie* they fragmented still further, with six political parties espousing liberal themes. This led to a marginalization of liberalism between the world wars. The present-day VVD (People's Party for Freedom and Democracy) was formed in 1948 to unite the liberal current and restore its political significance.

During the period of pillarization, the VVD saw itself as a referee for the general interest against the particular interests expressed through the pillars. Its 1948 party program stated that "the government should limit itself to a supervisory task, stepping in as guardian of the general interest whenever social organizations threaten to damage the general interest by becoming too preoccupied with the group interest." In recent times, as the predominance of pillar organizations has receded, the Liberals have focused much more on the issue of individual liberty in a highly regulated society. As the 1981 party program put it, "It is the task of the government to see to it that everyone enjoys the greatest possible degree of freedom."[14] This view makes the Liberal Party socially progressive, even though it is economically conservative (that is, oriented to the free market). The Liberals have, for example, favored abortion rights and legalization of euthanasia; they have also opposed discriminatory laws against women and gays.[15] The law that granted noncitizen immigrants the right to vote in local elections was written and championed by a Liberal Party minister.

In summary, the party system was for most of the twentieth century structured by four political currents: Protestant, Catholic, Socialist, and Liberal. These four currents spawned five major parties: two parties representing different strands of Calvinist political thought and one party for each of the other three ideological traditions. Each of these parties took as its role the representation of its own separate segment of society. Joseph Houska (1985) has written of the contrast between "hunter-gatherer" parties that move across the landscape seeking voters, and "cultivator" parties that stake out a portion of the electorate and tailor their appeals exclusively to that group. Dutch parties in the era of the pillars were highly successful cultivator parties with little interest in raiding rival pillars and mobilizing their voters, if only because there was relatively little likelihood of success in recruiting from the support bases of their rivals. Non-Catholics were not even allowed to join the Catholic party prior to World War II—a truly unusual restriction for a political party in a competitive democracy! As late as the 1970s, members of the Second Chamber rarely contacted voters, either during campaigns or between them; indeed, a survey of voters in 1956 showed that 65 percent preferred that candidates for office not contact voters during campaigns! In a period when most people had a standing party choice based on their pillar identity, such contacts were unnecessary.

That the cultivator strategy was the only strategy available to Dutch parties is shown by the one traditional party that from time to time sought to adopt a hunter-gatherer approach, the Labor Party. It was the dream of successive generations of social democratic leaders (the SDAP before 1945, the PvdA after) to unite the working class within their party, wooing away those religious members of the working class who voted for a Catholic or Protestant party. The search for support among religious members of the working class was much of the motivation for the socialists' nondoctrinaire approach to religious issues specifically and parliamentary democracy more generally. As SDAP leader J. W. Albarda wrote in 1939, "From the very day that the SDAP becomes a governing party . . . its position changes. Then a bridge will have been built over the abyss that now yawns between the religious and the socialist part of our nation. Then traffic will begin over this bridge. . . . The hitherto impregnable voting masses of the religious part of the nation will become potentially available for our efforts."[16]

Albarda's vision lasted into the postwar era, as the Labor Party drew upon the cooperative spirit of the time to seek the support of progressive leaders of the Catholic and Protestant parties. These efforts were rewarded in a series of coalition governments between Labor and the confessional parties under the leadership of PvdA leader Willem Drees. But they had little success in attracting the support of religious voters to the Labor Party, and its postwar election results were only a few percentage points higher than they had been a decade earlier.

The traditional parties continued to receive the support of their allied social organizations until the late 1960s. They were so successful that the votes of more than 70 percent of the electorate could in the 1950s be predicted from the bare facts of one's religion, church attendance, and social class. By 1998 those same demographic factors accounted for only 38 percent of vote choices. The strong connection between political parties and social groups is also suggested by the fact that fluctuations in party support between 1945 and 1969 were lower in the Netherlands than in any other democracy besides Switzerland (another country with a highly segmented electorate).[17] During the pillarized period, most parties saw their votes fluctuate within a band no more than two or three percentage points wide. In this environment of stability, swings of between four and five percentage points led to talk of landslide victories and disastrous defeats. Elections were, as Hans Daalder (1979: 177) put it, "incidents rather than decisive moments."

One result of the cultivator strategy is that each of the Dutch parties had an unusually homogeneous social base. Figure 4.1 provides information on the levels of party homogeneity in thirteen countries, using data collected between 1965 and 1975. The homogeneity index is based on the three primary cleavages that structure each national party system. The higher the homogeneity score, the more closely party support is related to the most significant social and political cleavages in that country. Thus, for example, the figure shows the exceptionally low level of homogeneity (in other words, the high degree of internal diversity) to be found in American political parties, which are classic hunter-gatherer parties in the breadth of their search for votes.

As we would expect, countries using proportional representation generally have more homogeneous political parties than do countries with district systems of election. Even among proportional representation countries, though, Dutch parties stand out as especially homogeneous. Only Finland and Belgium have a tighter linkage between party system and major social cleavages. The high level of party homogeneity in these countries means that each party appeals to a well-defined group in society.[18]

When parties are socially and politically homogeneous, and when each party is focused on the mobilization of its own segment of the electorate, they face little threat from parties representing other groups in society. Elections become less a competition for the hearts and minds of the voters than an occasion to mobilize one's "natural" base of support. But although competition between the pillars did not pose much of a threat to the established parties, they did have to be concerned about competition within the pillars. Given the ease with which new parties could be established, there was always the possibility that internal schisms might lead to the establishment of rival parties competing for support within the same pillar. I have elsewhere labeled these "challenger parties," because they challenge the right of the established party to represent a particular pillar in the Second Chamber.[19]

Each of the established parties was subject to challenges, though the greatest number of challenges occurred within the confessional pillars. Opposition to universal suffrage and dilution of the political status of the Dutch Reformed Church led the State Reformed Party (SGP) to split from the ARP in 1917.[20] The major Protestant and Catholic parties suffered defections whenever dialogue between them seemed to compromise the core pillar principle of separation. The Roman Catholic Party of the Netherlands (RKPN) was formed in 1972 not only in opposition to the growing dialogue between the Catholic People's Party (KVP) and leaders of the two Protestant parties, but also out of concern that the KVP was softening its opposition to abortion. To strengthen its own credentials to represent the Catholic pillar, the RKPN in 1972 adopted a platform identical to the platform of the KVP from the early 1950s!

The RKPN proved to be short-lived, which is typical of a challenger party. Between 1918 and 1972, at least fourteen new parties gained representation in the Second Chamber by challenging the right of an established party to represent a

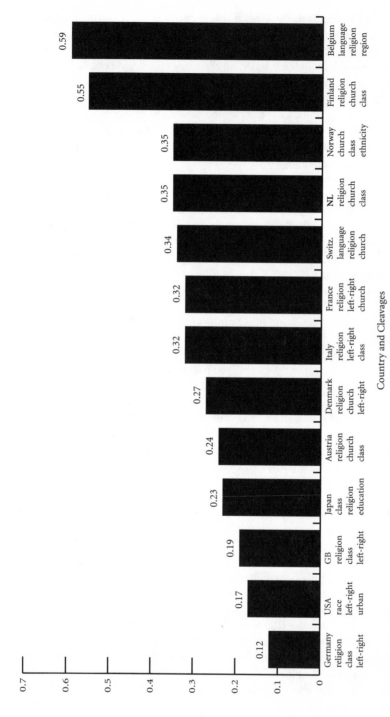

FIGURE 4.1   Party Homogeneity on Major Social Cleavages

NOTE: Data for this figure come from national election studies carried out between 1965 and 1975. Results for the Netherlands are from the 1974 *Political Action* Survey.

SOURCE: Rochon and Strate (1981).

particular pillar. Only four of those parties lasted longer than the life of a single parliament, however, and the longest any of them survived was three parliamentary sessions. This demonstrates that the established parties were always able eventually to reassert their dominance within the pillar, often by co-opting the ideas of the challenger. As long as the electorate remained united within their pillars, and as long as established party leaders remained adept in their appeals to pillar loyalties, no challenging party would succeed in becoming a significant political force.

The dominance of the five established parties in representing the four major political currents is illustrated in Figure 4.2, which shows the proportion of Second Chamber seats won by the five major parties in every election from 1918 to 1998.[21] For much of the period, both the extent and the consistency of major-party support are remarkable, again bearing in mind how easily a breakaway party can be formed. For nearly fifty years the vote and seat share of the five major parties hovered around 90 percent, a proportion left undisturbed by the economic and political chaos of the 1930s and by the ten-year electoral hiatus caused by World War II and the German occupation. Only in the 1960s did support for the established parties begin to decline, and this is the topic to which we next turn.

Change in the Electorate

As long as the Dutch electorate remained loyal to the pillar system in its voting patterns, the established parties would continue to thrive with almost no competition between them and with relatively little to fear from intrapillar challengers. And yet Figure 4.2 shows that the dominance of the established pillar parties began to erode in 1963. The trend was accelerated in 1967 when the Second Chamber seat share of the five major parties fell below 90 percent for the first time since 1948. In the two elections of the early 1970s, the five-party seat share fell to 75 percent. By the mid-1970s it was clear that there had been a fundamental break with the traditional party system.

The decline of established party dominance is mirrored by the success of a number of new parties in the late 1960s and early 1970s, to a degree that would have been unthinkable only a decade earlier. Moreover, though Figure 4.2 does not show this, there was also in this period increased movement of voters *between* the major parties. For example, former Catholic People's Party loyalists voted for the Labor Party in growing numbers, and there was movement as well from the confessional parties to the Liberals.

This transformation of the party system was the result of loosening ties between pillar loyalties and the major political parties. By the mid-1960s there was a growing pool of voters prepared to shop between the parties and to choose on the basis of issues presented in the campaign rather than on the grounds of long-standing subcultural commitments. This created problems for the pillar parties

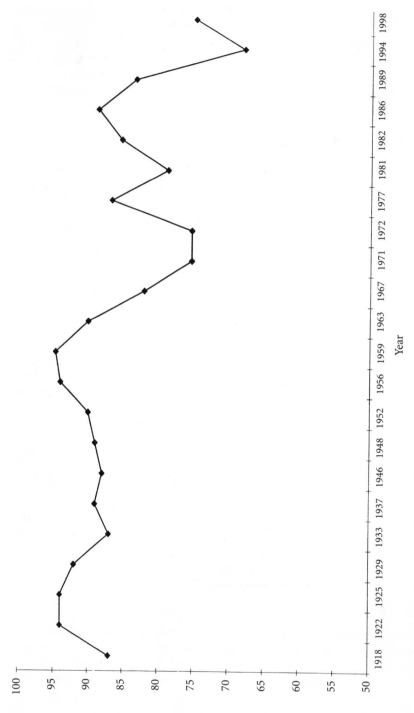

FIGURE 4.2   Percentage of Seats Won by Traditional Pillar Parties

because none of them were homogeneous on both economic and religious issues. In an early 1970s study of the issue positions of voters and members of parliament, Jacques Thomassen (1976b: 220–221) found that leaders from the Labor and Liberal parties represented well the views of their supporters on economic issues. But Liberal and Labor Party supporters were divided on abortion, making it impossible for party leaders to be representative on that issue. Leaders of the Catholic People's Party faced the opposite dilemma: There was a close correspondence between party leaders and supporters in their opposition to abortion, but divisions among party supporters on class issues made it hard for the KVP to formulate economic policies that would please everyone.

Independence from the traditional parties spread still faster as the voting age was lowered from 23 to 21 in 1967 and then to 18 in 1972. Van den Berg (1981) estimates that the floating vote grew during the 1970s from 10 percent of the electorate to 30 percent, a level that could not be ignored by any major party.[22] Elections in the Netherlands became contests between parties and leaders profiling distinctive issue packages. No longer were elections just "incidents" in the ongoing mobilization of pillar loyalists.

To understand this transformation of the party system, we must shift our perspective from the parties to the electorate. What changes in the electorate made possible such a rapid shift from pillar loyalty to competitive free-for-all? The answer to this question is, naturally, closely related to the societal shifts described in Chapter 3. The electorate was subject to three basic shifts in political orientation occurring at more or less the same time: secularization, deconfessionalization, and the decline of class conflict.

Secularization

The first shift in the values of the electorate came about as a result of the secularization of society. Secularization has been a general trend in European countries for the last forty years. Its impact on politics was especially marked in the Netherlands, however, because three of the five major parties made their primary appeals on the basis of religious belief and denominational loyalty. The support base for those three parties was composed of practicing members of, respectively, the Catholic Church, the Dutch Reformed Church, and the Reformed Churches.

As Table 4.1 shows, the proportion of the population describing itself as regularly attending services of the Reformed Churches fell by one-third between 1968 and 1971, and the proportion of practicing Dutch Reformed fell by 50 percent in that same period. The proportion of practicing Catholics fell by nearly two-thirds between 1968 and 1998. The liberalizing influence of the Second Vatican Council is often cited as a cause of the decline in Catholic adherence, though the fact that Protestant adherence declined more rapidly suggests that the causes are not specific to the Catholic Church.

TABLE 4.1   Change in the Group Composition of the Dutch Electorate

	1956	1968	1971	1972	1977	1981	1982	1986	1989	1994	1998
Catholic	30	30	24	25	24	20	16	16	14	13	11
Dutch Reformed	12	16	8	7	9	7	7	8	8	6	6
Reformed	10	12	8	7	9	8	7	5	7	5	7
Secular working class	33	25	29	28	28	30	27	26	24	23	21
Secular middle class	15	18	31	32	30	35	42	45	48	54	55
Total percentage	100	101	100	99	100	100	99	100	101	101	100

SOURCES: For 1956 and 1968: Lijphart (1974). All subsequent years: Dutch Parliamentary Election Studies.

Deconfessionalization

The reduction of church attendance from nearly 60 percent of the population in 1968 to less than 25 percent by 1998 posed a serious challenge to those political parties whose appeals were rooted in religious group identities. But the secularization of society was only part of the problem faced by religious parties. They were also affected by the process of deconfessionalization—a weakening of the link between political parties and the pillars. In 1956, 95 percent of practicing Catholics voted for the Catholic People's Party; but by 1972 KVP support had declined to 57 percent even among those still going to church. Among those who attended services in the Reformed Churches, loyalty to a Protestant party fell from 93 percent to 78 percent. Parishioners of the Dutch Reformed Church, never as completely integrated into "their" political party, reduced their voting support for a Protestant party from 63 to 55 percent.

The very concept of a confessional party, a party rooted in religious principles, was increasingly called into question by the public. Over two-thirds of the population believed in 1967 that there should be confessional political parties. By 1977 less than half the electorate supported the concept of a confessional party, and by 1994 only 38 percent thought confessional parties should remain (Andeweg 1995a: 119). Already by 1971, the segment of the population who agreed that "religious belief is a good guide to politics" was in the minority, and by 1998 this view had the support of only 39 percent of the population. These trends meant that not only were three of the five traditional parties challenged by a shrinking base of support in society, but also that there was a reduced level of loyalty within the pillars. The falling confessional-party vote resulted, in other words, from both a decline in religious sentiment and a loss of pillar loyalty among the still-faithful.

The Catholic People's Party faced the steepest decline. For decades the party had polled right around 30 percent of the vote, in conformity with the proportion of practicing Catholics in the population. In 1963 the KVP won 32 percent of the vote. In 1967 one of the Dutch bishops said publicly that Catholic voters did not need to support the KVP to be good Catholics, and the KVP vote share in that year dropped to 26.5 percent. Five years later, in 1972, the party's vote share fell to just under 18 percent, less than two-thirds the level of support it had received just ten years earlier. The 1972 election was the last national campaign the KVP would undertake.

The Protestant parties fared only slightly better in that tumultuous decade, 1967 to 1977. The Anti-Revolutionary Party, rooted in the stricter Calvinism of the Reformed Churches, held its own at about 9 percent of the vote. But the party of the Dutch Reformed Church, the Christian Historicals, had by 1972 lost 45 percent of its 1963 vote share. As Andeweg (1982: 196) concluded, the religious parties were all suffering from an erosion of orthodoxy among the faithful.[23]

Faced with an unprecedented loss of support, the Catholic and Protestant parties made a dramatic break from the past by running a joint party list in the 1977 national elections and then merging in 1980 into the Christian Democratic Appeal (CDA). Although Christian Democratic parties are common elsewhere in Europe, in the Netherlands the obstacles to forming such a party were substantial. Each denominational party had as its raison d'être the mobilization and defense of the interests of its separate pillar. Moreover, the confessional parties had developed substantially different traditions on such matters as how they dealt with class issues, the extent to which they cited the Gospels in developing policy positions, and whether they drew from the Gospels the progressive or conservative messages that have motivated Christian politics in other settings (Wolinetz 1988: 146–149). Even while they were negotiating a merger in the mid-1970s, confessional parties were divided between participants in the Labor-led den Uyl government (the Catholic People's Party and the Anti-Revolutionary Party), and opponents of the den Uyl government (the Christian Historical Union). Both the Catholic People's Party and the Anti-Revolutionary Party experienced internal schisms because of the merger, but today the CDA has taken the place of the three former confessional parties as the primary representative of confessional issues in politics.[24]

The Decline of Class Conflict

Shifts in the class structure also contributed to the demise of the traditional party system. Just as occurred with the confessional parties, the Labor Party has suffered from a shrinking base of support. There had been two countervailing movements affecting the size of the secular working class: movement into that category by formerly religious workers and movement out of that category by the growing proportion of the population who were adopting a middle-class outlook. However, movement from the working class to the middle class has outweighed the gains due to secularization. Table 4.1 shows that the secular working class declined from a third of the population in 1956 to barely more than a fifth by 1998.[25]

Like the confessional parties, the Labor Party has suffered an erosion of support within its traditional social base, as well as shrinkage of that base. The size of the Dutch working class has been declining faster in the Netherlands than in other countries as a consequence of the rapid shift toward a service economy. It is often claimed that increasing affluence of the working class in advanced industrial societies, and reduced income differentials created by the welfare state, reduce the salience of class conflict. The trend of working-class support for the Labor Party is consistent with this thesis. In 1956, 68 percent of the secular working class supported the Labor Party. Despite the polarization strategy of the 1970s, which should have increased working-class support by emphasizing the differences between Labor and other parties, PvdA support among the secular working class in 1972 dropped to 60 percent. By 1998, secular–working class support for the Labor Party was down to 50 percent.[26]

As we shall see later in this chapter, the PvdA has continued as a major player in Dutch party politics by expanding its support base beyond the secular working class. In particular, the party has embraced the agenda of the new left, which appeals primarily to younger, well-educated middle-class voters. This ideological shift has had profound consequences for the activist base of the Labor Party. Samuel Eldersveld (1998) has found that 27 percent of Labor Party activists in Amsterdam had a working-class or clerical background in 1976, but by 1993 the working-class/clerical activist base of the party had completely vanished. Instead, 65 percent of Labor Party activists in Amsterdam had a university education—a higher percentage than that found in either the CDA or the Liberal Party. The Labor Party continues to characterize itself as the representative of those who are least able to provide for themselves in the market, but in recent decades the reality of Labor Party support has been quite different.[27] As with the Christian Democrats, diversification of support is a prudent move for the Labor Party, given its diminishing success in its traditional working-class base.

The single social group to have grown over the last half century is the secular middle class—the traditional constituency of the Liberal Party. The Liberals have enjoyed the luxury of a dramatically expanding pool of "natural" supporters, from just 15 percent of the electorate in 1956 to over half in 1998. Not surprisingly, the Liberals have prospered in this environment, and are in fact the only major party to have increased its membership in the last forty years.[28] This has permitted the Liberal Party to improve its vote share while making fewer programmatic adaptations than have the other pillar-era parties.

The Challenge from New Parties

Even as religious belief and social class were declining in their power to structure the vote, other issues were becoming more important to the Dutch electorate.

New political parties sought, in some cases with considerable success, to redirect people's attention to issues that had tended to be neglected in a political system oriented to the defense of religious and class interests.

With the low threshold for entry into the Second Chamber, it has always been relatively easy for new parties to gain representation. But, as already noted, most new parties gaining entry to the Second Chamber prior to the 1970s were "challengers," parties that accepted the pillarized framework of politics but challenged the right of an established party to represent its pillar. Beginning in the 1960s, an increasing proportion of new parties were not challengers but instead "mobilizers," seeking to mobilize electoral support based on new issues. As I have pointed out in earlier research on the subject, "Mobilizing parties can succeed only among a public that is prepared to rethink its political identities. They require electoral dealignment" (Rochon 1985: 422).

Dealignment from the pillars was, of course, precisely the condition in the Dutch electorate beginning in the mid-1960s. As a result, eleven new mobilizing parties won seats in the Second Chamber between 1959 and 1982. Their names suggest the diversity of their programs: Pacifist Socialist Party, Farmers Party, Dutch Middle-Class Party, Evangelical People's Party, the Radical Party. A suggestion in 1994 by the leadership of the CDA that retirement pensions might be frozen led to the election of seven representatives from two parties appealing to pension recipients: the General Senior Citizens League (AOV) and Political Union 55+. A nationalist and xenophobic party of the far right, misleadingly called the Center Democrats, won a single seat in 1989 and expanded to three seats in the Second Chamber (2.5 percent of the vote) in 1994. This party has never received the kind of support enjoyed by far right parties in neighboring countries, and failed to retain its seats in the parliamentary election of 1998. The Center Democrats did succeed, though, in sparking a lively discussion over whether it is ever constitutional to prevent a political party from organizing public rallies.[29]

One of the earliest parties successful at mobilizing voters based on new identities was the Farmers Party, which entered the Second Chamber in 1963 to protest agricultural policies of the government. The protest broadened into opposition to big government more generally, and the party found its greatest support among small-business owners. The Farmers Party mobilized conservatives and others with an antistate orientation who could not support either the confessional parties or what they saw as the big-business orientation of the Liberal Party.

The most significant of the new mobilizing parties is the Democrats '66 (D66), which won a remarkable seven parliamentary seats in its first campaign in 1967 and has since that time remained a significant parliamentary force, including participation in several governing coalitions. D66 stresses the democratization of society and government, an issue that dominated Dutch politics for over a decade after the party's founding. The points of critique raised by D66 were essentially two. First, party leaders stressed the accountability between parties and their voters in the formation of governing coalitions. Second, D66 criticized the dominance of the pillar mentality, which put a premium on group loyalty and stifled consideration of issues that cut across the standard divisions of religion and class.

To American eyes it might seem that any system of five major parties and another half dozen minor parties would offer all the democratic options one could ask for. But critics of the party system point out that in some respects having a multiplicity of choices reduces the effectiveness of one's vote. Election outcomes in a multiparty system are indeterminate with respect to the formation of a governing coalition, for fragmentation of the vote typically makes it possible for a number of very different coalitions to form. As the founding manifesto of D66 put it, "The voters elect the Second Chamber of Parliament. Afterwards, the formation of a cabinet is initiated. You, being the voter, have no influence whatsoever on that formation."[30]

D66 called for structural change in the party system and the constitutional order to remedy these deficits. Party leaders proposed that parties form potential governing alliances prior to elections, a practice that would help voters know the coalition implications of their vote choices. They further suggested a constitutional revision that would permit direct election of the minister-president (prime minister), a measure that would establish popular control over the leadership of government. They also proposed instituting referenda to give the public a direct voice in legislation.[31] As a participant in the 1994–1998 coalition government, D66 authored a proposal to adopt an electoral system modeled on that of Germany, in which half the members of the Second Chamber would continue to be elected by proportional representation while the other half would be elected from five geographic districts.[32] This reform was proposed to strengthen the ties between individual members of parliament and their constituents.

Equally significant was the pressure for democratization *within* the parties themselves. D66 again led the way in the rules it adopted for its own party organization. All members are allowed to vote at party congresses, and all can vote on the rank order of candidates on party lists. In its early years, D66 went so far as to base important decisions on the opinions of a random sample of its members (Koole 1994: 285). This sampling technique for party decisions proved to be too cumbersome to retain, but the internal procedures of D66 nonetheless represented a significant advance in member participation over the practices of other parties.

The success of these new parties was helped by the fact that the electorate proved not to have deep attachments to the established parties. One might expect that the connection between parties and pillars would create a particularly close bond of loyalty between Dutch voters and their parties, but this was not the case. Instead, as found by Jacques Thomassen (1976a), party identification was not very stable or strongly held in the Dutch electorate in the early 1970s, despite the exceptional stability of the vote. The reason appears to be that the loyalty of voters was with their pillar, and the party was simply an expression of that pillar loyalty.

As Thomassen (1976a: 78) put it, for a Catholic voter "the identification was probably more with the Catholic subculture and much less an identification with the associated political party per se."

The Dutch political party system—stable for decades despite the absence of strong party loyalties among the public—reaped the consequences when subcultural loyalties themselves began to wane. The pillars had developed in the latter half of the nineteenth century in order to protect group rights, but by 1970 battles over universal suffrage and public funding of religious schools were distant historical memories. The combination of secularization, declining salience of class issues, and reduced support for pillarized parties meant that the major parties were faced with a fundamental challenge. The soil had become too infertile for the cultivator strategy to continue to work, and voters were ready for a more active role in an electoral process no longer dominated by pillar loyalty. Particularly among the postwar generation, it seemed apparent that politics should be about something else. A D66 representative on the Delft City Council captured this spirit in claiming, "Our party was founded in 1966 because a number of people thought that each era should solve its own problems, and not those of the last century."[33]

As the public became more independent in its political thought, party membership experienced a steep decline. In 1956 a remarkable 14 percent of the voting population were members of a political party, and the parliamentary parties had a combined membership of over 628,000.[34] By the 1990s the party membership rate had fallen to less than 4 percent and the parliamentary parties had a combined membership of just 326,000. The fall in membership was especially sharp among the confessional parties.[35] The Catholic People's Party had 430,000 members in 1955, but when the party definitively closed its books in 1980 membership was down to 50,000.

Public disengagement from the party system was not limited to the religious parties. Despite a 65 percent increase in the eligible voting population between 1963 and 1989, all major parties except the Liberals lost members in that period (Koole 1993). Attendance at party campaign meetings also dropped by a third between 1954 and 1977. By any measure, then, there has been a clear loss of willingness to get involved in party activities. On the other hand, those Dutch citizens who do become involved in parties do so today for more overtly political reasons. As Paul Lucardie (1993: 75) points out, "membership in political parties is no longer automatically coupled with a particular social class or religious denomination, but is seen more as a conscious personal choice for a political vision or a political career."

This distancing of the public from political parties worked to the disadvantage of new parties as well as the established parties. Although many new parties succeeded in entering the Second Chamber beginning in the mid-1960s, they usually found it difficult to sustain their initial levels of support. These parties, which had neither long traditions nor pillarized subcultures to draw upon, have not been able to build up stable clienteles. Their initial appeals were to the youngest voters; for example, one-half of Radical Party supporters in 1971 were under 25 years old. These voters are more weakly attached to their party choices, more likely to decide late in the campaign how to vote, and more likely to switch party loyalties between elections (Jennings 1972; Rochon 1985: 432–435). Even D66, the most successful of the new parties, has been labeled a "stopover party" by Galen Irwin and Karl Dittrich (1984), a temporary home for voters in the process of switching their support between two of the larger established parties.

The Rise of a New Issue Orientation

The instability and weakened loyalties of the Dutch party system were not due to people withdrawing from politics, but rather to a shift in emphasis to new political issues and new means of participating in politics.[36] Traditional issues concerning the role of religion in society have not disappeared, for controversies still arise on such matters as whether to allow stores to open on Sundays, whether it infringes on free speech when a municipality forbids swearing in public places, whether Dutch Reformed members of the royal family should take the Catholic Eucharist, and how to contain polio outbreaks when people in some parts of the country refuse to vaccinate their children out of religious considerations. But the emphasis that parties give to such issues in their platforms has declined significantly, as parties respond to shifts in public priorities.[37] For example, each of the proposals for constitutional reform championed by D66 enjoyed at least 60 percent support among the public at one time or another in the first ten years of the party's existence (Andeweg 1989: 54). Other new political parties such as the Pacifist Socialists (PSP) and the Radicals (PPR) brought the issues of the Provo youth movement into the political arena: rejection of established religious and political authority, decentralization of authority to municipalities and neighborhoods, greater personal freedom and relaxation of the church-inspired regulation of private life, environmentalism, women's rights, and protest against nuclear weapons (PSP 1982: 96–125).

The importance of new issues in Dutch politics is reflected in changing patterns of public concern. Issues of economic growth, jobs, and inflation often remain uppermost in people's minds when they are asked by pollsters to name the most important problems facing the country. But new issues have increasingly come to join these more traditional concerns. Of course, what constitutes a "new issue" can be open to debate, for some new issues are twists on matters that have long been important. An example would be access to abortion, which is a recent version of the long-standing concern about the role of the state in enforcing the viewpoints of a particular religious denomination. Even so, four issues stand out as central to the new political agenda. These are democratization of the political system, nuclear energy, environmental protection, and women's rights.[38] Public debate on these new issues began in the late 1960s and early 1970s, starting with democratization and then spreading to the other three issue areas.

The rapidity of growth in concern about these topics can hardly be overstated. Prior to 1967, very few among the public would have mentioned any of these issues as being among the most important problems facing the country. By 1971, 28 percent of the public mentioned at least one of these issues as being among the most important in the country. Among those who voted in the 1971 national elections, 43 percent mentioned at least one of these issues.

The traditional parties have certain advantages and disadvantages when such new issues as women's rights, the environment, democratization, and nuclear energy come along. Their organizational capacities and voter loyalties enable them to incorporate new issues into their electoral appeals. Yet these same factors create rigidities: Ideological traditions and voter loyalties can make it difficult for established parties to take a clear stance on new issues. This is particularly the case when the new issues do not map neatly onto the cleavage dimensions of class and religion that have traditionally defined the party system. The established parties were vulnerable to the rise of new political issues precisely because they were so closely associated with the religious and class groupings whose relevance to politics began suddenly to wane in the late 1960s. It is difficult for a confessional party to take a stand in favor of women's rights if this is interpreted to mean a reduction of support for traditional family structures and values. It is just as difficult for the Labor Party to come out in favor of environmental protection and against nuclear energy, if these standards are viewed as having an adverse impact on jobs and prosperity.

The impact of the new issues on the Dutch party system is shown in Figure 4.3. In this figure, parties are divided into the "new left,"[39] the Labor Party (PvdA), the Liberal Party (VVD), and the confessional parties.[40] Already in 1971, 17 percent of the "new issues electorate" had translated their concern into action by voting for one of the new left parties. Although the proportion of those in the electorate who mentioned new issues as an important problem declined over time, the relevance of those new issues for voting choice has steadily advanced since 1971.[41] In 1998 nearly one-third of the new issues electorate voted for one of the new left parties, compared to just 18 percent of the rest of the electorate.

Although the new left has taken an increasing share of the new issues electorate, their support has not come at the expense of the Labor Party. A strong stance in favor of democratization, environmental protection, and women's rights, and a more equivocal stance against nuclear energy, have helped the Labor Party maintain about a 30 percent share of the new issues electorate. The Liberals have received a smaller share of the new issues electorate, but their advocacy of equal opportunities for women generally—and liberalized access to abortion specifically—helps them with these voters. The biggest losers among the new issues electorate have been the confessional parties, whose share of the vote among this group has fallen steadily.

If we look at the distribution of the new issues vote in any given year, we can see the extent to which these issues have helped structure voting choice. Concern

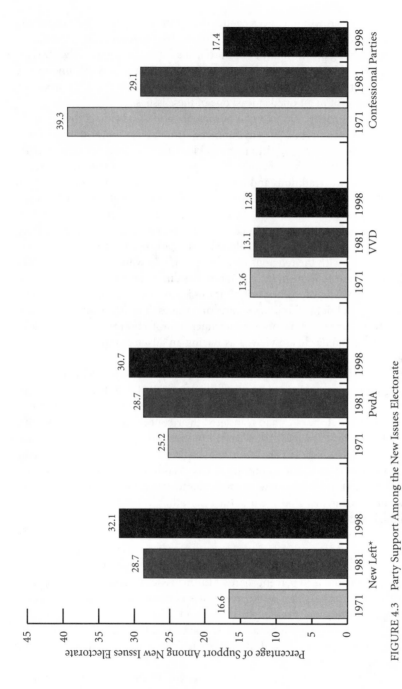

FIGURE 4.3   Party Support Among the New Issues Electorate

*In 1971 and 1981, "New Left" is PPR, PSP, CPN, and D66. In 1998, GL replaces PPR, PSP, and CPN.
SOURCE: Dutch Parliamentary Election Studies.

about new issues was quite widespread in 1971, but these issues made relatively little difference in how people voted. The confessional parties, for example, attracted more than twice as many votes among the new issues electorate as did the new left parties, whose programs were centered precisely on these issues. By 1998 those proportions had nearly reversed. Even though the total size of the new issues electorate was declining in those years, then, the significance of those issues for voting choice was rising. By 1998, the new issues dimension can be said to have joined religion and social class as a structuring element of the party system.

Figure 4.4 makes the same point in a different way, showing the trends in party sympathy among the new issues electorate compared to the rest of the electorate. In 1971 there was relatively little differentiation in party approval among members of the new issues electorate, resulting in a tight cluster of points on the left side of the graph. Over time, the Green Left has gained significantly in approval among the new issues electorate, while D66 and the Labor Party have maintained their earlier rates of approval.[42] The Liberals and the predecessor parties of the CDA had a relatively high approval rating among the new issues electorate in 1971, but their ratings had slipped into negative territory by 1994.

Changing Basis of the Vote

Changes in the society and changes in the party system have been mutually reinforcing. The increasing independence of voters from their confessional attachments drove party leaders to de-emphasize the links between their parties and the various pillars. This change in party strategy, in turn, has reduced still further the role of pillar identities in voter choice. The result of these changes can be seen in Table 4.2, which provides a summary of the reasons given by voters for their party choices in national elections. The data show a sharp decline in the percentage of respondents who say they chose their party because of the religious and class cleavages that structured the traditional party system. Similarly, the proportion of respondents who gave "principles" (personal philosophy) or "tradition" as the most important reason for their vote has also diminished. If these reasons are taken as emblematic of the logic of choice in the pillarized party system, then the total proportion of voters making a choice on traditional grounds fell from 57 percent in 1967 to 21 percent in 1998.

Many of the reasons given for one's vote choice have remained more or less constant through the decades, fluctuating from election to election as particular campaigns take shape. Thus, while the specific issues important to party choice have varied between elections, the proportion of the electorate choosing a party primarily on the basis of some issue has remained more or less constant. Similarly, it is often observed that campaigns in the age of television and diminished party loyalties put more emphasis on the head of the party list. Evaluations of party leaders do indeed figure prominently in the vote choices of those who are otherwise conflicted on the issues.[43] However, Table 4.2 shows at most a small in-

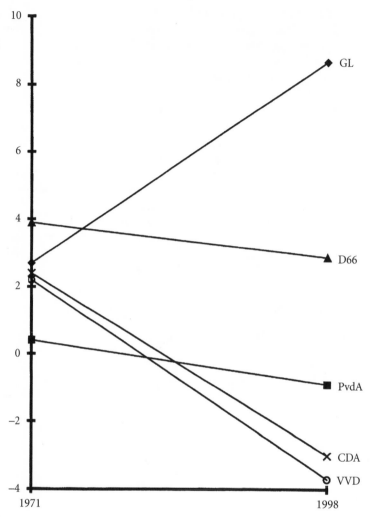

FIGURE 4.4   Party Sympathy Among the New Issues Electorate

NOTE: Entries are the sympathy scores of the new issues electorate minus the sympathy scores of the rest of the electorate for each party.

SOURCE: Dutch Parliamentary Election Studies.

TABLE 4.2   First Reason Given for Vote Choice

	1967	1972	1981	1982	1986	1989	1994	1998
Religion	18.8	11.6	11.8	8.6	4.7	6.2	4.5	6.5
Class or economic interests	17.1	11.4	12.7	11.7	7.9	6.8	6.0	3.8
Tradition or personal philosophy	21.0	9.8	7.6	6.1	6.4	7.6	10.1	10.3
Subtotal	56.9	32.8	32.1	26.4	19.0	20.6	20.6	20.6
Left-right ideology	na	5.6	4.9	4.9	5.0	5.9	1.9	3.7
Specific issues	11.8	12.1	7.3	13.3	10.4	11.0	10.2	10.4
Party leaders or candidates	3.5	6.6	3.4	3.4	8.4	5.6	5.7	9.7
Party or coalition performance	18.3	36.8	46.5	45.4	47.0	46.6	57.3	47.0
Other	9.5	5.9	5.7	6.5	10.2	10.2	4.3	8.6
Total percentage	100	99.8	99.9	99.9	100	99.9	100	100

SOURCES: For 1967: Sociaal-Wetenschappelijk Instituut (1967: 57). For all subsequent years: Dutch Parliamentary Election Studies.

crease in the proportion of the electorate naming party leaders as the overriding reason for their voting choice.

The single consideration that does stand out as having grown in importance over time is the performance of the parties themselves, and the desire to see certain parties in government or in the opposition. Answers in this category typically refer to the past or expected performance of a party, or to the party's general ideological perspective. It is no longer enough for a party to remind its voters of their social-group affiliations; today Dutch parties attract support based on their programmatic identity and performance.

It is an unfortunate accident of history that the extant series of Dutch election studies begins in 1967, just as the traditional party system began to collapse. As a result, we have no systematic reports on the motivations for voting choice from before the onset of rapid change in the party system. However, we can better understand how this change occurred by separating the electorate into different generational cohorts. Figure 4.5 tracks the prevalence of pillar-oriented vote motivations among three generational groups: those who first voted in 1959 or earlier; those who entered the electorate in the transition period between 1963 and 1972; and those who first voted in the 1977 election or after.

Generational studies of changes in party support have found that all age cohorts were part of the deconfessionalization trend.[44] Collapse of the confessional parties was, therefore, due to a society-wide shift rather than being a generational phenomenon. But although shifts in voting support may not have generational

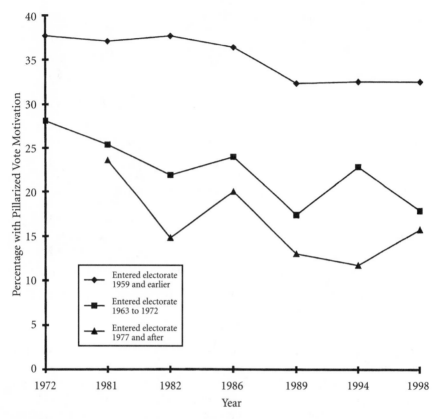

FIGURE 4.5   Generational Differences in the Reason for Vote Choice

SOURCE: Dutch Parliamentary Election Studies.

origins, shifts in the logic of voting clearly do. Older cohorts within the electorate are more likely than the younger cohorts to cast their vote based on the pillarized criteria of religion, class, and "tradition." Moreover, the pillarized cohort demonstrates a substantial degree of continuity in its logic of voting choice, as indicated by the gentle downward slope of the highest (oldest) cohort line in Figure 4.5. The middle cohort, which entered the electorate between 1963 and 1972, and the youngest cohort, which entered the electorate beginning in 1977, are not so stable. With each passing election these younger cohorts place less emphasis on a traditional reason for vote choice. Instead, these voters are part of what Cees van der Eijk and Kees Niemöller (1992: 281) call a "political emancipation of voters as individuals, who can now choose on the basis of their own political preferences and orientations, rather than merely express with their vote that they are part of a particular segment of society." The result, as Galen Irwin and Joop van Holsteyn (1997: 98) put it, is that "the structured [pillarized] model is no longer of much use in understanding the party choice of voters under age 40." As this cohort grows with each new increment of young voters, there will be a continuing shift in the electorate from the pillar logic of religion, class, and tradition, to one based on issues, leaders, and party performance in government.

Seeking the Postmaterialist Vote

The growth of concern about new issues and the shifting basis of the vote particularly by the postpillar generation have set the stage for a new era of competition between the parties. At the heart of that competition is the quest for support of the group most coveted by the major parties: the new middle class. Defined by their high levels of education and by their occupations of providing services in the public and private sectors, the new middle class is growing in size and is relatively independent in its partisan orientations—two traits that put them in play for party competition. Politically, the new middle class is likely to have postmaterialist values. They are secular, socially liberal, and concerned with such issues as social justice and environmental protection.[45] And, as we saw in Chapter 3, the number of postmaterialists is growing rapidly in the Netherlands, particularly among the young.

Any political party would love to capture the postmaterialist vote, and all parties have paid obeisance to such postmaterialist issues as protection of the environment.[46] The Christian Democrats have consistently taken between 15 and 20 percent of the postmaterialist vote, and about 10 percent of postmaterialists support the Liberals. That leaves roughly two-thirds of the postmaterialist vote for the Labor Party, the Green Left, and D66. Figure 4.6 shows that through the 1980s and into the 1990s, the Labor Party received high levels of postmaterialist support when it was in the opposition and much less support when it was part of the governing coalition. This suggests that the party is good at talking the postmaterialist talk, but has not yet been able to walk the walk when it is actually in a position to shape policy.[47] When postmaterialists abandon the Labor Party, they are likely to vote for D66 or the Green Left instead.[48] The continued shift of postmaterialist voters between these parties shows that the party system has not (yet) developed a stable alignment on postmaterialist issues.

Postmaterialism is a relatively new force in Dutch politics, but it is one that continues to increase in strength. Any political party that succeeds in capturing postmaterialist support on a stable basis will be in a commanding position in the Dutch party system—comparable to the position long enjoyed by the confessional parties through their domination of the religious vote.

Alternatives to Political Parties

The growing issue-based logic of voting and the rise of new issues among the Dutch electorate were not easily accommodated within the traditional pillar

94

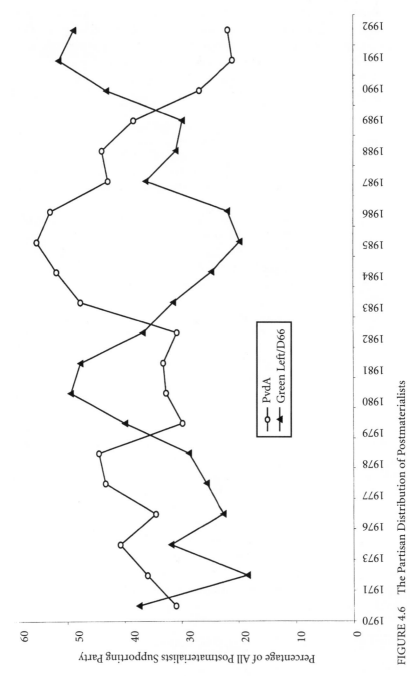

FIGURE 4.6   The Partisan Distribution of Postmaterialists

NOTE: Pearson's r=-.76.
SOURCE: Commission of the European Union: Eurobarometer surveys.

framework, or for that matter within the party system as a whole. Consequently, the established political parties lost the control they had previously exerted over the public agenda. Some challenges came from new parties, but others came from outside the party system entirely, through social and political movements.

Political protest is not a new phenomenon in Dutch society. The revolt from Spain established an honorable tradition of local political movements and resistance to central authority. The anti-regents couplet published in Groningen in 1748 could well have been penned by Provo in the 1960s:

> *There's none we see, to make us free,*
> *But we ourselves, the common folk.*[49]

The postwar wave of direct-action protest in the Netherlands began in 1965 with smoke bombs thrown at the royal wedding of Beatrix and Claus. But when the smoke cleared it turned out that something more significant was occurring: a widespread willingness to organize outside the conventional channels of participation in order to put new issues on the political agenda. Local "action groups" arose to take on issues ranging from redirecting traffic flows around a neighborhood to establishing solidarity committees with various Third World countries. Amsterdam's Kabouters were early pioneers in action-group tactics, setting up roadblocks to prevent cars from entering the city's central districts, occupying empty buildings to claim them as residential spaces, and sitting in at city hall to protest plans to build a new highway. By the end of the 1980s, over one-quarter of the population had taken part in a demonstration, six times the number who are members of a political party. Two cross-national studies show that the Dutch public is more active in non-institutionalized forms of political participation than are the publics of other countries.[50] As Ronald Inglehart and Rudy Andeweg (1993: 357) put it, "The Dutch may have started out as largely spectators in political life, but there is an undeniable trend towards a more participant political culture."

The use of nonparty channels of participation continues to grow. With the spread of protest experience, the skills of action-group organizing have been increasingly codified in the form of guides and handbooks (e.g., Korrel 1987). Each local movement—for women's rights, for environmental protection, and for cheaper housing in the major cities—has developed a national counterpart. Organizing for new left causes has become ever more institutionalized, as memberships in consumer, environmental, Third World/human rights, and women's organizations nearly doubled between 1980 and 1994. By the mid-1990s there were more than 16 million memberships in such organizations, just over one per capita (Koopmans 1996: 343). The four largest environmental organizations alone have grown to a combined membership of 1.5 million—about 15 percent of the adult population (Kriesi 1993: 182).

At their most radical, action groups challenge parliamentary democracy by attempting to force policy change through direct action, such as the occupation of an empty building to claim it as residential space, or the blockade of trains carrying nuclear waste. But in many cases action groups are also involved in political parties, particularly the Labor Party and small parties of the left (Kriesi 1989). The action group has thus become a parallel channel of influence used in conjunction with traditional political organizations and processes (Rochon 1982a). Indeed, the openness of the electoral system has encouraged many action-group activists to enter party politics, and the relative permeability of the policymaking system has not infrequently co-opted action groups into the policy process.[51]

It is easy to be overly sanguine about the influence of action-group protest on policy. A survey of the influence of protest on decisionmaking in the Second Chamber found only one instance in which policy was affected. The single exception was a protest of working youth under the age of 18 who sought a subsidy for continuing education. This particular protest was distinguished from others in the study by the explicit support it enjoyed from the trade unions, a fact that made it difficult to distinguish between influence of the unions and influence of the protest itself.[52]

But although action groups only rarely have a direct influence on national decisionmaking, they have had a major role in advancing the new issue agenda. They raise the visibility of new issues to the general public, creating pressure on the party system to respond. They have also been at the forefront of a widespread demand for more opportunities for direct participation in governance. The government has responded with a number of institutional reforms ranging from establishment of neighborhood councils (de Jong 1992), to public hearings in parliamentary committees (Veenstra 1976), to the creation of an ombudsman who may investigate any claim of mistreatment of a citizen by a civil servant or government organization (Bovend'Eert and Kummeling 1991: 320–321).

The New Party System Takes Shape

It is little wonder that many observers of Dutch politics in the 1970s predicted the complete breakup of the traditional party system. Given the ease of entry by new parties into the Second Chamber, a failure to adapt by the established parties would open the door to new parties whose programs captured the emerging issues in a changing society. The increasing issue focus of the electorate, combined with the growing tendency to pursue those issues outside the channels of party politics, added to the difficulties of Dutch parties in retaining their support in a rapidly changing social and political climate.

But review of Figure 4.2 shows us that the traditional parties have not become marginalized. Beginning in the mid-1970s, the major parties (now reduced from five to three by merger of three confessional parties into the CDA) halted their decline. At their best, as in the 1986 election, the traditional parties did almost as well as they had in the era of pillar stability. This recovery, however, has not meant a restoration of the old party system. Instead, the party system saved itself only by transforming itself.

Among the larger established parties, the response has been to abandon the exclusive focus on a single pillar in favor of a search for broader bases of support. Where once the major parties each enjoyed monopoly representation of "their" social group (subject to minor challenges from breakaway parties), they are now in direct competition with each other. The Liberals, the Christian Democrats, and Labor sought to become catchall parties of the center-right, center, and center-left, respectively.

The most pressing need for broadening was faced by the Christian Democrats. In their first election in 1977, 85 percent of the votes for the CDA came from churchgoing Catholics and Protestants, the natural base of the party. By 1994 only 49 percent of CDA voters were regular church attenders—a remarkable transformation in which the party has succeeded in broadening its appeal to secular groups.[53] Van der Eijk and Niemöller (1992: 280) conclude that even among religious voters, support for the CDA is now "predominantly a political choice rather than an identification with a particular segment of society." The Labor Party, also faced with a declining base of natural support in the secular working class, has made a similar transformation. In 1971, 60 percent of Labor Party voters were members of the secular working class. By 1998 that was true of under 30 percent of Labor Party voters. Only the Liberal Party, with the luxury of an expanding base of natural support, has continued to recruit a majority of its voters within its traditional support base. In both 1971 and 1998, 80 percent of Liberal Party voters were members of the secular middle class.

Overall, then, the altered basis of party appeals has caused an unprecedented social-group mixing in party support. Elections were once effectively a census of the relative demographic strength of religious and class groups in the society. Contemporary elections are instead a political competition based on party image, program, and performance. This transformation was thrust on parties as a consequence of social and political change. But it was also a transformation embraced by party leaders as they altered their appeals to remain competitive in a fluid strategic situation.

Organizational Change

For some of the established parties, responding to the pressures for democratization required a fundamental internal restructuring. The Christian Historical Union and the Liberal Party each originated as parliamentary parties in the nineteenth century, before expansion of the electorate required parties to develop extensive constituency organizations. They retained this legacy into the 1960s, having the character more of clubs of like-minded leaders than of mass parties with strong local organizations and extensive member participation. By contrast, the Catholic People's Party, the Labor Party, and the Anti-Revolutionary Party were each created by mass organizations as part of the development of the pillars. As a result, these parties developed more fully articulated networks of local chapters. Despite these differences in origins and structure, though, all major parties were in the 1960s effectively governed from the center, with executive *(partijbestuur)* control over the party program and the nomination of candidates for office.

The challenge to democratize caused each of the major parties to rethink these organizational structures. Involvement in the extensive network of subcultural organizations is no longer an effective strategy; the parties have developed instead into what Koole (1993: 179) refers to as a "modern cadre party." This includes an extensive internal structure that mobilizes member support and activism, combined with a professionalized central leadership attuned to the competitive situation as defined by voter preferences and rival parties. The parliament-centered parties also began aggressively to build local chapters.

All parties strengthened their national congress as a governing body, at the expense of the party executive. Party programs are written by a program committee, then discussed in local chapters where members can formulate amendments, and finally adopted at a national party congress (Zielonka-Goei 1992). Candidate selection has been decentralized to regional party organizations in all the major parties, although selection of the head of the party list remains the prerogative of a small group of leaders (Lucardie 1993; Koole 1994: 294–295). Parties have also embraced the growing women's movement by aggressively expanding the number of women nominated as candidates for election and appointed to the party executive. The proportion of women serving in the Second Chamber increased from less than 10 percent in 1956 to over 25 percent in the 1990s, and the major parties are pledged to meet still higher future targets for the recruitment of women (van de Velde 1994). The Labor Party was most affected by this revolution, pledging to reach 50 percent participation by women at all levels of party organization.[54]

Ideological Change

Democratization of party organizations and merger of the confessional parties were measures that helped lay the groundwork for survival of the existing party system in a period of rapid social change. But such reforms could scarcely have staunched the hemorrhage of popular support if they were not accompanied by a serious reappraisal of the ideological orientation of each party. By loosening the links between party and pillar, it became possible for people outside the pillars to consider voting for one of the major parties. But only by reforming their ideological appeals would the established parties be able to attract and retain a stable base of support in the more fluid electorate that was rapidly developing.

In the Labor Party, this ideological adaptation took the form of renewing an old social democratic dream: to break the confessional hold on much of the working class and to build a majority party of the left. Between the world wars and again immediately after the Second World War, Labor had tried to establish a "breakthrough" party that would transcend the pillarized division of society. The effort failed each time because too few religious members of the working class were willing to abandon their confessional party. This time would be different.

Beginning in the late 1960s, the Labor Party came increasingly to embrace the new issue agenda of greater democratization of political and economic institutions, a renewed commitment to social and economic equality, and a radicalized foreign policy that distanced the party from some policies of the NATO alliance.[55] In 1971 the Labor Party declared itself an "action party," dedicated to fostering social movements. The party gradually became more environmentally oriented during the 1970s, and in 1979 took the dramatic step (for a workers party) of coming out against nuclear energy. Finally, the PvdA sought to create a majority coalition of parties of the left, whose guiding idea was well summarized by the Labor Party slogan of the 1970s: "For the wider spread of income, knowledge and power."

By embracing these issues, the PvdA intended to woo new left or postmaterialist support as well as to accelerate the decline of the confessional parties. With confessional loyalties weakening, the Labor Party's goal was to make the choice between left and right as clear as possible. At about the same time, the Labor Party congress adopted a policy stating that the PvdA would not form a governing coalition with the Catholic People's Party, ostensibly in retribution for the decision of the KVP parliamentary leadership in 1966 to withdraw support from a KVP-PvdA coalition government. By forcing the Catholic People's Party to ally with the Liberals, Labor Party strategists hoped to increase their own support among the Catholic working class. A new wave of activists swept into the Labor Party, bringing with them an ideological and organizational style that turned the once-staid party of the working class into a "party of interminable meetings."[56]

The Liberal Party went through a different reasoning process to arrive at approximately the same conclusion. Like the Labor Party, the Liberals hoped to benefit from the decline of confessional voter loyalty. Unlike the PvdA, though, the Liberals enjoyed an expanding natural base of support in the secular middle class. For the Liberals, then, ideological polarization did not take the form of staking out a new issue terrain so much as of promoting their existing ideology more directly in opposition to Labor Party and Christian Democratic messages. As Galen Irwin and Joop van Holsteyn (1989a: 112) point out, this enabled the Liberals to appeal for the support of all secular voters opposed to socialism.

The same set of circumstances also triggered an ideological reassessment in the CDA, albeit one that appeared much less dramatic in the public pronouncements of party leaders. The task for confessional party leaders was twofold. First, ideological differences between the three major denominational parties had to be blurred so that cooperation between them and the transfer of confessional party support to the CDA would be facilitated.[57] Second, the CDA had to define for itself a broad center ground between the Labor Party and the Liberals. That center ground was to be generally Christian in inspiration but not explicitly tied to any particular denomination. These tasks did not create the kind of public fireworks characteristic of the issue-taking by such leaders as Joop den Uyl of Labor and Hans Wiegel of the Liberals, but they represented nonetheless a programmatic redefinition responsive to the loosening of confessional ties among the public.

The extent of ideological transformation among the major parties was remarkable. For example, all political parties incorporated environmental themes into their programs and increased the participation of women in their organizations. The established parties also took differentiated positions on the more contentious of the new issues, including abortion, income equalization, and defense policy. In a survey conducted in 1972, Jacques Thomassen (1976b) found that members of parliament took sharply distinctive positions on these and other issues. Taking their cues from these party leaders, members of the public also developed increasingly polarized evaluations of the parties between 1970 and 1972. The polarization of issue positions and party evaluations gave the party system a new ideological cast that came increasingly to supplant the idea of party choice as an expression of pillar loyalty.

It is normally thought that political parties cannot move past each other on the left-right ideological spectrum. As Anthony Downs (1957: 122) put it, the need to display "integrity and responsibility create[s] relative immobility, which prevents a party from making ideological leaps over the heads of its neighbors." Remarkably enough, there were several instances of Dutch parties making leaps over the heads of their neighbors between the late 1960s and early 1980s. Data on voter perceptions of the left-right placement of parties generated by Galen Irwin and Karl Dittrich (1984: 273) show that the Catholic People's Party was the most conservative of the three confessional parties in 1968. As it entered the period of rapid decline, the KVP moved rapidly to the center, passing the other two confessional parties and the Liberals in the process. When this strategy failed to halt its decline, the KVP began to converge with the other confessional parties by moving back to the right, again passing the Anti-Revolutionary Party. These programmatic peregrinations continued after merger of the separate confessional parties into the CDA. During the period of welfare state retrenchment in the 1980s, the CDA moved back to the center by articulating a concept of social solidarity that paid particular attention to the young, the handicapped, and foreign workers, and to the welfare of families. In the same period, from 1968 to 1982, the Liberal Party moved in a conservative direction, passing all three confessional parties to establish itself as the major party on the right side of the spectrum. The Labor Party's strategy of ideological polarization shows up in these data as significant movement toward the left, though Labor did not move past any other major parties during its ideological voyage.

This process of ideological redefinition and polarization among the parties had a number of effects on the Dutch political system. The long history of governance by compromise between pragmatic elites representing the various pillars was replaced almost overnight by a public and private politics of partisan invective. As Hans van Mierlo (1986: 113) notes, "Parliamentary debate between competing parties increased enormously; ministers flooded Parliament with policy plans provoking fierce public discussion." Increasing ideological differences between the parties, and the increasingly public way in which those differences were emphasized, made post-election formation of coalition governments steadily more difficult (see Chapters 5 and 6).

These difficulties in forming governments (and in holding coalitions together) were byproducts of the ideological polarization of the party system. The motivating purpose of that polarization was for parties to retain their traditional voters and attract new ones. To do that, the major parties increasingly defined their bases of potential supporters in ideological terms rather than as blocs delineated by religious belief and socioeconomic status.

The Color Purple

The polarization strategy was adopted for the specific purpose of giving the established parties a clear ideological profile in the altered climate of declining pillar loyalties and the rise of new political issues. By the 1980s this strategy had served its purpose. The established parties had weathered the challenge of social and political change and it became clear that they would remain the dominant members of the party system. The Labor Party captured a substantial portion of the environmental vote. Sentiment for a smaller welfare state, expressed elsewhere in Europe as support for anti-tax parties, was effectively absorbed by the Liberal Party. The solidarity of mainstream parties against the Center Democrats marginalized their anti-immigrant appeals and helped knock the party out of the Second Chamber in 1998. Only D66 and the Green Left among the new parties have retained a significant niche in the electorate.

Polarization between the parties has now come to be replaced by a greater degree of ideological convergence. The Labor Party, originator of the strategy of polarization, abandoned the strategy in the late 1980s. A series of party reports published in the 1980s articulated the view that the benefits of maintaining a distinctive ideological position must be balanced against the desire to be seen as a responsible party that can be entrusted with governmental finance (Wolinetz 1993). Samuel Eldersveld (1998: 338) finds that the new philosophy of depolarization penetrated even to the local levels of party organization. In Amsterdam in 1976, 46 percent of Labor Party activists and 47 percent of Liberal Party activists said that they became active in their parties for ideological reasons. By 1993 this was true of only 10 percent of Labor Party activists and 14 percent of Liberal activists.[58] As Ruud Koole (1993: 178) put it, "A call for 'no-nonsense' politics was heard in the 1980s, to counterbalance the adversarial style of politics of the previous years."

Since that time, governments of the center-left have replaced governments of the center-right with few discernible consequences for economic policy. In 1994, over one hundred years of confessional party participation in government was ended by a new coalition formed between the Labor and Liberal parties—a coalition quickly dubbed the "purple government" (combining red and blue political forces). This was an unthinkable combination just fifteen years earlier, and even as it was happening the idea was so dumbfounding that "many observers thought [the purple government] impossible until the new ministers were actually photographed with the Queen."[59] The purple government, then, marked the final step in the depolarization of the party system, now realigned to correspond to the new issue-based competition.[60] The Dutch party system proved its adaptability through an ideological convergence in the 1990s that was no less rapid than the polarization of the 1970s.

The receding tide of party polarization has left behind a permanently altered party system. One consequence of the independence of voters and the increased competitiveness between parties has been to foster the emergence of leaders who tend to personify their parties. From 1959 to 1971 no minister-president was also a party leader; instead, party leadership and governmental leadership were effectively separated.[61] Modern electoral campaigns are in large part contests between party leaders who compete as potential prime ministers, thus personalizing party choice to an unprecedented degree. Development of the media-centered campaign—including televised debates between the major-party leaders—has also contributed to the growing prominence of the party leader as articulator of the party's campaign themes.[62]

Voters have responded as never before to the appeals of particular leaders. These range from the youthful and "Kennedy-like" Hans Wiegel of the Liberal Party in 1982; to the sober, hardworking, and slightly rumpled Christian Democrat Ruud Lubbers in 1986 and 1989; to the fatherly, moderate, inclusive Labor Party leader Wim Kok in 1998. Each of these leaders led their party to unprecedented electoral success by attracting support outside the traditional constituency of that party. The Liberals fell back after Wiegel, and the Christian Democrats lost almost half their support in the two elections after the retirement of Lubbers. A similar fate may well await the PvdA after Kok's retirement.

Conclusion

The traditional party system in the Netherlands long had an especially close relationship to the dominant cleavages in society, with each major political party representing one of the pillars. From 1918 to the mid-1960s, the path to success for a Dutch party was to link itself to a particular social group and to champion that group's political rights and interests. In the last thirty years, though, secularization, the spread of middle-class prosperity and values, and declining pillar orthodoxy combined to challenge the traditional party system. The established parties, each closely tied to a particular social group, have been forced to adapt their organizations and ideologies in order to survive. Galen Irwin and Joop van Holsteyn (1997) refer to this transformation as the decline of the structured (pillarized) model of voting choice. In its place, they note, has come a greater emphasis on evaluation of party leaders, party programs, and economic conditions.[63]

The subsequent transformation of the Dutch party system recalls the experience of realignments of the American party system. The concept of party system realignment developed by V. O. Key Jr. (1955) and others involves a loosening of existing ties between voters and parties, a shift in the issues that are central to party competition, polarization between parties on those new issues, an increase in voter interest in politics, and a shift in the alignment of various social groups with particular political parties. Although party realignment is normally associated with changes in the strengths of existing parties and possibly with the rise of new parties, this need not be the case. The agility of party adaptation will be one factor that determines which parties survive the realigning era, and at what relative strengths.

The Dutch experience of the last three decades resembles the ideal-type pattern of realignment in many ways. Transformation of the party system was accompanied by a loosening of ties between voters and parties, and by a shift in the issues central to party competition. Realignment of the Dutch party system brought increased issue competition between parties, particularly for the support of those voters who came of age in 1977 and after. In addition, a new issue agenda became increasingly important to party choice, taking its place alongside religion and class as a structural dimension of the party system. Finally, the Netherlands experienced the ideological polarization typical of party realignments. If the traditional means of mobilizing support was to emphasize the party's linkage to particular social groups, the means of mobilizing support during the realigning era was to present a distinctive ideological profile.

In sum, the Dutch party system went through a realignment cycle between the mid-1960s and early 1980s. One striking element of that cycle is the rapidity with which the established parties adapted to a changed social structure and new political issues. Organizational and ideological traditions fell by the wayside as the parties confronted an electoral contest whose rules were changing from election to election. Prior to the transition, the established parties were enmeshed in a dense network of relationships with other organizations in their pillar, and operated as the political arm of a particular social group. The rapidity with which they were able to transform their organizational structures and ideological appeals from group mobilization to ideological mobilization is testimony to the power of strategic politicians to make rational adaptations to altered circumstances.

That said, the outcome of this adaptive behavior has not been to create a restored party system along the lines of the pillar era. The Green Left and D66 have become important parts of the party system, each embracing the new issues that are now permanently on the political agenda. The major confessional parties merged into the CDA, a startling development given the prior history of confessional pillar organizations. Even more significant than any of these changes in the party system itself, Dutch voters have developed a new independence from the structuring traits of class and religion. Elections are now fought on issues, the state of the economy, and the traits of party leaders. The result is substantially increased volatility between elections. An unprecedented thirty seats changed hands in the electoral earthquake of 1967 that inaugurated the new era of party competition. Thirty-one years later, in 1998, fifty seats (one-third of the parliament) shifted between parties. The Dutch party system has entered the era of permanent revolution.

NOTES

1. The *lijsttrekker* is literally "one who pulls the party list along."

2. One reason parties avoid solicitation of private gifts is that the acceptance of any such donation is treated as a scandal by the media, according to Andeweg and Irwin (1993: 66).

3. Reference will be made in this chapter exclusively to the lower house, or Second Chamber. The First Chamber (or "Senate") is indirectly elected every four years by an electoral college composed of members of the eleven provincial councils. See Chapter 5 for details on the Dutch parliamentary system.

4. The country is divided into eighteen electoral districts, and parties may vary the composition and ordering of the lists of candidates they submit in each district. This enables parties to feature local candidates more prominently on each district's ballot, and it is the party's vote tally in each district that determines which candidates will be elected.

5. The quota of votes needed to elect one member is determined by dividing the total number of votes by 150, the number of seats in the Second Chamber. Parties with fewer votes than the quota are eliminated from further consideration. The vote totals of the remaining parties are then divided by the quota to determine each party's number of seats. Any remaining seats are allocated to the party or parties with the largest remainders, that is, the most unused votes below the threshold of the quota. This procedure determines the number of people from each party list who will be elected.

6. Between 1945 and 1994, only three candidates placed below the party threshold on the ballot managed to get elected by the use of preference votes (Andeweg 1993: 81).

7. This is out of an electorate of about 11.75 million voters, and assumes a 75 percent turnout rate. Elections to the European Parliament also use proportional representation, though the threshold for election there is 4 percent since the Netherlands has just twenty-five seats in that body.

8. Those who did not turn up at the polls to mark a ballot were subject to a fine. Compulsory voting was repealed in 1970, as the pillars were in decline. In the fifty-three years that voting was legally required, turnout in national elections averaged about 95 percent (Irwin 1974: 293). Since repeal of the requirement, turnout in national elections has fallen to an average of 83 percent, and has recently fluctuated between 70 and 75 percent. This is still a very high figure compared to American presidential election turnout levels of just over 50 percent.

9. See for example Sinner (1973) and Lipschits (1977). For a discussion of how Dutch Christian democracy, social democracy, and liberalism compare to their sister movements in other European countries, see Mommen (1990).

10. The Liberals are a partial exception to the generalization linking major parties to the pillars of Dutch society. As the dominant party of the second half of the nineteenth century, the Liberals had no need for the kind of organizing and mobilizing effort of the Protestants, Catholics, and socialists. See Chapter 3 for details of pillar organization.

11. Cited in "Voorzitters SP en PvdA debatten over het socialisme," *De Standaard*, November 10, 1995, page 2.

12. During the nineteenth century the Liberals were considered to be on the left, compared to the conservative positions of the confessional parties. When social class became an electoral issue with the rise of the social democratic party, the Liberals came to be considered a party of the right. Even today, however, the Liberal party group sits to the left of the speaker of the Second Chamber.

13. Until 1887 only about one in eight adult males was eligible to vote (Daalder 1966: 205). In 1887 the electorate was expanded to about a quarter of the adult male population. From 1887 to 1913 the proportion of the electorate meeting the income requirements for the suffrage grew steadily to about 68 percent. By extending the vote to all males age 25 and over in 1917, the *Pacificatie* enlarged the electorate by about 50 percent over its previous size. Recent reforms have allowed prisoners and Dutch people living abroad to vote. Foreigners living in the Netherlands have been allowed to vote in local elections since 1986.

14. Both citations are from Lucardie (1982: 140).

15. See Daalder and Koole (1988: 169–170). Felling and Peters (1986) estimate that 71 percent of Liberal voters are "cultural progressives," meaning they are against governmental regulation of abortion and pornography and opposed to legal restrictions on gays.

16. Cited in Daalder (1966: 212).

17. This is according to a study by Rose and Urwin (1970).

18. Data for the Netherlands in Figure 4.1 were collected in 1974, nearly a decade into the period of social and political transformation. We can assume that the homogeneity of Dutch parties was even greater at the height of the pillar system. For details on the calculation of the homogeneity index, see Rochon and Strate (1981).

19. See Rochon (1985) for a listing of these parties and brief sketches of the issues that moved them to challenge the established party within their pillars.

20. Instead of universal suffrage, the SGP advocated the "organic suffrage," in which each head of a family would receive one vote on behalf of the family. See Lucardie (1988) for a review of the three extant "fundamentalist" Calvinist parties: the SGP, the Reformed Political League (GPV), and the Reformed Political Federation (RPF).

21. The system of proportional representation means that a figure tracing the votes won by the major parties would follow exactly the same track as in Figure 4.2, which gives election results in terms of seats won.

22. See also Daudt (1972) and Miller and Stouthard (1975).

23. See also van der Eijk and Niemöller (1983) and Houska (1985) for extensive analyses of the decline of cohesion within the confessional pillars. The only bright note for the confessional parties was that religious people continued to have higher turnout rates than the secular portion of the electorate. See Smeets (1995: 61).

24. Formation of the CDA prompted the founding of the Roman Catholic Party of the Netherlands and the Reformed Political Federation, each of which reaffirmed their commitment to separate denominational parties. Both parties achieved parliamentary representation, but neither flourished and only the RPF is represented in the Second Chamber today.

25. The measure of social class employed in Table 4.1 is self-identification. What is being measured, then, is the subjective perception of class location rather than the objective facts of income and occupation.

26. Three rival parties on the left—D66, the Green Left, and the Socialist Party—combined to win 28 percent of the secular–working class vote in 1998.

27. The Labor Party also dominates the votes of *allochtonen,* and (in local elections where they are permitted to vote) of noncitizen immigrants, according to Rath (1988: 635–636).

28. Liberal Party membership tripled between 1954 and 1990, from 30,000 to 90,000, according to Daalder and Koole (1988: 157).

29. Dutch courts have consistently ruled that the Center Democrats have the right to meet and demonstrate in public. In 1997, however, party leader and Second Chamber member Hans Janmaat was sentenced to a fine and four weeks in prison (with a suspended sentence) for racist speech that incited others to discrimination. *InterNetKrant,* March 29, 1997, page 1.

30. Cited in Gladdish (1991: 51).

31. D66's longtime desire for a constitutional amendment authorizing the referendum most recently took the form of a "corrective referendum," one in which voters could repeal a law passed by the Second Chamber. This amendment failed to obtain the necessary two-thirds majority in the Upper House in May 1999, leading to the fall of the second purple government.

32. The proposal was defeated in the Second Chamber in 1996.

33. Cited in the Delft City Council minutes, 1972, page 280.

34. See Koole (1993). These membership levels existed without the benefit of corporate membership, such as the automatic enrollment of all union members in the British Labour Party.

35. See Hippe et al. (1994: 26) and Koole (1993: 172). More precisely, the centrist confessional parties have suffered a great loss of membership. The smaller fundamentalist Calvinist parties—the SGP, the GPV, and the RPF—maintain exceptionally high member-to-vote ratios.

36. The proportion of people saying they were very or fairly interested in politics was 50 percent in 1954, rose to 61 percent in 1977, and reached 75 percent in 1998.

37. Dittrich (1987) finds that the confessional parties began reducing their emphasis on issues of traditional morality as early as 1959, a decline that continued through the next two decades.

38. See Chapter 3 for a discussion of the significance of democratization, women's rights, and environmental protection in Dutch society. Opposition to nuclear energy was a major issue in the Netherlands throughout the 1970s, and in the latter part of the decade several demonstrations with between 35,000 and 50,000 participants were held at a uranium enrichment plant at Almelo and at a joint Dutch-German fast-breeder reactor in Kalkar, Germany.

39. The "new left" parties are defined as D66, the Radicals (PPR), the Pacifist Socialists (PSP), and the Communists (CPN). Although the CPN was a relatively closed and even Stalinist organization in the 1970s, by the end of the 1980s it had merged with the PPR and the PSP to form the Green Left (GL). See Rochon (1991) and Voerman (1995) for accounts of the formation of the GL.

40. "Confessional" here includes the small religious parties the SGP, the GPV, and the RPF, as well as the CDA and its three predecessor parties. The small religious parties have allied with each other in local, provincial, and European elections where necessary to maintain legislative representation (Oppenhuis 1996). However, they have so far staunchly maintained their independence as separate parties in national elections.

41. For an analysis of the rise of new issue concern in the 1971 election, see Mokken and Stokman (1972). Concern about the new issues has decreased since the early 1970s, and part

of the rapid increase in new issue orientation proved to be a passing fad. In 1981 just 23 percent of the public, 34 percent of those voting, mentioned one of these issues as being among the most important in the country. By 1998, only 13 percent of the public and 14 percent of the electorate mentioned one of these new issues as being among the most important facing the country. The salience of nuclear energy and democratization of the political system fell off particularly sharply between 1971 and 1998, as did the proportion of those naming environmental protection as one of the most important issues (Jamison et al. 1990: 135, 152).

42. As a new party, the Green Left is able to stress the new issues of environmentalism, feminism, and democratization without the baggage of "old left" positions. A study of Green Left leaders by Lucardie and van Schuur (1994: 265) shows that less than half agreed that there should be income equality and less than a third said that large firms should be nationalized (two classic "old left" issues). By contrast, support for new left issues is unequivocal: 98 percent of the Green Left leaders agree that polluting products should be heavily taxed, and 85 percent agree that environmentally polluting industry should be phased out regardless of the effect on employment. These positions go beyond the environmental policies supported by the Labor Party.

43. See for example Anker (1992: chapter 5) and Irwin and van Holsteyn (1997: 103–111).

44. See Andeweg (1982), van der Eijk and Niemöller (1983: 80), and Need and de Graaf (1996).

45. Inglehart (1990: chapter 6). See also Middendorp (1977, 1991) and Felling and Peters (1986) for analyses of the changed ideological dimensions of Dutch political culture.

46. Dittrich (1987) finds that environmental protection quickly became one of the issues most stressed in the party programs of the 1970s, second only to social services in 1972 and 1977.

47. The Labor Party out of power, for example, developed extensive links with the movement against nuclear weapons; when in power, the party has been more cautious about the need to retain American nuclear weapons within the country as part of its NATO obligation. See Rochon (1988) and Kriesi (1989).

48. This is shown in the negative correlation between postmaterialist support for the Labor Party and postmaterialist support for D66 and the Green Left (Pearson's r = -.76). There is much less direct competition for postmaterialist support between the Labor Party and the confessional parties (r = -.41) and none at all between the Labor Party and the Liberal Party (r = .02). For further analysis of postmaterialism and the party system, see van Deth and Geurts (1989).

49. Cited in Rowen (1988: 174).

50. Sidney Verba et al. (1978: 58–59) find that the Netherlands ranks low among the seven nations they study on participation in campaign activities, but quite high in individual contacting of officials. Samuel Barnes, Max Kaase, et al. (1979: 169–170) find that compared to Britain, the United States, and Germany, the Netherlands ranks high in unconventional political participation, even though it scores relatively low in conventional political activities.

51. See Chapter 6 and van Praag (1991) for details of how social movement organizations are co-opted into the policy process.

52. Werkgroep Afdeling Politicologie (1971). This was a study of protests held outside the national parliamentary buildings, on issues of national concern. The influence of action groups at the local level may be much greater (Rochon 1982a; van Noort 1988).

53. Sixty-one percent of all CDA voters in 1998 were regular church attenders, as the party vote shrunk back to its core supporters.

54. Leijenaar (1993). The trend toward decentralization of decisionmaking and the desire to increase the number of women candidates on the party list have proven to be partially at odds with each other. In 1992 the Labor Party executive took back control over candidate selection from the regional party organizations to assure itself of the desired number of women candidates as well as to obtain the distribution of substantive expertise desired in its parliamentary group, according to Andeweg and Irwin (1993: 91).

55. For example, the 1969 party congress adopted a resolution supporting diplomatic recognition of the German Democratic Republic.

56. Kriesi and van Praag (1987: 334) found that 39 percent of active members in peace movement organizations were supporters of the Labor Party, versus 58 percent who supported one of the parties that later formed the Green Left. At the height of its engagement with social movements, the PvdA was known as a *"vergaderpartij,"* or party of meetings, according to Zielonka-Goei (1992). The PvdA held party congresses annually during the 1970s, a frequency matched among European social democratic parties only by the British Labour Party (Kitschelt 1994: 241).

57. On ideological movement of the three confessional parties as expressed in their election platforms, see Dittrich (1987: 224–226).

58. Activists in the CDA, which never participated in the polarization of the 1970s, were always less likely to say they had become active for ideological reasons: 14 percent in 1976 and 10 percent in 1993 (Eldersveld 1998: 338).

59. Irwin and van Holsteyn (1997: 94). Just three years before the purple government was formed, C. P. Middendorp (1991: 281) concluded from his study of elite ideology that "a coalition between Social Democrats and Liberals would be very difficult to envisage . . . because of their widely separated ideological stands."

60. The purple government's slogan of "jobs, jobs and more jobs" expressed an economic pragmatism comparable to U.S. President Bill Clinton's 1992 reminder to himself that "It's the economy, stupid."

61. Until the 1970s, parties often had no single *lijsttrekker,* instead placing different people in the number-one slot on the candidate lists they submitted in different electoral districts around the country. This practice has now disappeared, since, as Koole (1994: 295) points out, the era of the leader-centered television campaign "has made it absolutely necessary to emphasize the electoral appeal of one and the same leader."

62. Kleinnijenhuis and Pennings (1995: 33) find that the focus of media reporting of political affairs is more on the party leader during campaigns than between campaigns. Also, television focuses more on party leaders (35 percent of all reporting) than do newspapers (25 percent of all reporting). As people increasingly turn to television for their political information, then, the emphasis on party leaders grows. On the selectivity of media focus on issues during campaigns and the effect of media coverage on election outcomes, see also Kleinnijenhuis and de Ridder (1998).

63. See also Irwin and van Holsteyn (1989a). On the importance of party leaders in determining vote choice, see also Anker (1992). On the importance of evaluations of economic conditions, see also Middendorp and Kolkhuis Tanke (1990).

5

THE INSTITUTIONS OF DUTCH DEMOCRACY

"Everything from the past is forgotten. And forgiven."[1] These portentous words stood at the center of the proclamation of 1813 that restored sovereignty to the Netherlands and, paradoxically, set the stage for a modern democracy by establishing the first monarchy in Dutch history. Installation of King William I came at the behest of the allied victors over Napoleon, who sought a strong buffer state against a resurgent France.[2] As such, William's reign made permanent the transition from the decentralized Republic of the United Provinces to a unitary state.

This chapter will review contemporary constitutional arrangements of the Netherlands, including the roles of the legislative, executive, judicial, and administrative branches. We will also give consideration to subnational government, such as provincial and local governments, though these are of secondary importance in the unitary Dutch system. The king (or queen) no longer plays a significant role in determining the course of policy. In deference to the monarchy's role as symbolic head of state, though, we begin this chapter with a consideration of its constitutional origins.

The Constitutional Monarchy

Although William I and his successor William II were never absolute monarchs in the full sense, there was a steady growth of pressure during their reigns for greater accountability of the government to parliament. The revolution sweeping much of Europe in 1848 took the relatively tame form in the Netherlands of an election in which the Liberals gained a majority in the Second Chamber, the lower house of the Dutch parliament. Under duress, William II agreed to a proposal to appoint a committee of five Liberals under Johan Rudolf Thorbecke to write a new constitution. The work of this committee created the basic institutions that remain in the Netherlands today, including a constitutional monarchy whose ministers are responsible to the Second Chamber. The Second Chamber would henceforth be directly elected by all citizens whose tax payments were above a certain level. The First Chamber of the States General, formerly appointed by the king, was now to be elected by the provincial legislatures (known as *Provinciale Staten*).

A literal reading of the Dutch constitution, with its references to ministers being appointed and discharged by the king, gives a misleading sense of how a constitutional monarchy actually operates. To make sense of such language, H. M. de Jong (1992: 63) refers to "the constitutional King" as synonymous with the government, in which ministers take the leading role and the monarch is but their symbolic figurehead. This relationship has since 1848 been expressed in the constitution with the phrase that "the Monarch is inviolable; the ministers are responsible." This clause places the monarch outside of politics in the sense of not being responsible for the policy choices that govern the nation. Instead, the ministers *are* responsible. They are individually responsible for the decisions made in their respective departments; they are collectively responsible for the policies adopted by the government; and they are also collectively responsible for all words and actions of the monarch, for example in the annual Speech from the Throne and during state visits to other countries (de Jong 1992: 76–78).

The Dutch monarch has since 1868 been deprived of the power to name a cabinet that does not have majority support in the Second Chamber. Since that time the king or queen has exercised substantial political power only in the exceptional circumstances of World War II. During the German occupation, with the parliament suspended and many political leaders in prison or underground, Queen Wilhelmina signed or refused to sign decisions made by the government-in-exile based on her own judgment of what was needed. When after the war her successor Queen Juliana refused to sign the death sentences of fourteen Germans convicted of war crimes, Minister-President Willem Drees informed her that refusal would bring down the government and create a constitutional crisis. A compromise was ultimately reached, as the sentences were commuted to life in prison and the queen signed the documents.[3]

If the ministers are in fact responsible for making policy, this leaves the question of just what the role of the constitutional monarch is. To understand this role, it is useful to recall the distinction made by Walter Bagehot (1914: 72) between the efficient and dignified portions of government. The efficient portion of government is the decisionmaking authority, those institutions by which the government actually rules. The dignified portion includes those elements "which excite and preserve the reverence of the population," or those elements that remind citizens they are a unified people. As Bagehot pointed out, the executive office of the presidency in the United States combines the dignified and efficient executive functions, sometimes awkwardly, as when a president turns a ceremonial occasion into a partisan event. Parliamentary systems, by contrast, separate the efficient and dignified functions of the executive. In parliamentary republics such as Germany and Ireland, the prime minister is the "efficient" head of the executive branch and the president is the dignified or symbolic head of state. In constitutional monarchies such as the Netherlands and the Scandinavian countries, these roles are filled by, respectively, the prime minister and the monarch.

The primary task of the monarch, then, is to serve as a living reminder of those traditions and institutions that unite the nation. This is a particularly important matter in a country whose religious and class cleavages run deep. Because of the sensitivity of religious differences in the Netherlands, the connection between the royal family and religion has always been a delicate matter. We saw in Chapter 3 that the textbooks of Protestant schools proclaim William of Orange, patriarch of the royal line, as one of their own. Each successive generation of the royal family has been Protestant, though Queen Wilhelmina (1890–1948) and her daughter Queen Juliana (1948–1980) were both raised in a relatively small Protestant denomination as a way of avoiding the rivalries between larger denominations. The issue of religion and royalty nonetheless burst into the open in the 1960s, when Princess Irene, second in line for the throne, converted to Catholicism and married a prince who made claims to the Spanish throne. The subsequent debate in parliament on whether Irene should be removed from the line of succession focused on her potential involvement in domestic Spanish politics, but the unspoken question for many was the question of whether a Catholic could be king or queen of the Netherlands.[4] The same issue arose again in 1998 when Prince Maurits, son of Princess Margriet, married a Catholic. Some Dutch Reformed members of the royal family took the Catholic Eucharist at an interfaith ceremony consecrating the marriage, causing protest in both Catholic and Dutch Reformed circles. The episode shows how delicate controversies connected with the symbolic head of state can be.

The authority of parliament to limit the power of the monarch by making governmental ministers responsible to the Second Chamber was the central constitutional issue of the nineteenth century. Today, the monarch is no longer the effective head of state, but a symbol of the nation whose weight and meaning changes with the needs of each era. The symbol was a powerful one during World War II, and Nico Wilterdink (1990: 13) speculates that it may become so again as important elements of Dutch sovereignty are absorbed by the European Union. If Dutch national identity in a federation of European states becomes a key issue of the twenty-first century, the monarchy may indeed become an important symbol once again. Currently, the monarchy enjoys less symbolic weight, though the incumbent, Queen Beatrix, is greatly respected for her ability to walk the fine line of speaking out on moral issues without getting in the way of elected politicians or becoming ensnared in party disputes. As Wilterdink (1990: 9) concludes, the monarchy has become "less an object of both deep reverence and heavy criticism. Members of the royal family became more like other famous people, about whom the same kind of gossip began to appear in the popular press."[5] The Dutch monarchy has avoided the marital squabbles and sordid scandals that have recently plagued its British counterpart, though the media's limitless fascination with Crown prince William Alexander's love life and marital plans does not bode well for the monarchy's future ability to command the respect previously shown to Dutch kings and queens.

The Parliamentary System

The cornerstone of any parliamentary system is the legislative body or parliament. A parliamentary system differs in significant ways from the presidential system of government as found, for example, in the United States. The central distinction lies in the difference between separation of powers (characteristic of the presidential system) and parliamentary sovereignty. By electing directly both the president and representatives to the two houses of Congress, citizens of the United States spread effective political authority over two independent institutions.[6] Parliamentary sovereignty, by contrast, means that parliament has undivided authority, checked in principle only by the constitution and by election-day judgments of the voters. A coalition of parties comes together to form a majority bloc in the parliament, and that majority selects the prime minister and the ministers who together form the cabinet (also known as the government). The government continues in office only as long as it retains the backing of a parliamentary majority. The government, in turn, may dissolve the lower house of parliament and hold new elections before completion of its full four-year term. The practical impact of these arrangements is to create a far closer relationship of consultation and dialogue between the executive and legislative branches of government than is usually found in the United States. And, although there are certainly tensions between cabinets and parliaments, it is not possible in a parliamentary system for there to be the kind of oppositional relationship that is often found between a U.S. president and a congressional majority.

The parliament in the Netherlands is called the States General, a name inherited from the time when the national government was essentially a body composed of ambassadors from the sovereign provinces. As noted in Chapter 2, the powers of the States General were substantially increased during the French occupation under Napoleon, and those of the Provincial States correspondingly reduced. In partial compensation for this shift, the States General were also divided into two chambers under French rule, with the First Chamber intended to represent the provinces and the Second Chamber the will of the people. The Dutch parliament reflects this arrangement still today.

Organization of the Second Chamber

The 150 members of the Second Chamber are chosen directly by the voters in elections held no more than four years apart. Like all legislative assemblies, the

Second Chamber has developed elaborate internal organizations and processes to help it do its work.[7] It has a Presidium, composed of leading members of the various parliamentary parties, whose task is to decide on the daily order of business, the assignment of draft laws to particular committees, and so forth. In the nineteenth century, all proposals for law were assigned for consideration to each of five "sections," groups of randomly assigned members of the Second Chamber. This facilitated discussion of draft proposals, and each section leader would then report on their section discussion to the full chamber. The system was based on the idea that each deputy could form an opinion on every submitted bill. Those days are long gone.[8]

The two Dutch chambers now work through committees that each handle a particular policy area. There are about thirty standing committees in the Second Chamber that concern themselves with an area of policy, plus a number of other committees that make rulings on procedural matters and take care of various internal processes. The policy committees generally have a focus closely parallel to departments in the civil service, though there is no one-to-one match. For example, the Department of Social Affairs, which has responsibility for every aspect of the welfare state, is the concern of several standing committees in the Second Chamber. Other standing committees have no direct departmental counterpart, such as the committees on Civil Service, Minority Policy, Intelligence and Security Services, European Affairs, Emancipation Policy (concerned with the rights of women), and Handicapped Policy, as well as the Ombudsman committee.

Special committees may also be set up to handle areas that do not fall neatly into the domain of one of the standing committees. Some of these special committees are charged with investigating specific policy problems. A special committee established in 1990, called "Question Marks," was charged with examining a wide range of organizational problems in government and with proposing constitutional and procedural reforms that would make governance more effective.

As in the U.S. Congress, committees in both Dutch chambers are formed so as to reflect party strengths in the chamber as a whole.[9] But, unlike the U.S. Congress, committee chairmanships are also spread among the political parties in accord with their parliamentary strength, regardless of whether the party participates in government or not. In the Second Chamber elected in 1998, committee chairmanships were assigned to the Labor Party, the Liberals, and D66 (all governing parties), as well as to the Christian Democrats and the Green Left from among the opposition parties. Of course, no one party ever has a majority of members on the committee, so a committee chair cannot count on party discipline to get the work of the committee done. As a result, the power of the Dutch committee chair relies on persuasion and interparty cooperation to a far greater extent than is true in the U.S. Congress.

Most proposals are sent by the Presidium to a single committee for consideration, but controversial proposals may be sent to several committees at once. The proposal to accept cruise missiles as part of the Dutch NATO obligation in the early 1980s, for example, went to four committees: the standing committees on Foreign Affairs, Internal Affairs, and Defense, and a special committee on Constitutional Issues. The practice of multiple assignments has the effect of broadening member participation in deliberations even when the proposal is in committee stage. The collegial norms of the nineteenth century, when every member took part in the debate on every bill, are still reflected even in this age of greater specialization.

At the same time, increases in the volume and technical nature of legislation demand a growing reliance on expertise developed within committees. The Second Chamber is called upon to handle between 250 and 300 bills in a typical ten-month parliamentary session. Much of the detailed work on these bills is done in committees, whose total number of meetings per year has steadily increased over the last decades.

Plenary sessions are often of lesser importance when it comes to policy formulation. But it is in plenary session that the Second Chamber is best able to assert its more general prerogatives of control over the government. Questions are asked of ministers in plenary session, and this is where motions and amendments to legislative bills are submitted. The policy expertise of the Second Chamber is found in the work of the committees, but ideological vision is brought to the process through party debates in the plenary sessions.

Party Organization Within Parliament

As we saw in Chapter 4, there may be as many as a dozen parties represented in the Second Chamber, each with its own political vision. Elected members of a party form a group (known as a *fractie*) whose task is to coordinate the development of party positions on various issues. Development of the party stance on a particular issue rests chiefly with its policy specialists, whose expertise on a topic is recognized by other members of the party group. These members typically develop their policy interest and expertise before being elected to the Second Chamber, perhaps as leaders of interest groups or as civil servants in one of the departments.[10] Such members not only guide party policy in their area of expertise, but typically also join the chamber's committee dealing with that subject. Van Schendelen (1993: 197) points out that "Specialisation and division of labor are the key words for this structure of parliamentary decision making. Each member is preoccupied with just a few policy areas."

A concomitant development has been the significant increase in party discipline in voting on legislative proposals. Surveys of Second Chamber members show that they view themselves primarily as representatives of their party's voters, and consequently feel bound to vote the party line under most circumstances.[11] This is due in large part to the weight of the recommendations of the policy specialist, which tend to determine the legislative votes of his or her party group. Plenary debates on a bill before its final passage are typically debates between the policy specialists of the different party groups, with few other members participating (and often not very many in attendance) (Bovend'Eert and Kummeling 1991: 396).

It is worth noting that the importance of policy specialists poses especially difficult challenges for the small parties in the Second Chamber, which must choose between taking a generalist approach to legislation or having their members become expert on just a few policy domains. Small parties are unable to exert much influence on legislative bills not only because of their lack of parliamentary votes but also because of their lack of policy expertise in many areas.

The net result of these developments has been to shift more and more authority to the policy specialists of each party. The overall party program is generated from the perspectives developed by the party's policy specialists, while the party leadership is responsible for coordination of these positions and selection of the issues to be emphasized.[12] In this way the parliamentary party group develops integrated policy perspectives that link the broad ideological orientation of the party to the specific and often technical issues addressed in legislative proposals.

The First Chamber

Thus far we have considered only the Second Chamber of the States General, ignoring the fact that there is also a First Chamber (or "Senate"). The First Chamber is a key part of the legislative process, since all laws passed by the Second Chamber require its approval as well.

Bicameralism came to the Netherlands in 1815 with establishment of the First Chamber as a body appointed by the king. The purpose of the chamber was to guarantee the Belgian aristocracy a voice in government, since their territory had just been merged with the Kingdom of the Netherlands. This function was lost with Belgian independence in 1830, and the composition of the First Chamber was accordingly transformed in 1848 when royal appointment was replaced with election by members of the Provincial States.

The First Chamber is composed of seventy-five members elected for four-year terms by the members of the Provincial States (discussed later in this chapter). In principle this makes the First Chamber representative of the provinces, much as the U.S. Senate represents the American states and the Bundesrat represents the German Länder. However, in the Dutch case the number of representatives allotted to each province is proportionate to its share of the national population. Unlike the equal representation of each state in the U.S. Senate, the composition of the First Chamber does not differ significantly from that of the Second Chamber, either in regional balance or (as it turns out) in partisanship.[13]

With the constitutional change in 1848 that established direct election to the Second Chamber and the accountability of ministers to that chamber, the powers of the First Chamber were drastically reduced relative to those of the Second Chamber. The First Chamber considers legislation only after it has passed the Second Chamber, and it does not have the right either to initiate legislative proposals or to amend them.[14] Consequently, the choices faced by the First Chamber are essentially either to accept the bill as it stands or to reject it entirely, something that Ken Gladdish (1991) refers to as its ratification function.

As a result of its limited powers, the First Chamber does not subject legislation to the same exhaustive technical and partisan analysis that occurs in the Second Chamber. The First Chamber normally meets just one day per week, and 80 percent of its members pursue a career outside politics while serving as senator (Andeweg 1992: 130–131). Also, although senators are elected by the partisan members of the Provincial States and are themselves party leaders, they tend to be more independent of national party platforms than are members of the Second Chamber. They do not participate in the negotiations leading to cabinet formation and they are not bound to the policy program that emerges from those negotiations. These traits lead to a certain distinctiveness in the way the First Chamber views legislative proposals. As one senator put it, "We are people who are free from party discipline, who are not dependent on this Chamber for our livelihoods, who have a job in the society, and who can bring that experience to our work here. People sometimes say, 'You are amateurs,' and that is precisely our quality. That is precisely what we bring to it" (Andeweg 1992: 138).

As valuable as the alternative perspective brought by the First Chamber can be, it is an awkward fact of the Dutch democracy that an indirectly elected body—whose original reason for existence disappeared with Belgian independence—should have the right to deny legislation desired by the directly elected Second Chamber. As Rudy Andeweg (1992) notes, the First Chamber can be accused of unnecessary duplication of legislative scrutiny when it accepts a law as proposed, and of undemocratic interference with the directly elected Second Chamber when it rejects a law. In a First Chamber faced with these options, approval is by far the most common outcome. Even so, the First Chamber does on occasion reject major pieces of proposed legislation. In 1999 the first chamber failed to support by a two-thirds margin a proposed constitutional amendment that would authorize Dutch voters to repeal laws by subjecting them to a referendum. This action not only scuttled a constitutional amendment supported by the second chamber, but also caused the second purple government to fall after less than one year in office.

Surveys of the States General have shown that only about 60 percent of members of the Second Chamber support continued existence of the First Chamber. Ten percent of the members of the First Chamber itself agree that the body should be abolished![15] The First Chamber is controversial especially among parties of the left, and for a long time the program of the PvdA called for its abolition. As Andeweg (1992: 154) points out, "The most important reason that the First Chamber continues to exist is undoubtedly the fact that it exists already."

The Ministerial Council

Aside from the parliament itself, the second major actor in any parliamentary system is the government. The government is formally composed of the king or queen and the ministers. The ministers alone, without the monarch, are referred to as the ministerial council, or sometimes as the cabinet.[16]

As in other constitutional monarchies, ministers were originally advisers to the king, who consulted them as he saw fit. By 1823 the Dutch ministers had begun to develop autonomy by meeting collectively and formulating a common standpoint on policy questions. Their policy positions remained advisory until the constitutional revisions of 1848 turned decisions of the ministerial council into the effective policies of the government, while at the same time strengthening the accountability of the council to the parliament. Today, of course, the ministers remain in office only as long as they enjoy the confidence of a majority of deputies, as expressed by support for the government's major legislative initiatives (particularly the annual budget).

The responsibilities of the ministerial council include negotiating treaties and naming judges, provincial governors, and mayors. Most importantly, though, the ministerial council develops draft legislation to submit to the States General. It is in this function that the council is, in effect, the originator of governmental policy. Acting as a collectivity, the major function of the council is to foster coherence in the policies of various departments.

The ministerial council is composed of fourteen members, including the minister-president (or prime minister), twelve ministers who each head one of the bureaucratic departments, and one minister without portfolio whose task is to press for interdepartmental cooperation on assistance to Third World countries.[17] The functional areas of the ministers and the executive departments have varied over time as the activities of government have changed. Thus, a Social Affairs ministry was added in 1917 as the government became involved in the regulation of working conditions and the development of workers insurance programs. Economic Affairs was added in 1933 to coordinate governmental response to the global economic crisis of the 1930s. Postwar ministries attest to the issues of a densely populated and increasingly affluent country: Housing and Space Planning (1945); Culture, Recreation, and Social Work (1952); and Public Health and Environmental Protection (1971).

The task of the minister inherently involves both policy expertise and party-political skills. One of the primary functions of each minister is to bring the political vision of the government to the department, and conversely to represent the interests of the department in discussions in the ministerial council. The importance of departmental leadership is reflected in the weight given to policy expertise when choosing ministers. Each cabinet is a mixture of political leaders and policy experts, with some members having credentials in both areas. In some departments, prior political experience as a member of parliament is virtually a prerequisite; for example, 81 percent of postwar Ministers of Internal Affairs have come from the parliament. In other departments, prior experience in that policy area is crucial, as illustrated by the 82 percent of postwar Ministers of Education and 70 percent of postwar Ministers of Foreign Affairs who brought issue expertise to their post. To become Minister of Finance it is helpful to have both policy and political experience: 73 percent of postwar Ministers of Finance have had technical expertise, but 73 percent of them have also had national parliamentary experience.[18]

Despite these differences between departments, the policy expertise of the typical Dutch minister is a striking trait, at least when compared to members of the typical American or British cabinet. This expertise may be gained by having functioned as a policy expert in one of the party groups in the Second Chamber, by having been in the civil service, or by having worked as an academic with a specialty in that area of policy. The proportion of ministers with political experience rose beginning in the late 1960s, while at the same time the proportion with policy expertise fell. But even today, about two-thirds of ministers have prior expertise in the policy area of their department and only 15 percent of ministers can be described as having procured their posts through purely political appointments. The autonomy of each department and minister, the tradition of cabinet autonomy from parliament (see below), and the development of policy through negotiations between the civil service and leading interest groups (see Chapter 6) all argue for ministers with significant expertise in their policy areas (Bakema and Secker 1988).

Formally speaking, all ministers are equal on the council, and in fact there is a great deal of individual ministerial autonomy compared to other parliamentary systems. Ministerial autonomy is reflected in the fact that legislative proposals are generally prepared within a single department, drawing upon the network of advisory councils attached to it.[19] There have been suggestions in some governments that a "kitchen cabinet" exists, giving more authority to some ministers than to others (Andeweg 1988). Certainly the greatest responsibilities attach to the Ministers of Finance and Economic Affairs, as well as to the ministers in charge of the largest spending departments: Social Affairs (responsible for the programs of the welfare state), Domestic Affairs (employer of all civil servants), and Education. In a period dominated by the desire to reduce governmental spending, these ministries are bound to play a central role. In earlier periods, though, other ministries have been more prominent. In the years of postwar reconstruction, the Minister of Agriculture, Fishing, and Food Supply (Sicco Mansholt) was a powerful figure, as was the Minister of Foreign Affairs (Joseph Luns). The great flood of 1953 elevated the Minister of Traffic and Water Control to a central position in the ministerial council. In the early 1970s, the Minister of Housing, Space Planning, and Environmental Protection was very influential, since those issues were high on the government's agenda.

Although the ministerial council generally takes public positions as a collective body, this does not disguise the fact that it is composed of fourteen individuals whose policy views differ by virtue of their varying party backgrounds as well as their different departmental assignments. As van den Berg (1993) points out, a minister must balance three roles: as representative of a particular political party in the governing coalition; as head of a department in the civil service; and as member of the ministerial council itself. The first role requires that the party program be kept in mind in the formulation of policy; the second role requires strong managerial skills and taking to heart the perspectives of the department; and the third role requires the ability to negotiate and to blend the department's needs with those of other ministries.

Needless to say, these are partially conflicting tasks, and the relative importance of each has varied over time. In 1968, almost 80 percent of comments made in the ministerial council reflected the speaker's departmental affiliation.[20] Ministers from the various spending departments (such as Education, Development Cooperation, Defense, and Social Affairs) each press to defend and if possible increase their department's share of the overall budget. The ministries of Finance and of Economic Affairs, charged with overseeing the state's finances and the health of the economy, attempt to minimize the overall size of the public expenditure and to direct public expenditure in ways that will foster economic growth.[21] Each of the departments has priorities that conflict with those of other departments; the result is what Labor Party leader Ed van Thijn once referred to as "The Republic of Thirteen Disunited Departments," an ironic play on the name of the former United Republic of Eleven Provinces.[22]

Given the party polarization of the 1970s and 1980s (discussed in Chapter 4), it is not surprising that party ideology became more important during those years. Ministers from a given party began in this period to meet together prior to meetings of the full ministerial council. Their purpose was to discuss the pending agenda as a means of keeping the party vision clearly articulated in the ongoing press of business in the council. These meetings were generally confined to ministers of a single party, though Andeweg (1990: 31) notes that ministers of the Protestant and Catholic parties met together during the 1960s and 1970s in a pub near the parliament buildings. These meetings served to coordinate the thinking of the confessional parties. They surely helped produce the common perspectives that eventually led to creation of the CDA by merger of the three largest confessional parties.

The experience of consulting on a regular basis with others of the same party is a constant reminder to ministers that their party affiliations must not be left at the door when they enter the ministerial council meeting room. Inevitably, partisan disagreements arise in the ministerial council, particularly over issues that divide the governing coalition. When the Christian Democrats govern with either the Labor Party on their left or the Liberals on their right, such issues as abortion and euthanasia divide the coalition. These issues are less troublesome when the Labor and Liberal parties govern together, but then the ministerial council must deliberate at length on such issues as wealth and payroll taxes, or plans to reduce public health care benefits.[23]

In their study of ninety-six conflicts in the ministerial council that leaked into the press between 1973 and 1986, Timmermans and Bakema (1990) found that two-thirds of all conflicts between ministers were rooted in interdepartmental disagreements, and the remaining one-third in disagreements between political parties. Examples of interdepartmental disagreements included one in 1983 between the Minister of Economic Affairs and the Minister of Foreign Affairs on whether the Netherlands should sell submarines to Taiwan, and another in 1985 between the minister charged with water affairs and the minister charged with environmental protection on whether construction of the Markerwaard polder should continue. Conflicts between the Minister of Finance and ministers of the various spending departments on the size of departmental budgets for the coming year were most common of all. The importance of departmental perspectives as a source of conflict in the ministerial council is demonstrated by Rudy Andeweg's (1990: 33) finding that only three of seventy-eight former ministers believe that resolving interdepartmental conflicts is made any easier when the other department is headed by a colleague from the same party.

The ministerial council is, in short, called upon to adjudicate conflict both between departments and between parties. When the ministerial council is unable to reach agreement on a policy, one common form of compromise is to find a solution acceptable to the leaders of each party in the cabinet and to the ministers whose departments are directly involved in the decision. Gallhofer, Saris, and Voogt (1994) examined the cabinet decision process in forty-nine foreign policy issues between 1900 and 1955, and found that often no outcome achieved unanimous support.[24] In such cases, there was a tendency for other ministers to defer to the ministers most involved in the decision, namely the minister-president and those whose departments were directly concerned with the issue. Mutual deference, then, produces what Gallhofer and her colleagues call "secondary" unanimity—acceptance of a decision by the entire cabinet if the key ministers are all in agreement with it.

Resolving conflicts by majority vote occurs only as a last resort, because cohesion within the ministerial council may be damaged by a decision process that produces clear-cut winners and losers. Timmermans and Bakema (1990) found that 39 percent of the crises they examined were resolved with a clear-cut winner and loser. A further 42 percent of conflicts were resolved by compromise, and the remainder either were resolved by postponing a decision (14 percent) or failed to be resolved and subsequently developed into a cabinet crisis (5 percent). All but one of the conflicts that mushroomed into cabinet crises were rooted in interparty disagreements rather than in disagreements between departments. Party-based conflicts in the ministerial council are especially dangerous to resolve by majority vote, because a party on the losing side of the vote could withdraw from the coalition and bring down the government. Because of their potential for ending the life of a government, issues that cause interparty disagreements are very likely simply to be postponed until an acceptable compromise can be found (Timmermans and Bakema 1990: 188).

In such cases, the cabinet may decide not on a policy but rather on a process that will be used to resolve the issue at a later time. For the divisive issue of abortion, for example, it was decided in 1977 that either the ministerial council would present a proposal by January 1979 or else the Second Chamber would be free to take the initiative in drafting legislation (van Putten 1982: 177–178). This was essentially a means of motivating ministers from the CDA to accept a compromise or risk the possibility of the Labor and Liberal parties agreeing on far-reaching legalization. Similarly, the 1980s issue of bringing nuclear cruise missiles to the Netherlands was ultimately resolved by dropping the issue in the lap of the Soviet Union. Faced with divisions in the ministerial council, a wavering majority in the Second Chamber, and public hostility to cruise missile deployment, the council decided in 1984 that the missiles could be based in the Netherlands should the Soviet Union add to its own strategic nuclear force during 1984 and 1985.[25]

The focus of the ministerial council on resolving conflicts between governing parties has caused some observers to believe that the council pays insufficient attention to the development of an integrated policy (van Putten 1982: 190–192). The ministerial council is in some respects the apex of the elaborate system of policy negotiation that occurs primarily between administrative departments, interest groups, and advisory commissions of various sorts. That may be why meetings of the Dutch ministerial council take between twenty and thirty hours per month, compared to just six to nine hours per month spent in cabinet meetings by French and British ministers (Andeweg and Irwin 1993: 127).

Rudy Andeweg (1990: 35) has pointed out that the ministerial council is really two institutions: a council of party leaders and a council of departmental leaders. Each institution has "its own rules of the game, with different operating procedures, different pecking orders, and different means of solving disagreements." Clearly the potential for disagreements in the ministerial council—including disagreements that lead to the fall of a government—is very great. The ministerial council can function well only to the extent it is able to act collectively in developing a coordinated policy that articulates the political vision of the party coalition and meshes the perspectives of the various departments.

The Minister-President

Resolving disagreements and finding common ground in the ministerial council are primary responsibilities of the minister-president. The minister-president chairs the ministerial council as well as all councils and commissions connected to it. He[26] sets the agenda for the ministerial council and determines its schedule of meetings. The minister-president is also charged with concluding the council's deliberations on a given issue by formulating a resolution that will achieve consensus agreement among the ministers. Finally, the minister-president acts as Minister of General Affairs. This is not a regular department in the bureaucracy, but instead includes a cabinet of policy advisers and the staff of the ministerial council itself.[27] There are also three agencies within the Ministry of General Affairs: the Government Information Service, the Foreign Information Service, and the Scientific Council for Government Policy. These agencies give the minister-president control over the public information and media relations offices of the government. Indeed, the minister-president's office complex within the *Binnenhof* (parliament buildings) is adjacent both to the Government Information Service and to a state-of-the-art television studio.[28] The minister-president has long been the coordinator of policy within the ministerial council; in recent decades he has also become the articulator of policy to the rest of the world.

The powers of the minister-president have also grown by virtue of his role on the European Council, a body composed of EU heads of state that meets twice per year and sets the basic direction of EU policy. The Dutch ministerial council meets in advance of European Council summits to determine what the minister-president may and may not agree to during the discussions. But the fact that the minister-president is ultimately alone with the other EU heads of state in so-called fireside chats that lead to basic agreements means that "at such moments the premier *is* the Dutch government" (van den Berg 1990: 114).

Although the powers of the minister-president have grown, they still remain modest in comparison with the British prime minister or the German chancellor.[29] As head of a coalition government, for example, the Dutch minister-president cannot shuffle ministers with the impunity of a British prime minister, nor can he command a minister to follow a particular policy, as a German chancellor often can.[30] The minister-president cannot dissolve the Second Chamber and call a snap election at some politically propitious moment. The power of the minister-president stems instead from the ability to find policy formulations acceptable to all parties in the coalition and (ideally) all ministers in the cabinet.

The successful minister-president must above all be skilled in the art of identifying compromise positions. As Ruud Lubbers, who served as minister-president in three governments between 1982 and 1994, described the job, "I generally see the underlying motives of [contending parties] very quickly and from that I put together new proposals. People often argue in order to get their way; I argue primarily to find solutions that others can agree with."[31] Van den Berg (1993: 227) generalizes the same point with his comment that "The power of the premier lies in his ability to increase the stakes of a conflict; to bundle issues together and to arbitrage a compromise package; and in his ability to persuade." Arnold Blits (1989) offered an even pithier version when he described a successful minister-president as "The Great Lubricator."

Success in resolving conflicts requires both imagination and a delicate sense of timing. Sometimes a minister-president must heighten a conflict within the council in order to increase the pressure to resolve it. At other times it is better to keep disagreements quiet and delay decisions while working behind the scenes to develop potential avenues of resolution. Through his control of the weekly agenda, and by his ability to prolong meetings or bring them to a close, the minister-president can choose when to nudge the cabinet toward agreement on some issue.[32] What he cannot do is dictate a solution or replace ministers who refuse to accept his viewpoint. Unlike most heads of government in other parliamentary systems, the Dutch minister-president is still a "first among equals."[33]

Relations Between Government and Parliament

Formally speaking, legislation is a collaborative partnership between the government (composed of the monarch and the ministerial council) and the parliament (the States General, composed of the First and Second Chambers). The process as constitutionally prescribed is sequential, with legislation developed by the ministerial council; submitted via the Crown to the Second Chamber; reviewed, possibly amended, and then approved or rejected by the Second Chamber; approved or rejected by the First Chamber; then finally signed by the monarch and the responsible ministers, and published in the *Staatsblad* as the law of the land.

Such description would seem to give equal weight to each institution involved in the sequence, for any of them may exercise a veto by withholding approval. In fact, the institutions involved are very unequal in their influence. As we have seen, the constraints on a constitutional monarch do not permit refusal to sign a law approved by the States General. And although the First Chamber does sometimes deny approval to bills submitted to it, the fact that the body is indirectly elected means that rejection must be rarely used and carefully explained.

At the heart of the legislative process, then, is the relationship between the ministerial council and the Second Chamber. For a government to remain in office, it must retain the support of a parliamentary majority. This is not a trivial task. Since World War II the average cabinet length has been about two and a half years, so that the possibility of a coalition being overturned prematurely is quite real. Only eight cabinets between 1917 and 1998 have survived the full four-year parliamentary term (the last being the first "purple government" of Wim Kok, 1994–1998). On nearly all other occasions, the life of a government was ended prematurely because of a partisan split in the coalition, either between the ministers or between the parliamentary parties. When the coalition majority is particularly thin, even few members of parliament may bring down a government.

The power of the Second Chamber to judge governmental policy stems from the Dutch constitutional principle of dualism, according to which the ministerial council develops policy proposals and the Second Chamber reviews and approves of that policy. This dualism between cabinet and parliament echoes the separation of powers characteristic of a presidential system of government such as that in the United States, though it does so in the context of a parliamentary system in which the cabinet is ultimately responsible to the legislature. Dualism is reflected in the fact that members of the Dutch government cannot also serve in the Second Chamber: If they are members of the Second Chamber, they must resign their seats upon taking ministerial office. In fact, only about 60 percent of the members of a typical cabinet come directly from the Second Chamber, and a quarter of the ministers have never been in parliament.[34] The Second Chamber, in turn, does not have the right to initiate a vote of confidence whose failure would force resignation of the cabinet. Support for the cabinet is instead shown solely in the passage of the annual budget and in any other legislative proposals that the cabinet chooses to regard as indicative of confidence in the government. In addition, ministers do not routinely attend parliamentary sessions or take part in debates; when they are present they sit at a separate table facing the members of parliament. This arrangement stands in clear contrast to the front-bench/back-bench arrangement of ministers and parliamentary parties in Great Britain and in most other parliamentary democracies.

Each of these elements of the relationship between cabinet and parliament is indicative of dualism, or a relatively strong separation (for a parliamentary system) between the executive and the legislature. The philosophy behind the arrangements of dualism lies in the origins of the cabinet as a body of advisers to the king. Ministers were expected to embrace the interests of the country rather than the interests of particular political parties. Even those ministers whose careers originated in party politics were expected to keep their distance from the parties after joining the cabinet. As Nicolaas Pierson, a nineteenth-century Minister of Finance, put it, "the closer to the Throne, the less a party man."[35]

The distinct roles of ministerial council and Second Chamber are also reflected in the operation of the Second Chamber. Nearly all draft laws examined in the Second Chamber are developed in the bureaucratic departments and reviewed in the ministerial council before being formally submitted to the Second Chamber. Although the Second Chamber has the right to initiate legislative proposals on most topics, it does so only about a half dozen times per year.[36] Fewer than one hundred Second Chamber–initiated bills have been passed since 1813, though the majority of these have been passed in the last thirty years. Most of the parliamentary bills that are approved deal with symbolic issues that enjoy broad consensus, though in 1972 a member-initiated bill to lower the voting age to 18 achieved the two-thirds support required in each chamber for passage as a constitutional amendment.

Such member-initiated successes are, though, the rare exception in the overall legislative agenda, which is largely developed by the ministerial council. Ninety-eight percent of all legislative proposals in the Netherlands are initiated by the government, compared to an average of 58 percent in other European parliamentary democracies (Peters 1991b: 80). Moreover, approval of the government's draft bills by the Second Chamber is almost certain. About 95 percent of the 250 to 300 bills submitted annually by ministers are ultimately passed, though many of them only after being amended.[37] M.P.C.M. van Schendelen (1993: 195) estimates that 30 to 40 percent of amendments are adopted, though this figure includes many minor changes in wording that are readily accepted by the minister responsible for the bill. Andeweg (1991a: 247) points out that Second Chamber amendments in 1985 altered only 0.06 percent of the budget proposed for the coming year. The last time an entire section of the budget was denied by the Second Chamber was in 1919, when the budgetary request for the navy was turned down as a means of forcing the Minister of the Navy out of office. The budget was fully restored following his resignation (Bovend'Eert and Kummeling 1991: 267). It is clear, then, that the Second Chamber does not have a great deal of influence on legislation once it has been developed in draft form and submitted for consideration.[38]

This dominance of the ministerial council comports with the idea of dualism, in which the job of the ministerial council is to propose legislation and the job of the Second Chamber is to review and enact it. Van Schendelen (1993: 190) finds that oversight of government and influencing government policy proposals are the two most important tasks in the eyes of members of the Second Chamber; originating legislation is far down the list. For some Dutch constitutional scholars, extensive involvement of the legislature in the formulation of policy proposals (as occurs in the United States) is undesirable, because a parliament too deeply involved in policy formulation will not be able to carry out its primary function of being a watchdog.

Staff Resources

There are practical as well as philosophical barriers to a more active parliamentary role in drafting laws. The power of any legislature is closely tied to the level of staff resources at the command of its members. In that respect, the U.S. Congress has long had a substantial advantage over all European parliaments, with extensive staffs directed by each member of Congress in addition to the staffs of congressional committees and the research staffs of the Library of Congress, the Congressional Budget Office, and the General Accounting Office. The staff expertise available to the Second Chamber is far more modest, though it has been greatly strengthened in recent years. In 1968, one-third of the members of the Second Chamber had no staff or secretarial support whatsoever, and another quarter had only self-financed or part-time volunteer assistance, often from their wives (Daalder 1975: 73). Today, each party group has its own staff, and each member of the Second Chamber has a staff assistant. Even with these improvements, though, Guy Peters finds that Dutch members of parliament are lacking in personal and research staff compared to other European countries. Parliamentary committees are, by contrast, reasonably well staffed (Peters 1991b: 81). The bias toward committee staff and away from personal and research support again underscores the Second Chamber role in reviewing government policy, as opposed to developing its own policies.[39] By contrast, the ministerial council is served by a number of special councils of policy experts, including the Council for Economic Affairs, the Council for Space Planning, and the Council for European Affairs.

Prerogatives of the Second Chamber

When the constitutional engineers of 1848 created the dualistic system and as-signed the Second Chamber the task of reviewing and approving government policy, they also gave the Second Chamber a number of tools for carrying out its tasks. One of those tools is the right of interpellation: the ability to summon a minister to appear and answer questions concerning policy. A request for inter-pellation must receive majority approval in the Second Chamber, since it requires an interruption of scheduled chamber business. The member or members re-questing the interpellation place their questions before the relevant minister, who is obliged to answer them. The interpellant then has a chance to speak in reply, af-ter which the subject is opened for general debate. Although interpellations are generally submitted by members of the opposition parties as a means of calling attention to perceived shortcomings of government policy, a chamber majority can be found for most interpellation requests. Like the right of unlimited debate in the U.S. Senate, most members of the Second Chamber will rally around the institution's right to interpellate ministers even when the purpose of a particular interpellation is not to their liking. In a recent year-long parliamentary session, there were nine interpellation requests, all of which received majority support in the Second Chamber.[40]

Short of requesting an interpellation, members of the Second Chamber can simply question ministers, orally or in writing, during a regularly scheduled "question hour." The question hour, a device borrowed from the British House of Commons, limits both questions and ministerial replies to a few minutes, a prac-tice that can make for a lively debate. Despite these limits, ministers are required to answer fully; if they cannot do so on the spot they must reply in writing within a reasonable length of time.[41] The number of questions posed has risen from fewer than a hundred per year in the early part of the century, to over two thou-sand at the height of the period of party polarization in 1972–1973. More re-cently, the number of questions put to ministers has fallen to under one thousand per year, but the questions are still an important means of bringing details of gov-ernment policy to light. The minister is expected to answer all questions unless to do so would "harm the interests of state."[42]

Questions and interpellations are two means by which the Second Chamber may obtain the information about government policy to which it is constitution-ally entitled. The third and strongest tool for gathering information is the parlia-mentary investigation.[43] The parliamentary investigation was rarely used until re-cently, as there was only one held between 1886 and 1980. In the last twenty years, however, investigations have become an important tool for examining govern-mental policy, particularly when there is an apparent failure of government pol-icy. The first recent instance was in 1982, when the Rijn-Schelde-Verolme (RSV) shipbuilding concern went bankrupt despite massive government subsidies in the immediately preceding years. The parliamentary investigation focused on the fact that the Second Chamber was unaware of the extent of public subsidies, and the investigative report took Finance Minister Onno Ruding to task for concealing information in testimony to the Second Chamber. But the investigation also criticized the Second Chamber itself for insufficient attention to the details of public expenditure. The RSV investigation was generally hailed as an evenhanded and useful exercise, one that led to constructive reform of the budget process. Further investigations have followed, covering subsidies in the housing construction industry (1986) and the so-called passport affair in 1988, in which the Dutch government spent a considerable sum of money to design and issue a "counterfeit-proof" passport, only to find that the new passport was as easily duplicated as the old. Parliamentary inquiries in the 1990s have included one in 1993 on social welfare, which has been influential in guiding reform of the system (see Chapter 7); one in 1995 on Dutch involvement in the UN mission in the Bosnian safe haven of Srebrenica (see Chapter 8); and one in 1999 on the crash of an airplane into the Bijlmer neighborhood of Amsterdam.

The common theme of these investigations is inquiry into policy failures, making the parliamentary inquiry a means of Second Chamber oversight of the government and civil service. Because a parliamentary inquiry can be established only with majority support of the members of the Second Chamber, it is not possible for the opposition to use this device as a means of attacking the government, at least not without the consent of some parliamentary members of the majority coalition. This, too, increases the prestige of the parliamentary inquiry as a vehicle of Second Chamber influence.

Questions, interpellations, and investigations enable the Second Chamber to develop the base of information necessary to serve as an independent check on government policy. Of course, it is also important that the Second Chamber be able to act on the information it collects. Because passage of member-initiated proposals is rare, the Second Chamber often instead passes a parliamentary motion expressing its viewpoint on some policy. A motion is not a law and it does not bind the government to any course of action. However, passage of a motion critical of some policy sends a very public message of disagreement with that policy. The Dutch constitution does not permit the motion of no-confidence found in other parliamentary democracies, but passage of a motion enables the Second Chamber to express its policy preference without forcing a change of government.

As with the frequency of questions and interpellations, the number of motions submitted in the Second Chamber has risen and fallen with the tides of party polarization. There were just nine motions submitted in the 1963–1964 parliamentary year, of which one was passed. Late in the period of party polarization, in 1983–1984, over 1,200 motions were submitted and 485 were passed (Gladdish 1991: 115). By the end of the 1980s the number of motions submitted had fallen to about 400 in a year's sitting.[44]

The End of Dualism?

Although the Dutch parliamentary system is founded on the principle of dualism, the extent of dualism in practice has waxed and waned. Rudy Andeweg (1991a: 243–245) observes that the theory of dualism evolved at a time when parliament was composed of individual representatives elected from districts, who had relatively little party organization and who formed no cohesive majorities in support of the government. At that time, ministers were named by the king and had few ties to the parliamentary leadership. Between 1848 and 1967, only 35 percent of ministers were members of the States General at the time of their appointment (Andeweg and Irwin 1993: 128). The relationship between ministerial council and Second Chamber was distant, in accord with the dualist perspective.

Today, governments rely on the support of cohesive parliamentary majorities. This creates a far closer relationship between ministers and parliamentary party groups. Three-quarters of ministers—including virtually all ministers in the most powerful departments—have had parliamentary experience prior to joining the ministerial council. In all nine of the cabinets formed between 1971 and 1990, more than 60 percent of their members were drawn directly from the Second Chamber; this was the case of only seven of the forty-seven cabinets formed between 1848 and 1970 (Bakema and Secker 1990: 76). Since the early 1970s it has also become normal for parliamentary party group leaders to join the ministerial council. Prior to that time, party leaders frequently preferred to remain in parliament, in the belief that this was the best way to influence policy across a wide range of domains. Some parliamentary party leaders still remain in parliament rather than becoming ministers; in the Kok government of 1994–1998, the leader of the Liberal Party and the leader of D66 both kept their parliamentary seats rather than enter the government. What was once the general rule, though, has now become the exception.

It might not matter that the ministerial council tends to be drawn from the parliamentary leadership, if it were not also the case that ministers and party groups of the majority coalition maintain close contact after the government is formed. Since the 1970s, ministers have consulted with their parliamentary party groups prior to meetings of the ministerial council (Andeweg 1988: 135). The minister-president also has weekly meetings with the parliamentary leaders of all governing parties. These discussions have forged a closer link than has ever before existed between the ministerial council and the parliamentary party groups in the majority coalition. They are an acknowledgment that the Second Chamber is more than an external check on governmental policy, instead giving the parliamentary majority a role in the development of that policy.

Increased coordination of ministerial council and parliamentary parties was made necessary by the heightened degree of party polarization in the Second Chamber, which made it more difficult to hold together parliamentary coalitions in support of the government. The effect of greater Second Chamber activism (expressed in an increased number of questions, interpellations, motions, and amendments) was to force the ministerial council to take fuller account of parliamentary sentiment in the formulation of draft laws. The ironic result is that the Second Chamber may be today more influential than it has ever been, but that influence is not seen in the legislative process as it unfolds in the chamber itself. Influence occurs rather by close consultation between the government and the majority parties of the Second Chamber in the development of policy. As H. M. Franssen (1982: 3) put it, "The constitution still recognized two independent bodies, the Crown and the States General, but . . . the division is no longer watertight; in practice the dividing line is between the government parties and the opposition parties."[45]

There is nothing inevitable about these trends, and the relationship between the ministerial council and the Second Chamber is to some extent reconstituted with each new government. The purple government of 1994–1998 (renewed for a second term after the elections of 1998) reduced the amount of parliamentary consultation that had become the norm in previous parliaments, and was unafraid to propose policies for which there was no clear parliamentary majority. The Liberal Party group in the Second Chamber took an especially independent stance toward the purple government, and several major policy proposals (including one to alter the electoral system and another to create new regional governments) were defeated with the help of defections from the coalition parties. Two of the three coalition party leaders remained out of the cabinet, and an unusually large number of ministers were drawn from outside the Second Chamber—two further indications of a partial restoration of the dualist tradition.

These developments are unlikely to herald a return to dualism in its full nineteenth-century sense, but the norm of an independent Second Chamber that reviews and judges governmental policy proposals remains a powerful philosophical underpinning of the Dutch parliamentary system. Dualism continues particularly in the symbolic interaction between ministers and parliament. For example, ministers do not usually attend parliamentary sessions unless they are defending a policy proposal emanating from their own department. The minister-president is also rarely present.[46] When ministers are present in the Second Chamber, usually to defend a legislative proposal from their department, they sit at a table at the far end of the room, clearly separated from the party groups (Gladdish 1991: 112). This is different from the front-bench location of the British government. Also, when the Minister of Finance stands before the Second Chamber on the third Tuesday of every September and delivers a briefcase containing the proposed budget, the action symbolizes the role of the government in proposing policy and of the Second Chamber in reviewing it. But this action is only symbolic. The main elements of the draft budget are already known in the Second Chamber because of preliminary discussions begun in the middle of August, and the briefcase does not even contain the budget![47]

Forming a Government

Given the dualist tradition of Dutch governance, the high point of Second Chamber influence on the government comes during negotiations leading to the cabinet formation. These negotiations produce an agreement between the coalition parties that becomes the touchstone of government policy for the life of the cabinet. Although the negotiations leading to formation of a cabinet are one of the most important aspects of politics in the Netherlands, they are also among the least understood because of the secrecy that surrounds the process.[48] But although specific negotiations are confidential, the general process by which governments are formed are well known.[49]

Responsibility for forming a government belongs formally to the monarch, who appoints and dismisses ministers. But, as P. F. Maas (1986: 217) points out, "it [is] highly undesirable for the monarch to be actively involved in Cabinet formations . . . because it would drag monarchs into party struggles and intrigues, which would be incompatible with their neutral position." Consequently, the process of government formation has been devolved to two intermediary figures. The *informateur* is appointed by the monarch to gather information about possible governing coalitions in parliament. The *formateur* is then appointed to act on this information by putting together the government and, usually, by becoming its minister-president. In this way, the potentially damaging involvement of the monarch in political controversy is reduced, though it can never be eliminated. Queen Beatrix (who has a degree in political science) surely went too far when she said, "I am no more than a letter-box; the advice comes in and the formation mandates come out."[50]

On the advice of the presidents of the First and Second Chambers, of party leaders, and of personal advisers, the monarch first appoints the *informateur,* who makes the rounds of party leaders to determine which parties might participate in the upcoming government coalition. In theory, the monarch may exercise significant political influence through the choice of an *informateur* who will be inclined to certain coalition possibilities rather than others. In practice, though, party leaders are sufficiently vocal about their coalition preferences both before and immediately after the election that the most likely composition of the government is fairly obvious.[51] After all, it is ultimately up to the party groups in the Second Chamber to determine which coalition possibilities they are willing to support and which they will not; the monarch cannot frustrate their will by choosing an *informateur* with a different opinion. The people who have been appointed *informateur* are a diverse group, including professors and retired politicians as well as prominent members of parliament. The one general rule is to avoid choosing a parliamentary party leader who could potentially become minister-president, though even this rule has its exceptions.

The task of the *informateur* is to gather information about likely coalition prospects and report back to the monarch. This task has become more complex since the early 1970s, as the *informateur* is now also charged with drafting elements of a possible coalition program. The consultation process has also become more open and inclusive in recent decades. Leaders of the unions, business associations, and other interest groups are consulted along with leaders of the parliamentary parties. As soon as the *informateur* develops a sense of the desired composition of a majority cabinet and the main areas of policy agreement within that coalition, he submits his report to the monarch. Perhaps the most important part of this report is the nomination of a *formateur*, who will complete the government formation and, most likely, become its minister-president.

Based on the advice of the *informateur*, the monarch then names the *formateur*, whose task is to put together a government along the party lines indicated by the *informateur*. Among the tasks of the *formateur* are to develop further the governing program and to achieve agreement on the specific division of ministry seats between governing parties, including agreement as to the particular individuals who will occupy those seats.

The division of ministerial portfolios between the governing parties is often a contentious point. Ministries must be fairly divided between coalition partners, taking account of those that are more and less powerful. Sometimes a party will insist on controlling a specific ministry, or insist that a rival party not control a particular ministry. The major economic portfolios of Finance, Economic Affairs, and Social Affairs are usually divided between coalition partners, as are the major international departments of Defense and Foreign Affairs. To ease the process, state secretaries (or junior ministers) are appointed to give parties some control over departments where they do not have a minister. Although the number of ministers is relatively invariant between fourteen and sixteen, the number of state secretaries has varied from eight to sixteen in recent decades, depending partly on the complexity of the coalition and the amount of interparty balancing needed (Gladdish 1983: 172–173).

The phase of developing a governing program *(regeerakkoord)* may last a long time or it may be brief. In recent years the program has become more and more explicit in spelling out the major policies that will be adopted. Andeweg and Irwin (1993: 112) note that the 54-page governing program developed in 1989 contained "detailed proposals for legislation, ranging from environmental protection to commercial television, and set strict limits on the size of the budget deficit and the level of taxation." On issues that require a longer period to negotiate between the coalition parties, the program will not spell out the policy to be adopted but will instead indicate procedures for further study and negotiation. This enables the coalition to defer consideration of issues on which it is unable to reach advance agreement.

Though governing programs may vary in their particulars, the element common to all of them is that they are vehicles for increased parliamentary influence over the policies of the coalition government. At the same time, participation in the negotiation of a governing program commits the majority coalition in parliament to support of that program. As Bovend'Eert put it, "The governing program has on the one hand resulted in increased parliamentary involvement with the formation of government policy, but on the other hand it has more or less bound the majority to the points of the government's policy, which reduces the Chamber's freedom of movement during the life of the cabinet."[52]

The negotiation process leading to formation of a government sounds rather involved, and indeed it must be in order to take account of a Second Chamber containing ten or more political parties, even the largest of which will have fewer than one-third of the parliamentary seats. As a result of this complexity, the sequence of *informateur* to *formateur* to completed coalition is not always smooth. Formation of the first purple government in 1994 required six *informateurs* and over three and a half months to complete.

Polarization between the parties in the 1970s made coalition formation even more difficult than it had been previously or has been since. Between 1946 and 1973 the average coalition formation period was forty-seven days. Formation after the 1973 elections took a bit longer than five months, and it took almost nine months to form a government in 1977. In the fifty years between 1946 and 1996 the Netherlands was governed by an interim cabinet for 1,788 days, or nearly five years. Roughly half of the time spent under an interim government occurred during the fifteen-year period of party polarization, from 1971 to 1986.[53] In the 1980s and 1990s, coalition governments were typically put together in two months or less. Even today, though, the negotiations are made lengthier by the fact that parliamentary parties and leading interest groups view the formation period as their best opportunity to influence governmental policy in the coming four years. Bernard Grofman and Peter van Roozendaal (1994) found that the longer it took to put a government together in the first place, the more likely it was that the coalition would come to a premature end. The more difficult the birth, the less easy the life.

The coalitions that result from this formation process have proven resistant to successful prediction using the theories that work elsewhere in Europe. Abram de Swaan's (1982) study of Dutch governing coalitions between 1946 and 1981 found that only twelve of twenty-two were minimum-winning (i.e., containing no unnecessary members) and ideologically connected (i.e., containing parties adjacent to each other on the left-right spectrum).[54] One reason for the lack of predictive success appears to be the coexistence of economic, social, and religious issues in the Netherlands. This places the Christian Democrats, for example, in the middle of the party spectrum on some issues and at the polar end of the spectrum on others. Even more important is the propensity to form coalition governments containing more parties than the minimum necessary to secure majority support in the Second Chamber. Almost two-thirds of the twenty-two governments formed between 1945 and 1999 had at least one "extra" party in them. As long as the Christian Democrats dominated the center of the party spectrum, it was strategically advantageous for them to include parties to their left and right in governing coalitions and then play them off against each other as policies were negotiated (de Swaan 1982; van Roozendaal 1993). The tradition of consensus democracy in the Netherlands was also supportive of oversized coalitions.[55]

With ten parties represented in the Second Chamber and a great deal of voter movement between different parties from one election to the next, it is not always clear what the mandate of the election might be. In 1994, for example, Hans van Mierlo of D66 argued that the two parties winning the most new votes in the election (D66 and the Liberals) should govern together with the largest of the losing parties (the Labor Party). Wim Kok of the Labor Party, by contrast, pointed out that those who change their votes should not be counted more heavily than those who continue to support the same party. Kok reasoned that the Labor Party and the CDA remained the two largest parties in the Second Chamber and should continue their coalition, together with D66.[56]

Such arguments could continue indefinitely; the point is that a number of coalitions are possible after the election, and there is no prima facie reason to claim that some coalitions reflect the election result better than others. Each parliamentary party leader uses the coalition formation period to press for the coalition and governing program most advantageous to their party. It is little wonder that van den Berg (1993: 218) refers to the formation period as "the supreme moment of parliamentary influence on government policy."

The Bureaucracy

As in all modern democracies, government would not be possible in the Netherlands without a large professional body of career civil servants who give continuity to policy formulation and implementation. The largest group of civil servants are the "street-level bureaucrats," who determine whether an application for welfare assistance is correctly filled out or whether a complaint of criminal wrongdoing merits further investigation. Despite the importance of that group, we will here focus on a much smaller group of senior civil servants, the *ambtenaren,* who are involved in the development of public policy.

The civil service is organized into departments, each led by a cabinet minister and, in the case of the larger departments, one or two state secretaries (junior ministers). The ministers and state secretaries are selected as part of the cabinet formation process, and the top civil servant in each department (the secretary general) reports to them. The departments themselves are organized in a hierarchical branching structure, including several directorates that are in turn divided into divisions *(afdelingen),* offices *(bureaus),* and sections *(secties).*

Senior civil servants are nearly always careerists who have worked their way up the organizational ladder of their departments. More than two-thirds of them enter the national civil service directly from school—there is relatively little recruitment from industry, political and social organizations, or academia. There is also little recruitment from the ranks of the municipal or provincial civil service (van der Meer and Roborgh 1993: 245–247). Instead, promotion takes place almost exclusively within the department. By the time civil servants reach the highest levels of a department, then, it is typical for them to have spent their entire careers immersed in the department's work and perspectives. This is an effective strategy for maintaining an autonomous organizational culture within each department. Eldersveld, Kooiman, and van der Tak (1981: 85–86), for example, find that the social affairs and welfare ministries have more politicized, activist orientations than the technical ministries of Agriculture, Justice, Economic Affairs, and Interior.

The departmental civil service has expanded by a factor of more than ten during the course of the twentieth century, from 13,500 in 1900 to a peak of just below 155,000 in the mid-1980s (van der Meer and Roborgh 1993: 69). Part of this growth in the size of government is due to increases in the Dutch population. But the number of government employees has also more than tripled with respect to the total labor force, from 27 per 1,000 workers in 1899 to 99 per 1,000 workers in 1979 (van der Meer and Roborgh 1993: 103). There have been two waves of particularly rapid growth in the twentieth century. One occurred between 1900 and 1920, and was associated with expansion of the state's mining operations and the postal and telecommunications service. The second wave of growth came between the early 1960s and the mid-1980s, and was the result of rapid development of the welfare state (see Chapter 7).

In a modern state, the bureaucracy inevitably wields a great deal of influence. Consider the plight of a Dutch minister whose job it is to develop legislation in a particular policy area for submission to the Second Chamber, as well as to oversee implementation of the laws by the department over which he or she presides. Although Dutch ministers are more likely than their British or American counterparts to have prior expertise in the department's policy area, the technical demands of drafting legislation and the sheer volume of regulations make it impossible for the minister to keep abreast of all developments within the department. After all, the parliamentary system was developed in the Netherlands in the middle of the nineteenth century, at a time when the annual governmental budget was 70 million guilders. By the turn of the century, the budget had doubled to 150 million guilders, indicating a level of governmental activity that was still within the bounds of direct ministerial oversight. By the 1990s, though, the governmental budget had exceeded 200 *billion* guilders—a thousandfold increase in nominal terms and a more than fourfold increase in relation to the entire economy. The tasks undertaken by the government today have been expanded to include such activities as preparing economic projections, reducing economic inequality, controlling the use of land through urban policy and agricultural regulation, protecting the environment, and providing education, health, and sociocultural services. There are few aspects of life that are not subject to governmental regulation, and the scope of the civil service has expanded accordingly.

Given that ministers and state secretaries cannot know all that happens within the department, they must rely upon senior civil servants to anticipate decisions that are important or that may become politically sensitive, and to bring these is-sues to the minister for a final decision. Research into the beliefs of senior civil servants shows that most of them accept without question this duty to their polit-ical bosses (Aberbach et al. 1981; Eldersveld et al. 1981). This does not mean, though, that senior civil servants abdicate completely their own judgment on such matters. Moreover, a senior civil servant who disagrees with the minister on the desirability of some new policy can have a great deal of influence on that pol-icy. As one senior civil servant put it to Eldersveld et al. (1981: 73), it is "always [possible] to come up with technical problems and difficulties which make it desirable that a certain decision be postponed for half a year."

It is little wonder that studies of the Dutch bureaucracy have found it to be very influential. Jan van Putten (1980), together with his colleagues, examined eight laws and regulations across a variety of policy areas to determine which institu-tions and organizations wield the most influence. Among their findings were that civil servants are the most important force in development of legislation. This is not unexpected, given the tradition of dualism that defines the parliament as a check on policy rather than as initiator of policy. The influence of the dualist sys-tem is also clear in the finding by Aberbach et al. (1981: 97) that Dutch civil ser-vants are especially likely to endorse for themselves the roles of policymaker (90 percent versus 70 percent on average elsewhere in Europe) and legalist (52 per-cent versus 33 percent elsewhere in Europe).

The dualist system is also reflected in the fact that a single civil servant is typi-cally entrusted with drafting any given regulation. In most cases, these regulations will never be reviewed by the ministerial council or the Second Chamber.[57] As we shall see in the next chapter, such regulations go through an extensive process of review and negotiation before being promulgated. Even so, responsibility for de-termining the scope and general thrust of a regulation—a source of considerable power—most often lies with the senior civil service.

The power to draft regulations is further increased by the growing importance of regulations in the lawgiving system. This is due to increasing acceptance by the Second Chamber of "framework laws" *(kaderwetten)*, which set general standards and procedures of policymaking in an area and then designate the departments and agencies that will provide regulatory detail. The development of framework laws has been a response to the sheer growth of governmental activism and law-making over the last fifty years, which makes it impossible for the Second Chamber to review and formally endorse all governmental decisions. The growth of framework laws, which constituted over 40 percent of all laws by the 1970s,[58] has been a periodic source of alarm among observers of Dutch politics, for frame-work laws indicate that the Second Chamber no longer oversees legislation to the extent that is constitutionally required of it. Attempts to reduce the number of framework laws have met with some success, and the Second Chamber will some-times write into a framework law the requirement that major regulations drafted in accordance with the law must receive subsequent parliamentary confirmation.

Even with these safeguards, though, the framework law is yet another indication that the power of the senior civil service is greatly expanded in an era of activist government.

Increasing volumes of technical regulation would overwhelm even the senior civil service if it were not able to grow to meet this demand. Data collected by van der Meer and Roborgh (1993: 186) show that the rate of growth in the senior civil service has been twice that of the overall rate of growth in the governmental bureaucracy. This trend represents a continuing professionalization of the bureaucracy, indicative of its ever-increasing involvement in policymaking. In contrast, the number of ministers has remained relatively constant for 150 years. The Second Chamber was increased from 100 members to 150 members in 1956, but this increase has done little to improve parliament's ability to cope with the mushrooming of legislative and regulatory activity.

These trends of increasing legislative complexity and growth of the senior civil service are not, of course, unique to the Netherlands. In the Netherlands as elsewhere, there has been concern about the growing political power of what Mattei Dogan (1975) once called "the Mandarins of Europe." The real question is whether increasing reliance on the civil service for policy development as well as implementation should be a matter of concern.

One way in which scholars have approached this question is to examine the extent to which senior civil servants are closely representative of the Dutch public as a whole. In some respects, such as in their level of education, the senior civil service is quite distinctive from the general population. In the mid-1970s, 93 percent of senior civil servants had attended university compared to just 3 percent of the general population.[59] That civil servants are highly educated is neither surprising nor troubling. More significant may be the social origins of the senior civil service, 15 percent of whose members come from working-class families. Though this figure is lower than the proportion of working-class families in the general population (46 percent), it still represents a significant degree of heterogeneity.[60]

Given the pillarized history of Dutch society, religious representativeness is a matter of particular interest. There are modest discrepancies between the religious composition of the senior civil service and that of the population. As the pillars began to decay, Catholics were underrepresented among senior civil servants by about one-half (40 percent of the population but only 21 percent of the senior civil service), while those professing no religious beliefs were overrepresented by one-third (23 percent of the population but 36 percent of the senior civil service).[61] Differences between the civil service and the public in party preferences are also relatively modest, with the Liberals somewhat overrepresented and the Christian Democrats and Labor Party somewhat underrepresented (Eldersveld et al. 1981: 46). More significant may be the uneven distribution of partisanship between the various civil service departments. Labor Party adherents are primarily found in three departments: Social Affairs; Welfare, Health, and Culture; and Employment, Housing, and Land Planning. The Labor Party is significantly underrepresented among senior civil servants in the Ministry of Defense (van der Meer and Roborgh 1993: 400).

The two groups most underrepresented in the senior civil service are women and ethnic minorities. The proportion of women in the senior civil service has grown steadily and in 1990 stood at 27 percent (van der Meer and Roborgh 1993: 286), as compared to the 36 percent share that women then had of the entire Dutch labor force. However, only 57 percent of women civil servants were employed full-time, compared to 96 percent of male civil servants (van der Meer and Roborgh 1993: 293). Despite this underrepresentation, Joyce Outshoorn (1994) finds that feminists have brought new perspectives to the civil service, and have helped change policies toward women.

Ethnic minorities are also underrepresented, constituting 2 percent of the national civil service but 4 percent of the population. The Dutch government undertook an aggressive program between 1987 and 1990 to increase the number of minority civil servants by 50 percent. The program fell short of its goals, though it did lead to a substantial increase of minority representation in many departments. The new employees are, however, generally at the lowest end of the pay scale, and their prospects for advancement are often limited by their educational attainments. If gender parity will require a change of social values with respect to full-time participation in the labor force by mothers, ethnic parity must await the more complete integration of minorities into the educational system.

The representativeness of the senior civil service is important not only because of a concern for social justice, but also because a civil service reflective of the population will presumably share more fully the beliefs and concerns of that population. The representativeness of the senior civil service may be less of a concern if civil servants embrace the norm of being responsive to politicians in the Second Chamber, and more generally to political parties, interest groups, and other organizations that express public policy demands.

There is a relatively smooth relationship between politicians and civil servants in the Netherlands, facilitating cooperation between these two groups. This is partly because of the tradition of making civil service appointments in proportion to the relative strengths of the pillars. Although the pillars have waned in influence, civil service appointments are still today made partly with an eye to religious and partisan proportionality. Equally significant is the large number of ministers and members of the Second Chamber who are former civil servants themselves. The norms of proportional appointments and the movement from civil service to political service have given politicians and civil servants assurance that their views and concerns will be taken into account each by the other.

Smooth interaction between the civil service and politicians is also facilitated by the fact that there is a great deal of contact between senior civil servants and various political groups such as ministers, members of the Second Chamber, political party officials, interest groups, and action groups. These contacts occur through the many standard consultations that are legally mandated parts of the policy process. The negotiations between civil servants, politicians, and interest groups that occur in the development of policy will be explored in greater detail in Chapter 6. Here it is worth noting simply that such interactions have a major effect on the political values of senior civil servants. Samuel Eldersveld (1980: 179) finds that 80 percent of civil servants who interact regularly with members of the Second Chamber believe that political factors should take precedence over the technical, compared to only 66 percent of civil servants whose contacts with politicians are more sporadic. As Eldersveld (1980: 180) summarizes, "contact with MPs creates a more politicized, conflict-acceptant view of the political process."

Extensive contacts between senior civil servants and politicians, and the consequent acceptance within the departments of the political dimension of policy-making, suggest that the classic Weberian distinction between politicians as formulators of policy and civil servants as implementers of policy is not a realistic model for the contemporary Dutch state. Instead, the best characterization of the civil servant–politician relationship in the Netherlands is what Joel Aberbach and his colleagues (1981: 16–19) call the "pure hybrid model," which involves a blurring of the roles of senior civil servant and national politician. The senior civil servant must have a great deal of political acumen to be able to draft regulations that will survive parliamentary and interest-group scrutiny. The minister, and for that matter the parliamentary politician as well, must be possessed of a significant degree of policy expertise to deal with the technical challenges of mounting volumes of legislation. Politicians, senior civil servants, and interest-group representatives are all involved in extensive negotiations over the shape of legislation. These negotiations begin with the concept for a new law and continue through to its final passage in the Second Chamber. The distinctive roles of the political and the technical are substantially blurred in such a process.

The Judicial System

The process of drafting, enacting, and implementing laws is dominated by the senior civil service, the ministerial council, and the Second Chamber. The judiciary in the Netherlands is not directly involved in the legislative process, for unlike the United States, Germany, and some other democracies, the Netherlands does not grant to its courts the power of judicial review. No court, in other words, has the power to set aside legislation passed in the States General because that legislation does not conform to the constitution. The constitutional instruction that courts "are not to engage in judgment of the constitutionality of laws or treaties" (*Grondwet*, article 120) is in keeping with the tradition of the French Revolution, according to which ultimate constitutional and lawgiving power rests with the elected representatives of the people. In this sense, the Dutch constitution means whatever the States General decide it means.[62] There is an extensive consultation process before submission of a draft law to the Second Chamber, in which the

Council of State (*Raad van State,* established in 1531) offers advice on the constitutionality, technical legal quality, and likely effectiveness of the proposed law. This advice is influential in the drafting of legislation, but it is nonetheless advisory.

Although the judiciary is not a lawmaker, it is an important institution for determining how the law should be applied to particular disputes. For disputes between individuals, the civil and criminal courts come into play. There are four layers of these courts, ranging from the sixty-two local *(kanton)* courts to the supreme court of the Netherlands, known as the High Court *(Hoge Raad).* Criminal proceedings in the Netherlands do not involve juries, but are instead initiated by the prosecutor's office and decided by the judge assigned to the case. This makes the selection of judges a particularly important matter. About half of all judges enter the profession in the manner of French and German judges, that is, by taking training as a magistrate upon completing a law degree. The other half are chosen in the manner of American and British judges, by appointment after having practiced as a lawyer. During the period of the pillars, much attention was paid to the religious composition of the judiciary, which remained about one-third Protestant, one-third Catholic, and one-third secular (de Groot–van Leeuwen 1992). The proportion of women serving as judges has gradually grown, and reached one-fifth by the early 1990s.

Because the government acts as prosecutor, the independence of the judiciary from political influence is a crucial matter. This is guaranteed by the life appointment of judges (whose retirement age is fixed), and by allowing only the High Court to bring proceedings against judges for removal from office. The High Court itself consists of three justices appointed for life. Although new appointments are made by the ministerial council on the advice of the Second Chamber, the practice has been to accept nominations for new members made by the High Court itself. This practice offers a further guarantee of judicial independence.

Extension of the reach of Dutch government to virtually all areas of life has made disputes between citizens and government (rather than between citizens) increasingly common. Laws are not subject to judicial challenge, but regulations promulgated by the civil service may be taken to court. As noted above, the growth of regulatory law has been a source of concern about the loss of parliamentary authority. Ironically, that very grant of authority to the bureaucracy also empowers the population, because regulations promulgated in a department of the civil service can be challenged in court in a way that legislation passed by the Second Chamber cannot.

Disputes over regulations are handled differently in different countries. In France there are independent administrative courts, specialized in particular areas (tax appeals, welfare claims, zoning and land use planning), to which one may appeal any given regulation or ruling. In Germany these functions are unified in a single system of administrative courts. There are no administrative courts in the United States or the United Kingdom; instead, one may appeal to higher levels within the same department or take the case to the regular (civil) courts. The

Netherlands has long combined all three systems. There are administrative courts, the possibility of appeal within a department, and under certain circumstances the opportunity to take a case to the civil courts. These channels give citizens an opportunity to contest regulations they believe are outside the scope of the law or unfairly applied to their situations. The major drawback has been that the system is so complex—with many channels of appeal but usually only one channel appropriate to a particular appeal—that the task of initiating a challenge can be daunting. Recent reforms, though, have merged the administrative courts into the regular court system, making it easier for the citizen to know where to initiate a case (Helder 1992). In the early 1990s, administrative courts heard over 50,000 cases per year (Cohen et al. 1993: 302).

The criteria used by administrative courts in their judgments about the validity of a regulation are whether the department has sufficiently taken all affected interests into account in formulating a particular regulation, and whether the regulation is within the scope and purposes of the legislative act from which it stems. An example of a regulation overturned for being outside original legislative purposes occurred in 1980, when the administrative court in The Hague set aside a decision to create a salary cap for medical specialists working in the publicly financed health care system. The court noted that the intent of the framework law permitting salary caps was to foster a better distribution of income, but that the purpose of the regulation was to fight inflation (Cohen et al. 1993: 306).

A third, much broader criterion for administrative review was added in 1950: whether the regulation is in conflict with "the principles of proper government." This third test was inspired by the experience of the German occupation during World War II, when the administrative courts upheld many regulations promulgated in accordance with laws passed by the puppet government of the Nazis. As long as those regulations were in conformity with the law, the administrative courts had no basis for overturning them.

The addition of the "principles of proper government" test opened the floodgates for other criteria to be developed in the scrutiny of regulation. Added criteria have included the test for equal treatment of equally situated individuals, and the principle that the impact of a regulation must reasonably be expected to achieve the goals of the regulation. The proliferation of tests that any regulation must pass has greatly enlarged judicial discretion in determining the acceptability of a particular regulation. In effect, the courts have come to exercise a power analogous to judicial review when it comes to the scrutiny of regulations (van Koppen 1992).

The power of the courts to scrutinize governmental action is expanded still further by the constitutional provision that the judiciary may test laws against international treaties into which the country has entered, including the Treaty of Rome (founding the European Union) and the Human Rights Treaty of the United Nations. In other words, the courts may not declare a law invalid due to incompatibility with the Dutch constitution, but they may do so on the grounds of incompatibility with international treaty obligations.[63] Since the basic civil and political rights guaranteed in the Dutch constitution are all restated in similar terms in treaties to which the Netherlands is signatory, the power of testing laws against treaty obligations is a significant one. The Treaty of Rome and subsequent commitments to the EU have successfully been used as a means of attacking a number of laws and regulations related to equal pay for men and women, as well as equal benefits from the social insurance system. For example, a law that prevented married women from receiving unemployment benefits was rejected by the Dutch courts on the grounds of its incompatibility with international treaty obligations in the area of equal rights (Traag 1990; Helder 1992: 144–145; Olson 1995). The courts have also been active in environmental protection disputes, drawing upon their power to enforce EU directives (Betlem 1993).

As with courts in the United States, Dutch courts must be careful to limit their involvement with political matters if they are to maintain the high esteem in which the public holds them. The attempt of some peace organizations to use the courts to prevent the Dutch government from accepting NATO nuclear cruise missiles in the early 1980s was rejected by the High Court as a matter outside its competence. Similarly, the power to declare departmental regulations invalid is used with care in order to avoid the claim that the courts are hindering implementation of the laws. Even so, the expanded power of judicial discretion over regulations and the increased significance of authority to review laws in light of international treaty obligations mean that the constitutional prohibition against judicial review is no longer the absolute and straightforward provision that it once was. Dutch courts do get dragged into political issues.

An example is the case of euthanasia, or assisted suicide. Euthanasia has over a period of several decades found growing social acceptance in the Netherlands in cases of painful, terminal illness.[64] Its practice began to spread before there was ever any law permitting euthanasia or defining the conditions under which a doctor could legally assist in the death of a patient. Nor was it likely that any Dutch government that included confessional parties—meaning all Dutch governments between 1917 and 1994—would ever act to legalize euthanasia even under restrictive circumstances. As a result, pressure was put on the Department of Justice to decide which cases could be prosecuted as well as on the courts to develop a set of principles that would govern their findings of guilt or innocence. An early euthanasia case brought before the Rotterdam court in 1981 resulted in the conviction of a layperson who had assisted in a suicide, but at the same time resulted in the enunciation of nine conditions under which an act of euthanasia would not be legally punished.[65] In 1992, the Second Chamber passed a law protecting doctors from criminal prosecution if they followed guidelines similar to the conditions enunciated by the Rotterdam court in 1981. In effect, the law was catching up to judicial practice.

The flexibility given the Dutch legal system on the decision to prosecute means that although the judiciary does not have a de facto role in lawmaking, it does sometimes develop by default a de jure influence. That is, although the courts cannot declare euthanasia legal, they can declare it a nonprosecutable offense. As Carlos Gomes (1991: 121) summarized, "The language of the courts ... does not give a permission to perform euthanasia, but it suggests instances in which physicians who practice euthanasia will be excepted from punishment. ... [I]n admitting to having practiced euthanasia, a physician admits to a crime, and it is his or her task to prove *not innocence* but mitigating circumstances." As long as public opinion supported euthanasia under restricted circumstances, and as long as the ministerial council and States General were unwilling to define a set of criteria for legal euthanasia, the prosecutor's office and courts were left to make their own decisions.

Much the same pattern of judicial influence on legislation occurred twenty years earlier with respect to abortion. In the 1970s the Justice Department stopped prosecuting abortion clinics despite a restrictive law that made abortion illegal under nearly all circumstances (van Koppen 1992). As Joyce Outshoorn (1986: 69) put it, "The Netherlands had a most restrictive statute until 1981, but probably had the most liberal and easily available abortion situation except perhaps for Sweden and Denmark." The combination of restrictive law and liberal practice continued until 1981, when the Second Chamber (including the CDA) accepted the need to make the law conform to popularly accepted practice.

Euthanasia and abortion (along with drug use, discussed in Chapter 9) have in common the trait of being moral issues of especially great sensitivity in a country with one large confessional party and several small ones. Laws on such matters have not always kept pace with changing social practices. The pragmatic Dutch solution in such cases has been to allow a distinction between legal prescription and everyday practice. This is a solution whose tradition reaches back all the way to the legal restrictions on, but de facto acceptance of, Catholic religious practice in the seventeenth century. The Dutch refer to such allowances as "tolerance policies."

Regardless of how one feels about the extralegal acceptance of abortion during the 1970s and of euthanasia during the 1980s, tolerance policies allow social practice to move ahead of legal acceptance without convulsing the political system in acrimonious and stalemated debates. The judicial system makes tolerance policies possible by defining the permissible boundaries of social practice. It is not a solution that everyone is happy with, particularly because an unelected judiciary takes the lead in formulating policy.[66] But it is a solution that works when the government and Second Chamber fail to produce clear legislation in an area of changing social values and practices.

Subnational Government

To the American eye, it inevitably seems anomalous that the people of a country as small as the Netherlands could have strongly felt regional differences and identifications. And yet, Dutch history has created a number of forces for localism. The tradition of town governance goes back nearly a thousand years. Local autonomy was defended against Burgundian rule and was one of the key issues leading to the Dutch revolt. Already at the time of the revolt, the strongest traditions of governance were those of the water control boards—governing councils with legal powers to tax in order to build and preserve dikes and dams, as well as to undertake land reclamation projects.

These traditions of local and regional government belong largely to the past, visible today only in such symbolic remnants as the fact that passports are still formally issued by the mayor.[67] The Netherlands has been a fully centralized state since 1800, when Napoleonic conquest brought with it the French pattern of highly centralized government. The Dutch state retained this centralized form even after the French had been defeated and sovereignty restored; as Theo Toonen (1996: 618) put it, "The political élites seemed to have become weary of endless quarrels and battles" between the United Provinces.

Despite the centralization of formal power, the pillar system created a significant degree of functional decentralization of government. During the heyday of the pillars, there was substantial delegation of policy decisions to organizations linked to the various pillars. Policies were developed in consultation with pillar organizations. In such key areas as social welfare, pillar organizations also helped implement those policies (see Chapters 6 and 7). Theo Toonen (1996: 626) goes so far as to call the pillar organizations "para-governmental institutions" that "fulfill executive tasks in policy areas often viewed as the domain of regional governments in other countries: education, welfare, culture, health, labour-market policy, etc." Although governance in the Netherlands still takes place through an extensive process of consultation with various social groups, the decline of the pillars in recent decades has loosened the grip of social organizations on development of public policy, and contributed still further to the power of the central government.

Even the water control boards are losing their venerable authority. They were created at a time when draining swamps and building protective dikes was done in relatively localized areas. The water control projects of the last few generations have been costly national affairs decided in the ministerial council and Second Chamber. Moreover, pollution has joined physical protection as a major issue for Dutch waterways, and this too has had a centralizing influence. The first Dutch water pollution–control act, passed in 1969, was ineffective because power to implement water pollution taxes rested with the local water control boards. European Union directives in the 1980s changed that, forcing the national government to take a direct hand in the control of surface water pollution in order to implement EU policy. Graham Bennett (1986: 91) concludes that "the transfer of responsibilities from local water authorities to central government is a fundamental re-ordering of the balance of power in Dutch administrative institutions— and, it must be said, an unwelcome development to many of those directly involved in water management."

The tax system gives a good indication of the degree of governmental centralization. Public spending in the Netherlands divides into about one-third for social insurance and transfer payments, one-third for the national government, and one-third for all subnational government (including provincial and local governments as well as special agencies such as the water control boards). Despite this apparent equality in expenditures, though, 98 percent of all taxes are collected by the national government—the highest percentage found among twenty-one democracies studied by Arend Lijphart (1984a). This central control of taxation means that local governments receive about 85 percent of their revenues in the form of grants from the national government.[68] Roughly 60 percent of all national grants are given with specific instructions from the national government on how to spend them.[69] The tasks of municipal government are thus broadly determined by the national government, and they tend to center on social services, education, land use planning, and housing (Denters 1993: 325). Most of these tasks are shared with the national government, which provides detailed instructions on the policies to be followed. The centralization of tax revenue collection is thus reflected in the centralization of power in the Dutch governmental system, even though many tasks are carried out at the municipal level. This leads observers to refer to the Netherlands as a "decentralized unitary state" (Toonen 1987; de Jong 1992).

The Provincial States

Prior to the nineteenth century, the Provincial States were the dominant force in Dutch government. When these sovereign provinces signed the 1579 Union of Utrecht, thereby establishing the Dutch Republic, they retained for themselves the rights to decide the form of their individual governments, to choose separate sovereigns, to have separate currencies, and to regulate their own social and economic affairs. The original provinces continue to exist,[70] but their autonomy does not.

The first significant surrender of provincial power to a central authority was for the war effort, as William of Orange and then his son, Maurice, were given authority over disposition of the armies and navies of the various provinces. Today, the twelve provinces of the unitary Dutch state form the weakest of the three layers of government in terms of autonomous power. All laws passed in the Provincial States must be approved by the national government, and their annual budgets must receive approval from the Second Chamber.[71]

The Provincial States have between thirty-nine and eighty-three members, who are elected for a four-year term and are presided over by a six-member executive council called the Deputized States. The Deputized States are led by the Commissaris of the Queen, who is appointed by the ministerial council in the name of the monarch. The Commissaris of the Queen is expected to be a delegate of the national government and to retain a national perspective in decisionmaking. This is a role somewhat similar to that of the French prefect.[72]

The powers of the Provincial States reside largely in their capacity to influence the other two levels of government. The Provincial States review budgets submitted by municipalities, making sure that the budgets are in balance and that they incorporate national policy mandates. The Provincial States also have an important role in fostering the development of regional land use policy.[73] Although municipal space plans are the only binding decisions on land use, the provincial government can send back for revision any submission that is not compatible with the regional plan.

When it comes to the national government, the Provincial States exert influence through their role in selecting members of the First Chamber. As noted earlier in this chapter, the First Chamber does not have the independence of the U.S. Senate or the German Bundesrat. But it can and does act autonomously when provincial interests are at stake. This has been the case, for example, with respect to plans to increase the number of provinces. Over the last several decades there have been designs for 13, 24, 26, or even 40 provinces, with boundaries drawn so as to facilitate economic and environmental planning. The most persistent variant on this theme has been a plan to separate Rotterdam and its surrounding area from the rest of the province of South Holland, in recognition of the distinctive issues facing Europe's largest port. The First and Second Chambers have at various times stymied each of these proposals, though one proposal was submitted to a referendum in 1997. Though the referendum was unofficial,[74] the proposal was soundly defeated and the Second Chamber dropped it from further consideration.

Local Government

There were over six hundred municipalities in the Netherlands in the mid-1990s, a large number for a country of its size but nonetheless a number only about half what it was one hundred years earlier. Amalgamation of cities, towns, and villages in an effort to gain greater efficiencies continues to reduce this number.[75]

The institutional structure of Dutch local government mirrors in many ways that of the national government in The Hague.[76] A municipal council, which may have from seven to forty-five members depending on the size of the municipality, is elected for a four-year term by a party-list system of proportional representation.[77] The council then elects from its ranks a number of aldermen *(wethouders)*, who hold full-time positions as heads of various departments in the local administration. The aldermen are functionally equivalent to ministers at the national level.

Like the Commissaris of the Queen at the provincial level, the mayor of a municipality is appointed for a six-year term by the Crown on the advice of the Ministry of Internal Affairs. As Rudy Andeweg (1989: 43) notes, "it is symbolic of Dutch centralism that in no other democracy are provincial governors and municipal mayors still appointed by the central government rather than elected locally." Although the religious and partisan composition of a municipality is taken into account in the selection of a mayor, the residents of a city do not make the ultimate selection.[78] This appointed mayor is supposed to play no role in local party politics, but rather act as an impartial executive. Indeed, a 1974 study of forty mayors showed that they have a bureaucratic conception of their role, emphasizing the provision of municipal services (Faber 1974). This attitude, prevalent in the 1970s, carries forward to the pragmatic 1990s.

The aldermen and the mayor are referred to by the collective title of the College of B & W *(Burgemeester en Wethouders)*. They constitute the executive branch of the local government and are responsible for its daily operation. Since the College of B & W develops the entire legislative program set before the municipal council, choosing the aldermen is one of the most important decisions a council is called upon to make. In most cases, major parties are represented in the College of B & W in proportion to their strengths in the council. This so-called mirror college turns the College of B & W into a reflection of the entire council. In the last few decades, though, municipal councils in the major cities have frequently selected a College of B & W with support from a majority coalition of parties, rather than as a reflection of the entire council. Leaders of the various parties bargain with each other over the program to be adopted by the coalition. This more party-political form of College of B & W is called a program college, since it is based on a governing program rather than being a mirror of the municipal council.[79] The process of creating a program college is closely parallel to the creation of cabinets and governing programs at the national level.

The transition from mirror colleges to program colleges in the municipal councils of the larger cities reflects an increased politicization of local government. As party groups within the council began to insist on a greater role in policy, they were forced to increase their degree of professionalization. The role of the standing committees in the municipal councils has been strengthened, with more frequent meetings and fuller scrutiny of the policy plans developed within the College of B & W. Colleges of B & W have been obliged by the municipal council to submit white papers and long-term plans in which their priorities and policies are clearly spelled out. Party delegations in the council have also increased their own technical expertise by adding part-time research staffs and increasing their contacts with the municipal bureaucracy. Increased technical support makes it possible for parties to submit proposals and even whole budgets in opposition to those of the College of B & W. These changes have led in some instances to a dramatically more activist role for municipal councils. In 1977, for example, the budget proposed by the College of B & W in the city of Breda was amended over college objections for the first time in the seven-hundred-year history of the city.

Despite these changes, though, the balance of power between college and council has certainly not been tipped toward the council. The superior expertise of the full-time aldermen and their staffs compared to that of the part-time council members means that the college can reject many council proposals with the claim that they are not feasible.[80] The College of B & W also creates advisory commissions that work with administrative departments in formulating laws and regulations. Despite the increase in partisanship and programmatic orientation in local politics, the general tenor of local government is still more one of management than of politics. Denters (1993: 333) points out that about 70 percent of municipalities continue to have mirror colleges, a reflection of the extent to which local government is still seen as a matter of wide political representation and sound technical management. The Dutch public would seem to agree, for they are much more likely to contact local officials about some problem than they are to contact national officials.[81] At the same time, their voting rates in local elections are low (by Dutch standards) and in decline.[82] The reason appears to be cynicism about the relative powerlessness of local government, as well as belief that local parties are too much alike (Leijenaar and Niemöller 1997: 115). Local government in the Netherlands is centered on the delivery of services rather than on political choices.

Conclusion

The political institutions and authority patterns of any country are a synthesis of historical experience and the present-day requirements of decisionmaking. Increasing transfer of effective political authority from the monarchy to the Second Chamber during the nineteenth century, and the adaptation of the First Chamber to its current role of cautious check on Second Chamber policymaking are two examples of this.

There are currently two areas of ongoing institutional adaptation in the Netherlands. One such area is in subnational government: the provincial and municipal governments and the water control boards. These bodies have become increasingly marginalized in policymaking, even as the issues with which they are traditionally concerned have become more important. The Netherlands has the most rapid rate of land transfer from agriculture to other uses of all countries in the European Union.[83] This pressure on land use puts a premium on space allocation plans, which are primarily the product of local and provincial governments. The scarcity of land, particularly of areas reserved to nature (among European Union nations, only Ireland has less forested area than the Netherlands), has led to conflicts over such projects as laying high-speed train lines and expanding Schiphol airport. Construction of a new artificial island of up to 2,000 hectares in the Maas River delta near Rotterdam has been stalled for years in the planning stages, largely due to the struggle between advocates of land use for industrial expansion, recreation for city residents, and nature preserves.[84] These are conflicts that local and regional governments are best suited to resolve.

Similarly, legislation to impose a tax on effluents discharged into surface waters originally empowered the water control boards to design a permit process, monitor discharges, and collect the tax. As Gjalt Huppes and Robert Kagan (1989) point out, no other governing bodies have the detailed knowledge of every canal, pipe, and ditch necessary to make the legislation work. And yet while housing, education, regional planning, and environmental protection are of growing significance to people's lives, the power to make decisions in these areas has moved increasingly to the national government and the EU. As a result, local Dutch politicians are more likely than their counterparts in Sweden and the United States to see their policy problems as serious, but they are the least likely to say they have the power to act on those problems (Eldersveld et al. 1995: 238). Centralization of the Dutch political system makes local elites conscious of an authority deficit as they grapple with the policy issues they see as most pressing.

The second area of current institutional change is in the relationship between the Second Chamber and the ministerial council. The breakdown of pillarization and elite political accommodation has pushed this relationship from one of dualism—in which the Second Chamber acts as an independent judge of government policy initiatives—to one of government versus opposition. Ministers and their parliamentary party groups have closed ranks, the Second Chamber has become more involved in policy development, and the dualistic separation of government and parliament has been reduced. The Dutch parliamentary system is today more like the parliamentary systems of Britain and Germany, though the complexity and range of Dutch governing coalitions continues to make the Government-Parliament relationship in the Netherlands more nuanced and variable than that found in other parliamentary systems.

It is not inevitable that these trends in political authority and relationships be carried forward. The strategy of party polarization that so transformed interactions between the ministerial council and Second Chamber lasted just fifteen years. Regional government has the potential for renewed vitality in land use planning and environmental protection. The elaborate formal and informal patterns of institutional behavior described in this chapter should not be allowed to obscure the capacity of the Dutch political system for adaptation when faced with new social demands and policy challenges.

NOTES

1. Cited in Daalder (1991: 54).

2. William took the title "Sovereign Prince" in 1813 out of respect for Dutch republican sensibilities. With the accession of Belgium to the Netherlands in 1815, however, William became a king in title as well as in function.

3. Andeweg and Irwin (1993: 142). A parliamentary commission of inquiry was established in 1947 to review the circumstances surrounding the Dutch surrender to the German army in 1940, the subsequent establishment of the government-in-exile in London, and the decisions of the government-in-exile between 1940 and 1945. The committee worked for nine years and, as summarized by Bovend'Eert and Kummeling (1991: 306), its nonpartisan and often unanimous conclusions served to "make clear the disadvantages that are attached to a situation when ministers must govern without the necessity or possibility of being held responsible by the parliament."

4. This is constitutionally permitted, but it would be a controversial matter in some circles were a Catholic actually to accede to the throne.

5. See Gladdish (1991: 218–224) for a brief history of the monarchy in the nineteenth and twentieth centuries, and Newton (1978: 222–225) for an account of the family troubles of the monarchy in the 1960s and 1970s.

6. The presence of judicial review in the American system creates, of course, a third branch of national government with autonomous powers.

7. I am indebted to Bovend'Eert and Kummeling (1991) for the information in this section.

8. Though not so long gone as one might expect. The general sections for discussing pending legislation were abolished in favor of specialized committees only in 1953.

9. Party strengths in committees reflect only approximately their chamber strengths; since some of the parties in the chamber are quite small, it is impossible to represent them on every standing committee. The rule of proportional representation on every committee was deliberately set aside during the height of the Cold War, 1948 to 1966, when members of the Communist Party (CPN) were excluded from the committees on Defense, Trade, Nuclear Energy, and Civil Defense (Bovend'Eert and Kummeling 1991: 206–207).

10. Eldersveld et al. (1981). About 35 percent of members of parliament (MPs) come from the civil service, with another 35 percent from educational, political, or social organizations. There is a striking lack of movement from the business world to the Second Chamber and, compared to the United States, there are relatively few lawyers. See Daalder (1992) and Leijenaar and Niemöller (1997) for discussion of the occupational and educational backgrounds of members of the Second Chamber.

11. Thomassen and Zielonka-Goei (1992); Andeweg (1997). Party discipline in the Second Chamber is so great that, as Bovend'Eert and Kummeling (1991: 409–413) point out, few recorded votes are even taken. Party discipline leaves no drama to the outcome of most votes; when the Second Chamber wishes to assert itself vis-à-vis the government, it does so in other ways, as described later in this chapter.

12. Party leaders then articulate these positions to the public and to the government.

13. The last time the majority coalition of parties in the Second Chamber did not also have a First Chamber majority was 1904, prior to the innovation in 1917 of the system of proportional representation. A First Chamber election could in theory result in a majority different from that in the Second Chamber. But since national party platforms and loyalties dominate provincial elections, a split between the national majority and provincial majorities is not a likely event.

14. When the First Chamber does find problems in the draft of a law, it may indicate these to the minister in charge of shepherding it through the process. If the argument is persuasive, the minister may amend the draft accordingly and resubmit it to the Second Chamber. This is called a *novelle,* and represents a kind of back-door possibility of amendment by the First Chamber.

15. These figures are from Andeweg (1992: 143). Abolition of the First Chamber is not likely, since it would require two-thirds agreement in the First Chamber itself.

16. The Dutch often use the two words "government" *(regering)* and "cabinet" *(kabinet)* interchangeably, forgetting that the monarch is part of the government but not of the cabinet. This is due to the small role of the king or queen in actual governance.

17. Engels (1990: 160–163) notes that ministers without portfolio have no means of compelling interdepartmental coordination in their area, other than to bring issues to the ministerial council for collective resolution. During the 1970s a minister of science policy was named in several successive cabinets, but was never able to overcome the barriers to interdepartmental cooperation. This ministry was abolished in 1981. Successive ministers of Development Cooperation have had greater success due to the political commitment to foreign aid by successive ministerial councils and to consistent support in public opinion for foreign assistance (see Chapter 8).

18. Hence, about half of postwar Finance Ministers have had experience both in public finance and in parliament. These figures are from a study of the background of cabinet ministers between 1948 and 1989, reported in Bakema and Secker (1990). See especially page 88 of their study.

19. See Chapter 6 for a detailed account of the policy process and the role of external advisory groups.

20. Andeweg (1990: 27). A ministerial council from the late 1960s was studied because of the twenty-year lag before summary notes taken in council meetings are released.

21. In the era of big government and substantial deficits, minimizing expenditure and crafting a budget for economic growth are typically seen in the same terms.

22. Cited in van den Berg (1993: 223).

23. As we shall see later in this chapter, contemporary ministerial councils are formed after party groups in the coalition have agreed to a detailed governmental program (*regeerakkoord*). One might think that partisan disagreements in the ministerial council would be avoided when governments take office on the basis of extensive policy agreements. Although the governing program is used as a guide to policy priorities, however, it does not always say exactly what the government plans to do on a particular issue. The governing program may actually be a hindrance to political unanimity when its promises force the ministerial council to take up a divisive issue.

24. Their study ends in 1955 because of the time lag before records of ministerial council meetings become available.

25. See Chapter 8 for a more complete account of the cruise missile controversy in the Netherlands.

26. As of 1999, no woman has ever served as minister-president.

27. The Ministry of General Affairs is by far the smallest department, with just over three hundred employees. The Department of Finance (including the tax collections office as well as the budget development office) is the largest department, with 41,000 civil servants (Rosenthal 1993: 237).

28. Since the late 1960s, the minister-president has always held a weekly press conference and television interview in which cabinet policies are explained and discussed.

29. Van den Berg (1990: 104–111) and Andeweg (1991b) provide historical overviews of the development of the minister-president's office. For much of the nineteenth century it was a weaker position than today, involving primarily coordination among powerful and relatively autonomous ministers. The growth of party discipline increased the power of ministers-president who were also leaders of large, cohesive parties. The activist leadership of such ministers-president as Abraham Kuyper and Hendrik Colijn has also shaped the modern institution, much as the leadership of Abraham Lincoln and Franklin Roosevelt did for the U.S. presidency.

30. As van den Berg (1990: 112–113) points out, a coalition of two large parties (as usually occurs in the Netherlands) requires far more delicacy in mediating party interests than does a coalition in which one party is much larger than the other (as is usually the case in Germany).

31. Cited in Blits (1989: 17).

32. The minister-president can also influence the consideration of an issue by creating a special interdepartmental committee to make a recommendation on it, and by appointing particular ministers to that committee. See Andeweg (1985).

33. Baylis (1989: 143–163) finds that only the Swiss government acts on a more collective basis (i.e., has less prime ministerial authority) than the Netherlands. See also Andeweg (1991b).

34. Andeweg and Nijzink (1992: 168). Andeweg (1991b) points out that only thirteen of forty-three ministers-president between 1848 and 1999 had previous experience in the parliament and cabinet before being named to their post. The last minister-president never to have been in the Second Chamber was Andries van Agt (1977–1982).

35. Cited in Joustra and van Venetië (1993: 105).

36. The Second Chamber may initiate legislation on any topic except succession to the throne, the scope of royal authority, the budget, and mobilization of the army. These were, of course, the most important legislative matters of the eighteenth and nineteenth centuries.

37. About half of all bills are not enacted during the parliamentary year in which they are submitted, but (contrary to practice in the United States) these bills are simply carried over for consideration in the following year rather than being resubmitted to begin the legislative process again. Though overt rejections of submitted bills are quite rare in the Second Chamber, then, it is somewhat more common for bills to languish beyond the bounds of a single parliamentary session before enactment. Andeweg and Irwin (1993: 143) note one case in which a bill was passed twenty-six years after being submitted to the Second Chamber!

38. Taking into account the right to amend legislation, and the structure and staffing of the budget committee, Peters (1991b: 83) concludes that the Dutch parliament is among the weaker European parliaments, along with those of France, Britain, and Greece.

39. Though the size of the staff available to a member of the Second Chamber remains very small compared to the U.S. Congress, it must be remembered that each member of Congress devotes a great deal of staff effort to helping constituents in their home districts. This is a task that members of the Second Chamber—who are elected by proportional representation from a party list—do not face. Van Schendelen (1993: 196) reports that legislative and committee work takes 60 percent of a member's time, while contacts in the country on behalf of the party take about 35 percent. Legislators elected from geographic districts must pay far more attention to the needs of their constituents.

40. In the first decades after World War II, interpellations were not common; there was just one in 1966–1967. In the politically polarized period that followed, there was a sharp rise in the number of interpellations: Twenty-nine were held in 1979–1980. There were less than ten per year by the end of the 1980s (Bovend'Eert and Kummeling 1991: 275).

41. The norm is for written replies to be received within a month of the question being posed, according to Bovend'Eert and Kummeling (1991).

42. Bovend'Eert and Kummeling (1991) note that ministers sometimes refuse to give information on other grounds, such as the desire to protect the privacy of an individual. In such cases, the Second Chamber must decide whether the reason is justifiable, having as recourse the power to initiate a motion of censure against the minister.

43. When parliamentary investigations are authorized on a particular issue, the special committee set up to pursue the investigation has the right to take sworn testimony from any citizen or foreign resident in the Netherlands, including ministers themselves. A parliamentary investigation continues even if the Second Chamber is dissolved for new elections before the investigation is complete. See Visscher (1976).

44. Andeweg and Irwin (1993: 149). The First Chamber may also hold interpellations and submit motions, but it rarely does so. There were just four interpellations in the First Chamber between 1945 and 1990, about the number the Second Chamber would hold in six months. Although the First Chamber may also institute parliamentary inquiries, it has never done so.

45. Dualism is still present in parliamentary inquiries, when the division runs between cabinet and parliament rather than between governing parties and opposition parties.

46. The minister-president attends only to defend proposals that engage the collective responsibility of the cabinet, such as the annual policy debate that follows the Queen's Speech from the Throne each October. In keeping with the general philosophy of equality of ministers, most legislative proposals are considered to be the responsibility solely of the minister from whose department they come (Bovend'Eert and Kummeling 1991: 402–405).

47. The briefcase is empty because there is no briefcase large enough to contain (at least in printed form) all the documentation related to a governmental budget in the modern era.

48. As K. de Vries of the Labor Party remarked while working on the formation of the first Kok government after the 1994 elections, "If you turn the light on while in the dark-room, you spoil the photograph." Cited in Andeweg (1994: 152).

49. Indeed, the procedures for consultation leading to government formation are constitutionally specified. See Andeweg, Dittrich, and van der Tak (1978) for a thorough account.

50. Cited in Vis (1983: 158). A motion initiated in the Second Chamber in 1970 proposed that the Second Chamber itself appoint an *informateur* by convening immediately after the election. This was tried in 1971, but each party group voted for their own candidate for the position and no individual was able to win a majority. The queen went ahead with her own appointment. This experiment in parliamentary initiative has not been repeated, but it exposes the central dilemma of government formation in the Netherlands: The monarch cannot legitimately be a political actor, and yet there is no one else in a position to initiate and shepherd the process of government formation. The system of *informateurs* and *formateurs* protects the monarchy by putting its role at one remove from the actual process of negotiation.

51. The election itself usually sends clear signals as to which parties should be in the government and which party leader should become minister-president. However, those clear signals need not always be followed. In 1977 the Labor Party concluded a term in government with a resounding electoral victory, gaining ten seats. The general expectation was that Labor would return to office, and indeed a Labor *informateur* appointed by Queen Juliana recommended exactly that. Four and a half months later, negotiations with the CDA to form a center-left government collapsed. Within days a new *informateur* was appointed, followed by a Christian Democratic *formateur* who soon had agreement on a coalition between the CDA and the Liberal Party.

52. Cited in Denters (1992: 97).

53. See Hoogerwerf (1993: 34) for a listing of interim governments.

54. If de Swaan's analysis were updated to 1999, the score would improve slightly, with sixteen of twenty-eight cabinets conforming to the theory that coalitions are minimum-winning and ideologically connected. On strategic models of coalition formation, see also Andeweg (1994).

55. Indeed, Lijphart (1989) has shown that when consensus politics was replaced by party polarization, oversized cabinets were replaced by minimum-winning cabinets. Before 1967, just 13 percent of cabinets were minimum-winning; after 1967, fully 71 percent of coalitions had no extra parties. For a further account of Lijphart's analysis of consensus democracy, see Chapter 6.

56. Andeweg (1994: 157). Van Mierlo's desired coalition of Labor, Liberals, and D66 was eventually formed.

57. Of course, the more significant regulations will be reviewed by one or both bodies.

58. Andeweg (1991a: 247).

59. Eldersveld et al. (1981: 44). The proportion of the population that has completed a university education has now increased to 9 percent, according to the 1998 Dutch Parliamentary Election Study.

60. Van der Meer and Roborgh (1993: 337). Van der Meer and Roborgh also find that the percentage of civil servants with a working class background has grown steadily in the postwar period. The percentage of the population that is working-class has, by contrast, declined sharply (see Table 4.1).

61. Eldersveld et al. (1981: 44). The population now resembles the senior civil service more closely because it has become more secular.

62. The courts do have an active review function with respect to local laws, in contrast to legislation passed by the States General. City councils may pass any law that is "made necessary by the interests of the municipality" and that is not in conflict with a national law. It is up to the judiciary to determine whether these conditions are met.

63. In Britain, Italy, and Germany, by contrast, treaty obligations do not have force within the country unless and until they are embodied in national law, according to de Winter (1991: 139–140).

64. In 1995, 35,000 people requested euthanasia "when their time came," 10,000 of whom were requesting it "in the short term." Nearly one-third of those 10,000 requests were honored, resulting in 3,200 recorded cases of euthanasia in that year. *InterNetKrant,* November 27, 1996, page 1.

65. The conditions are that there must be unbearable suffering on the part of the patient, that the desire to die must emanate from a conscious person, that the request for euthanasia must be voluntary, that the patient must be given alternatives and have time to consider them, that there must be no other reasonable solutions to the patient's problem, that the death must not inflict unnecessary suffering on others, that there must be more than one person involved in the decision, that the euthanasia must be performed by a physician, and that "great care" must be exercised in reaching the decision. See Gomes (1991) and Griffiths et al. (1998) for excellent accounts of the moral, legal, political, and policy issues connected to the practice of euthanasia in the Netherlands.

66. Hans van Mierlo of D66 has observed that "The country is governed by judges because the government formulates defective laws." Cited in Molenaar (1990: 20).

67. Localism is also seen in the fact that local parties typically win between 15 and 20 percent of the vote in municipal elections. These parties are unaffiliated with the national parties and often revolve around a local personality or an issue such as preventing development of open spaces.

68. This level of dependency on national government revenues compares to only 13 percent dependency in the United States (Peters 1991a: 47).

69. Andeweg and Irwin (1993: 162) note that municipal governments in the early 1980s received an average of twenty instructions per day from the departments of the central government.

70. The one exception is the division of the province Holland into North Holland (including Amsterdam, Haarlem, and Leiden) and South Holland (including Rotterdam and The Hague).

71. This is, of course, a complete reversal of the power relations during the days of the United Provinces, when all expenditure by the States General required provincial approval.

72. The typical commissaris is, however, a senior politician stepping down from a national career rather than a civil servant, as is the French prefect.

73. The provinces have recently enlarged their role in encouraging economic development by use of tax incentives and investment grants, according to Tömmel (1992).

74. There is no constitutional provision for popular consultation on proposed legislation.

75. At the same time, the effective number of local governments may be considered to be larger than the number of municipalities, since some larger cities (including Amsterdam and Rotterdam) have created neighborhood councils. These councils are directly elected by residents of the neighborhood and have been delegated certain tasks by the municipal government (de Jong 1992: 122–124).

76. For further detail, see Daalder (1966: 194–196), Weil (1970: chapter 3), and de Jong (1992).

77. Foreigners resident in the Netherlands for at least five years are also eligible to vote in municipal elections.

78. The purple government promised in 1998 to develop legislation that would permit residents of a municipality to express their opinions on candidates for mayor in a consultative referendum (*InterNetKrant*, June 4, 1998, page 1). If implemented, this could significantly increase the role of local opinion in the appointment of mayors. Accounts of the recruitment and careers of mayors under the existing system may be found in Andeweg (1975) and Andeweg and Derksen (1978).

79. See Morlan (1974) for an account of the issues surrounding mirror and program colleges, as well as other issues in municipal government.

80. Aldermen are also part-time functionaries in towns with populations of less than 30,000.

81. Twenty-nine percent of the Dutch population have contacted a local official about some problem, compared to only 11 percent who have contacted a national official (Denters 1993: 327).

82. The proportion of eligible voters turning out for local elections is now under 50 percent in the larger cities.

83. Eight percent of agricultural land was built upon or turned to recreational purposes between 1960 and 1980, according to Briggs and Wyatt (1988).

84. The change in values with respect to land use is suggested by the change in allocation decisions made for successive polders in Lake IJssel. Just 5 percent of the land created in the *Wieringermeer* and the Northeast Polder (completed in 1940 and 1962, respectively) was allocated to woods and nature, with nearly all the rest going to agriculture. Over 10 percent of East Flevoland (completed in 1980) is a nature preserve, and that will be the case of one-quarter of South Flevoland, which is not yet completed (van Lier 1988: 96).

6

THE POLICY PROCESS

In the last chapter we identified the institutions of government that wield political authority in the Netherlands. In this chapter we will look more closely at the ways in which these institutions interact with each other and with organized groups in society to arrive at policy decisions. David Easton (1971: 128) has defined politics as those activities that influence the authoritative decisions made for a society. These authoritative decisions are made by formal and informal rules according to which various groups bring their interests and influence to bear, whether in face-to-face negotiations or by marching in the streets. The ideal outcome of the policy process is to arrive at laws and regulations that will be accepted by all as legitimate and binding, and that will improve the welfare of the national community.

Despite a few dramatic exceptions, the means of expressing political interests and demands in the Netherlands lies nearly always in face-to-face negotiations and is hardly ever achieved by marching in the streets. The task of reaching a legitimate and binding policy decision, though, is complicated by the existence of highly mobilized social and economic groups that differ significantly in their interests and perspectives. For much of the twentieth century, Dutch policymakers had to steer a course through the competing demands of the various pillars. More recently, the mobilization of postmaterialist interests and the demand for political access by new organizations representing professional associations, consumers, women, environmentalists, ethnic minorities, and others have added still more complexity to the policymaking process.

One useful way to put the policy process of any country in perspective is to employ Arend Lijphart's (1984a) distinction between majoritarian and consensus democracies. The majoritarian model of democracy employs a unitary system of government, a strong political executive, a unicameral legislature, and a two-party system, which together invest the majority party with near-exclusive control over governmental policy. Majoritarian democracy is government by majority rule, a process that leaves the political minority relatively powerless. Of course, in a majoritarian democracy the minority party or parties are able to contest the next election in order to become a majority bloc. In the meantime, though, they are relegated to the role of critic of policies supported by the majority party.

Lijphart argues that majoritarian democracy is suitable for homogeneous societies in which the differences between majority and minority parties are relatively slight. Majoritarian democracy is also suitable when the minority party has a realistic chance of becoming a majority party in the foreseeable future, that is, when becoming a majority party is simply a matter of adjusting one's electoral platform to better match the policy preferences of the median voter. Under these circumstances, majoritarian democracy produces a competitive two-party system with periodic rotation in the control of government.

The chances of becoming a majority party are much reduced when the minority bloc is a regional, religious, or ethnic group. Under such circumstances the institutions of majoritarian rule can be deeply frustrating and alienating to minority groups. As Lijphart (1984a: 23) points out, "What these societies need is a democratic regime that emphasizes consensus instead of opposition, that includes rather than excludes, and that tries to maximize the size of the ruling majority instead of being satisfied with a bare majority."

Minority groups may be included in the policy process by multiplying the number of venues in which policy decisions are made, by establishing a separation of powers between branches of government, by territorial and functional decentralization of power, by creating a bicameral legislature with regional representation in the upper house, by using proportional representation to foster a multiparty system, and by requiring enhanced majorities for changes to the constitution (thus giving the minority effective veto power). Lijphart calls this "consensus democracy," a pattern of governance that protects minority power and so enables permanent minorities to accept the uncertainties of democratic rule.

Consensus Democracy in the Netherlands

Given the divisions in Dutch society along lines of religion, class, and ideology, it will come as no surprise that the Dutch political process tends more to the pattern of consensus democracy than to the pattern of majoritarian democracy. The process that has evolved in the Netherlands to deal with these circumstances is one marked above all by consultation and negotiation. The *Pacificatie* of 1917— the agreement between major political forces that settled the schools question and the suffrage issue—created a proportional electoral system that all but guaranteed that no single party would ever gain a majority in the Second Chamber. As we saw in Chapter 4, election results typically give representation to ten political parties, about half of which are plausible candidates for participation in the governing coalition formed after the election. We also saw in Chapter 5 that the government is formed after agreement is reached on an extensive and detailed set of policy prescriptions. These negotiations encompass not only the coalition parties but also the representatives of leading interest groups. The low threshold for election to the Second Chamber provides legislative seats even for relatively small societal groups that seek representation through their own parties. Finally, the practice of distributing committee chairmanships among all but the smallest parties spreads opportunities for policy leadership beyond the governing coalition.

Provisions for altering the constitution also follow the logic of consensus democracy, because a minority group is perfectly able to block a proposed constitutional amendment. Amendments may be initiated by the ministerial council or by a member of the Second Chamber, just as with regular legislation. Any proposed amendment must be submitted in draft form to various advisory commissions and to the Council of State for commentary and advice, after which it must *twice* receive a two-thirds majority in each of the First and Second Chambers. After the first vote on the measure, the chambers are dissolved and new elections are held. This gives the electorate (and, in the case of the First Chamber, the provincial governments) a chance to revise the composition of the two chambers in accord with their views on the constitutional amendment.[1] In the second reading, held after the election, both the First and Second Chambers give the proposed amendment an up-or-down vote in which approval by a two-thirds majority is required. This is a demanding threshold, for it means that the measure must enjoy broad support across the ideological divides of Dutch politics. In 1999, for example, the First Chamber blocked by one vote a constitutional amendment that would permit voters to repeal legislation through a referendum. In so doing, they negated the support for this measure of more than two-thirds of the Second Chamber and a majority of the First Chamber.[2]

In short, many of the procedures for lawmaking in the Netherlands are designed to protect minority rights—the hallmark of a consensus democracy. The protection of minorities is enhanced still further by the fact that even some majoritarian institutions in Dutch politics operate according to the principles of consensus democracy. For example, although the Dutch constitution does not give courts the authority to subject laws to judicial review, the power of the administrative courts to scrutinize regulations and of the High Council to test laws against the commitments made in international treaties has created a substantial judicial protection of individual and group rights.

The essence of consensus democracy in the Netherlands, though, does not lie in the country's governmental institutions.[3] Rather, consensus democracy in the Netherlands is most purely expressed through a policy process rooted in consultation with the leaders of political, economic, and social organizations. As we have seen in earlier chapters, this habit of negotiation has been present since the early days of the United Provinces, fostered by the existence of sizable minorities whose interests could not be ignored without endangering the unity and hence the very survival of the country. The need for compromise became especially acute in the late nineteenth and early twentieth centuries, as Liberals, Conservatives,

158 The Policy Process

Catholics, Protestants, and Socialists maneuvered to reach agreement on the issues of importance to them. From the 1860s to 1917, a series of agreements between these political forces resolved such fundamental issues as the power of parliament over colonial policy, expansion of the suffrage, and governmental support
for religious schools. The demands of reconstruction after World War II further
reinforced belief in the efficacy of elite negotiation and compromise. It was a period of policymaking by consensus at all levels of government. One of the most
striking examples may be the "Chairman's Club" of local party leaders that existed
in the city of Delft from 1946 to 1948. According to one of those involved:

> This club of party chairmen discussed in a sort of conclave all important local issues,
> before the elections as well as after the elections, talked about points before the
> Council meetings, [and] before important committee meetings. . . . We often sat up-
> stairs [in a house], in a small room; there was no air and no light, only a small trap-
> door to let some air in, and we met and talked over all the large important questions.
> Entirely different political beliefs, but [we spoke] with a complete honesty and open-
> ness. We learned from each other which motions we would submit, which amend-
> ments we would submit, which proposals we would make, and it never occurred to
> any of us to make any misuse of this procedure.[4]

Belief in the need for elite cohesion is readily apparent in this tale of conspira-
torial local party leaders plotting a common strategy for the governance of the
city. Much the same phenomenon occurred throughout the country, at all levels
of politics, though usually not in an attic. The experience of economic crisis in the
1930s and of the German occupation during World War II had left Dutch political
leaders determined to put the policy process on the most collaborative and consultative footing possible.

Revitalized elite collaboration across the pillars was, in turn, made possible by
acceptance of the idea that policymaking would be developed to the greatest extent possible in technical rather than political terms. This was the motivation behind founding of the Central Statistical Bureau (CBS) and the Central Planning
Bureau (CPB) after World War II, both of which were charged with developing a
systematic statistical picture of the Netherlands that would provide information
relevant to policy planning and coordination. In subsequent decades the
Scientific Council for Governmental Policy (WRR, founded in 1972) and the
Social and Cultural Planning Bureau (SCP, founded in 1973) extended the information and policy-planning function from economic and regional planning to
the study of long-term social trends and their implications for governmental policy.[5] Jan Tinbergen, a Nobel laureate economist, was the first director of the
Central Planning Bureau, and the economic projections of this body were put to
immediate use in informing contract negotiations between employers and
unions.[6] A half century after World War II, the Netherlands continues to have a
"broadly shared faith in the possibility and blessing of technical solutions for political controversies" (de Beus and van Kersbergen 1994: 7).

Arend Lijphart (1975: 209–219) calls this pattern of governance "consociational democracy"—a form of rule adopted in countries whose democratic stability is presumed to require collusive collaboration between leaders of differing backgrounds and ideologies. In the Netherlands, this collusion originated in the need to find consensus between the leaders of rival pillars, and during the era of pillarization it included a substantial element of elitist and even secretive politics. Today the Dutch policy process is far more open to public inspection and participation. But the most important element of consociational democracy still remains: the inclusion of a great variety of groups and interests in the policy process, coupled with the effort to base public policy on the widest possible consensus. Politicians and senior civil servants in the Netherlands are far more likely than their counterparts in other countries to subscribe to the view that the interests of different groups in society can and should be reconciled cooperatively.[7]

Parliamentary Influence on Policy

We saw in the last chapter that it is the task of the ministerial council to prepare legislation for consideration in the States General.[8] The two chambers of the States General then review, perhaps amend in the case of the Second Chamber, and ultimately adopt the proposed legislation set before them. Since a majority in the Second Chamber is responsible both for keeping the ministerial council in office and for passing legislation, this would seem to be a classic example of majoritarian democracy at work.

What this skeletal outline of the policymaking process conceals, however, is the means by which a proposal for new legislation is developed in the first place, before it is ever considered by the ministerial council and submitted to the Second Chamber. The process of preparation is a lengthy one. It involves formal and informal consultation with a wide range of groups, in government and in the society, in the ruling coalition and outside it. In this section we will review this extensive process of consultation, paying particular attention to the involvement of advisory councils.

The idea for preparing a draft law usually originates with the cabinet, either as a result of the government's program or because an individual minister has come to believe that a particular law is needed.[9] Despite the concentration of legislative initiation in the executive, though, the steps leading to formulation of a draft law bring different perspectives into play. The relevant department of the civil service is asked to prepare a report on existing legislation and regulations connected to the subject, as well as to determine whether a new law is necessary and what form it should take. A policy concept paper is then developed based on this research, and is sent to one or more advisory commissions (*adviescolleges*) for consideration and recommendations. Submission to an advisory commission is in many cases required by law, and in some instances there are constitutional mandates for solicitation of advice from specific bodies.[10] The advice of these commissions is taken into account in putting together a legislative proposal, which is then circulated widely among interest organizations to assemble their comments and viewpoints. The reactions of these groups not only influence further development of the policy proposal, but also enable the ministerial council to anticipate likely objections to the version that is formally submitted to the Second Chamber. Based on written reactions from interest groups and advisory commissions, the ministry prepares a memo listing key issues and questions *(vraagpuntennota)* connected to the policy proposal. This memo is submitted to relevant committees in the two chambers for their own reactions and commentary.

These consultations occur in advance of drafting the actual legislation. If the proposed law still seems like a good (and politically feasible) idea at this point, a full draft of the legislative text is prepared along with a summary of the main issues connected to it *(memorie van toelichting)*. The written documents prepared by the various advisory commissions are also included. These documents provide information on the legal issues raised by the proposed legislation, as well as reactions of the major interest groups affected by the proposal. At this point, the proposal is reviewed by the ministerial council for conformity with the policy goals of the government. Approval by the ministerial council sends the proposal to the Council of State, which certifies that the law would be in accord with international treaty obligations if enacted. The Council of State also advises on conformity of the bill with the Dutch constitution, and comments on whether the legally specified process of consultation for development of the proposed law has been followed.[11]

After approval by the ministerial council and the Council of State, the proposed law is sent to the monarch, who is formally responsible for its submission to the Second Chamber. The text of the proposed law is accompanied by its explanatory documents, which describe the general purposes of the law and its various provisions. The net effect of this procedure is to put proposals for new laws through an extensive test. By the time a proposal is submitted to the Second Chamber, by the time it is even fully drafted, it has been thoroughly vetted by experts in the policy area and by interest groups that would be affected by the law. It is not enough that the ministerial council considers the proposal to be desirable, though this is clearly necessary.

As we saw in the last chapter, this extensive process of preparatory consultation both with interest groups and with the governing party groups in the Second Chamber leads to a better than 90 percent approval rate for measures proposed by the ministerial council. Although the Second Chamber may amend a bill significantly or may even show such antipathy to it that the minister removes it from consideration, these are unusual events. By the time the Second Chamber receives the draft law and the *memorie van toelichting* summarizing the advice of relevant groups, its room for maneuver is substantially reduced. After all, what can members of the Second Chamber say about a draft bill crafted through intensive discussions between civil servants and a range of interest groups and experts? One example is the approval of the National Environmental Policy Plan (NEPP). The NEPP was adopted in 1990, seven years after it was first drawn up in concept form. In the intervening years, details of the plan were worked out in negotiations between departments and in consultations with several advisory commissions. Although parliamentary members of every major party had reservations about the plan, the Second Chamber accepted it with only minor revisions (Bennett 1991; van Zijst 1993).

Nor does the Second Chamber have the right to consult directly with advisory commissions, for example to test reactions to desired amendments. If members of the Second Chamber seek further information from an advisory commission, they must do so by sending a request to the responsible minister, to be forwarded at his or her discretion. Debates in the Second Chamber, then, often make heavy use of the reports compiled from advisory bodies by the ministerial council itself.

Despite these limitations on parliamentary maneuvering, advance discussion between the minister responsible for the policy and the parliamentary leadership (including relevant parliamentary committees) give the Second Chamber significant influence at an early and informal stage in the development of policy. By the time the bill is formally submitted, all parliamentary party groups represented in the ministerial council are normally on board. The high rate of acceptance of government proposals should not be equated with parliamentary impotence in the policy process.

Interest-Group Influence on Policy

The consultative process by which policy proposals are developed gives interest groups a central role, both directly and as participants in advisory commissions. Of course, interest groups have a great deal of influence in any democracy. Government has become so complex that we should no longer think of it as a sovereign and unified entity making decisions for the society; it is rather a process of consultation and negotiation that reaches decisions by developing a working agreement between various public and private organizations. The range of interests that come into play during the process of policy development includes those of private organizations, departments of the civil service, and national and subnational government.

The Dutch policy process is distinctive in the variety of groups involved in policy discussions and in the extent to which such groups are also involved in the actual implementation of policy. These are the characteristic traits of a corporatist policy process—one that incorporates interest groups by giving them specific rights of consultation and roles in implementation. Corporatism is sometimes described primarily as a centralized tripartite bargaining relationship between government officials, representatives of labor, and employers. Their negotiations cover such issues as economic policy and private-sector wage agreements. This economic summitry also exists in the Netherlands, but Dutch corporatism involves much more than centralized wage negotiations.[12] The essence of corporatism lies not so much in the existence of specific central institutions as in the conviction that the relationship between government and leading interest groups is one of social partnership.

Corporatism generally can be contrasted with pluralism as practiced in countries such as the United States, where interest groups also lobby any governmental body that might be amenable to influence. But while interest groups under pluralism have only the right to *attempt* to get a hearing for their viewpoints, under corporatism the government is legally obliged to solicit interest-group perspectives and—in some instances—to involve those groups in the execution of policy. Robert Cox (1993: 44) points out that "Corporatism awards privileged representation to functional interests whereas pluralism relegates all private interests to the status of lobbying organizations that must compete with one another for influence over policy." Pluralism, then, maintains a clear boundary between interest groups as supplicants (though sometimes as quite powerful supplicants) and the state as final authority. Corporatism blurs the line between state and society by guaranteeing access to officially recognized groups.

Prior to the rise of the religious pillars in the nineteenth century, interaction between interest groups and government in the Netherlands more closely resembled the pluralist model of interest-group lobbying. This was the case, for example, with a campaign mounted in the nineteenth century by the Amsterdam Chamber of Commerce, which lobbied the Second Chamber not to legislate restrictions on the use of child labor.[13] In the early part of the twentieth century, though, there was a blossoming of interest groups connected to the pillars. As the pillars developed their networks of organizations in the fields of education, health care, and social services, it became clear that any government seeking to make policy in these areas would need the consent and participation of these societal organizations. Dutch neutrality during World War I also challenged the unions, employers associations, and government to work together. Union leaders were given seats on the National Emergency Relief Committee and obtained governmental backing for their participation in collective bargaining. The government also subsidized recognized unions by providing matching funds for dues the unions collected from their members. These efforts at co-optation of the union movement paid off, as the only major strike (by coal miners) during World War I was opposed by the unions themselves (Windmuller 1969: 44).

The development of direct channels of consultation between executive departments and organized interest groups continued during the 1930s, as the state tried to cope with the global economic crisis. After World War II, faced with the task of reconstructing the country and building the welfare state, the corporatist network reached its full density as new institutions were created for consultation and coordination between leading interest groups and the government.[14]

Because the pillars each had their own political party, political influence was for pillar organizations less a matter of lobbying an external authority than of working out specific policy perspectives with leaders of their pillar party. The corporatist networks of the confessional pillars thus became a way of imprinting onto the state Protestant ideas of "sovereignty in one's own circle" and the Catholic idea of subsidiarity.[15] Robert Cox (1993: 206) notes that "In the Dutch context corporatism was a way to limit the degree of state meddling, whereas in other countries corporatism is often perceived as a way to manage state intervention."

The domination of corporatist policy networks by confessional organizations, indeed the development of those networks in order to give political voice to confessional interests, has given Dutch corporatism a character distinctive from that of other small European countries. Dutch corporatism stands in particularly sharp contrast to that of the Scandinavian countries, where corporatism is rooted in the power of labor. Corporatism in the Netherlands, by contrast, is primarily confessional in nature rather than being an expression of class interests. Catholic and Protestant groups embraced corporatism as a means of muting class conflict and of giving confessional organizations direct access to government policymaking. The division of both workers and employers along religious lines prevented any general mobilization around class differences and further enhanced the political power of the confessional pillars.

The distinctive origins of Dutch corporatism are also reflected in the nature of corporatist negotiations. The Scandinavian model of corporatism is focused on centralized wage negotiations and government provision of social services. In contrast to the corporatist pattern under which the peak associations of labor and employer organizations meet with government officials, Dutch corporatism extends well beyond the domain of labor relations to permeate all areas of social and economic policy, and involves many more groups than just the peak associations of workers and employers.

The Dutch corporatist pattern mitigates some disadvantages of the more centralized style of corporatism dominated by economic interests. One general difficulty with corporatist systems is that they are not very flexible in the interests they represent.[16] Corporatist countries must of necessity distinguish between recognized and nonrecognized groups in determining whom to invite to the process. In the prototypical social democratic corporatism, organized labor and employers groups negotiate with state agencies. Dutch corporatism is more flexible on the specific interests represented, with economic, confessional, and ideologically-based groups negotiating side by side. Even Dutch corporatism, though, involves official recognition of particular groups as representative of societal interests. There are, for example, "recognized" and "nonrecognized" labor unions, farm associations, and environmental organizations. The communist Unity Labor Center (EVC) was not accepted as a participant in the Foundation of Labor after World War II, even though it was larger than the Protestant National Trade Union Federation (CNV) at the time. Deprived of any possibility of influence, communist labor organizations withered.

Within the pillars, leaders of officially recognized groups not only had privileged access to "their" political party but were also able to put their representatives on the party list for election to the Second Chamber.[17] Policy specialists within a parliamentary party group frequently come directly from the interest groups active in that policy area. Even ministers and state secretaries may be recruited directly from these interest groups (van Goor 1993: 113).

This system was effective in negotiating policy decisions between the leading interest groups as long as the pillars remained the preferred type of social organization. As we have seen, though, changes in political values and the economic structure of society have altered the bases of social organization. This is partly a consequence of the decline of the pillars, but also results from changes in the economy. Where once pillarized labor unions represented most employees, today the service sector has given rise to many occupational groups whose interests are expressed through professional associations rather than through unions. These professional associations have created their own relationships with governmental officials, bypassing the regular corporatist channels. For example, when associations of the self-employed began to press for a disability program that would cover them, they went directly to the parliament and the social affairs ministry rather than trying to interest the Socio-Economic Council in their issue (Cox 1993: 159).

In the last few decades, as the grip of the confessional pillars on Dutch society and politics has loosened, corporatism has been transformed into a new hybrid phenomenon that might best be called "pluralistic corporatism." The basic features of this new form of corporatism are that it involves a wide variety of interest groups in policy consultation, that it operates differently in different policy domains, and that it is flexible in its ability to admit new members to the negotiating table.[18] With the decline of the pillars, the role of the state in setting the policy agenda and directing the corporatist process has also become greater (van Mierlo and Gerrichhauzen 1988). The element of formally guaranteed access to the policy process is retained from classic corporatism, but sectoral variability and temporal flexibility, characteristics of pluralism, have been added. As we shall see, this multiplication of and fluidity in corporatist networks enables a strategic minister to manipulate the consultation process in a way that increases the cabinet's ability to enact its own agenda.

External Advisory Commissions

The flexibility of the Dutch corporatist system derives from the involvement of external advisory commissions (EACs) in policymaking.[19] The government creates EACs by bringing together representatives from interest groups as well as academics and civil servants considered to be experts in the policy area. EACs are asked to advise on government policy whenever a new initiative in that area is being considered. Depending on the topic, advisement may occur once every few years or a thousand times in a single year, as is the case with the Council of State.

The median number of requests for advice is about five per year (van Delden 1993: 155). The number of members of an EAC ranges from five to about thirty, and each EAC is staffed by a civil servant from the department concerned with the particular policy area.

As of the mid-1990s there were between 150 and 200 permanent external advisory commissions, and another 25 or so ad hoc external advisory commissions. Over three-quarters of these EACs were established after 1960 in connection with the rapid expansion of policymaking into new areas of economic regulation and social welfare. Some of them are primarily groups of experts in the specific policy area (most often a mixture of academics, researchers, and civil servants); others are composed so as to represent the major societal stakeholders on the issue. Some EACs have wide mandates that span an entire sector of policy, such as the Education Council or the Water Affairs Council. Others are organized around much narrower concerns, such as the Chamber for Trade in Garden Seeds and the Railroad Accident Council.

About 30 percent of all EACs have tasks that go beyond the provision of advice. Some are named in framework laws as the bodies empowered to issue guidelines and regulations in conjunction with those laws. Others are given responsibility for particular aspects of policy implementation, such as determining eligibility for grants and subsidies. The influence of these advisory commissions has waxed and waned over time, depending on the predilections of a specific ministerial council. As a more "businesslike" style of government came to replace the party polarization of an earlier era, many interest-based EACs were disbanded and more expert EACs were established.

EACs are a flexible form of corporatist consultation because individual commissions are readily created and abolished. As the number of confessional organizations in society has declined, for example, the role of confessional organizations in EACs has shrunk in favor of EACs composed of representatives from various professional associations. Large, intersectoral issues of reform may be assigned to ad hoc EACs, created to develop (it is hoped) a unified policy perspective rooted in a broad cross section of experts and interested parties. The Dekker Commission on health care reform and the Oort Commission on reform of the tax code are two recent examples of ad hoc EACs. Reform of the EAC system itself was examined by an ad hoc EAC, the van der Ploeg Commission. Koppenjan, Ringeling, and te Velde (1987: 284) find that ad hoc EACs tend to have more influence than standing EACs, and that the influence of EACs is greatest in policy areas that present unfamiliar problems. Their study shows that in such areas as noise pollution, women's rights, and urban renewal, EACs helped define the problem and identify solutions in the early phase of agenda formation. "But as soon as the problem area becomes institutionalized, departmental actors move to the foreground," and the role of the EACs is reduced (Koppenjan et al. 1987: 250).

Policy development through consultation with EACs has proven to be so useful that it is regularly extended to new areas of policymaking. For example, a number of advisory commissions were created in recent decades to advise the government on policy toward ethnic minorities (Rath 1988). Growing public interest in environmental protection was also followed by creation of an EAC for environmental issues, called the Council for Environmental Management, within which environmental groups could air their views alongside representatives of employers, farmers, labor, and consumer organizations (Goverde 1993: 57–58). Creation of an environmental policy network led, predictably, to a shift of attention within environmental organizations from grassroots mobilization to preparedness for detailed dialogue with the ministry. The result, according to a staff member in the Association for Defense of the Environment, was that "we began to play a role in decision-making, which meant that we had to become more realistic in our demands. What realistic was to mean was not determined by us, but by our opponent: the government. Because the work became therefore more practical, ideological discussions were held less often."[20] Despite the pessimism implicit in these words, organizations jostle to become part of the consultative network in their area, and once they are included they may seek to exclude organizations with other viewpoints.

External advisory commissions are a key feature of the Dutch system of pluralistic corporatism. Whether permanent or ad hoc, whether based in interests or on expertise, and whether issue-specific, sector-specific, or intersectoral, EACs give government the capacity to draw upon the insights and perspectives of a wide variety of individuals and social groups in the formulation of policy. A 1977 study of EACs by the Scientific Council for Governmental Policy (WRR) found that one EAC drew upon over 9,000 individuals. This extreme case of wide involvement occurred in a review of nuclear energy policy. A commission was created to develop a broad social discussion of the future of nuclear energy in the Netherlands. Any organization interested in studying the issue received a subsidy, and their conclusions were compiled into a report that was then subject to discussion in over 1,800 community meetings. As Rudy Andeweg and Galen Irwin (1993: 39–40) point out, the effect of this procedure was to cool off an issue that had excited intense passions when the process began.

Formalization of the role of EACs in the policy development process—that is, making them part of a corporatist system—also has the side benefit of making it unnecessary for interest-group representatives to pour money into politics in order to gain access to the policy process. The relatively low cost of Dutch electoral campaigns is due to many factors, including the prominence of party lists over individual campaigns for office (see Chapter 4). But the availability of institutionalized access to the policy process also contributes to the small role of money in politics by eliminating much interest-group incentive to make contributions to political parties or individual candidates.

Despite these advantages of pluralistic corporatism, the impact of EACs on the quality of policymaking is often questioned. Policies predicated on wide consultation are certainly rooted in a rich understanding of the issues, and are developed with a high level of organized consent. But this very advantage of the consultative policy process is also one of its weak points. When ministerial departments must seek advice from a range of EACs as part of the development of policy proposals, it becomes difficult to avoid stalemate. The potential problem of policy gridlock stems from the requirement that every policy proposal run such an extensive gauntlet of advice. Although there is no requirement that each of the consulted groups actually agree with the policy proposal, the process puts them in a relatively strong position to water down objectionable proposals, or even to block them.[21]

Opposite the Scylla of policy gridlock lies the Charybdis of micropolicy proliferation. EACs are, after all, an institutionalized means of identifying policy problems and urging the government to address them. In an era when government is actively involved in so many areas of life, it may be hard to resist having a policy on everything. Such EACs as the Council for Adult Education, the Advisory Commission on Issuing Mussel Bed Licenses, and the Commission for Advice on Work and Rest Times for Crews of Freight Airlines will inevitably urge policies that protect the interests of their constituents. This problem had been foreseen in 1922, when a constitutional amendment (initiated by the social democrat Troelstra) was passed mandating that EACs be formed only with parliamentary permission. In practice, though, there proved to be no way to prevent the government from establishing EACs and consulting them. By the 1980s, fewer than 40 percent of EACs had been established with parliamentary consent (van Putten 1982: 180).

A final problem of pluralistic corporatism comes from its very flexibility—the fact that there are distinct advisory networks for each area of policymaking. This creates a tendency for policy to be formulated independently within each issue sector, a problem that the Dutch call *"verkokering"* of the policy process.[22] Fragmentation of policymaking begins with the ministers and their departments, but is also fostered by the EACs, nearly all of which pursue policy interests within a single department such as Education, Transportation, or Social Affairs. When participation in policymaking is divided along departmental lines, it becomes difficult to develop an integrated perspective that conforms to the political vision of the governmental coalition. Jan van den Berg and Henk Molleman (1974: 30–39) refer in this context to the "closed circuits" of Dutch policymaking, consisting of the minister or state secretary, top civil servants specialized in the policy area, specialists from the party groups in the Second Chamber, and the EACs for that policy area. Rosenthal (1993: 258) points out that within these closed circuits, "people know each other, they know the jargon, they understand each other's viewpoints and problems. . . . Anyone who opposes the system is deprived of information."

Even though there will be differences of opinion about policy directions within a particular advisory network, all members of the network are interested in preserving the network itself. It is as if, in the words of Jelle Visser (1990: 232), "societal corporatism was replaced by many little corporatisms, each capturing some state agency and holding the others in check." The autonomy of each individual minister and the weakness of the ministerial council as a collective body result in part from an implicit pact of nonintervention in each other's policy circuits. Van den Berg and Molleman (1974: 38–39) go so far as to conclude that policy in a given area is merely the residue of consultations that occur within the closed circuit.[23] Policy initiatives that require coordination across departments, in the form of pooled information or a sharing of responsibilities, are less likely to happen. In short, closed circuits of policymaking work against the development of a unified policy perspective.

These difficulties led to the creation of the van der Ploeg Commission in 1983 to examine the role of EACs. To combat the closed circuits, the commission proposed elimination of 170 advisory committees whose mandate was confined to a single policy sector, and suggested instead greater reliance on intersectoral committees (van Delden 1993: 161). These recommendations were accepted, and the subsequent reduction of the number of EACs by one-half had the additional advantage of saving time and money in the preparation of legislative proposals. It is noteworthy that the option of abolishing EACs altogether was never considered, for within the Netherlands the very legitimacy of public policy relies on the extent to which social interests are involved in the formulation of policy proposals.

The recent shift toward intersectoral advisory commissions is reminiscent of the corporatist policy process as it originally developed in the first decades after World War II. At that time, the emphasis was also on a few broad advisory bodies rather than a multiplicity of EACs. However, these advisory bodies were restricted to the peak economic organizations of workers and employers, and were also limited to organizations affiliated with one of the pillars. The most important of these consultative bodies are the Foundation of Labor and the Socio-Economic Council.

The Foundation of Labor

The Foundation of Labor *(Stichting van de Arbeid)* is not a corporatist organization in the strict sense because it does not include formal governmental representation. Established in secrecy during World War II with representation of employers, workers, and farm organizations, the Foundation of Labor does have the core corporatist trait of being the site of centralized negotiations between interest-group representatives on matters that have implications for public policy. Employers participating in the Foundation of Labor agreed to collective bargaining with the unions and to the goal of full employment, in exchange for which labor organizations made a no-strike pledge and removed codetermination (labor voice in the management of the firm) from their list of demands (Klein 1980). Wage agreements reached in the Foundation of Labor by representatives of the unions and of employers associations were applied throughout the economy in the first fifteen years after World War II, when the priorities of reconstruction were a bigger factor than market considerations in setting wage rates.

Central coordination of wages through the Foundation of Labor continued with relatively little friction between employers and labor representatives until the early 1960s. The postwar spirit of reconstruction and the development of an extensive welfare state made possible agreement on wage increases that were level with inflation but well below the growth in productivity. By the end of the 1950s, Dutch wages were 20 to 25 percent below those in Belgium and Germany. What workers did not receive in increased wages, however, they received in the form of new programs of social insurance. Similarly, employer acceptance of the payroll taxes that financed new health and retirement programs was facilitated by the guarantee of modest growth in wages and the near-absence of strikes.

Centralized wage bargains like those concluded in the Foundation of Labor were also possible because of widespread belief in the complementarity of interests between social classes, or what the Dutch tellingly call "the social partners." This is to a great extent the legacy of labor organizing by confessional unions, but the attitude has outlasted the era of pillarized union federations. In a survey conducted in the mid-1980s, Adam Szirmai (1988: 319) found that just over half the working class believed that "If [different occupational classes] cooperate, it is to everyone's advantage."[24] Ten percent of Dutch workers believed that "The top class decides what happens in politics and the economy [and this] is as it should be"! Belief in a class-conflict perspective of the kind normally championed by socialists is found in just 15 percent of the Dutch population.

Like the pillar system of social organization more generally, the success of the Foundation of Labor sowed the seeds of its own demise. Viewed from the perspective of economic growth and labor peace, the Foundation of Labor was during its heyday in the 1950s a model of the efficacy of centralized bargaining between employers and employees. And yet the centralized process of wage determination brought with it problems that became steadily more serious. Wage restraint meant high profits and full employment; it also meant labor shortages and eventually a misallocation of labor due to artificially low wages. As Paulette Kurzer (1993: 48–49) points out, "One drawback of the policy of low wages was that it subsidized the least efficient firms and hampered the ability of expanding firms to hire skilled or specialized personnel."

As it became obvious that wages were being artificially depressed, many workers began to question the system. By the end of the 1950s, wage increases had already outpaced price increases by two to one. Union representatives in the Foundation of Labor had an increasingly difficult time guaranteeing the support of their own constituents for the wage agreements reached, and it did not help that union membership was steadily declining.[25]

Several large unauthorized strikes in the early 1960s shattered the postwar labor peace. When employers responded to some of these strikes by paying wages above those agreed in the Foundation of Labor, the centrally guided wage policy fell apart. Union leaders began taking a harder line in the annual negotiations, and wage increases averaged almost 13 percent per year between 1963 and 1965. As wages surged ahead, negotiations in the Foundation of Labor became more laborious. No central agreements were reached between 1964 and 1970, and the government began to take a hand in the negotiations by specifying maximum wage increases.[26] The government was driven to intervene partly because of the linkage of social welfare benefits to private-sector wage movements (see Chapter 7), which meant that as much as 60 percent of the government budget was determined by the outcome of collective bargaining in the private sector (Visser 1990: 211).

Viewed from an international perspective, the Dutch retained a remarkably high level of labor peace even after the breakdown of the central wage negotiation system. In the relatively turmoil-filled years between 1967 and 1976, the Netherlands lost fewer workdays to labor disputes than did Sweden and Germany (two other countries with low levels of labor strife). The Dutch strike rate was barely more than one-twentieth that of the United States!

Though labor conflict remained low by international standards, the Foundation of Labor was no longer able to produce sectoral wage agreements. With the employment crisis in the 1980s, unions once again moderated their wage demands in exchange for a shortened workweek and a commitment to job creation by the employers.[27] However, the era of the central wage bargain has not returned in the form that existed shortly after World War II. Although 75 percent of all private-sector employees are covered by a collective agreement, many of these agreements are negotiated within a particular firm rather than for a sector of the economy. Given the number of very large firms in the Netherlands, this means that there still is a great deal of centralization in the collective bargaining process.[28] Now, however, centralization is driven by lead firms in the economy rather than by a strategic determination of the importance of various sectors for economic growth.[29]

The Socio-Economic Council

The Socio-Economic Council (*Socio-Economische Raad,* or SER) was established in 1950 as a classic tripartite organization in the corporatist mold. It is composed of ten representatives from the unions, ten representatives from employers associations, and ten "Crown members," most of whom are academics with training in business or law.[30] The composition of the council marked a significant shift in Dutch politics. As de Jong (1959: 24) put it, the SER brought with it "the disappearance of the de facto monopoly of access to government by employers and their organizations prior to 1940, replaced by what is in principle an equality of involvement by employees in the political process since 1945."

Between 1950 and 1995, all proposed legislation with significant implications for the health of the economy, labor laws, the distribution of income, and the system of social insurance was by law sent to the SER for advisement. The Second Chamber was also given the right to ask the SER to consider a particular issue, and the SER may of its own volition write an advisory report on any matter it deems important. Early in its existence, the SER formulated five general goals that would inform its policy prescriptions: full employment, economic growth, the distribution of income, equilibrium in the balance of payments, and price stability.

As long as the top civil servants, union leaders, business leaders, and policy experts in the SER were able to reach agreement, their status as representatives of leading organized forces in society lent their views extraordinary weight. As Ken Gladdish (1991: 144) observes, "[The SER's] recommendations, for much of the 1950s and 1960s, had a status which even the cabinet as a whole could not readily contest." The SER was at the core of what came to be known as "the consultation economy," a collaboration between government and the private sector that combined features of a market economy and a command economy.[31]

Until the 1970s, the operations of the SER approximated the corporatist ideal of broadly based central consultation with a spirit of coordination and compromise in the conclusions reached. A survey of SER members by Wazir Singh published in 1972 revealed a great deal of satisfaction with the operation of the council and with its influence. Employer, employee, and Crown members of the council agreed that the SER operated in a collegial fashion to bring out the pros and cons of various policy ideas. They agreed that discussions tended to lead to a convergence of views, and that the most important forces for developing agreement were a spirit of compromise and thoughtful consideration of factors brought up in the discussion. Furthermore, Singh found that SER members were of the unanimous opinion that their advice was highly influential with the ministerial council, parliament, political parties, and interest groups. Even when their policy advice was not taken, according to the SER members, they succeeded in generating a serious discussion of the issue.

Singh's study captured the end of an era. Since the early 1970s the SER has found it more difficult to reach agreement on policy proposals set before it. Frustration grew between the "social partners," and the unions boycotted SER meetings in 1969 and 1973. Between 1977 and 1984 the SER produced a consensus advisory statement on fewer than half the issues it considered (Visser 1990: 233). Failing to reach agreement, the SER offered divided advice or even failed to formulate any response at all.[32] Even when faced in 1989 with a proposal to take control over social insurance implementation away from the unions and employers associations—the same organizations that compose the majority of the SER—the council was unable to formulate an alternative (Cox 1994).

These divisions and delays substantially reduced both the usefulness and the influence of SER advice. As transformation of the Dutch welfare state and labor laws continued in the 1980s and 1990s,[33] the government found itself acting more and more autonomously—without meaningful partnership with the organizations represented in the SER (Scholten 1987). In some major decisions, such as restrictions in the duration of unemployment benefits, the government did not even wait for the SER to complete its deliberations. The final blow was struck in 1995, when the legal requirement that the SER be consulted on pending legislation was abolished.

The decline of the SER's influence is traceable in part to the loss of cohesion in the pillars. When the pillars were internally cohesive, workers and employers were able to reach agreement in part because of the common interests inherent in their mutual pillar affiliation. As the confessional pillars were dismantled, the ability of labor and employer organizations to bridge the class divide was progressively reduced, until the SER was no longer able to prepare unified advisory documents for the government.

A second factor in the loss of SER influence is the proliferation of organized social interests outside the pillar context. By the 1980s the SER—being composed primarily of unions and employer associations—was no longer representative of all the relevant interests in society. As the degree of union organization continued to decline, the very idea that the SER could be representative of society became less plausible. Professionals and service-sector workers are less likely to be unionized and are therefore underrepresented in the SER.[34] Nor is there any representation of consumer interests on the council. Client groups ranging from pension recipients to drug addicts expect to have their own voice in policy (van Goor 1993: 104), but work through EACs rather than in the SER. And although the SER declared in 1989 that it would thenceforth give priority to environmental considerations in its deliberations, this declaration has not been fully persuasive without the direct representation of environmental organizations. In short, the interest-group map for the year 2000 is very different from the interest-group map of 1950, when the SER was created.

With the SER generally divided and sometimes paralyzed, and a growing number of other interest groups clamoring for policy influence, Dutch corporatism has become a more decentralized phenomenon, diffused among many bodies. The number of EACs has mushroomed, and ministers now often consult them in preference to the SER. Consultation of the Dutch central bank *(De Nederlandsche Bank)* has also increased in recent years because of the policy requirements of maintaining the Dutch guilder in the European Monetary Union (Kurzer 1993: 141–151).

Growing complexity in the Dutch corporatist process has, in other words, diminished the influence of any one avenue of corporatist consultation. The proliferation of social groups and venues of corporatist consultation has created new strategic opportunities for ministers seeking to negotiate the policy development process with minimum damage to their own preferences. This phenomenon had already been witnessed, for example, in the mid-1960s, when Minister of Social Affairs Gerard Veldkamp consulted with organizations in the medical field on his ideas for a new disability program, bypassing an SER that he knew would be unwilling to accept the kind of program expansion he desired.

This phenomenon is similar to the "venue shopping" described by Frank Baumgartner and Bryan Jones. As they point out, "where venues change, the terms of the [policy] debate may be altered" (1993: 38). The existence of multiple venues in which a given policy could be formulated creates a strategic opportunity for the shopper, who may select from among them the venue most likely to secure the "right" outcome. Venue shopping in the United States is carried out by interest groups seeking the best political forum to air their views. In the Dutch case, however, it is the government that engages in venue shopping. As Robert Cox (1993: 131) points out, government officials can choose between "bipartite institutions in which state officials had no representation, tripartite institutions supervised by ministries, and tripartite institutions on which independent councillors, rather than the state, [serve] as the third party. Without a clear hierarchy among the various bodies, reform-minded ministers [move] from one to the other searching for support for their proposals" (Cox 1993: 131). Paradoxically, the very multiplicity of consultative venues through which the government may seek policy advice from social groups—combined with the fact that the government is no longer legally required to consult any given organization—increases the ability of the government to control the policymaking process.

The Unwritten Rules of Policymaking

We have to this point examined the range of governmental institutions and societal groups involved in the policy process, as well as the formal rules of consultation and mutual influence that govern their interactions. The formal institutions of Dutch governance have had an exceptionally high degree of continuity throughout the twentieth century, interrupted only by World War II. The most significant change in the policy process in that time has been the proliferation of external advisory commissions and the decline of confessional domination through the corporatist consultation process. When we turn to the informal patterns of behavior—the unwritten rules—that govern Dutch policymaking, we see a more fundamental shift.

All polities have an elite political culture that shapes policymaking or, as Arend Lijphart (1975) has called it, a set of "rules of the game." The left-hand column of Table 6.1 summarizes the rules of elite behavior during the period of pillarization, as described by Lijphart. These rules reflect the domination of pillar elites over the policy process, as well as their desire to prevent escalation of political differences into a broader ideological conflict. The rules concerning "businesslike" politics (rule 1), tolerance (rule 2), and depoliticization (rule 3) are really orientations to policymaking, reflecting a determination to strip issues of symbolic divisiveness and find a compromise acceptable to representatives of all pillars. The rules of summit diplomacy (rule 4), secrecy (rule 5), and "the government governs" (rule 6) specify a means of accomplishing those policy goals, namely by having the ministerial council operate with relative autonomy from the Second

TABLE 6.1   Rules of the Game in Three Eras

The Pillarized Era	*The Polarized Era*	*Depoliticized Competition*
1. Businesslike politics	Unmasking establishment; critical ideology	Businesslike politics
2. Agree to disagree	Contestation and conflict	Agree to disagree
3. Depoliticization	Politicization	Symbolic politicization
4. Summit diplomacy	Grassroots autonomy	Selective elite consultation
5. Secrecy	Openness	Selective openness
6. The government governs	Assertation of parliamentary power against a government and civil service believed to be too powerful	Governing parties rule; dualism replaced by shared governance between cabinet and Second Chamber
7. Proportionality	Party polarization and majority formation	Proportionality

SOURCES: For rules of the pillarized era, see Lijphart (1975); for the polarized era, see Daalder (1974); for the era of depoliticized competition, see van Praag (1993).

Chamber. Finally, the rule of proportionality (rule 7) is a statement of expected outcomes. The expectation of proportionality allowed pillar leaders to count on a share of governmental support proportionate to their strength in the population. A typical policy based on proportionality was the decision to give public funds to religious and secular schools alike based on enrollment.

As the pillars declined in salience for the Dutch public and as the political parties grew more competitive with each other, the rules of the game characteristic of the pillar period came under challenge. We have already seen in Chapter 4 that there was an increase in the independence of voters from political parties in the 1970s, and that this was accompanied by polarization between the political parties themselves. Weakened party attachments and increased citizen participation wore through the insulation that once shielded elite actions from close public scrutiny. In the midst of these developments, elite consensus on the pillar-era rules of the game was shattered.

The result was substitution of a new set of rules of the game that were in many respects virtually the opposite of those of the pillar era. Hans Daalder (1974) summarizes these rules as described in the middle column of Table 6.1. The three rules concerning the style of decisionmaking were inverted: from businesslike considerations to ideological thinking, from accepting disagreement to heightening conflicts, from depoliticization of issues to politicization. The three rules concerning primacy of the government in policymaking were countered with a demand for openness and power at the grass roots. Perhaps the most significant departure in the rules was rejection of proportionality in policy outcomes. Rather than ensuring that governmental policy treated all major social groups on an evenhanded basis, the new rule was to use party polarization as a means of forming a majority coalition in the parliament. That majority would then push through the policies it favored without regard to other social groups now relegated to the minority. Efforts by a coalition of leftist parties in the 1970s to achieve a national parliamentary majority never bore fruit, though at the local level many "mirror colleges" (representative of all parties on the municipal council) were replaced by "program colleges" (composed of a mere majority of parties and put together to pursue a specific policy program).[35]

The pillar-era rules of the game were never rejected by all political parties. A study of the beliefs of middle-level party activists in 1978 showed that the new rules of ideological polarization, openness, and majoritarian policymaking were supported by most local leaders of the Labor and Radical parties, but that the pillar-era rules still had substantial support among local leaders of the Christian Democrats and the Liberals (Rochon 1982b). As Arend Lijphart (1975: 207) comments, the PvdA had by the mid-1970s "essentially become an anti-accommodation party," one that rejected the pillar-era rules of the game. With the decline of the pillars and the development of party polarization, Dutch politics became a game played by two sets of rules, one for the left and one for the right.

Eventually, the rules of the pillar era were reasserted, as summarized by Philip van Praag (1993) in the right-hand column of Table 6.1. A series of governing coalitions including the Christian Democrats and Liberals under the leadership of Ruud Lubbers in the 1980s reestablished the businesslike orientation to politics that had been characteristic of the pillar era. Political parties continued to profile themselves with ideological clarity in order to offer choices to an electorate still inclined to shift its allegiances from election to election (see Chapter 4). But van Praag characterizes this as a symbolic politicization, lacking the bitterness of party disputes a decade earlier. Robert Cox (1993) adds that party groups in the Second Chamber continued to polarize on such issues as reform of the welfare state, while the ministerial council became increasingly consensual and businesslike in its orientation to those same issues.

The secrecy and elite domination of the political process during the pillar era could hardly be restored, but there was at least a partial restoration of elite rule as the wave of protest movements and party polarization receded. One significant shift in the post-polarization rules of the game is that it is no longer the government that rules, but rather the governing parties. As noted in Chapter 5, the dominance of the ministerial council in developing legislation has been replaced by a more intensive relationship between ministers and parliamentary parties of the governing coalition. Despite the majoritarian orientation of the policy process, though, proportionality has been reasserted as the guiding rule for many policy decisions. The policymaking environment is more competitive than in the pillar era, but also less politicized than in the era of polarization. We might, then, call the current period one of "depoliticized competition."[36]

There have been three eras of policymaking in the Netherlands over the last half century, each with distinctive rules of the game. Clearly then, it is possible for the policy process to change quite drastically without alteration in the formal institutional structure. Crucial to such changes in the rules of the game are the behavior and mutual expectations of political leaders. At the same time, the politics of accommodation has been a hardy survivor in the elite political culture. The polarization rules were never completely accepted, but were instead adopted mainly by the left parties and ultimately on a temporary basis. When the polarizing strategy of the left failed to generate the majority needed to take power, the left parties returned to an updated version of the old rules.

The ultimate significance of the unwritten rules of policymaking is that these extra-constitutional aspects of the policy process affect the way policies are developed and the kinds of policies that are possible. To see even more clearly how the policy process differed between these three eras, we will take a look at the nature of political leadership during the hegemony of the pillars, in the period of party polarization, and in the present era of depoliticized competition.

A Tale of Three Social Democrats: Drees, den Uyl, and Kok

We saw in the last chapter that the role of the minister-president is primarily one of coordination and consultation: holding the governing parties together in the ministerial council and holding the council as a whole to the lines of the governmental program. The position of minister-president can be a powerful one, but it does not have the formal powers enjoyed by the German chancellor and the British prime minister. Rather, the office of minister-president is very much what the incumbent makes of it—and what his colleagues in the ministerial council allow him to make of it. For this reason, the style of governing employed by a given minister-president makes an excellent prism through which to examine the policy process at that point in time.

In this section we will look at the styles of three social democratic ministers-president. They happen to be the only three Labor Party leaders to have served as minister-president during the twentieth century, and the fact that each served in a different "rules" era creates an opportunity to examine the impact of the elite political culture on leadership styles. The first is Willem Drees, who headed three consecutive coalition governments between 1948 and 1958, during which time he became synonymous in the minds of many Dutch people with the postwar reconstruction. The second is J. M. "Joop" den Uyl, whose five-party coalition between 1973 and 1977 was an expression of the high tide of party polarization. The third leader is Willem "Wim" Kok, minister-president beginning in 1994, whose "purple government" with D66 and the Liberal Party culminated the return to a less ideological style and at the same time ended nearly a century of confessional party participation in government.

Willem Drees and the Politics of the Pillars

In 1904, an 18-year-old SDAP party member named Willem Drees attended a Congress of the Socialist International in Amsterdam. He was captivated by Jean Jaurès, the French socialist leader who argued, unsuccessfully to the congress but powerfully to Drees, that socialists must join coalitions with nonsocialists in order to participate in government. "In that moment," writes H. A. van Wijnen (1984), "the first year socialist Drees became a social democrat."[37] By World War II, Drees had risen from a seat on the municipal council in The Hague to SDAP party group leader in the Second Chamber. During the war he was interned by the Germans at Buchenwald for his political activities. Released after a year because of ill health, Drees promptly became a coordinator of resistance activities within the Netherlands and a communications link between the resistance and the government-in-exile in London.

Drees was 62 years old when he first became minister-president in 1948. He was fabled for his extensive knowledge of every facet of Dutch government and political history. When a topic came up for discussion in the ministerial council, Drees could cite from memory the current policy in that area, the considerations that had led to adoption of that policy, and the changes in conditions that might bear on a reconsideration of the policy. Ruud Lubbers, whose lengthy service as minister-president made him the 1980s version of Drees, liked to tell the story about how Drees would draft a memo summarizing discussion of some issues in the ministerial council *before* the council meeting took place. Drees would produce the notes at the end of the debate and ask if they reflected the views that had been expressed. They did.[38] His grasp of budget detail was particularly amazing to his ministerial colleagues. In the midst of budget discussions in the ministerial council, Drees once drew attention to a subsidy for an association of harmonica players. As one of his ministers later reported, Drees "approved of this form of leisure activity, but believed that the musicians could pursue their inexpensive hobby without government subsidy."

As a social democrat, Drees advocated nationalization of some key industries and extensive government supervision of others. He also supported a heavily redistributive tax system (Cox 1995). And yet the three Drees governments did none of these things, instead laying the basis for a system of income guarantees that rested on a social insurance principle rather than on redistribution of wealth. In place of government control over industry, Drees oversaw establishment of the SER and other institutions of corporatist consultation with employers and unions. In foreign policy, Drees accepted the KVP's hard line against Indonesian independence and agreed to send Dutch troops in 1947 and 1948 in a vain effort to put down the independence movement, despite significant opposition within his own parliamentary party group (Lijphart 1966: 251–257). As Robert Cox (1995: 114) points out, "Drees's role in the conflict gave him the dubious honor of being one of the few socialist prime ministers to fight a colonial war."

The reason for these compromises, of course, was that the PvdA was not in a position to carry out policy plans on its own. The Labor Party received about 30 percent of the vote in postwar elections and had only one-third of the seats in Drees's first cabinet. The three governments over which Drees presided between 1948 and 1958 contained social democrats, Catholics, Protestants, and, for the first four years, the Liberals. True to the spirit of accommodation politics, Drees's three governments rested on parliamentary majorities of between 73 and 87 percent of the Second Chamber. At the core of these coalitions was the "Roman-Red" alliance between Labor and the Catholic People's Party.

The Roman-Red coalition proved to be both durable (lasting until 1958, when the final Drees government broke up and the KVP began to govern with the Liberal Party) and fertile in transforming the role of the Dutch government in society. What makes this accomplishment so remarkable is that it was not based on a close ideological proximity between Labor and the KVP. On the contrary, the two parties were bitter rivals, with a rivalry that grew in intensity while Drees was in office. The Labor Party, capitalizing on Drees's popularity and claiming credit for the progress of the country between 1948 and 1952, gained seats at the expense of the KVP in the 1952 elections. These losses led directly to the 1954 *Mandement* of the Dutch bishops, in which Catholic supporters of the PvdA were urged to return to the KVP or be at risk for their souls. With these voters at stake, the two parties—by then coalition partners for eight years—waged a campaign in 1956 that is still remembered as bitter and hate-filled. One pamphlet produced for the KVP implied that a Labor Party victory would lead to Catholic churches being sent up in flames. From the PvdA side came suggestions of exploitative child factory labor in the southern, Catholic part of the country. Acts of sabotage against each other's campaign meetings were reported in the weeks leading up to the election (Koole 1992: 359). D. J. Elzinga and G. Voerman (1992: 99) conclude that "Other themes were pushed to the background by this 'propaganda violence.'" Both sides characterized the election as a choice between the two party leaders: "Drees or Romme."

The campaign was, by the standards of any era, a bitter one, but the election itself was something of a standoff. Both the PvdA and the KVP maintained their preelection strengths. What happened next, though, was truly remarkable, for the Roman-Red coalition simply continued as though nothing had happened. As Arend Lijphart (1975: 178) observes, "Both [parties] depicted the contest as one between their top leaders: 'Drees or Romme.' . . . But the two parties patched up their differences and entered the new cabinet together. The voters were asked to choose between the two, but they got 'Drees *and* Romme.'"

Twenty years later the effects of bitter election campaigns were carried over into the process of coalition formation, but in the era of the pillarized rules of the game it was understood that there was a difference between campaign slogans and the business of governing. The fact that there was still a clear dualism between the ministerial council and the Second Chamber greatly helped in maintaining the distinction. Ministers in those years did not meet regularly with the party groups in the Second Chamber, and in fact it seems there were relatively few bilateral meetings between ministers themselves. Jelle Zijlstra, Drees's minister of economic affairs and later minister-president himself, reports that Drees may have called him on the phone about once per month—their business was conducted in the weekly meetings of the ministerial council (Joustra and van Venetië 1993: 18–19). By handling the business of government collectively, party divisions could be minimized and the collective viewpoint of the government could be developed. Drees himself expressed it with the words "I am a socialist, but first I am minister-president of the country." This phrase captures well both the nonpartisan spirit and the independence of ministerial councils in the era of accommodation politics.

Joop den Uyl and the Politics of Polarization

Competition between the PvdA and the KVP for the votes of free-thinking Catholics in 1956 was just a skirmish compared to the campaigns of the late 1960s and early 1970s. Presented with the opportunity to attract working-class voters previously tied to the confessional pillars, as well as the votes of the newly enfranchised postwar generation, the Labor Party went on an ideological offensive to profile itself against the other political parties. In those heady days, it even seemed possible that the "progressive alliance" of Labor, the Radicals, and D66 could win a majority of the seats in the Second Chamber, thereby putting themselves in a position to dispense altogether with the rules of accommodation that had been developed between the pillars.

The leader of the Labor Party in this era was J. M. "Joop" den Uyl, an economist by training and a socialist by temperament, who rose to party leadership in 1967 in part because of his early grasp of the potential of social democracy to unite the classic socialism of the working class with the new left ideas of the postwar generation. Den Uyl may have been that rarest of political animals: an ideologically-oriented policy wonk. Having been director of the party's research bureau between 1949 and 1962, den Uyl was a sponge for economic and social statistics and was always intrigued by the details of crafting policy solutions to particular problems (Wolinetz 1995). Arendo Joustra and Erik van Venetië (1993: 39) report that den Uyl kept the current volume of figures from the Central Statistical Bureau at his elbow and loved to cite figures from it. At the same time, he enjoyed a good argument over the broad directions of policy. One civil servant who was a policy adviser to three consecutive ministers-president said of den Uyl that "He liked you more to the degree you went to him and said his ideas were utter nonsense." Joustra and van Venetië (1993: 21) conclude that "Joop den Uyl . . . had a political mission: reform the world, beginning with the Netherlands."[39]

Den Uyl presided over a coalition of five political parties, including the Radical Party on the far left, the Labor Party, D66, and two of the confessional parties of that era, the Catholic People's Party and the Anti-Revolutionary Party. Formation of the coalition took 164 days, a Dutch record to that time. Most of the time was spent coaxing the party leaders simply to negotiate with each other, and particularly to overcome the antipathy that had developed between the Labor Party and the Catholic People's Party in the mid-1960s over the breakup of a governing coalition.[40] When the government was finally formed, the two confessional parties declared their "tolerance" of the coalition rather than their full allegiance to it.

The rules of the game during the era of party polarization were not conducive either to forming a government or to implementing its program. The ministerial council was said to have "rolled out of its meetings and continued fighting in the street" (Timmermans and Bakema 1990: 176). This is just colorful language, but there appears to have been plenty of disagreement in council meetings. The ministerial council met regularly till deep into the night because of the coalition's ideological diversity and the range of policy targets that the government sought to address. There were repeated threats of a cabinet crisis over issues ranging from water control efforts in the Oosterschelde, to government support for abortion clinics, to the development of nuclear energy at home and the export of nuclear reactors abroad. Remarkably, though, the government survived to within a few months of its maximum length of four years.

The era of party polarization was also not conducive to easy relations between the ministerial council and the Second Chamber. Although den Uyl favored centralization of decisionmaking in the ministerial council, the era of polarization was the period in which detailed consultation between ministers and their party groups began. With four party leaders in the cabinet, the custom developed of reviewing the council agenda with parliamentary party groups prior to council meetings. Even this degree of consultation, though, did not guarantee a happy fate for the government's legislative proposals. In a study of the legislation that emanated from the Ministry of Internal Affairs during the den Uyl government, H. M. Franssen (1982) found that major reforms were largely stymied. Constitutional amendments were proposed to directly elect the *formateur*, establish a district system for Second Chamber elections, elect the First Chamber directly, and set up four super-regional governments. All were defeated by a shifting coalition of opposition parties and defectors from the governing parties. Of the thirty-one legislative initiatives from this ministry that did receive approval during the den Uyl government, nineteen were amended, seven of which significantly so. Franssen concluded that the den Uyl government survived the life of its mandate thanks to adroit use of shifting majorities, at times including the coalition parties and at other times losing the confessional parties but picking up support from the Liberals on issues related to personal freedom.

The era of party polarization was not, then, a period of stalemate. But it was a period in which the rules of the political game became more combative, more visible to the public, and hence more difficult to harness to the development of a successful program of legislation. As D.F.J. Bosscher (1987: 59) notes, Joop den

Uyl personified the core traits of the era—"the openness, the polarization, and a socialism that reflected the ethos of that energetic period."

Wim Kok and the Restoration of Accommodation

"A pragmatist. A politically talented statesman. Manager of 'Netherlands Incorporated.' . . . A team leader and bridge builder. There is in the end just one qualification he does *not* have: idealist." These words by Niels Rood (1989: 8) were written in praise of Ruud Lubbers, but they could equally well have been written of Willem "Wim" Kok, who has completed the restoration of pragmatism and compromise (begun by Lubbers) as the means by which policies are negotiated.

Wim Kok came to the leadership of the Labor Party through the union movement—a career path more common at the beginning of the twentieth century than at the end. His first contacts with the inner circles of power came in the late 1970s when he was chair of the federation of socialist unions, the NVV.[41] During wage negotiations and other policy discussions in the SER, Kok was known as a particularly tough-minded individual for his defense of social insurance programs in an era when government spending was being trimmed. Although he clashed repeatedly with Ruud Lubbers, then minister of economic affairs in the van Agt government, Lubbers characterized Kok as "open and business-like, savvy and expert" (Joustra and van Venetië 1993: 62). The choice of words is telling, for a businesslike and expert approach to politics was central to the rules of the game in the pillar era, and was about to become so again.

Kok became party leader of the PvdA upon den Uyl's retirement, and promptly moved to mend the breech between the Labor Party and the CDA that had opened with the fall of the den Uyl government in 1977 and the failure to renew the Labor–Christian Democrat coalition later that year. He was a coauthor of the 1988 party report advocating that the PvdA abandon the polarization strategy of the previous fifteen years (Wolinetz 1993: 104). In 1989 the Labor Party entered a coalition with the Christian Democrats, and Kok became the vice minister-president and minister of finance in the third Lubbers government. The Lubbers-Kok team disagreed on a range of policy issues relating to the continued drive to reduce public expenditures, and there were reports of growing friction between Lubbers and Kok personally. Kok's embrace of financial reform of the social insurance system also led to a major demonstration of union members against the government and a wave of resignations from the Labor Party, whose members nearly mandated an end to the coalition in a special party congress. In other words, abandoning polarization for the compromises involved in government participation was not easy for Wim Kok personally or for the Labor Party leadership more generally. Even so, Kok and Lubbers held the coalition together for its full term by developing the habit of checking informally with each other on policy ideas. The extensive consultation that developed between Lubbers and Kok recalls the government-centered decisionmaking pattern that was dominant during the period of accommodation, before the polarization era.

In the early 1990s, Kok began preparing the way for what would become the purple government by stating publicly that the PvdA was open to an alliance with the Liberals. This openness came to fruition in 1994, when the PvdA, D66, and the VVD established the purple government with Wim Kok as minister-president. It was the first time since 1918 that a coalition had formed without confessional party participation.

There was a great deal on which Labor and the Liberals had to "agree to disagree" in order to make the purple government work. Like Drees before him, Kok focused the coalition on those issues that united it, specifically a commitment to job creation, moderate wage increases, and restraints on social spending.[42] Although the PvdA-VVD relationship was founded on pragmatism and compromise, it did not represent a restoration of the earlier era of accommodation between the pillars. For one thing, the Second Chamber continues to be deeply involved in the preparation of policy proposals, and the ministers of all three coalition parties have had to work assiduously to develop parliamentary support for their proposals. "Wim Kok is energetic in his advance preparations. Much more than his predecessors, Kok wants to nail down the PvdA party group on all topics before they formally arise" (Joustra and van Venetië 1993: 80). The habit of extensive consultation with parliamentary party groups developed in the period of polarization still remains, though the experience of the purple government in its first five years has been that independence of the parliamentary party groups (particularly the Liberals) continues the recent pattern of Second Chamber assertiveness.

The decade of the 1990s has been a period of international economic constraint and domestic political restraint. Wim Kok has succeeded as a leader in this decade because he understands the former and embodies the latter. Kok's most remarkable achievement thus far as leader of the purple government may have been that after four years of the coalition, employers and Liberal Party supporters preferred him as minister-president to the leader of their own party![43]

"Sound and sober" read the headline profile of Kok in the conservative newspaper *NRC Handelsblad* on the day the formation of the second purple government was announced. The article went on to say that if you ask Wim Kok about his vision of the future, "you get a story about train lines, bridges and neighborhoods. A story about equal opportunity, justice, security. Ideals that politicians of all stripes can share."[44] Such ideals are the mortar of coalition politics in the era of depoliticized competition.

Conclusion

Willem Drees, Joop den Uyl, and Wim Kok governed in different political contexts, shaped in each case by the state of the public's engagement in politics, the nature of party competition, and the elite rules of the game characteristic of their eras. In the pillarized period of the politics of accommodation, there were certainly intensely partisan electoral campaigns, exemplified by the competition between the PvdA and the KVP for working-class Catholic votes in 1956. But those struggles were not allowed to interfere with the business of governing, and the pragmatic collaboration between Willem Drees and C.P.M. Romme continued after the election.

The breakdown of the pillars liberated many Dutch voters from a standing political choice based on religion and social class, and opened up the possibility of party competition. The revised rules of the game in the era of party polarization were a strategic choice made by the secular parties to take advantage of the new competitive possibilities in the electorate. The three parties of the progressive alliance (PvdA, D66, PPR) sought to build a majority bloc of parties on the left and to govern without inclusion of the confessional and Liberal parties.

It turned out that building a majority alliance was not possible, both because of the balanced distribution of the Dutch electorate between left and right and because of the continued vitality of the Christian Democrats. Moreover, the experience of the den Uyl government illustrated the pitfalls of the polarization strategy. It was difficult to obtain approval in the ministerial council for the wide-ranging policy goals championed by Labor, the Radicals, and D66. Though most of those goals were eventually articulated in legislative proposals set before the Second Chamber, it proved impossible to shepherd them through a parliamentary body that had blasted through the wall of dualism without having yet developed the party discipline that would sustain governments beginning in the 1980s.

The present era of depoliticized competition represents a new synthesis built upon a strategic climate that is unchanged from the period of polarization. The electorate remains flexible in its loyalties, and ready to judge parties based on their performance in the immediately preceding parliament. The Second Chamber remains activist in its approach to policymaking, eschewing dualism for an extensive role in the development of legislative proposals.

At the same time, party leaders now know that this flexibility will not lead to the development of a majority party bloc. Collaboration across the great divides of social democratic, confessional, and liberal must continue. This knowledge has restored the pragmatic, businesslike approach to politics that had for so long been a hallmark of Dutch politics. Party leaders continue to differ from each other on policy questions, but these differences are now taken simply as a starting point from which pragmatic bargains must be struck. Wim Kok was schooled in the Socio-Economic Council in the art of getting as much as possible without making an enemy of your counterparts on the other side of the fence. He exemplifies the trait, common to most successful Dutch leaders, of being willing to put all issues on the table for negotiation.

It is one of the great riddles of history whether Willem Drees, Joop den Uyl, and Wim Kok could have risen to the leadership of their parties in an era whose rules of the game were less suited to their respective personalities and convictions. One hint may lie in the later career of Willem Drees, who lived for thirty years after his retirement from politics in 1958 at 72 years of age. Mr. Drees became a respected elder statesman and an occasional adviser to the Labor Party during the 1960s. But the polarization strategy adopted later that decade so distressed Drees that in 1971 he resigned from the party he had helped found twenty-five years earlier!

The corporatist process of interest-group consultation and the informal rules by which political leaders reach policy agreements are all part of the general template of the policy process. Of course, the real purpose of any policy process is to arrive at decisions that move the political life of the country forward. In the next two chapters we will look at two substantive areas of policy. The development and continued modification of the welfare state will be the subject of Chapter 7, and foreign policy will be covered in Chapter 8.

NOTES

1. Bovend'Eert and Kummeling (1991: 230) point out that constitutional changes are often voted on just before a regularly scheduled election. In the subsequent campaign, parties focus on their usual issues and constituencies rather than using the election as a referendum on the proposed constitutional amendment. This makes the provision for dissolving parliament between the two votes less effective than it might otherwise be. Even so, a controversial amendment would likely lead to an altered party composition of the new Second Chamber, which would then decline to pass the proposed amendment on its second reading.

2. The deciding vote, cast by Senator Hans Wiegel of the VVD, caused the fall of the second purple coalition (of Labor, D66 and the Liberals) because it rejected a piece of legislation that D66 considered a cornerstone of its program. This was the first time that the First Chamber had caused a government to fall, though it did so only because the government chose to regard this measure as a question of confidence.

3. In fact, Lijphart (1984a: 215–220) finds the Netherlands to be something of a mixed case in institutional terms—predominantly a consensus democracy but with such majoritarian features as a strong central government, a powerful cabinet rooted in a parliamentary majority, and weak bicameralism due to the relative impotence of the First Chamber.

4. Delft City Council Minutes, 1973, pages 369–370.

5. See Chapter 7 for further discussion of social welfare policy and the SCP.

6. In recent years there have been complaints that the growth and employment projections of the Central Planning Bureau are too conservative, giving employers an unfair edge in bargaining over contracts. Despite that concern, political parties routinely ask the CPB to assess the cost and the growth implications of their platforms, and these evaluations play a prominent role in electoral campaigns. For details of the CPB, see de Vries (1978: 102–108), Griffiths (1980b), van Vught (1993), and the essays in Dutt and Costa (1985).

7. See for example Eldersveld et al. (1981: 179–184). Although the Netherlands remains strikingly consensual in its policy process, it stands out from other countries less today than it did prior to the 1970s. See Lijphart (1989) and Mair (1994).

8. I am indebted to the detailed account of the Dutch parliamentary system in Bovend'Eert and Kummeling (1991) for the material in this section.

9. Although the ministerial council and the bureaucracy dominate legislative initiatives, the idea for the draft law may come from interest groups, from members of the States General, from the judiciary, or from international organizations like the European Union.

10. Until recently for example, the Socio-Economic Council (SER) was consulted on all legislation dealing with social and economic regulation. See the discussion of the SER later in this chapter.

11. Since the Council of State is consulted after the ministerial council has given its preliminary approval to the proposal, only some dire flaw will prompt ministers to revisit the process of pulling together political and social interests behind the draft. The Council of State is consulted so late in the process of policy development because it was once an advisory body to the monarch, charged with submitting its opinion only on proposals already passed in the ministerial council. The king could then decide whether to submit the proposal for consideration by the States General. This provision added to the power of the Council of State in the days of a stronger monarch, but it diminishes that power today since the monarch must automatically transmit to the Second Chamber all proposals submitted by the ministerial council.

12. Despite the common emphasis on central wage negotiations, definitions of corporatism are invariably broader in scope. Schmitter's (1979: 13) classic definition of corporatism stresses interest representation that is "singular, compulsory, noncompetitive, hierarchically ordered, . . . recognized or licensed (if not created) by the state, and granted a deliberate representational monopoly within their respective categories" of policy. For a history of corporatism in the Netherlands, see Albeda and ten Hove (1986).

13. De Jong (1959: 14). The effort was not successful, as child labor was banned in 1874.

14. A junior minister for corporatist reform was appointed in 1948, and a minister for corporatist reform joined the cabinet from 1952 to 1956 (Andeweg 1988: 131).

15. See Chapter 3 for details of the rise of the pillars and their views of the proper role of government.

16. Under pluralism, invitations are self-generated: The interest group itself decides to try to influence legislation. Not all interest groups will have equal influence, but all can participate. This makes pluralism more adaptive in the representation of new groups than are corporatist systems of policy bargaining.

17. For example, late in the pillar era (1963), nineteen current or former union officials were members of the 150-seat Second Chamber. Most larger parties still today reserve some of their parliamentary seats for specialists in a particular policy area, the so-called quality seats *(kwaliteitszetels)*. These policy specialists often come from social organizations active in that area of policy.

18. Another phrase sometimes used to describe these shifts in the corporatist process is "meso-corporatism," meaning corporatism that does not involve peak associations of labor and employers. See Cawson (1985).

19. "External" in this context means that more than 50 percent of the commission's members are not government employees.

20. Cited in Cramer (1989: 115–116). The Dutch environmental movement ultimately bifurcated, with one wing involved in consultation with government while other organizations focused more on direct action and public education (Cramer 1989; Jamison et al. 1990: chapter 4).

186   *The Policy Process*

21. For this reason, crisis policymaking in the Netherlands has a much more centralized and less consultative character. See the case studies of crisis decisionmaking in Rosenthal (1986).

22. *"Verkokering"* is literally the segmentation of policy into separate "tubes." See van Vught (1993).

23. See also Koppenjan et al. (1987: 14–21).

24. A further 23 percent believed that the interests of the different social classes only "sometimes" clash.

25. Only the printing industry has a closed shop in the Netherlands, so membership in a union is nearly always voluntary. The proportion of the labor force that belongs to a union has declined sharply in the postwar period, from a high of 44 percent in 1951 to just 29 percent in 1996, after hitting a low of 25 percent in the 1980s. The shift to a service economy accounts for part of this decline, but there has also been a decline in membership in sectors of the economy that were once highly organized. This is, of course, yet another manifestation of the disappearance of the pillars.

26. Between 1972 and 1982, central agreement in the Foundation of Labor was reached only twice, and the government set wage limits eight times.

27. See Chapter 7 for details.

28. Ninety percent of all Dutch firms employ less than ten workers, while three percent of firms employ half the labor force. See Kurzer (1993: 109, 114).

29. Centrally reached agreements cover wages and set guidelines for working hours. These central agreements are augmented by local bargaining within specific plants on other aspects of working conditions, training, and employee consultation (Visser 1990: 229).

30. The head of the Dutch central bank is automatically one of the crown members of the SER. Employer representatives are distributed among the employers associations for large enterprises, small businesses, agriculture, trade, and finance. The labor representatives come from the largest union federations. Employers, unions, and the Crown each had fifteen representatives when the SER was founded, but the number was reduced to ten in 1996 as part of the general downgrading of the SER in favor of other forms of corporatist consultation.

31. See Scholten (1968), Albeda and ten Hove (1986: 110–111), and Visser (1989).

32. The longest lag in replying to a request for advice was the seventeen-year delay in responding to the minister of social affairs regarding a proposed reorganization of the social insurance program.

33. See Chapter 7 for details on reform of the welfare state and labor market.

34. This problem was only partly mitigated by admission of the Union of White Collar and Senior Staff (VHP, representing about 9 percent of all union members) to the SER in 1977 (Visser 1990: 200–201; Visser and Hemerijck 1997: 83–84).

35. See Chapter 5 for details.

36. Van Praag (1993: 173) also notes that two new "rules" have been added in the postpolarization era. First, governing coalitions are no longer changed without dissolving the parliament and holding new elections. This rule is an informal understanding that resulted from public discontent with a series of coalition changes in the mid-1960s. Second, the largest governing party now provides the minister-president. This latter rule has been observed consistently for several decades, though this is so only because the leader of the largest party has always wanted to be minister-president.

37. Quoted from book jacket.

38. Cited in Joustra and van Venetië (1993: 123).

39. This is a play on the slogan of the Interchurch Peace Council (IKV) in the 1980s, which sought to "Rid the world of nuclear weapons, beginning with the Netherlands."

40. The Cals government broke up in 1966 in the so-called Night of Schmelzer, named for the KVP leader who withdrew support for the cabinet and caused it to fall. This proved to be a watershed event in Dutch politics, alienating the Catholic union movement and resulting in informal agreement that any breakup of a government must be followed by new parliamentary elections.

41. The NVV later joined with the federation of Catholic unions to form the Federation of Dutch Unions, or FNV, which Kok also chaired. See Rochon (1984) for an account of the formation of the FNV.

42. See Chapter 7 for details of these policies, collectively known as the "Dutch model."

43. *InterNetKrant,* February 24, 1997, page 3; January 16, 1998, page 3.

44. *NRC Handelsblad,* "W. Kok: Degelijk en sober," July 30, 1998, page 3.

7

THE WELFARE STATE

The political economy of the Netherlands in the sixteenth and seventeenth centuries offers a great deal of support for those who believe in a link between minimal government and economic growth. The unanimity rule of the States General in the Republic of Seven United Provinces meant that the scope of central government remained confined to the necessities of military defense during the Eighty Years War. The provinces and the leading towns largely governed themselves, and their ruling councils were dominated by the merchant class. The republic flourished, both economically and culturally.

The role of the government in steering the economy is very different today. The constitution assigns to the central government responsibility for guaranteeing economic security, health care, and education to every citizen, as well as for maintaining employment and the economic welfare of the people. This means, of necessity, that the government has developed into a welfare state. As Jan van Deth (1992: 34) comments, "a welfare state is a constitutional order [*rechtsstaat*] in which the government explicitly strives to better the welfare and well-being of the citizenry, in addition to guaranteeing their [political] freedom and equality. That requires the government to intervene in the economy whenever employment, inflation or the distribution of welfare suffers."

The Netherlands has become widely known for being one of those countries that, like Sweden, has a particularly extensive and generous welfare state. As we will see in this chapter, the Dutch welfare state is committed to abolishing poverty and to buffering the population against the risks of unemployment and sickness. Although the economy is decidedly capitalist on the production side, with full rights of private property, the welfare system gives the distribution of incomes something of a socialist tinge. All people are expected to work to their capabilities, but incomes have been made partially independent of the job one does—or indeed whether one works at all.

As with other aspects of politics and society, the Dutch welfare state has been marked by extensive international influences. Policymakers patterned their retirement and disability insurance programs for workers (passed in 1913) on the German model created by Bismarck. In postwar extensions of the welfare system to include retirement pensions and health care, the Dutch borrowed from the British (Beveridge) model of universal coverage. The system of financing social insurance through payroll contributions was adapted from the social security program in the United States. International influences even account, indirectly, for the scope of the Dutch welfare state. David Cameron (1978) and Peter Katzenstein (1985) have argued that economies open to trade develop large welfare states in order to cushion the workforce against the vagaries of international markets. This pattern certainly fits the Netherlands, which is exceptionally dependent on trade and which has one of the most extensive welfare states in the world.

Despite these international influences, the welfare state in the Netherlands is nonetheless distinctive to that country. This is particularly true in the extent of religious influence on both the growth and the organization of social insurance programs. In contrast to the welfare state in Sweden, which was the product of social democratic thought, social democracy in the Netherlands had only a supportive role compared to the dominant influence of the confessional pillars and particularly the Catholic People's Party. While the Swedish welfare state is actually run by the state, in the Netherlands private organizations—many of them originally rooted in the confessional pillars—dominate the provision of social services. And while the corporatist policy process played a significant role in Sweden as the means by which key social welfare policies were negotiated, in the Netherlands corporatism actually impeded development of the welfare state.

The net effect of these distinctive elements has been to make the Dutch welfare state organizationally complex and relatively slow to develop. Indeed, until the 1960s the Netherlands was a welfare-state laggard, comparable to the United States and Japan. Rapid growth of the welfare state began only in the late 1950s, not long before corporatist institutions started to break down. Once begun in earnest, though, the Dutch welfare state grew rapidly. By the mid-1960s the proportion of GDP spent on social welfare transfers in the Netherlands had outdistanced that of other European countries (Rochon 1992: 74).

The Dutch welfare state developed in four stages, of which the first three all involved growth in programs and expenditures. In the first stage, spanning approximately the first half of the twentieth century, governmental involvement in the provision of social welfare was limited and indirect—channeled through the maze of social-work organizations that developed within each of the pillars. In the second stage, from 1957 to 1976, governmental provision of social services was expanded to include all the programs of the modern welfare state. The role of pillar organizations in shaping social services policy was reduced in this second period, a development that paralleled the general decline of the pillars. The extensive social insurance programs developed during the second stage of the welfare state enabled the government to engage in social engineering to a greater extent than is common in other democracies. In the third stage, which began in the late 1960s and gathered momentum in the 1970s, the Dutch developed a new philosophy of social participation that replaced the logic of minimum income maintenance previously guiding welfare state policies. At the peak of this third stage, the welfare state sought to give all citizens the opportunity to participate fully in the society, regardless of the jobs they held or whether they worked at all.

The fourth stage of welfare state development represents a trend-break from the earlier phases of expansion. Retrenchment of the welfare state began in 1981 with the installation of a center-right government determined to restore budgetary balance. What began as a budget-cutting exercise, though, soon developed into a shift in the very logic of public services. The previous emphasis on citizen entitlements gave way to a new focus on economic efficiency. The language of solidarity, which stressed collective accountability for the welfare of each member of society, was supplemented by an emphasis on the need to maintain incentives for work.

In this chapter we will review the origins of the Dutch welfare state, looking particularly at the contribution of the confessional pillars in creating what was elsewhere a social democratic phenomenon. We will then examine the rapid development of the welfare state in the 1960s and 1970s as it matured into its pioneering form of the social welfare state. Finally, we will look at the welfare retrenchment of the 1980s and 1990s. In this period the problems inherent in the social welfare state model have become apparent, and the Dutch have been challenged not only to reduce costs but also to rethink the very philosophy of the welfare state.

Social Welfare Before the Welfare State

Recall from Chapter 2 that the Dutch did not enter the modern world as convinced statists. Unlike France, England, and China (among others), the Netherlands had no tradition of strong central government. There was on the contrary a deep suspicion of and resistance to centralizing tendencies. This was expressed during the era of the Dutch Republic as an unwillingness to grant tax authority to the States General, despite the clear and present danger of reconquest by Spain during the Eighty Years War. Later, after a unitary government had been established, religious groups organized to limit its power, particularly in regard to the regulation of domestic affairs.

"Sovereignty in one's own circle" was the Calvinist formula expressing the expectation of churches that they would control community life among the faithful. For Dutch Catholics the idea of subsidiarity expressed a comparable demand that the Church would govern itself to the greatest possible extent, leaving national defense and international affairs to the national government. Calvinists and Catholics formed the confessional pillars precisely in order to defend their autonomy in such areas as religious worship, education, and family life. Certainly when it came to assistance for those in poverty, the churches expected to take care of their own. The Calvinist leader Guillaume Groen van Prinsterer could have been speaking for the Catholic Church as well when he said that "only the Gospel contains the true principles . . . of philanthropy and constructive humanitarianism."[1] By the time governmental involvement in social welfare became an issue late in the nineteenth century, the confessional pillars were sufficiently entrenched to guarantee that they would have an important role in shaping welfare state legislation.[2]

Urgency in creating the pillars was enhanced late in the nineteenth century by the arrival of the industrial revolution. Despite the prosperity and the high degree of urbanization in the Netherlands in the seventeenth century, the country was actually a late industrializer whose cities became smaller during the eighteenth and nineteenth centuries.[3] The seventeenth-century economy had been founded on trade, shipping, finance, and agriculture, and the lack of raw materials in the country meant that Dutch investors who became involved in industrial production sent their capital abroad. For a long time thereafter, many shared the view of Johannes Goldberg, who opined in 1799 that "because of our geographical location, Holland is destined to be a warehouse where merchants in every corner of the world send their goods. It would not be wise to sacrifice our strategic advantages with regard to commerce and trade for the uncertain and imaginary benefits of industry."[4] This may have been a self-fulfilling prophecy for the Netherlands, for by 1850 Belgium, an early industrializer, had five times as many railroad lines and steam-powered industrial enterprises (Gladdish 1991: 18).

Late in the nineteenth century, though, the Netherlands did enter a period of rapid industrialization, centered on shipbuilding, the manufacture of engines and vehicles, food processing, and production of chemicals (de Vries 1978: 19). In 1871 an international butter dealer, Antoon Jürgens, bought the patent for a product he named margarine, and was soon employing thousands of workers (Newton 1978: 84–85). A bit later, in 1890, the Philips brothers began to make light bulbs in the town of Eindhoven.

The growth of an industrial working class posed a new challenge to the churches, which did not want to lose working-class loyalty to socialist influences. In order to maintain working-class support, the confessional pillars guarded for themselves the right to provide social assistance to their own communities. The churches had long been active in the provision of relief for the poor through affiliated organizations. This community-based relief system provided a basic level of income support and was administered primarily by private charities whose money came from the churchgoing middle and upper classes.

The Dutch public has always been particularly sensitive to the problem of poverty. The seventeenth-century terms *behoeftigen* (the needy) and *armwezen* (the poor) did not stigmatize poverty in the manner of contemporaneous words in England like "pauper" (Gouda 1995: 38–39). A. T. van Deursen (1991: 56) notes that statutes passed by the authorities during the seventeenth century to limit beggars from asking for alms were actually circumvented by a public determined to assist the less fortunate among them.[5] At the time of the French invasion of the United Provinces in 1672, the king of England claimed that he "was of the opinion that God would preserve Amsterdam from being destroyed if it were only for the great charity they have for the poor."[6] Two English visitors in the same period commented on Amsterdam's

> neat and distinct Almes-Houses for Men and Women, which a man would think were rather rich Merchants habitations. . . . Their Guest-house, for Sick poor men and women are well furnished with all Necessaries. . . . Their Dul-houses, or Bedlams, for the distracted; their Tuchthouses, or Houses of Corrections for the stubborn and idle, are generally fair with all means used to reclaime the first to their Wits, the other to their Honesties.[7]

Suggestions that the state assume responsibility for the poor were rebuffed with words like those of P. J. Elout, who wrote in 1846 that "the church never humiliates the indigents by providing poor relief in public. The church maintains the voluntary nature of charity and leaves room for the altruistic compassion of the giver and the warm gratitude of the receiver."[8] With these ideals of private initiative in poor relief, it is perhaps no surprise that a population of just 5 million supported 7,476 organizations engaged in social or charitable work at the turn of the twentieth century (Timmermans and Becker 1985: 87).

Over time, however, the demand for poor relief support grew beyond the resources of private charitable associations. The responsibility of the churches for poor relief could at times be heavy. The period of French rule was especially hard on Dutch cities, and as much as one-third of Amsterdam's population and one-half of Rotterdam's population were on "winter relief" in 1808. In 1811, 10 percent of the national population relied on charity, in part or in full (Gouda 1995: 72–73). A potato fungus in 1845–1847 brought on a famine that further stretched the resources of private charity. Despite these stresses, it was only with industrialization later in the nineteenth century that church funds for poor relief were overmatched by the level of need. Industrialization brought with it business and employment cycles, while reducing the number of farm owners and workers who could generally provide for their own basic maintenance in hard times.

As the demand for poor relief grew in an increasingly urbanized and industrialized country, religious organizations called upon governmental assistance to supplement their own charitable resources. In 1910, 41 percent of public assistance was still being raised by private charitable organizations, but late in the depression decade of the 1930s private funds accounted for only 12 percent of all income relief (Timmermans and Becker 1985: 88).

Even as the national government became involved in poor relief, though, confessional organizations retained control of the program's administration. Already in 1854, a new poor law shepherded through parliament by J. R. Thorbecke and the Liberals had supplemented the efforts of private charities and local governments with a state guarantee of assistance. Thorbecke's reform was originally intended to take control over poor relief away from the churches, on the grounds that Christian charity could be capricious and dependent on the wealth of a parish. But his proposal met with great hostility in the churches. Abraham Kuyper would call a later proposal to establish a national social insurance agency "un-Dutch, socialistic, and bureaucratic." "This proposal is worse than anything anyone has ever dared suggest," Kuyper continued, "it is a web spun over the entire country, with the governmental agency as the huge spider in the middle, pulling all the strings."[9] Ultimately, then, the Poor Law of 1854 "developed into a system of public subsidization of private charities whereby the state paid for poor relief but had almost no control over how the programs were administered. The various charities were free to establish their own criteria for benefit entitlements, the only legal restriction being vaguely defined as a requirement that they operate in the public interest" (Cox 1993: 82).

Confessional organizations involved in poor relief administration solidified their position by establishing their own federation, the Dutch Association for Social Work, whose "purpose was to coordinate the way poor relief was dispensed and provide a unified voice for the charities vis-à-vis the state" (Cox 1993: 72). This confessional association, in turn, established the Dutch Council for Social Work, a permanent advisory body whose members were the only recognized recipients of governmental subsidies for poor relief. The poor relief system that resulted gave private (mainly religious) associations a great deal of control over the implementation of public policy. In this way, confessional organizations retained control over poor relief even as the industrialization of society put the scope of the task beyond the reach of purely private charitable efforts.

The Netherlands entered the twentieth century with a local, decentralized, and religiously controlled system of poor relief, one that already looked antiquated in comparison to neighboring states. The lack of a more extensive array of social insurance programs was due in no small part to the determination of confessional pillar leaders to avoid any aggrandizement of the role of the state in ordering social relations and economic life. And yet the experience of neighboring countries, particularly Germany, was that state-run programs of social insurance helped reduce class conflict generally and the appeal of socialism in particular. Leaders of the confessional pillars consequently came to support the development of workers insurance programs for disability and retirement. The Dutch modeled their welfare laws on the social insurance plans developed in Germany twenty years earlier. As Robert Cox (1993: 84) notes, much of the original legislation for Dutch social insurance was translated directly from the German laws. Unlike Bismarckian social insurance, though, Dutch programs were implemented by representatives of the confessional employers and labor associations. The administration of worker disability and illness insurance programs thus ended up in the hands of private industrial insurance boards. In this way, the confessional forces in society effectively preempted the socialist labor movement, retaining the support of much of the working class and preventing the emergence of a unified working-class organization. As we shall see, confessional power in this early phase of the welfare state was an important force in shaping both the benefits and the administration of postwar social insurance programs.

Development of the Postwar Welfare State

Despite the continued importance of the confessional pillars as agents for implementing poor relief, the Dutch were already in the early twentieth century moving toward the welfare state as an entirely new system for taking care of the needy members of society. The distinction between poor relief and welfare state rests on changes of scope and agency. The scope of welfare state guarantees extends well beyond the temporary provision of minimal assistance to the deserving poor. And the agent carrying out this enlarged welfare state function is no longer private charity but rather the government. As Harold Wilensky (1975: 1) put it, "The essence of the welfare state is government protected minimum standards of income, nutrition, health, housing, and education, assured to every citizen as a political right, not as charity."

The second stage of welfare state construction began in the Netherlands, as elsewhere, with the experience of the Great Depression and World War II. Because of its reliance on international trade, the Netherlands was hit even harder by the depression than were most other countries. The Dutch unemployment rate averaged 25 percent between 1932 and 1939, with as much as one-third of the labor force out of work. The experience of mass unemployment created a general expectation that government take greater responsibility for maintaining high and stable levels of employment. In 1937, for example, the minister of labor was given the power to extend a negotiated contract to an entire sector of the economy as a means of resolving disputes, or to declare invalid parts of a negotiated contract if the agreement was deemed bad for macroeconomic conditions (Windmuller 1969: 73).

The increased power of government in labor relations was further augmented by spreading acceptance of an expanded set of publicly provided social services. This was in part due to the development of Keynesian thinking on the potential of government to maintain full employment by means of countercyclical spending. Social welfare policies that provide income replacement for the unemployed are countercyclical by nature. As governments adopted the principles of Keynesian economics, then, more extensive social welfare policies not only became theoretically feasible but were considered good policy. "The ideal of the Minister of Finance," according to A. A. van Rhijn in 1944 (258), "can no longer be that of the thrifty housewife."

Yet another push for expanded welfare state programs came from an increase in public expectations as a consequence of the war. The extreme demands made by governments on their citizens for the war effort established a more intimate link between public and private spheres than had previously existed. Postwar Dutch politicians accordingly felt obliged to retain a number of public relief measures that the German rulers had decreed during their occupation of the Netherlands (van Kersbergen 1995: 129–130). The rigors of reconstruction and the artificially low level of wages in the first postwar decade also argued for an extension of publicly provided social services.

Consequently, the wartime government-in-exile charged A. A. van Rhijn with developing a plan for a post–World War II social welfare system. Given its location in London, the van Rhijn Commission was greatly influenced in its thinking by social welfare blueprints in other countries, particularly by the report of the Beveridge Commission in Great Britain.[10] The van Rhijn Commission followed the lead of the Beveridge Commission in recommending that the Dutch welfare state be universalized to the entire population rather than being limited to the current system of workers insurance. According to van Rhijn in 1945, "The community, organized in the form of the State, is responsible for the social security of all its members and for protecting them from want, provided that the members themselves take reasonable measures to ensure their own social security and protection from want."[11]

In the postwar era, then, government in the Netherlands followed the international trend as it grew and changed its functions from those of the night watchman state to those of the welfare state. The night watchman state kept the public order and defended international borders. The welfare state continued these tasks but also took on the additional responsibilities of stimulating economic growth, maintaining employment, and providing material subsistence for all. The Dutch welfare state paralleled its counterparts elsewhere in pursuing these objectives. In the Netherlands, though, continuation of the power of the confessional pillars meant that development of a network of social welfare programs would not occur by creating a large national welfare bureaucracy, as happened in Great Britain and Scandinavia. The Dutch welfare state could grow only in a form that respected the confessional traditions of Dutch politics. This meant avoidance of social insurance plans financed through general taxation or administered by the state bureaucracy. Instead, financing for new welfare state programs after World War II came primarily from payroll deductions paid into a series of "social funds" dedicated to each of the insurance programs—sickness, disability, retirement, unemployment, widows and orphans, and so forth.[12] The programs that benefited workers and their dependents were administered by special boards composed of representatives from the unions and employers associations. The flat-rate programs available to all citizens, whether employed or not—the old-age pension, widows and orphans fund, and minimum income relief—were administered through a government agency. And the universal health care system was administered through private associations linked to the pillars.

These developments resulted in an unwieldy system that was publicly funded but whose administration and implementation were largely in private hands. As

Kees van Kersbergen (1995: 129) concludes, "this [administrative] solution mirrored the pillarised organizations of society to a large extent and, in effect, reinforced the political significance of pillarised social associations." The welfare system created entitlements not only for the Dutch citizenry but also for the pillar organizations, which were able to block proposals of administrative reform for the next fifty years.

Even this mixed system of public and private implementation, though, represented significant concessions by the pillarized social welfare organizations. Acceptance of a state role in administering social welfare became even more marked in 1963, when the earlier system of poor relief was replaced by an expanded program guaranteeing a minimum income for all Dutch residents (the *bijstand*). By then, confessional organizations long dominant in poor relief were also changing their thinking. Confessional social welfare agencies began to be populated by trained social workers whose interests were primarily in community organizing, counseling services, and job-skills training (Cox 1990: 94–96). Running an income assistance program had much less appeal for postwar confessional welfare organizations, and turning administration over to a state agency no longer seemed as threatening as it had in earlier decades. As Robert Cox (1993: 144) points out, "many [confessional] charities had already discovered new tasks they could perform, such as promoting awareness of eligibility among the poor, providing assistance in filling out forms, and acting as intermediaries in negotiations between applicants and municipal agencies. . . . Though direct financial aid had been taken out of their hands, they continued to be subsidized for their new activities."

Once the confessional welfare organizations were on board, the government rapidly created an extensive array of welfare state programs, including universal social insurance for retirees, the disabled, the sick, and widows and orphans. The Public Retirement Pensions Act in 1957 represented the first step in universalization of the welfare state—that is, extension beyond those workers who paid into the social insurance pool. The most consequential of the universal programs was the Worker's Disability Act in 1967, which replaced existing accident and disability insurance for on-the-job injuries with a general guarantee of income replacement in the event of partial or full disability. The previous legislation had become controversial in some circles because of cases that raised questions about what constitutes an "on-the-job" injury. Robert Cox (1994: 147) reports one case of denial of benefits to an employee who was injured while on a social excursion organized by the employer. In another case, in which someone was injured while riding his bicycle to work, the administrative court ruled that the accident was due to careless bicycle riding and that the employee was not entitled to a job disability benefit. The denial of benefits in these cases meant that the individuals were forced to turn to public assistance rather than receiving the more generous income replacement under the disability law.

Under the Worker's Disability Act, disability was defined as incapacity to continue in the same or similar work due to health problems. The injury could be sustained on the job or in activities unrelated to the job; it could be a physical injury or stress-induced psychological damage. The extent of disability could be great or small, as long as the disability itself prevented one from earning the same wage as "a comparable completely healthy person." Benefits were related to earnings; for workers deemed completely disabled (i.e., unable to work at all), the benefit was equal to one's last wage. The duration of the benefit was indefinite until one reached retirement age, at which time the benefit shifted to the retirement program. The high-water mark of the Dutch welfare state was reached when the Worker's Disability Act was generalized from the labor force to the entire population. This 1976 extension in effect gave all individuals the right to an income for life if they were disabled, whether or not they had ever been part of the workforce.[13]

With passage of a full range of welfare state programs, the size of the public sector began to grow rapidly. Governmental expenses and social insurance payments grew from 31 percent of national income in 1950 to more than 60 percent in 1990. The size of the bureaucracy grew as well. Measured in full-time-equivalent work years, the civil service expanded from 20,000 in 1850 to 69,000 in 1900, and has since expanded to 750,000.[14]

Even with this growth, the Dutch welfare state has not generated a public bureaucracy as large as that found in other European countries. In the Netherlands the government employs just 16 percent of the workforce, compared with public bureaucracies of 38 percent in Sweden, 30 percent in Denmark, and 18 percent in Germany. In fact, growth of the Dutch civil service was less rapid during postwar construction of the welfare state than was growth of the civil service in the United States in that same period, despite the more limited expansion of public services in the United States (van der Meer and Roborgh 1993: 109–110).

The relatively modest growth of the civil service—at least when compared to growth in the welfare state programs themselves—occurred because of the extensive implementation responsibility that is even today left to private organizations. For example, health insurance in the Netherlands, though publicly funded, operates through a network of private medical practices, clinics, and hospitals.[15] Many schools, though also publicly funded on a formula tied to their enrollments, are privately run. These schools and health care delivery networks generally originated as pillar organizations, though they tend not to have an exclusively Catholic, Protestant, or secular identity today.

As Gøsta Esping-Andersen (1990) has pointed out, welfare states differ not only in the magnitude of their expenditures but also in the extent to which they alter market outcomes by levelling incomes. Although the Dutch welfare state is quite extensive, its primary emphasis is on income maintenance rather than income redistribution. As a result of this emphasis on income replacement and minimum income guarantees, the percentage of people living in poverty in the Netherlands was in 1979 the lowest in the European Union (Ellman 1984: 196). At the same time, the Netherlands has experienced a relatively small decline in income inequality during the postwar period, closer to conditions in Germany than to the more extensive income-equalization conditions in Sweden and Denmark (Kraus 1987: 204). In 1990, minimum social welfare benefits in the Netherlands averaged just 57 percent of the maximum benefits available. This compares to a more homogeneous and egalitarian system in the Scandinavian countries, where basic benefits averaged 81 percent of maximum benefits.[16]

The impact of the welfare state on Dutch society has been not so much to flatten the market-driven distribution of income as it has been to remove as much variation as possible from an individual's expected income during the life-span. This program design fits with the argument by Cameron (1978) and Katzenstein (1985) that welfare states in small, open economies are a means of shielding the labor force from the vagaries of international markets. The lack of emphasis on income redistribution also reflects the confessional rather than socialist origins of the Dutch welfare state. It is consistent with pre–welfare state traditions of poor relief as well as with Dutch cultural values, which favor assisting those in the lowest decile of the income ladder but do not support a more general program of collapsing all incomes toward the mean.

Of course, the goal of eliminating poverty does entail some degree of redistribution to those with the lowest incomes. The public assistance program in the Netherlands accomplishes exactly that, and it is the one form of social insurance financed by general revenues rather than by employee payroll deductions. Moreover, both the minimum wage and the poverty line that triggers public assistance are set at a relatively high level; in the early 1980s the poverty line stood as high as 80 percent of the average net income of a laborer (Idenburg 1985: 132).

In Gøsta Esping-Andersen's (1990) terms, the commitment of the Dutch welfare state to sustaining a high level of income for those who cannot work or who work at minimum wage creates a significant degree of "decommodification," or severance of the link between labor and income. Decommodification is a trait of the social democratic welfare state, the most elaborate of the three welfare state regime types described by Esping-Andersen. At the same time, the Dutch welfare state resembles Esping-Andersen's conservative welfare state regime in that it does not significantly alter the income distribution as determined by market forces. As dramatically expanded as the Dutch welfare state is today compared to one hundred years ago, the same logic of social insurance that informed those small beginnings is still the underlying principle.

The Dutch welfare state is a hybrid of Esping-Andersen's three categories, and its proper placement has generated substantial debate.[17] No matter what we call it, the Dutch welfare state was by the mid-1970s the largest in the world if measured by the yardstick of spending as a proportion of the national economic product. At its peak, over one-half of the Dutch GNP traveled through the public sector, and about half of that amount was collected for redistribution by social welfare agencies to the sick, the disabled, the elderly, or the unemployed.[18] This is a far higher percentage than that found in Sweden and Denmark (45 percent of GNP) or the United States (25 percent of GNP).

In the thirty years from 1946 to 1976, the Dutch welfare state developed from the provision of minimum income relief to the poor, to the guarantee of a minimum income as well as insurance against income loss due to sickness, disability, unemployment, death of the head of household, or retirement. Figure 7.1 shows that these programs have succeeded in alleviating worries about serious illness and unemployment among the Dutch public, compared to residents of other advanced industrial societies.[19] This "no worries" attitude exists despite an unemployment rate as high as 16 percent in the decade preceding this survey! Other survey data show that only 39 percent of Dutch people say that money problems would be their main worry if they were unemployed, compared to an average of 58 percent in nine other countries (International Social Science Program 1989).[20]

The goal of the welfare state is to develop effective programs of social insurance that create a true sense of material security, and Figure 7.1 suggests that the Dutch have achieved this goal. In the process of implementing universal social insurance programs, though, the very logic of the welfare state began to change. The emergence of a new philosophy of social participation forms the backdrop for the third—and most distinctive—stage of the twentieth-century Dutch welfare state.

From Welfare to Well-Being

Completion of the programmatic repertoire of the welfare state did not end the development of the welfare state, or even its expansion. Although the panoply of state guarantees and services was largely in place by the mid-1960s, the period of fastest growth in welfare state spending was yet to come. This late burst of spending came about not because of continued development of new services, but rather because the principles of the welfare state were changing. What had once been a matter of keeping people above the economic level needed for minimum subsistence now became a more ambitious guarantee of income sufficient to allow full participation in society.

Development of the Dutch welfare state has followed the path originally described by T. H. Marshall in terms of the evolution of citizenship rights. Marshall ([1950] 1992) described citizenship as being initially confined to the grant of civil rights, such as the right to a fair trial. In the nineteenth century, the idea of citizenship was expanded to include political rights such as the right to vote. During the course of the twentieth century, according to Marshall, the concept of citizenship grew once again to encompass social rights, meaning the right to full participation in the society. Elements of social citizenship, according to Marshall, include guaranteed access to education, health care, legal aid, housing, and other social services.

In the Netherlands, Marga Klompé, minister of culture, recreation, and social work in the 1960s, saw her role as moving the country toward social citizenship. "After the fight for political equality and for the right to economic welfare for everybody, the aim to achieve the wellbeing of society as a whole and of every in-

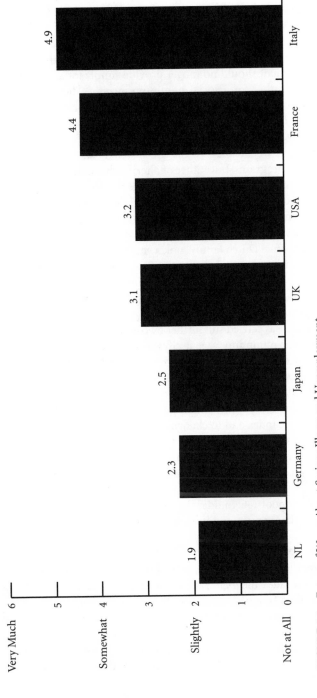

FIGURE 7.1 Extent of Worry About Serious Illness and Unemployment

NOTE: These survey data were collected between 1987 and 1993.
SOURCE: Hayashi et al. (1992).

dividual citizen is beginning to emerge. This wellbeing is not the fringe of economic welfare but the essence."[21] Minister Klompé incorporated this idea into the Public Assistance Act of 1963, which specified that the level of public assistance benefits must be based on "social existence" *(bestaansonderhoud)* rather than on material subsistence *(levensonderhoud)* (Cox 1990: 95). During the 1970s the idea spread that government should no longer provide simply for an economic minimum income, but rather for a social minimum income. The idea of the "social minimum" entered the Dutch welfare state vocabulary, creating a gradual shift from the original concept of the welfare state to a new concept that might be called the "social welfare state."[22]

The shift from the welfare state to the social welfare state was not a matter of implementing new programs, but rather of altering the nature of income guarantees found in existing programs. In the area of general income assistance, for example, there was an increasing concern that public assistance recipients should live in a way that mirrors broader social patterns, even if on a modest scale. For example, public assistance benefits were augmented in 1964 to include a vacation allowance; if the normal Dutch family took a vacation every year, then the logic of full social participation demanded that those on public assistance also have the means to take a vacation.[23] More recently, local governments decided to offer a daily newspaper to those on public assistance, again with an eye to the conditions necessary for full social participation.[24]

In 1970 this logic was carried still further by coupling public assistance to the net minimum wage. The minimum wage itself was set at 80 percent of the net average wage. This had the effect of maintaining a constant (and relatively modest) gap between public assistance and the lowest-paid jobs, and between the lowest-paid jobs and the average job. A further step in development of the social welfare state came in 1976, when sickness, disability, unemployment, and retirement benefits were all tied both to the price index and to changes in the wages of private-sector workers. As wages rose, so would social insurance payments. As prices rose, both wages and social insurance payments would be adjusted. In 1979 this automatic indexation was extended to those receiving public assistance benefits, completing the guarantee that all citizens would share in the increasing levels of prosperity. The minimum subsistence goals of poor relief under the welfare state were now completely abandoned in favor of the far more ambitious goal of making public assistance indistinguishable from a modest working wage. This coupling of benefits to wage levels cut the link between work and consumption, creating (in Esping-Andersen's terms) extensive decommodification. The result was, in the words of former education minister J. A. van Kemenade, "the high water mark of [Dutch] civilization."[25]

The social welfare state should not be thought of simply as the welfare state with a little extra money; instead, the social welfare state integrates all previous roles of government in society. The older functions of government in providing justice and national defense are part of the social welfare state, because no one can participate fully in society if their physical security is threatened. Nineteenth-century liberal expansions of the state to provide universal education are also part of the social welfare state, since education provides access to one's cultural heritage. Finally, the universal social insurance of the twentieth-century welfare state is a key element of the social welfare state, because material existence is also a prerequisite for social citizenship. In addition to integrating these roles of government, the social welfare state adds the element of participation. In the social welfare state, a citizen has the right to effective participation in the political, economic, and cultural life of the society.

The concept of the social welfare state is nicely illustrated by Michael Ellman's (1984: 193–194) accounting of major Dutch welfare state programs:

- employee works councils that have extensive rights of information about the firm, including the right to review financial records. These works councils participate in such major decisions as reorganization of the firm and the naming of a new CEO;[26]
- security of employment, that does not permit dismissal without approval of the local Employment Exchange;
- affordable housing, guaranteed by rent control and rent subsidies to people of modest incomes;
- a high quality education system, with both "general" schools and religious schools publicly funded on an equal basis;
- universal access to medical care through insurance programs (compulsory for all but the highest wage earners) that subsidize those with the lowest salaries;
- a minimum wage that is not far below the average wage and is indexed to the average wage;
- a public assistance program that guarantees all people, working or not, a minimum income. For a couple, the guaranteed minimum income is set at the net minimum wage;
- earnings-related benefits in the event of unemployment, illness or disability, with a high level of income replacement;
- a universal and indexed old age pension system;
- a child benefit program;
- pensions for widows and orphans, with the widow's pension equal to a single person's old age pension.

A striking feature of Ellman's list is that it includes elements that one might not normally think of as being part of welfare state programs, such as works councils, job security, education, and a high minimum wage. Note, however, that each element of this list enables people to participate more fully in the political, economic, and cultural life of society. The social welfare state rests not just on guarantees of a minimum income, but also on access to education, health care, cultural events, and quality options for leisure.

Development of the social welfare state entailed an extension of the government's roles in society. For example, the guarantee of full participation in social life makes the government responsible for supporting a rich cultural life in which people can take part. As the Cals-Donner Commission on social welfare put it in 1971, "The government is responsible for the livability *[leefbaarheid]* of the country and . . . creates conditions for leisure time activities and cultural development."[27] This responsibility has led to an extensive policy of subsidizing social and cultural organizations ranging from ballet companies, theater groups, and orchestras, to stamp-collecting clubs, sport associations, and youth groups. Over 80 percent of the price of a theater ticket is paid for by the government, as is 10 percent of the price of a movie ticket (Sociaal en Cultureel Planbureau 1993: 299). The policy of subsidizing a wide range of social and cultural activities led novelist Harry Mulisch to write a satirical passage in his 1973 novel *Last Call.* When the subsidy for a theater group is threatened with termination, the ensemble holds a meeting. One actor complains that loss of the subsidy would threaten his "social security," to which another retorts that "as an actor he has a fixed income which we writers have never had, and which if the worst comes to the worst will be replaced by state benefits consisting of eighty per cent of the last received wage. . . . What exactly are you? Artists, or a bunch of embittered petty bourgeois bellyachers?" (Mulisch [1973] 1989: 129).

One of the most radical perspectives of the social welfare state philosophy is its redefinition of the meaning of work. With a guaranteed right to a level of public assistance not far below the minimum wage (and a minimum wage that is itself pegged to remain not far below the average wage), the monetary incentive to work is significantly diminished. Under the social welfare state, work is a form of economic and social participation as well as a means of earning money. The quality of the work experience becomes more important; the monetary rewards of work become less important.

This element of the social welfare state owes its origins partly to the influence of Provo and the youth movements in the 1960s, which sought to redefine the meaning of work from economic production to personal fulfillment. Such values fly in the face of the Calvinist heritage of the Netherlands, which stresses work and material success as signs of God's grace. And yet there is evidence that the Dutch today place a great deal of emphasis on the nonmaterial aspects of work. Figure 7.2 shows that the Dutch are less focused on work as a means of earning money than are the publics of other advanced industrial societies. The Dutch are five times more likely to emphasize having a feeling of accomplishment at work than having a good salary, and they are much more likely than other publics to believe that the way one earns money is more important than how much money one earns.

Figure 7.2 shows a seven-nation mean score for each of the three items, based on the ratio of nonmaterialist answers to materialist answers. For comparison, the American responses are also included in the graph, and they hew quite closely to the seven-nation average. One question not shown in Figure 7.2 on which Dutch

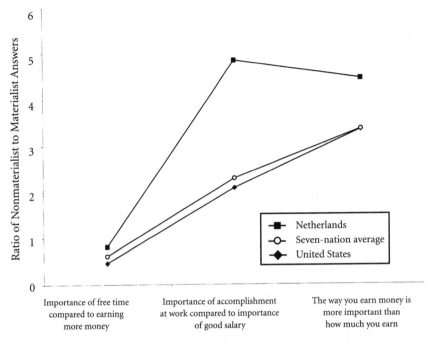

FIGURE 7.2   Attitudes Toward Work and Money

NOTE: These survey data were collected between 1987 and 1993.
SOURCE: Hayashi et al. (1992).

and American values converge regards the importance of teaching children the value of money. The Dutch, along with Americans, are the least likely to think one must teach children that money is important.[28]

Although there are national variations in how particular questions are answered, the overall picture is quite clear: The Dutch are one of the least work- and money-centered publics in the world. Of the seven nations surveyed, the Dutch gave the least money-centered answers on two of the three questions shown in Figure 7.2, and the second least money-centered answer on the other.[29] These findings are generally congruent with the studies conducted by Ronald Inglehart (1990) over the last thirty years, which show that the Dutch are the most postmaterialist population in the world.

The philosophy of the social welfare state does not imply that work is an option one may or may not choose. But it does embody the belief that a person should have the opportunity to work at a job suitable to his or her own tastes and skills. Thus, those receiving unemployment benefits are expected to seek a new job, but they are not expected to seek or accept work below the level of their qualifications or past work experience.

The most extensive realization of the idea of suitable work for everyone in the social welfare state occurred in the form of the Fine Arts Program. Art has always had a special place in Dutch culture, and numerous observers have testified to the ubiquity of original works of art in Dutch homes. "He that hath not bread to eat hath a Picture," according to two seventeenth-century English visitors to the country.[30] The Dutch take pride in their artistic traditions, as exemplified by the Dutch masters of the seventeenth century (Rembrandt, Vermeer, Steen, Hals, and others) and continued by Vincent van Gogh in the nineteenth century and by M. C. Escher, Piet Mondriaan, and Karel Appel in the twentieth century.

The private market for art collapsed during the economic crisis of the 1930s. To sustain the community of artists during that period, the government began a program to purchase works by designated artists. This policy continued after World War II, and despite the return of prosperity to the country the program expanded over time. By 1960, 200 artists were supported by the governmental purchase program. Ten years later, following 1969 legislation inspired by the ideals of the social welfare state, the number of Dutch artists whose primary customer was the government had quadrupled to 800. By 1980 the number had nearly quadrupled again, to 3,000 artists, and national and local governments were purchasing 20,000 works of art per year under the program. This compares to only thirteen Dutch artists who were able in 1973 to earn as much as 50,000 guilders per year (US$17,860) by selling their work on the free market.[31] The Fine Arts Program thus significantly expanded the number of artists who were able to support themselves through their work. Further assistance to artists came indirectly, through a governmental subsidy available to private purchasers of Dutch art. A total of 200,000 works had been purchased by the early 1980s, 60 percent of which at any given time was on display in governmental offices or on loan to exhibitions. As expressed by Marga Klompé, former minister of culture, recreation, and social work and theorist of the social welfare state, "Art is in the end part of one's lifestyle, and it is part of a pleasant lifestyle. I call that well-being *[welzijn]*."[32]

The place of the Fine Arts Program within the social welfare state should not be exaggerated. Its total cost in 1980 was 100 million guilders (about US$3 per capita), just 0.11 percent of the total government budget. While it existed, though, the program was a symbol of the kind of society that the social welfare state sought to create.

Such an extensive reconceptualization and extension of the traditional welfare state can only be undertaken with substantial popular support. Already in 1958, a survey of 5,000 Dutch people between the ages of 18 and 30 had shown that the social services of the welfare state constituted one of the strongest points of pride in their country, second only to the dike and levee system of protection from the water (Goudsblom 1959: 82). Expansion of social services and improvement of social justice through universal insurance were the most discussed issues in party platforms between 1946 and 1977, even ahead of economic issues (Dittrich 1987). Adam Szirmai (1984: 122–123) found in the early 1980s that 82 percent of the

Dutch population, including 67 percent of the highest income decile, would accept additional cuts in the highest incomes to maintain purchasing power among the lowest.

Sensitivity to the distribution of opportunities for social participation is also high in the Netherlands, at least by the standards of American political discourse. There has been a great deal of attention paid in recent years to the disparity between those who are able to use digital technology and those who are not. This is partly an economic issue of being able to afford computer equipment and access to the Internet. But it is also a matter of age and education, for surveys of the population show that older people and those with less education are not comfortable looking for information on the Internet, sending e-mail, or completing automatic transfers of money via computer.[33] Making information technologies available to everyone is considered to be, in part, a public policy problem that grows out of the government's commitment to full social participation by the entire population.

Of course, not everyone is equally enthusiastic about the social welfare state. Politically, these developments were most strongly championed by the confessional parties. In contrast to what they painted as the narrowly materialistic welfare state desired by the social democrats, the confessional parties supported a welfare state that would enhance social participation and therefore, they hoped, preserve the importance of religious communities in Dutch society. The Catholic People's Party, for example, replaced its advocacy of subsidiarity with "solidarity"—a variant on the socialist theme that "emphasized empathy of individuals for one another, especially empathy of the privileged for the less privileged" (Cox 1993: 136). Long-standing confessional ideas about mutual responsibility between the classes were now used to justify a social welfare state with far more ambitious goals than those found in most other welfare states. The Labor Party, though not part of the governing coalitions that accelerated welfare state development in the 1960s, certainly supported the development of universal social insurance programs. However, Labor leaders occasionally found themselves in the anomalous position of arguing that proposed increases in entitlements were too expensive to be fiscally responsible!

One reason why the religious forces sought a relatively high level of benefits lies in the traditions of church-sponsored poor relief. In bygone centuries, relief was granted not to an individual but to a family in need. Poor relief was subject to a "right of recovery" *(verhaalsrecht)*, by which private charitable agencies could collect financial support for an indigent from other family members (Cox 1990: 88). As the twentieth-century welfare state developed, church leaders—especially the Catholic bishops—maintained this focus by stressing the right of workers to an income sufficient to maintain a family (van Kersbergen 1991: 282). As a result of this perspective, benefit levels came to be predicated on the assumption of a traditional family unit with the husband as breadwinner and the wife and children as dependents of a single income. Thus, for example, there are pensions for widows and orphans but not for widowers. And when an old-age pension was enacted in the mid-1950s, the pension for an unmarried worker was set at 70 percent of the pension for a married worker. The assumption of a male breadwinner was embedded in the former rule that married women had no right to a pension at age 65 unless their husbands were retired. Compensation levels for minimum wage and unemployment benefits were also set relatively high in the belief that these benefits would typically be granted to an individual responsible for the expenses of a family (van Kersbergen 1995: 131, 190).

The confessional, and specifically Catholic, inspiration behind the Dutch welfare state is also visible in the policy on child subsidies, which in 1963 were extended from the first two children in a family to all children. This in one of the most densely populated countries in the world! In other respects, confessional power limited the generosity of the welfare state, which long refused to offer child care facilities for working mothers.[34] As Wil Albeda, social affairs minister from 1977 to 1981, put it, "The breadwinner principle in our system of social insurance was based upon the widely held belief that married women should stay home and care for the house and the children. Child payments and public housing proceeded from this same view."[35]

These policies were founded on long-established social patterns in which married women stayed at home to raise a family. As we saw in Chapter 3, only about a quarter of Dutch women worked in 1960, including only 3 percent of married women. This percentage of working women had remained unchanged since 1889![36] As recently as 1989, 18 percent of Dutch people said that family responsibilities should be a consideration in deciding one's pay at work.[37] Changes in society since 1960, though, have reduced the proportion of the population living in nuclear families under the financial protection of a single breadwinner. There are more single-parent families, more people living alone, and more families headed by two individuals who are not married to each other.[38] In 1975, 85 percent of all married men were the sole earners in their families; by 1994 this was true of just 50 percent of married men (Visser and Hemerijck 1997: 42).

These trends have combined to shift the focus of state-sponsored financial support from families to individuals.[39] In this individualized version of welfare state income guarantees, all that is relevant is the financial situation of the adult individual—without consideration of the means of family members who might contribute to that person's support. As a consequence, benefit levels that were originally set on the assumption that there would be one claimant per family have since come to serve as individual entitlements. Although the individualization of benefit payments enhances personal autonomy and equality, it has also created some problems. There has been a doubling of women's participation in the labor force, meaning that two members of a family often make social insurance contributions and may consequently apply for benefits. Though many working women are part-timers, they are entitled to full benefits. In some families, husbands, wives, and young adult offspring may each receive social insurance payments set at a level originally designed to support the entire family.

Development of the social welfare state also posed implementation challenges to the civil service. According to the General Subsistence Law of 1963, Article 1, section 1:

> To every Dutch person residing in the country who falls into circumstances or threatens to fall into circumstances such that he does not have the means to provide for the costs of existence, public assistance *(bijstand)* will be given by the Mayor and Wethouders [of the municipality].

Though the words are clear, their interpretation leaves significant problems of implementation. Civil servants are charged with determining what constitutes the costs of existence, who is threatened with not being able to meet those costs, and how large the amount of public assistance will be. Freedom of the frontline bureaucrat to decide (within specified limits) the level of payment to each eligible applicant is important, because some needs (e.g., a disability) require more support than others.

When the welfare state shifted in logic from providing "the costs of existence" to guaranteeing "full participation in society," these implementation problems only increased. Specifying a poverty line for welfare programs intended for basic subsistence is difficult enough. But how many theater tickets are required to meet the standards of social participation? If one citizen likes to go to the ballet and another likes to watch television in a corner bar, do they have different financial requirements to meet the social participation standard? The regulatory answer to this question is yes—and it is an answer that requires civil servants to make detailed individual assessments, leading to an extraordinary customization of welfare state benefits.[40]

These implementation issues of the social welfare state have led to the development of research programs to understand people's leisure choices. Bakker (1986), for example, reports that income and occupation are unrelated to the number of visits one makes to museums and theaters in the Netherlands—a sign of success of the social welfare state. Social class differences in the number and range of leisure activities have not been eliminated, but they are strikingly modest.[41] For government to promote social participation by subsidizing cultural life requires that the state have a thorough understanding of the needs and interests of the young, the old, cultural minorities, the disabled, and all other groups in the population. The need for information about social amenities and desired patterns of participation led the government to set up a new advisory body in March 1973, called the Social and Cultural Planning Bureau (SCP). This agency carries out research on the quality of the housing stock, health, work, and leisure. It develops projections of demographic and economic trends, their implications for the provision of social services, and the need for government subsidies.[42]

The social welfare state is an ambitious endeavor, one of the most complex projects of social engineering ever undertaken by a government. The scope of this project necessarily occasioned mistakes, such as granting subsidies to youth groups that turned out to be more like youth gangs. For a number of years the Hell's Angels in Amsterdam received an annual subsidy of about US$25,000. But the greatest problem of the social welfare state has been trying to pay for it. The endeavor to guarantee all citizens an income that would permit full social participation, and that would moreover increase benefit levels in tandem with wage movements in the private-sector labor force, created an enormous burden for the Dutch taxpayer. That burden was bearable as long as the number of income earners exceeded the number of benefit recipients by a factor of eight to one, as was the case in 1960. By 1983, though, there were only 2.2 workers paying into the social funds for each benefit recipient. As the earner/recipient ratio became less favorable, a financial crunch loomed on the horizon and the social welfare state became an unsustainable dream.

Beyond the Social Welfare State

As the social welfare state developed, it became clear that its realization would require an ever escalating commitment to those who did not work or who worked in very low-paying jobs. T. H. Marshall had foreseen that granting social rights of citizenship would carry with it an obligation that every citizen work to their capacity. "When social relations were dominated by contract," he noted, "the duty to work was not recognized" ([1950] 1992: 46). Social welfare state guarantees, by contrast, could only be funded by a general commitment to employment.

Like the social security system of the United States, Dutch social insurance is on the "pay as you go" system, with today's payments from workers used to cover today's retirees, sick, disabled, and poor. Maintenance of this system requires a stable balance between the number of benefit recipients and the number of workers. The fiscal problems of the Dutch welfare state started when the ratio of workers to benefit recipients—the labor force participation ratio—began to fall.

There were a number of reasons for this unfavorable movement in the labor force participation ratio. Foremost among them was a rapid increase in the unemployment rate during the 1980s. The welfare state was developed in a time of full employment, for the unemployment rate averaged just over 1 percent between 1964 and 1973.[43] As the welfare state was transformed into the social welfare state in the 1970s, the unemployment rate edged up to an average of 5 percent. This could at first be written off as a temporary problem stemming from the global recession of the 1970s. But, as economies elsewhere were recovering in the 1980s, Dutch unemployment continued to rise, hitting a peak rate of 16 percent in 1984.[44]

Employment in the Netherlands failed to recover in tandem with the world economy partly because of the structure of the Dutch economy. As Paulette Kurzer (1995) points out, escalation of union wage demands in the 1960s and 1970s gave the Netherlands a high-wage/high-productivity/high-unemployment economy. Indexing moved the minimum wage steadily upward, and by the mid-

1980s the Netherlands had the highest minimum wage in the world. Contributions to the social insurance funds added to high labor costs, for premiums rose twice as fast as wages between 1960 and 1980.[45]

Steady increases in the minimum wage and in the cost of labor forced the Dutch economy into ever more capital-intensive and high-value-added activities. Development of a single market within the European Union has also increased the degree of specialization within member-state economies, especially the smaller ones. In the Netherlands, this meant an increase in such capital-intensive activities as dairy farming; it also moved the largest industrial firms to put even more emphasis on their global investment networks. The largest half dozen Dutch firms, which together account for over a quarter of all employment, have more employees outside the Netherlands than they do within the country.[46] This movement of jobs outside the country has only accelerated in recent decades.

As a consequence of these developments, the fastest growth sectors in the Dutch economy in the 1960s and 1970s were technologically advanced, capital intensive, and relatively light in the use of labor to produce value. These sectors include such industries as chemicals, metallurgy, electronics, and oil refining. At the same time, between 1963 and 1980, the share of the labor force in traditional industries declined substantially as firms responded to escalating labor costs by moving their low-skilled industrial jobs abroad. Jelle Visser and Anton Hemerijck (1997: 121) note that "in the second half of the 1960s, coal mining was shut down, the textile, clothing, footwear and leather manufacturing industries all but disappeared, and shipbuilding began its long-term decline."[47] By 1980 there were only 40 percent as many jobs in low-technology industrial sectors as there were in high-technology sectors.[48] The industrial share of the labor force fell from 36 percent in the early 1970s to 27 percent in 1987 (Kitschelt 1994: 43).

Although the strategy of rapidly escalating minimum and median wages is good for economic transformation and productivity, those who have less education and those who work in declining industries pay the price with high rates of unemployment. Since 46 percent of the unemployed in the early 1980s had only an elementary school education (de Roos et al. 1980: 182), the strategy of forcing high-technology industrial growth was bound to create a significant problem of structural unemployment due to the mismatch between the needs of the economy and the training of the unemployed. Between 1947 and 1963, when central bargains between unions and employers kept wages artificially low, full employment was defined as just 2 percent unemployment. During the 1980s unemployment averaged 10 percent.

Adding to the fiscal stress created by burgeoning unemployment has been an increasing rate of disability in the workforce. In 1967, when the Worker's Disability Act was passed, there were about 225,000 workers receiving disability payments. By the time of the 1976 extension of the act, this number had reached 400,000. By 1982, fifteen years after the insurance program's inception, the number of disability claimants had exceeded 700,000 (Cox 1993: 154). Nearly one-sixth of the labor force claimed disability benefits in the early 1990s, a rate two and a half times that in the United States and three times that in France (van der Veen and Trommel 1997; Sociaal en Cultureel Planbureau 1993: 137). The work-eligible population of the Netherlands had become the most disabled in the world.

This high rate of disability is not due to a particularly unhealthy labor force. Surveys of Dutch workers have shown them to be as satisfied with the safety of their working conditions as are publics from other wealthy democracies.[49] The increase in disability claims is, then, less a reflection on the health of the population than a consequence of the lure of permanent income replacement. Claiming disability was made even more tempting by a relatively lax qualification procedure that required only a doctor's statement. Robert Cox (1993: 168) points out that "the entitlement was available for not only physical but also psychological disabilities. Especially in the construction industry, many older workers were granted benefits simply because they claimed fatigue. Doctors, in turn, were unwilling to assume the task of policing the program and were lenient in their assessments of patients." In 1988 more than one-quarter of those claiming disability received benefits for stress-related or psychological problems (Andeweg and Irwin 1993: 205). Employers may often have abetted such claims by older workers, since a grant of disability benefits allowed them to replace older (more expensive and perhaps less productive) workers with younger ones at governmental expense.[50]

A third factor that has moved the labor force participation ratio in an unfavorable direction is the increase in the number of retired people, both those over 62 (the age at which one can earn full retirement benefits) and those taking early retirement. The 62-plus population is growing steadily due to the aging of the Dutch population as a whole.[51] To combat unemployment in the 1980s, partial retirement benefits were made available to employees at age 55, and in some companies full benefits were made available at age 571/2.[52] This resulted in a wave of early retirements, so many in fact that retired workers under age 62 have their own group name—Vutters.[53] By the mid-1980s, just over a quarter of people between the ages of 55 and 65 continued to work.

The combined effect of high unemployment, high rates of disability, and a growing population of retired people has exerted steady pressure on the labor force participation ratio. Between 1960 and 1970 the percentage of the work-eligible population receiving benefits of one kind or another doubled. Between 1970 and 1980 the benefit population increased by another 37 percent, led by increases in the number of people receiving unemployment and disability benefits. In the mid-1980s only 52 percent of the population between ages 15 and 64 was employed.[54] One-quarter of all union members were unemployed, on disability, or in early retirement (Visser and Hemerijck 1997: 13). Observers began to refer to the Dutch labor market's "exit bias," a bias created by incentives embedded in the programs of the social welfare state. Ruud Vreeman, vice chair of the Labor Party and a specialist in employment issues, stated the problem with just a bit of exaggeration when he claimed in 1995 that "In the Dutch labor market we throw out everyone over fifty years old. That was always the case with disability insurance, [and] today it is also true of unemployment insurance and the early retirement program."[55]

For a while, the effects of declining labor force participation on the financial viability of the welfare state were cushioned by the windfall received by the Dutch government in the wake of the 1973 oil price shock. The value of Dutch natural gas reserves tripled overnight, bringing the government an enormous amount of unanticipated revenue. The gain in revenue at first enabled the government to continue social insurance benefits at levels originally set under much more robust economic conditions (de Wolff and Driehuis 1980). But the same developments caused an overheating of the economy. A surge in wages in the energy sector echoed throughout the labor force because of centralized bargaining and wage-coupling agreements. This made exports more expensive, and also caused the Dutch guilder to appreciate on international money markets. As exports declined, firms shed labor.[56] The jump in natural gas revenue proved to be a two-edged sword.

Ultimately, there was no way to overcome the sheer demographic force of increasing numbers of benefit claimants and decreasing numbers of workers paying into the social insurance system. With unemployment peaking at 16 percent in the early 1980s, another 15 percent of the labor force claiming sickness or disability benefits, and a growing army of pensioners, those remaining in the labor force could not be asked to pay for all those who had left. The situation was made even more precarious by rapid increases in benefit levels. Although wages stagnated between 1974 and 1981, the indexation of social insurance benefits to inflation meant that benefits actually rose two and a half times faster than the average working wage.[57]

As a consequence of these developments, government expenditures began to rise precipitously, both absolutely and as a percentage of GDP. In 1950 public expenditure expressed as a percentage of GDP was about the same in the Netherlands as it was in the United States. In the wake of building the social welfare state, the Netherlands had by 1970 the highest public expenditure rate in the world, and in 1980 the Netherlands was second only to Sweden.[58] As a consequence, the government deficit ballooned. Figure 7.3 shows that a balanced budget in the early 1970s yielded to deficits on the order of 11 percent of national income by the early 1980s, resulting in a doubling of public debt between 1970 and 1987. Given that social insurance payments constituted about half of total government expenditures, it was clear that something had to be done about the welfare state.

The governmental response to this crisis can be divided into two phases. The first phase, which began in 1981, was a wide-ranging search for ways of limiting spending. The second phase, which began later in the 1980s and has continued to the present, has involved a revision of the very concept of the social welfare state.

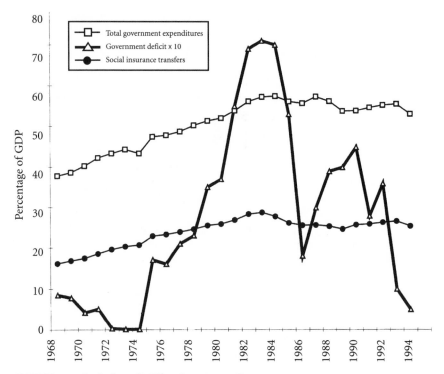

FIGURE 7.3   Evolution of Welfare State Expenditures

SOURCE: Transfers and expenditures: OECD Historical Statistics (1996). Government deficit: International Monetary Fund.

The first-phase objective of limiting spending required an austerity program affecting all social spending. The maximum duration of full unemployment benefits was reduced from two and a half years to six months. Unemployment and disability benefits were cut by 3 percent in 1984; pensions and family allowances were frozen for three years beginning that same year. Support payments in the Fine Arts Program were reduced in 1983, and the program itself was eliminated a few years after that. Income-tax allowances for the old and disabled were abolished and child allowances were cut. Even the benefit payments to widows and orphans were reduced by making them means-tested and by declaring orphans over age 18 and widows over age 50 no longer eligible for benefits (Sociaal en Cultureel Planbureau 1993: 116). These changes were all made under the leadership of Minister-President Ruud Lubbers during the course of the 1980s, causing Margaret Thatcher to remark that Lubbers's cuts in the Dutch welfare state were a disaster for her own reputation as the Iron Lady.[59]

The disability program was a particular target for cost reductions, with the main focus being to reduce the number of claimants. Doctors have been required since 1993 to indicate not only the extent of disability but also whether the individual is capable of seeking alternative work. All disability beneficiaries are now reexamined periodically to ascertain whether they remain unable to work; the original program was designed with the assumption that one remained disabled indefinitely (Cox 1992). The maximum benefit has also been reduced from 80 percent to 70 percent of the last earned wage, making disability benefits equivalent to unemployment benefits.[60] The duration of disability benefits has also been limited. Between 1981 and 1986 the purchasing power of individual disability payments fell, on average, by more than 20 percent (Rochon 1987: 68). These measures succeeded in reducing the number of disability claims. In 1996 there were 737,000 full-equivalency disability claimants, almost 9 percent fewer than in 1992, when the number of claimants peaked at 806,000.

Even the minimum income guaranteed by public assistance (the *bijstand*) was reduced. In 1995 the guarantee was divided into a basic benefit and supplementary benefits, the latter to be offered under such special circumstances as an imminent loss of home or shutoff of utilities.[61] Municipalities—which administer the public assistance program—may set the basic compensation level at anywhere from 85 to 120 percent of a national norm. They receive compensation from the national government at the level of the national norm, but must finance bonus amounts themselves. This decentralization creates an incentive for municipalities to economize both on the basic stipend and on special payments beyond the minimum (Cox 1998: 408–409).

The 1980s were ultimately a period of dramatic plans and reasonably dramatic results in welfare reform. Robert Cox (1993: 176) estimates that retrenchment plans developed during the decade advocated 9.7 billion guilders in spending reductions, and that about 59 percent of those cuts were actually achieved. However, not all cost-cutting undertaken in the austerity phase was directed at social spending: The direct costs of government were also examined. Six so-called great efficiency operations were undertaken during the 1980s to reduce the costs of government. Civil service salaries were frozen in 1983, reduced by 3 percent in 1984, and then held in place for three years.[62] Civil service reorganizations resulted in the abolition of one department and a sharp reduction in the number of external advisory bodies used in policy formulation.[63] In 1987 the size of the civil service peaked at 746,000 full-time-equivalent work years, and by 1990 had shrunk through attrition to 743,000 work years (de Kam and de Haan 1991: 9). Regulations were examined for potential reduction and simplification, a task undertaken not only to reduce the cost of government but also to restore public trust and—it was hoped—to increase regulatory compliance. Because of the fragmentation of responsibility between different agencies, for example, a firm previously had to submit applications for permits to several different agencies before undertaking a project such as building a plant. The permit system has now been simplified by bringing better coordination to the approval process. The ultimate goal is to require just one comprehensive permit for most projects.[64]

Finally, the governments of the 1980s sought greater efficiencies through privatization. The PTT (Postal and Telephone Service), the governmentally owned postal savings bank, the national airline (KLM) and rail system, the state mining company (DSM, which now produces chemicals), the studios of the public broadcasting service (NOS), the governmental purchasing bureau, and the state publishing house (which publishes the text of parliamentary debates, laws, regulations, official studies, and policy papers) have all been partially or fully privatized. Competition has also been introduced into the domains of telephone service, cable television, and public transport. Netherlands' Railways (NS) has accordingly lost its monopoly on intercity train transportation.

The results of the great efficiency operations were mixed, with the greatest changes coming through privatization and the least change in the areas of program cuts and size reductions in the civil service.[65] However, the cumulative impact of these operations was to alter the very conception of the relationship between government and society. As former minister-president Ruud Lubbers (1991: 140–141) points out, reorganization of government agencies was originally undertaken with the goal of increasing policy coordination. With the beginning of the wave of privatization and deregulation, the emphasis soon shifted to revitalizing the state-society relationship and reducing the autonomous power of government. In environmental protection, for example, there has been a shift from regulation to market incentives in the form of taxes on undesired activities and subsidies for environmentally sound practices. The result is simplified regulation and an option for firms to choose the level of resources they want to devote to environmental protection (Goverde 1993). Former minister-president Ruud Lubbers (1991: 141) concludes that "the idea of the state with one center of power has been replaced by an image of a complex of governmental institutions, each interwoven with their counterpart social institutions." It is easy to hear in such phrases a twenty-first-century echo of the nineteenth-century confessional ideas of subsidiarity and sovereignty in one's own circle, for the state becomes once again a partner in governance with private institutions rather than a sovereign grantor of the rights of social citizenship.

Through a variety of paths beyond simple cuts in expenditure, then, the size of the government has been reduced. The effect of efforts to brake the growth of social welfare spending and the total cost of government can be seen in Figure 7.3. Between 1983 and 1986 the government cut public spending by nearly 8 percent and drove its annual deficit below 8 percent of national income (from 10.7 percent in 1983). Moreover, this was done in a time of continued high unemployment.[66] By the end of the 1980s, the government had also been able to reduce the top corporate tax rate from 48 percent to 35 percent, and the top personal income tax rate from 73 percent to 60 percent.[67]

But cost-cutting measures could not be taken very far before the participation guarantees of the social welfare state were called into question. For example, a regulation introduced in 1985 mandated a 10 percent reduction in public assistance for people who share a household. Though based on the reasonable assumption that two can live cheaper than one, this reform in effect ended the individual basis of social insurance entitlements and reintroduced the criterion of the extent to which one can depend on others for assistance. The reform required inspectors to find out who was living alone and who was not; these officials were quickly dubbed "toothbrush inspectors" because counting toothbrushes was one means of determining the number of members of a household (Cox 1993: 186).

As the program of cuts continued during the 1980s, many Dutch people began to worry that the basic commitments of the social welfare state were themselves being eroded. Reacting to a steady diet of austerity measures, the percentage of the public saying that social insurance benefits should increase rose steadily during the 1980s, from just 21 percent in 1980 to 57 percent by 1989 (Sociaal en Cultureel Planbureau 1993: 111). Adam Szirmai (1988: 100) found that over 60 percent of the Dutch public believed in 1980 that income differences in the Netherlands were too large, a finding that suggested limited tolerance for further cuts in social services.

Responding to this climate of concern about the fate of the social welfare state required a change of direction from cutting costs to a greater emphasis on rethinking the basic principles of the social insurance system. From the social welfare emphasis on government as guarantor of social participation, there has now come to be more of an emphasis on partnership between the state and social institutions. In this evolving philosophy, the government has been able to take advantage of the existence of hundreds of private organizations responsible for delivering welfare state services. These organizations, a legacy of the pillar system, each serve their clienteles within the parameters of state regulations and then bill the government for services performed and payments made. As long as each was guaranteed its own niche in the provision of social services, these private organizations were an obstacle to change. By putting these implementing agencies in competition with each other, incentives in the emerging social insurance system were suddenly altered in favor of efficiency.

The central strategy in forging a new partnership between government and social organizations, then, has been to take advantage of the presence of multiple implementing agencies to introduce competition into the provision of social services. The Social Insurance Council, a body composed chiefly of employer and labor representatives, was closed down in 1994 after administering social insurance systems for over forty years. In its place, a competitive system was created in which private organizations bid for the right to administer particular social insurance programs. For example, a private agency was designated in Amsterdam in 1999 to pay unemployment benefits and to serve as an employment agency. When it successfully places people into jobs, the agency is allowed to keep a portion of the money earmarked for unemployment benefits.[68]

The private clinics, hospitals, and administrative organizations that deliver health care have also been given greater freedom of operation, subject to government standards on quality and universal access. This has slowed the rate of increase in health care costs by eliminating a reimbursement structure that encouraged health care organizations to provide too many services to some patients.[69] Similar incentives have been put into place for employers with respect to the disability program. As of 1998, disability premiums paid by individual employers are dependent in part on the number of claims for occupational disability made by their employees. Employers who hire workers off the disability rolls, on the other hand, receive a wage subsidy paid by the government for four years. Employers also have the option of purchasing disability coverage in the private insurance market rather than paying into the government's insurance program (van der Veen and Trommel 1997). This package of measures creates a disincentive for employers to use the disability program to shed older workers from their payrolls, and it puts the government's social fund in competition with private insurance.

The most sustained focus of reform has been in the area of job creation and keeping people in the labor market. It has been understood since early in the 1980s that the social welfare state could be sustained only if labor force participation remained high. And yet the incentives of the social insurance system pulled some people out of the labor market, while others were pushed out by increasing unemployment. Despite high unemployment, wage rates continued to escalate because of indexation against inflation. Escalating private-sector wages, in turn, were automatically coupled to increases in public-sector salaries and in social welfare benefits. Paying those increased wages and benefits required the government to raise income and payroll taxes, further increasing the cost of labor to employers. Increased costs of labor, in turn, led to increased unemployment. It was a perfectly designed and perfectly vicious circle.

That circle was broken in the early 1980s by Wim Kok, then leader of the largest union federation (the FNV), and Chris van Veen of the largest employers association (the VNO, now VNO-NCW). They agreed in 1982 to trade a scheduled 2 percent wage increase granted as price compensation in exchange for reduced working hours. It was the hope of union leaders that shorter work hours would lead to the creation of new jobs. This "Wassenaar Accord" (named after the place in which it was concluded) between unions and employer organizations set the stage for two decades of wage moderation in exchange for employment growth.[70] These negotiations restored the tradition of nonbinding central agreements between unions and employers, which serve as guidelines for contracts concluded within the firms.[71]

The success of these agreements has become known as the "Dutch model." The two most dramatic trends associated with this renewed collaboration between unions and employers are a slow rate of wage increases and a rapid growth of employment opportunities. Real wages grew in the Netherlands at a rate of just 1.5 percent per year between 1984 and 1990, and between 1991 and 1996 real wages did not grow at all.[72] In the same period, the rate of job growth increased sharply. In just over a decade, the Netherlands had gone from having what Göran Therborn called "the most spectacular employment failure in the advanced capitalist world" to having a job creation record that has attracted international acclaim.[73] Between 1982 and 1996 the Netherlands experienced 1.6 percent job growth per year, the same rate of job creation enjoyed in the United States and four times that experienced elsewhere in Europe (Visser and Hemerijck 1997: 20). By 1998 unemployment in the Netherlands was hovering just above 5 percent, half the average in the European Union and one-third of the peak Dutch unemployment rate in the mid-1980s.

Although wage moderation and job growth are due above all to compacts between leaders of the unions and employers associations, the government has also contributed by altering its policies with respect to employment. The labor market was deregulated by extending the probationary period for new employees and relaxing the conditions that must be met before someone is terminated from a job. The right of those receiving unemployment benefits to refuse employment beneath their qualifications has also been restricted. An unemployed college graduate, for example, must now accept unskilled labor after two years without work. The long-standing rule that one must actively seek a job while receiving unemployment benefits is being enforced more strictly, and an applicant must now prove that he or she did everything possible to avoid the loss of a job in order to be eligible for benefits. As a result of this stricter stance, the percentage of benefit recipients receiving sanctions due to insufficient search activities increased from 7 percent in 1987 to 17 percent in 1994. Romke van der Veen and Willem Trommel (1997: 20, 27) note that these new policies "have changed the administrative culture [of the Ministry of Social Affairs]: from lenient and friendly it has gradually become more rigorous and coercive."

The efforts of the Dutch government to foster increased employment have traditionally been limited to such macroeconomic measures as holding down the rate of wage increases and granting subsidies to troubled firms as a way of keeping their workers employed.[74] In social democratic countries such as Sweden, the government has long had an active labor-market policy that includes retraining of the unemployed. The Dutch government has only recently begun to create programs to get people into jobs, focused on those least likely to find jobs on their own. Youth unemployment has been a particular target, along with unemployment among ethnic minorities. Both groups are overrepresented among those unemployed for two years or more, a condition that often leads to permanent exclusion from the labor force. Among the recent reforms is a ruling that young adults under age 21 no longer have the right to claim unemployment benefits. They are expected instead to go to school for further training if they cannot find a job, or to work in a youth employment program that combines a minimum-wage job with time-off provisions for extra schooling. The largest program resulting from the purple government's pledge to create "jobs, jobs, and more jobs" has been the development of so-called Melkert jobs. Named after Ad Melkert, social affairs minister from 1994 to 1998, these are subsidized positions in hospitals, daycare centers, and homes for the elderly. They are available only to those who have been unemployed for at least twelve months, and are intended as a bridge to regular employment (Visser and Hemerijck 1997: 168–174).

These efforts of the central government have been echoed in pilot programs developed in a number of municipalities. An experiment in Rotterdam in 1996 allowed those on public assistance to work for the city two to three days per week at minimum wage, with the salary deducted from their public assistance benefits as per the normal policy. In exchange for accepting this employment, participants may work the rest of each week without reduction of their public assistance benefits.[75] The goal of this program is ultimately to entice public assistance beneficiaries off the welfare rolls altogether.

The government has also fostered employment by reducing payroll taxes for social insurance programs, severing the automatic cost-of-living adjustments for social benefits, and allowing the minimum wage to lag behind the private-sector wage index.[76] The most effective measure to foster labor force participation may have been the simplest: the decision to provide free daycare for single mothers on public assistance, enabling them to seek work.[77]

These efforts have been rewarded with an increase in the proportion of those between ages 15 and 64 who work in paid employment, from 52 percent in the mid-1980s to 63 percent in 1996.[78] This is due mainly to increased employment among women, since the popularity of early retirement continues to reduce male labor force participation. The participation of women aged 15–65 in the labor force rose from 29 percent to 54 percent between 1974 and 1991. Women's labor force participation in the Netherlands is still below the European Union average, but continuation of the trend will soon obliterate those differences.[79]

Increased labor force participation has occurred in the context of a transformed economy. Despite wage moderation, the loss of industrial jobs has continued unabated. Jelle Visser and Anton Hemerijck (1997: 105) estimate a loss of 100,000 jobs in manufacturing, 10 percent of the total, between 1992 and 1994 alone. Nearly all the jobs created in the last decade are in the service sector, which now employs almost 70 percent of the workforce. These jobs, many of them in retail and social services, do not pay as well as the manufacturing jobs they replace, and they have little scope for productivity gains and wage increases. Moreover, a startling number of the new jobs are part-time or temporary. By 1996, 37 percent of all jobs in the Netherlands were part-time, more than double the rate of part-time work in neighboring economies.[80] About three-quarters of Dutch women in the labor force work part-time, the highest rate of part-time work in the twenty-four countries on which the OECD collects data.

This changing profile of the labor force represents a fundamental break from the previous emphasis on high-skill/high-wage jobs in the Dutch economy. Compared to France, Germany, and Italy, the average real wage in the Netherlands peaked in 1976 and has been declining since then. As Visser and Hemerijck (1997: 12) point out, the Dutch model has produced "nearly full part-time employment" rather than a high rate of full-time employment.

It is important to be cautious about such labels as the "Dutch model," for it was not so long ago that political steering of the economy in the Netherlands was being called the "Dutch disease." Even so, recent innovations do represent a significant shift in welfare and labor market policy, and are being cited elsewhere in Europe as a synthesis of American-style job creation with European-style social solidarity. The leader of the German Christian Democratic Union, Wolfgang Schäuble, summarized this development in 1997 by saying that "The Dutch appear, after 15 years, to have largely succeeded in reforming their economic system without forfeiting the solidarity which is characteristic of their society."[81]

Schäuble is correct that solidarity has not only been retained but also in some ways strengthened compared to the deadlock between unions, employers, and government characteristic of the 1970s. But the Dutch model has not evolved without significant conflicts. One million workers took to the streets of The Hague in 1991 to protest the policies of a government containing their nominal ally, the Labor Party. It was the largest demonstration in Dutch history, beyond anything even the peace movement had put together a decade earlier.

One reason for the disappointment of union leaders is that wage moderation, although dramatically improving the employment picture, has not been able to stave off continued cuts in social benefits. Between 1991 and 1994 there were reductions in rent subsidies, deletions of some dental costs from the public health-insurance package, and reductions in the level and duration of benefits in the sickness and disability programs. An even more profound disappointment has been the disestablishment of both unions and employers from their former role as overseers and implementers of social insurance programs. Recall that the social partners were placed in charge of implementing workers insurance programs for sickness, disability, and unemployment. This was a necessary concession by architects of the welfare state to persuade the pillar organizations to accept a significant expansion of social insurance after World War II.[82]

Control of these programs by the social partners began to be questioned as all three insurance programs grew far beyond expectations in scope and expense. An investigative committee of the Second Chamber concluded in 1993 that the social insurance programs had been mismanaged and that the disability program had mushroomed because of its use by unions and employers as an alternative to layoffs or early retirement. The response of the purple government was to reduce the importance of the Socio-Economic Council as a policy adviser and to replace the bipartite Social Insurance Council with a new advisory body, the Supervisory Board for Social Insurance (*College van Toezicht Sociale Verzekeringen*), whose members are appointed by the government. As noted above, implementation of the social insurance system is also being reformed through competitive subcontracting to private agencies. These changes constitute a revolution in the administration of social welfare, giving the state more control over the system at the expense of the central organizations of unions and employers.[83]

Reform of the social insurance system represents a significant departure from past practice in the Netherlands. The social partners of business and labor have been largely disestablished from their former role as administrators of social insurance and replaced by private agencies. There has been a new emphasis on job creation in labor-intensive industries, often at lower skill levels and rates of pay, and often part-time. Social insurance benefit levels, the duration of benefits, and the permissive entitlement to benefits have all been scaled back. These reforms have ended the individual basis of entitlement and terminated the system under which benefit recipients automatically participate in increasing labor force prosperity. Studies of public assistance beneficiaries suggest that payments are no longer high enough to provide the kind of social participation once promised to all citizens.[84] The net result has been a significant departure from the ideals of the social welfare state. And that leads us to our final consideration in this chapter, which can be phrased as a question.

What Is Left of the Social Welfare State?

Reaction against changes of the last two decades has been strong in some quarters. Bishop Muskens of Breda spoke out on several occasions against what he termed "growing poverty" in the Netherlands, which created (according to some) increased health problems in the poorer parts of the major cities. And yet, even after retrenchment of the social welfare state, the system remains an extensive bulwark of protection from the income consequences of sickness, disability, unemployment, and old age. After a decade of cuts from 1981 to 1991, pension recipients still received 82 percent of the average disposable (post-tax) income of a worker, disability claimants received 96 percent of average disposable income, and the unemployed received 65 percent of average disposable income.[85] If the poverty line is defined as having one-half or less of the median household income, then 3 percent of Dutch families are in poverty compared to 18 percent in the United States. Moreover, Dutch families spend a shorter period of time in poverty than their American counterparts (Visser and Hemerijck 1997: 42). The Dutch welfare system also continues to be particularly sensitive to the issue of how to avoid giving public assistance recipients the feeling of being second-class citizens. Use of the social insurance format guarantees that there is as little ostracism of a Dutch recipient of disability benefits as there is of an American recipient of social security.

The Dutch model of labor market flexibility and a renewed emphasis on job creation and employment have themselves come to be part of the revised vision of the social welfare state. Development of a more active labor market policy means that the earlier stress on the rights of citizenship is now modulated by added emphasis on the individual's duties in a social welfare state. This is partly due to realization that development of a passive mentality as a client of the welfare state does not foster the kind of social citizenship envisioned under the social welfare state. H. te Grotenhuis and J. Dronkers (1989: 27) found that "Despite a guaranteed

State income, being out of work can introduce tensions and frustrations within the family . . . unemployed and occupationally disabled fathers sometimes feel themselves to be useless and marginalised." Grotenhuis and Dronkers found that this effect persists even into the next generation, as the children of benefit recipients have lower achievement scores at school. Policies to get people back to work thus have a principled basis as well as being a pragmatic necessity for public finance. Social participation is fostered by providing the incentives and opportunities to work in paid employment.

In some respects, developments of the last two decades have actually increased the potential to achieve the goals of the social welfare state. Wage moderation and the commitment to full employment have made possible a contingent recoupling of social benefits to wages. That coupling was severed in 1982 in order to let private-sector wages move ahead of benefit levels. In 1992 a new law reestablished coupling as long as wage increases do not exceed anticipated increases in inflation and productivity, and as long as the ratio of benefit recipients to those in paid employment remains below a specified threshold. This contingent coupling preserves the principle of maintaining the relative economic position of those receiving benefits, while also recognizing that the desired goal must at times give way to macroeconomic conditions. Between 1996 and 1998, unemployment levels sank, the ratio of benefit recipients to workers moved in a favorable direction, and coupling was restored.[86]

Even the development of extensive part-time work and the massive overrepresentation of women in part-time jobs represent an accommodation between the ideals of the social welfare state and the Dutch tradition of a relatively sharp division of labor between men and women. In two-income households, men work in a paid job on average eighteen hours more per week than do women. Women, in turn, spend eighteen hours more per week on housework than do men (Visser and Hemerijck 1997: 43). This division of labor may not be to the taste of every couple, but the Dutch labor market makes it a viable option for those who choose it. As Jelle Visser and Anton Hemerijck (1997: 182) note, the spread of the "one-and-a-half income family" reduces the household's dependency on one head-of-household/breadwinner, while also serving as a defense against child poverty.

The Netherlands is moving, step by step and in an unsystematic way, toward a society in which paid employment, family responsibilities, education, and leisure are chosen by the individual in a mix that may be altered at different times in the life cycle. Part-time employment opportunities are plentiful, and even full-time Dutch workers are on the job only 1,400 hours per year, compared to 1,500 hours per year in Germany and 1,900 hours per year in Japan (Münchau and Cramb 1997). "Labor market participation" has thus come to mean not simply putting more people in the labor force, but also altering the labor market itself in ways that accommodate diverse aspirations. The "Dutch model," then, might be thought of less as a retreat from the social welfare state than as a midcourse correction. It continues to soften the link between paid employment and income, while paying greater attention to T. H. Marshall's cautions about the importance of work as part of the meaning of citizenship in the social welfare state.

Conclusion

The Dutch welfare state has gone through several distinct cycles in the twentieth century, corresponding not only to changing ideas about the role of government in distributing economic goods but also to the organization of society, the health of the economy, and cooperation between social classes. The early Dutch welfare system was shaped and limited by the confessional pillars, and specifically by their determination to contain the power of the state. The postwar welfare state was made possible by the widespread desire to transcend class conflict and rebuild the economy. This led to development of an elaborate set of corporatist institutions that simultaneously defused class conflict, eased confessional fears about growth of the state, and professionalized the social welfare field. The social welfare state of the late 1960s and 1970s was, in turn, rooted in the social and political activism of a postwar generation that proclaimed the inadequacies of a welfare state concerned with bread alone. It was also founded on the seemingly uninterrupted prospect for increasing prosperity that was prominent in the Netherlands until the mid-1970s. Finally, the phase of retrenchment was driven by an understanding that the ideals of the social welfare state are not realizable if a growing number of benefit recipients are funded by a shrinking workforce. The government has responded by incorporating paid employment into the concept of social partnership, and by attempting to put people into jobs with the same vigor it uses to put people into theater seats.

One constant through these changes has been the commitment of both government and public to assist the poorest members of society—the "socially weak," to use the Dutch term. This record of support for the social welfare state puts the Netherlands in sharp contrast with countries ranging from Sweden and Denmark to the United States, with their periodic tax revolts and welfare backlashes. Despite the low electoral threshold, no new political parties have gained entry to the Second Chamber based on the demand that the welfare state be reduced or dismantled. Even among the Liberals, the most conservative of the mainstream parties, the basic concepts of the social welfare state are widely accepted. The neoconservative critique of the welfare state that has taken hold in other advanced industrial democracies has had relatively little impact on the Netherlands. Extensive support for the social welfare state, both in public opinion and among political leaders, has enabled the country to continue at the forefront of the effort to link national prosperity to individual security of income and the construction of a more just social order.

NOTES

1. Cited in Gouda (1995: 190).
2. See Newton (1978: 91–97) for an account of early social reform and social welfare legislation.

3. The Netherlands was an early industrializer in such sectors as textiles and shipbuilding, but these sectors went into a steep decline in the nineteenth century with the loss of trade markets and the development of mercantilist protection among European neighbors. See Boxer (1990: 322–331) and Chapter 8.

4. Cited in Gouda (1995: 130).

5. This tradition continues. In 1998, Dutch churches were welcoming refugees who had been denied asylum in other European countries and were ineligible for consideration by the Dutch government. *InterNetKrant,* October 19, 1998, page 1.

6. Cited in Haley (1972: 157).

7. Johnson and Marsh (1664: 55–56). See also Boxer (1990: 61–65).

8. Cited in Gouda (1995: 173).

9. Cited in Riemen (1992: 20).

10. The Beveridge Commission, named for Sir William Beveridge, was appointed by the British government in 1942 to draw up plans for a postwar social welfare policy. Among the chief recommendations of the Beveridge Commission was development of the National Health Service.

11. Cited in Idenburg (1985: 133). The recommendations of the van Rhijn Commission became the basis for policy proposals developed under the Labor-Catholic (Roman-Red) coalitions of Willem Drees, not least because A. A. van Rhijn came to be state secretary for social insurance in the Ministry of Social Affairs for much of this period. C.P.M. Romme was a member of the van Rhijn Commission as well and therefore also remained supportive of the recommended changes in policy when he came to be leader of the Catholic People's Party.

12. Today, Dutch workers contribute between 20 and 25 percent of their income to the funds that support the retirement pension, widows and orphans fund, health insurance, employment insurance, and disability insurance programs. These contributions account for over 90 percent of the money paid into the social funds, making the Dutch system the most heavily reliant on employee contributions of any advanced industrial society.

13. See Cox (1993: 104–128) for a detailed account of the passage of postwar welfare state legislation.

14. These numbers do not include another half million full-time-equivalent work years in private but collectively financed occupations including public transport, health care, and social services.

15. For a review of the networks of private organizations involved in policy formulation and implementation in health care, housing, and old-age policy, see the essays in van Mierlo and Gerrichhauzen (1988). Maynard (1975), Juffermans (1982), and Boot and Knapen (1986) also provide detailed accounts of the pillar-era health care system.

16. The U.S. welfare system avoids income redistribution by pegging the basic benefits at just 22 percent of the maximum allowable benefits (Esping-Andersen 1990: table 3.1, page 70).

17. See for example Kloosterman (1994) and van Kersbergen (1995).

18. At the beginning of the 1950s, before development of the welfare state, a mere 8 percent of GNP was spent by government on social services.

19. These data are from a seven-nation survey conducted between 1987 and 1993 by Chikio Hayashi and his colleagues (1992). The focus of the survey is the cross-national comparison of cultural values. This is a notoriously difficult area to study because questions formulated about cultural values typically have a larger level of "noise," or random

response, than do questions on such concrete matters as which party one voted for in the last election. Even so, the data of the Hayashi survey are uniquely valuable because of the relatively large number of questions on values connected to money and work, and because the seven-nation sample gives us a good sense of where the Dutch stand in relation to other publics.

20. The other countries surveyed include Austria, Hungary, Ireland, Israel, Italy, Norway, the United Kingdom, the United States, and (former) West Germany.

21. Cited in Idenburg (1985: 138).

22. In Dutch, the traditional welfare state came to be contrasted with the *"verzorgingsstaat"*—literally, the "caring state."

23. Partly as a consequence, the Dutch have the highest holiday participation rate in the European Union (Sociaal en Cultureel Planbureau 1993: 302).

24. *InterNetKrant,* January 7, 1998, page 1. There was even debate at one point about whether social participation requires that those on public assistance be given an automobile, though this issue was ultimately decided in the negative.

25. Cited in Rochon (1987: 59).

26. See also Albeda (1988) and Visser (1993) for discussion of the rights of employees within the firm.

27. Cited in van den Berg (1980: 33).

28. Just 16 percent of the Dutch and 17 percent of Americans agreed with this proposition, compared to 21 percent of the British, 25 percent of the Italians, 27 percent of the Germans, 42 percent of the French, and 49 percent of the Japanese.

29. The Germans gave fractionally less materialistic answers than the Dutch on the importance of free time compared to earning more money.

30. Johnson and Marsh (1664: 68). See also Boxer (1990: 190–192).

31. Valkman (1982: 37). The criteria for subsidy under this program were both economic and artistic. An applicant was first screened by the Ministry of Social Affairs, which ascertained that the individual did not have a sufficient income from activities other than art creation. After certification by the ministry, the work of the applicant was judged by a committee of three artists, three art experts, two civil servants from the Ministry of Social Affairs, and an adviser to the Fine Arts Program. It is sometimes claimed that the program was lax in its standards (e.g., Cox 1993: 167). Certainly the number of supported artists expanded significantly between 1960 and 1980, but this was not for lack of an extensive selection process.

32. Cited in Valkman (1982: 26).

33. *InterNetKrant,* May 3, 1998, pages 1–2.

34. The Dutch government has recently begun to promote child care as part of its drive to increase labor force participation by women, but "the gap between demand and supply is still growing," according to de Jong Gierfeld and Liefbroer (1995: 104).

35. Cited in Visser and Hemerijck (1997: 127). See also Becker and van Tiel (1990) and van Kersbergen (1995) for discussions of the family-centered ideology in what van Kersbergen terms "social capitalism."

36. Goudsblom (1967: 48–49).

37. Only 7 percent of Americans and 4 percent of British shared that view (International Social Science Program, 1989: 72), variable 20.

38. Between 1960 and 1994 the population grew by 30 percent but the number of households grew by 93 percent. The average number of people per household declined

from 3.9 to 2.35 in that period, and 31 percent of all households are now single-person households (Centraal Bureau voor de Statistiek 1996: 47).

39. European Union regulations on nondiscrimination in the provision of social services also forced the Dutch to abolish distinctions between men and women, and between unmarried and married men, for purposes of social welfare benefits.

40. One recipient of public assistance sued the state for an extra condom allowance, claiming that his existing benefit levels did not permit he and his girlfriend to make love as often as they wanted. Upon review of testimony concerning average frequency of intercourse in the relationship, the administrative court agreed to increase the client's living allowance.

41. Education, on the other hand, correlates closely with cultural activities, a finding that has led to concern about the distribution of educational opportunities. See de Graaf and de Graaf (1988) and Sociaal en Cultureel Planbureau (1993: 307, 309). Farah et al. (1979: 413) find that the Dutch public is highest among the five countries they surveyed in support for governmental provision of a quality education.

42. See Timmermans and Becker (1985: 93–100) and Ester and Nauta (1986).

43. Job vacancies exceeded the number of unemployed in most years between 1954 and 1972, according to Pinder (1976: 30).

44. These unemployment data are from Organisation for Economic Co-operation and Development (1996).

45. According to André Mommen (1986), the average gross salary of a Dutch worker was 25 percent higher than that of an American worker in the mid-1980s, while the net wage was 25 percent lower.

46. Paulette Kurzer (1993: 110–114). According to Kurzer, 48 percent of Unilever employees, 67 percent of the work force of Royal Dutch Shell, and 79 percent of the Philips labor force are employed outside the Netherlands. Voorhoeve (1979: 87) finds that of the five largest Dutch companies, only KLM has a majority of employees within the Netherlands.

47. In 1970, 5 percent of all Dutch industrial jobs were in shipbuilding. By the mid-1980s the last of the major shipbuilding yards had collapsed, unable to compete with labor costs that were 50 percent lower in Japan (Stråth 1987). Similarly, the number of textile and clothing manufacturing jobs was reduced from 60,000 to 20,000 between 1968 and 1978 (Katzenstein 1985: 57–59).

48. Calculated from de Roos et al. (1980: 179).

49. See International Social Science Program (1989: 124–126), variables 72–74. The Dutch also claimed to be more satisfied with the state of their health than did other national populations, according to Hayashi et al. (1992).

50. The "early retirement" usage of the disability program is suggested by the fact that the number of disability claimants between the ages of 55 and 65 in 1986 became greater than the number in that age group still working in a paid job. See Visser and Hemerijck (1997: 138).

51. The birthrate has fallen rapidly in the last generation, so sharply that de Jong Gierfeld and Liefbroer (1995) refer to a "second demographic transition." Dutch women are having their first child at a later age, no doubt due in significant degree to their increased levels of education and labor force participation. The resultant low birthrate, combined with the low death rate, means that the Dutch population is aging faster than that of any other advanced industrial society except Japan.

52. Andeweg and Irwin (1993: 93). Government employees could until recently retire on full salary at age 61.

53. Vutters are named after the Dutch initials for "early retirement": *Vervroegd UitTreding*. Early retirement benefits were abolished in the 1990s, though the continuation of benefits for those already receiving them means that the labor force participation rate of those between 55 and 65 will begin to climb only gradually.

54. This compares to the 70 percent of Americans between ages 15 and 64 then working in paid employment (Organisation for Economic Co-operation and Development 1996). See also Sociaal en Cultureel Planbureau (1993).

55. Cited in Smits (1996).

56. See Lubbers and Lemckert (1980) and Kurzer (1993).

57. Indexation of social insurance benefits to wage movements was largely responsible for a tenfold increase in the basic old-age pension between 1953 and 1977 (de Wolff and Driehuis 1980: 31). See also Szirmai (1988: 24–25).

58. Peters (1991a: 77). Tax revenues also rose, from 22 percent of GDP in 1950 to 46 percent in 1980, resulting in the highest total tax rate in the world outside of Scandinavia (Peters 1991a: 27).

59. Cited in Blits (1989: 19).

60. By 1994, 85 percent of employees had negotiated "gap insurance" into their contracts—a restoration of benefits to the 80 percent level in the event of disability. This frustrated government efforts to eliminate the distinction between disability and unemployment, but it also shifted some costs of the disability program from the public to the private sector (van der Veen and Trommel 1997).

61. *InterNetKrant*, October 28, 1997, page 1.

62. Between 1978 and 1987 civil service pay lagged behind wages in the private sector by 10 percent (Visser 1990: 223).

63. See Chapter 6 for discussion of the role of external advisory bodies in the policy process.

64. Proponents of regulatory streamlining claim that compliance will actually increase as cumbersome and expensive procedures are eliminated (Hanf 1989). A pressing example in the environmental area is the effective processing of manure on Dutch farms. Dairy and chicken farms in the Netherlands are intensive operations whose manure production threatens to overwhelm the capacity of the soil to absorb ammonia, nitrate, and phosphorous compounds. Faced with a threat to the quality of both surface and ground water due to the leeching of these compounds into the water supply, the government has attempted to control manure production by taxing animals above a certain number per hectare (Huppes and Kagan 1989; van Geleuken 1990). The number of manure-producing animals in the Netherlands continues to rise, and finding a policy that will effectively encourage environmentally sound manure reprocessing remains one of the most pressing tasks in the Netherlands.

65. Of course, simply arresting the growth of the civil service must be counted as a significant accomplishment. For an assessment of the six operations (reorganization, reduction, decentralization, deregulation, privatization, and program discontinuation), see de Kam and de Haan (1991).

66. With unemployment around 5 percent in the mid-1990s, the government deficit was reduced to just 1.4 percent of GDP.

67. The Dutch still retain one of the highest VAT (sales tax) rates in the European Union. Although value-added tax increases the price of goods sold in Dutch stores, it does not increase the cost of exported goods (as do taxes on incomes and corporate payrolls). Despite its regressivity, then, the VAT is a preferred form of taxation for a country seeking to maintain export competitiveness.

68. This program was modeled on a U.S. experiment first tried in Wisconsin, which resulted in a 75 percent reduction in the number of unemployment benefit recipients (*InterNetKrant*, August 1, 1998, page 1).

69. For example, the health insurance system paid for 80 percent of the cost of care in a hospital but only 67 percent of the cost of ambulatory care. As a result, in 1987 the average length of a hospital stay in the Netherlands was 35 days, compared to only 17 days in Germany and 10 days in the United States (Organisation for Economic Co-operation and Development 1990: 89, 150). These perverse incentives are removed under the new health care system.

70. Although the agreements reached between leaders of union federations and employers associations were not binding on the contract negotiations carried out in particular firms across the country, they were influential as pattern agreements that were usually replicated in specific contracts.

71. In contrast to the period between 1963 and the end of the 1970s, these agreements were reached without central government intervention, though in a number of years the threat of a wage-price freeze or other governmental wage limits provided the stimulus for agreement between unions and employers.

72. See Visser and Hemerijck (1997: 99) and Münchau and Cramb (1997).

73. Therborn is cited in Visser and Hemerijck (1997: 9).

74. The RSV, a shipbuilding firm that employed 30,000 workers, received 2.2 billion guilders in subsidies over a ten-year period and then collapsed anyway in 1983. Succeeding governments drew the lesson that it does not pay to grant public money to firms in trouble. See Andeweg and Irwin (1993: 203).

75. *InterNetKrant*, November 15, 1996, page 2.

76. The minimum wage was 64 percent of the average wage in 1980. Severance of automatic coupling of the minimum wage to other wage increases left the minimum wage at just 51 percent of the average wage in 1997, according to Visser and Hemerijck (1997: 41–42).

77. In 1999 the Christian trade union federation CNV claimed that the growing number of women receiving disability benefits due to stress was a result of the continuing shortage of daycare options. An increase in state-subsidized daycare would thus reduce the disability rolls as well as the level of unemployment, according to the CNV (*InterNetKrant*, January 12, 1999, page 2).

78. Organisation for Economic Co-operation and Development (1996); Münchau and Cramb (1997). In line with the emerging philosophy concerning part-time jobs, the Central Statistical Bureau began in 1989 to count those working less than twelve hours per week as employed. All comparisons of labor force participation from before and after 1989, then, must be attentive to this shift in definitions.

79. According to Kloosterman (1994), Dutch women under 25 are already as likely to work as their northern European counterparts.

80. An additional 3.5 percent of the labor force in 1996 worked in temporary jobs, also a rate substantially higher than in neighboring countries.

81. Cited in Münchau and Cramb (1997).

82. When a universal disability program was passed in 1967, administration of that program was also given to the unions and employers.

83. Visser and Hemerijck (1997: 149). See also Toonen (1996).

84. One such study showed that public assistance recipients had to choose between paying their utility bills and buying fresh fruit (Cox 1993: 186–187).

85. Sociaal en Cultureel Planbureau (1993: 364). See also Visser (1992: 62).

86. The target was set at 82.8 benefit recipients per 100 workers. Restoration of coupling in 1996 showed that the target is achievable if unemployment is contained. But aging of the population will in the future put added pressure on the recipient/contributor ratio even if unemployment remains low and the disability program is brought under control. In the year 2000 there will be just over 5 workers for every retiree receiving a pension, but by 2040 it is projected that there will be only 2.4 workers per retiree—a ratio that is about 25 percent less favorable than that projected for the United States (Peters 1991a: 85).

8

SMALL COUNTRY IN
A WORLD MARKET

In the mid-1950s, faced with the problem of balancing ministerial portfolios
between governing parties, Willem Drees named two ministers of foreign affairs.
J. W. Beyen was given the portfolio for European affairs and Joseph Luns was given
responsibility for the rest of the world. Asked by a colleague from another country
about the reason for this arrangement, Luns replied, "Because our country is so
small, abroad is very large."[1]

Luns's explanation of the divided portfolio was facetious, but the Dutch do
have cause to appreciate more keenly than most the scope and importance of foreign relations. Over half the GDP in the Netherlands is traded abroad, making the
country twice as reliant on trade as is Great Britain and five times as reliant as is
the United States. One telling example of the Dutch reliance on trade is that 78
percent of the 692,000 tons of Gouda, Edam, and other cheeses produced annually in the Netherlands is sold abroad.

The classic pattern of Dutch trade has been to import raw materials and export
finished goods. The country was the leading shipbuilder and maritime power in
the seventeenth century, despite having to import virtually all the timber that
went into those ships. Today, exports of meat and beer are made possible by large
quantities of imported grain.[2] At a time when the chief products of the Dutch
multinational corporation Philips were light bulbs and radios, it was observed
that "the only material of real Dutch origin ... [was] the vacuum of the lamps
and the energy of the founders."[3] Without access to world markets, the Dutch
economy would be a barely recognizable shell of what it is today.

Security policy and trade policy are always linked, but in the Netherlands they are
deeply intertwined. As the Dutch political scientist and former minister of defense

Joris Voorhoeve put it, the foundations of Dutch foreign policy can be summarized in three words: peace, profits, and principles.[4] What Voorhoeve did not say, but what will be shown in this chapter, is that profits have played the greater role in motivating Dutch foreign policy making. The Netherlands has extensive international investments (it is the second largest foreign investor in the United States, after Japan) and trade relationships on which its prosperity depends. The broad lines of foreign policy have therefore been developed with a keen awareness of the extent to which the country's prosperity depends on maintaining a stable set of trade and investment relationships in an international order that is itself stable.

To be sure, principles have always been central to the Dutch style of foreign policy making. No sooner had the Netherlands terminated its colonial war in Indonesia and granted that country its independence in 1949 (under considerable pressure from the United States and the United Nations),[5] than the Netherlands became an ardent advocate of the end of colonialism and the rights of newly independent states. During the Cold War period, the Dutch government viewed itself as the "conscience of NATO," taking independent and critical stances within the alliance on a number of occasions. A moralistic style of foreign policy rhetoric has a venerable tradition in the Netherlands; already in the nineteenth century, the Liberal leader Johan Rudolf Thorbecke had claimed, "The Dutch policy, being itself free from lust for power, is the most impartial judge of other nations' lust for power."[6] Brand (1980: 274) put the matter unkindly but not inaccurately when he wrote, "It appears to be part of the Dutch character to judge itself by its motives and others by their actions."

Principles rather than interests routinely inform the language of foreign policy in the Netherlands. Rozemond (1983) found that the word "interest" was used by foreign ministers in parliamentary speeches only thirty-three times between 1971 and 1982. And yet the dichotomy between principles and interests must not be overdrawn, for it is in the Dutch interest that its foreign policy be articulated on a principled basis. If a small country like the Netherlands is to impress its point of view on the international system, it must do so through persuasion based on principled argument. The more forceful alternatives open to major powers have not been available to the Dutch since late in the seventeenth century. For the same reason, the Dutch are deeply committed to international law. This commitment is reflected in the siting of the International Court of Justice (colloquially known as the World Court) in The Hague, as well as in the clause in the Dutch constitution stating that all national laws must be in conformity with international treaties. The Dutch identity came to include the trait of being, as Queen Wilhelmina put it at her installation ceremony in 1899, "a small nation, but one great in deeds."[7]

One need not look far beneath the core principles of Dutch foreign policy to find national interests. For example, Hugo de Groot (better known by his Latin name Grotius) in the seventeenth century drew upon his training as a lawyer and classical scholar to develop a natural-law argument for freedom of the seas. "Can the vast, the boundless sea, be the appanage of one country alone, and it not the greatest? Can any one Nation have the right to prevent other nations which so desire from selling to one another, from bartering with one another, from communicating with one another?"[8]

Grotius's arguments for free trade and freedom of the seas commanded general respect; Sweden named Grotius its ambassador to France in 1634 despite the fact that he was Dutch. And yet, Grotius's ideas on free trade were clearly motivated by Dutch national interests, for at the time he wrote them the Dutch were expanding their commercial empire and encountering armed resistance from Portugal and Spain. Sent later in life to negotiate with England on English access to Dutch trading posts in the East Indies, Grotius took a more restrictive stance. He justified his about-face by suggesting that the Dutch had earned preferential treatment in the East Indies because of their efforts in discovering and building up trading sites (Hyma 1942: 93–95). After Grotius's death, when the Netherlands had become the leader in global trade and England was threatening to take away its most lucrative trading routes, the principles of peaceful free trade fell away and the Dutch became fierce defenders of their local monopolies. As the founder of the Dutch United East India Company trading center in Batavia (Indonesia), Jan Pieterszoon Coen, put it, "You cannot have trade without war or war without trade."[9] Or, to put the matter in the words of those patriotic Dutch pirates, the Sea Beggars, "Help thyself, and God will help thee."

Profits have consistently come ahead of both principles and peace in Dutch foreign policy. That said, the route to profits in the Netherlands has generally been via trade rather than conquest, and the path to lucrative trade relationships has in nearly all circumstances been through peaceful coexistence with others. Johan de Witt, leader of the Dutch Republic during the Golden Century, stated baldly that "The interest . . . of this State [is] posed in this: that calmness and peace be everywhere and that commerce may be carried on unhindered."[10]

The extent to which trade rather than force became the guiding principle of Dutch foreign policy is suggested by the ability of the Netherlands to maintain a trading relationship with Japan after the Portuguese and Spanish were thrown out by Shogun Tokugawa Ieyasu for Christian proselytizing. The Dutch accepted remarkable privations in Japan with humility. They remained confined to the island of Deshima, near Nagasaki; they made no display of their religious symbols; and they paid regular tribute to the Japanese authorities.[11] According to D. W. Davies (1961: 75):

> When a vessel entered the harbor of Nagasaki, it was boarded by soldiers and officials. The soldiers remained guarding the ship night and day until it sailed for its home port. The officials seized all swords, cutlasses, firearms, and gunpowder and returned these articles to the Dutchmen only when the ship was ready to depart. All aboard were strictly questioned and examined lest there be a lurking Catholic priest among them.

What makes acceptance of these conditions even more amazing is that it was on behalf of a trade relationship that was subject to changing terms imposed by the shogun, a relationship that was very profitable in some years but only marginally profitable in others (Hyma 1942: 44, 159–170).

The objective of furthering trade has, in short, been the single constant in Dutch foreign policy, and under most (but not all) circumstances the desire for expanding trade also led the Dutch to seek international peace. Until the German invasion of 1940, the Netherlands could look back on over one hundred years of successful avoidance of European conflicts through a policy of neutrality. Unable to generate the military power necessary to defend their colonies, their trade routes, or even their home territory, the Dutch deemed a neutral stance between themselves and the great European powers to be the only available policy.

The Dutch desire to minimize international tensions has sometimes been interpreted as a neutralist or pacifist spirit. In the early 1980s, Dutch reluctance to see new nuclear missiles placed in Europe under NATO auspices led some to criticize the Netherlands for a "head in the sand" approach to the military threat posed at that time by the Soviet Union. Walter Laqueur coined the term "Hollanditis" to refer to a loss of nerve in defense policy that, in his view, had striking parallels with the neutralism practiced by the Netherlands and other small states in the 1930s. The Dutch were said by Laqueur (1981: 19) to have had "a desire to keep out of world problems and an aversion to spending money on defense."

Dutch neutrality is not, however, a passive policy of isolation; there is nothing in the Netherlands comparable to the isolationist spirit that occasionally surfaces in U.S. foreign policy. The prosperity and even the survival of the country require a significant engagement with the outside world, specifically that the Netherlands be open to trade with its neighbors and that those neighbors be both prosperous and at peace. Moreover, Dutch security historically was sufficiently precarious that it constantly had to be adjusted to a changing environment. Some observers date Dutch neutrality policy back to 1648 and the end of the Eighty Years War.[12] However, neutrality was periodically abandoned during the next two centuries in favor of alliances concluded alternately to repel French invasions and to contain British naval power. Jan Siccama (1985: 115) describes this phenomenon of the nineteenth century in noting that, "The term 'neutral' is slightly misleading when referring to Dutch policy during this period. From 1839 to 1866 Dutch neutrality was anti-French, from 1866 to 1901 it was anti-Prussian, and from 1870 on it was anti-German." Consequently, the Dutch viewed their neutrality from 1814 to 1940 not as a policy of isolation but rather as a means of promoting stability in the European balance of power.

Dutch engagement with the international system, in short, has long had a different character than that of the United States in the twentieth century. The United States has been a leader, periodically sounding the call to arms both literally and figuratively. The Netherlands has been more of a broker, a mediator seeking to lower tensions and avert flash points by searching for workable compromises that might avert conflict. The United States has itself moved toward a mediator role in the post–Cold War era, as U.S. foreign policy has been reoriented toward moderating the effects of international tensions rather than leading one bloc of nations in an effort to contain the influence of a rival bloc.

In this chapter, we will examine the pattern of Dutch engagement with the international economic and security system. We will focus particularly on the seventeenth-century trading system and the contemporary roles of the Netherlands in NATO and in the European Union.

The Seventeenth-Century Trade Network

Development of the global Dutch trading empire during the seventeenth century not only put the country temporarily in the first rank of world powers, but also laid the foundations of the global economy as we know it today. Many of the trends toward globalization of economic production began with the Dutch, who first saw the full possibilities of multilateral networks linking sovereign nations. It is therefore worthwhile to take a close look at the development of the Dutch trade network during the seventeenth century.

Already in the third century A.D., Frisian inhabitants of the region had taken advantage of their location at the juncture of the North Sea and the great European rivers to trade goods. The Frisians began a coastal trade with the Danish peninsula and an inland trade up the Rhine River with the German regions, sending their cattle for German grain and for Danish amber, slaves, furs, and timber (Lambert 1971: 46).

A major boost to Dutch trade activity came late in the fourteenth century, when Willem Beukelszoon of Zeeland discovered an improved means of curing fish with salt. The Dutch fishing fleet harvested herring off the coast of Scotland and England throughout the summer and fall, using the first "factory ships" ever built. The herring were salted and barreled on board as they were caught, enabling the fleet to remain in fishing waters for months at a stretch. Exports of salted fish (primarily herring) to France, Flanders, and England grew rapidly, and the profits from salted fish enabled Dutch merchants to expand their fleets and become carriers of products not their own.[13] Dutch ports began to supplant those of the Hanseatic League—Hamburg, Bremen, Lubeck, and others—as centers of the European carrying trade. By the middle of the fifteenth century, the Dutch merchant fleet was twice as large as the fleets of all the Hanseatic League ports combined.

From the Middle Ages to the seventeenth century, international commerce was a mixture of trade, plunder, and empire-building. Spanish and Portuguese ships sailed around the world with the prime mission of exporting Catholicism and bringing back gold and silver bullion. During the course of the seventeenth century, however, the Dutch developed multilateral trade networks in which they were carriers and warehousers for a variety of goods whose origins and final destinations were outside the Netherlands itself. The warehouses of Amsterdam and

Rotterdam filled with grain from northern Germany and the Baltics, Norwegian wood, coals from Newcastle, copperware from Hamburg, canvas from St. Petersburg, Swedish pitch and tar, wines from France, Germany, and the Mediterranean, soap from Marseilles, English leather and lead, olive oil and honey from Spain. Leiden became Europe's leading textile center by weaving Spanish wool. Italian pasta was made from Baltic wheat brought to Italy in Dutch ships in exchange for the marble that went into the stately houses of Amsterdam.

These trade relations were solidified by a complex set of commercial arrangements and political ties—what Immanuel Wallerstein (1980: 38) called "the first core state of the capitalist world system"—that prefigure the interdependence of the contemporary international economy. For example, Dutch banks made loans to the Swedish crown using that country's copper mines as security. Dutch merchants purchased mine and timber concessions in Sweden and Norway, and in Iceland the Dutch undertook every phase of investment, extraction, and refinement of sulphur. Russian exports of caviar, tar, hemp, oil, salmon, and wool were all Dutch monopolies. The Dutch operated the mint in Poland, giving them complete control over the currency. In short, the Dutch created relationships with their neighbors that would today be described as neocolonial, although it was a neocolonialism that predated the colonial era itself.[14]

Although the Dutch did everything they could to maintain their trade dominance, they did not do so as a means of developing a dominant position in the manufacture of goods they traded. This stands in contrast to the subsequent English trading empire, whose purpose was to maintain a global network of outlets for goods manufactured in England. The Dutch, uniquely, saw potential in the activity of trade itself. Daniel Defoe is known today primarily for his fictional character Robinson Crusoe, the ultimate autark who learned all the skills necessary for a materially comfortable life after being shipwrecked on a remote island. In real life, though, Defoe was keenly appreciative of the benefits of the Dutch trade network. He believed that "The Dutch must be understood as they really are, the middle Persons in Trade, the Factors and Brokers of Europe . . . they *buy* to *sell* again, *take* in to *send out,* and the greatest Part of their vast Commerce consists in being supply'd from All Parts of the World, that they may supply All the World again."[15]

How did a small country, a newcomer to the world of sovereign European states, come to play such a prominent role in international trade? Many Europeans asked themselves that question during the course of the seventeenth century. And the reply is pretty much the same answer one can give to account for any startling instance of rapid success: The Dutch trading empire flourished because the Dutch were in the right place, they were the first to see potential in a number of technical and organizational innovations, and their timing was impeccable.[16]

That the Netherlands would be a key player in European trade was guaranteed by the position of the country at the mouth of three major rivers that reach into the European interior: the Rhine, the Maas, and the Schelde. Dutch ships could bring goods to French, Flemish, and German cities for as little as one-tenth of the cost associated with a land voyage. By the beginning of the seventeenth century, three-fourths of the mercantile shipping tonnage in Europe was owned by the Dutch (Brand 1980: 252).

European trade always remained the profitable backbone of the Dutch trading empire, and the oceanic trade with the East Indies never accounted for more than 10 percent of the total value of the trade of the United Provinces.[17] But the money, experience, shipping fleet, and financial institutions developed for the European trade were soon employed in seeking the profits available from trade elsewhere around the globe. Until late in the sixteenth century, the Spanish and Portuguese had dominated ocean navigation and intercontinental trade. Spain maintained bases in Central and South America from which gold and silver were collected for shipment to the king. The Portuguese pioneered in trade with Asia on the route around southern Africa. Portuguese outposts in Malaysia supplied the European market with a variety of spices so rare in Europe that they were expensive luxuries. Peppercorns, for example, were known in Portuguese as "grains of paradise" (Phillips 1990: 50), and one still sometimes hears the Dutch say that something is "as expensive as pepper."

Dutch merchants were determined to gain a share of the Portuguese spice trade, and two developments at the end of the sixteenth century gave them their opportunity. One was completion in 1594 of the first Dutch *fluyt*, a new kind of ship specifically designed for long-distance trade. The *fluyt* sacrificed speed for size, and had a much greater cargo capacity than existing ships. Spain and Portugal traded with heavily armed ships, little different from warships, as one might expect given the blurry line that separated trade and plunder. The Dutch *fluyt* was not only more lightly armed but also carried a much smaller crew than other trade ships. With the crew's wages accounting for over half the expense of a long-distance voyage, the ability of the *fluyt* to carry 450 tons of cargo with a crew of fifteen made the Dutch ship substantially more efficient than its rivals.[18] The *fluyt* (which became widely known as the "East Indiaman" in deference to its use in the Asiatic trade) was eventually adopted by the English trading fleet, and its design was not superseded until 1793—after a nearly two-hundred-year run as the most efficient of long-distance cargo ships. Yet the *fluyt* was but one, albeit the most successful, of a number of specialized ships that made the Dutch the greatest shipbuilders on the continent. The Dutch developed a number of standardized ship designs that they were able to produce more cheaply than their continental rivals, earning them a reputation comparable to that of Henry Ford in automobile production three hundred years later (Wallerstein 1974: 212).

The second development that allowed the Dutch to enter the oceanic trade was the publication in 1595 by John Huyghen van Linschoten of a book called the *Itinerario*, a description of the Portuguese trade with the Spice Islands accompanied by an account of trade routes and navigational conditions. Portuguese domination of the spice trade had depended in no small part on their ability to keep this information secret (the Dutch themselves kept for two hundred years the secret of their process for curing fish). Van Linschoten had worked for the Portuguese in East Asia, and publication of his book (which was translated into English and Latin within a few years) opened up the region to fierce competition between Portugal, the Netherlands, and England for control of the spice trade. It was a competition that the Dutch would win.

In the seven years following publication of the *Itinerario*, Dutch merchants outfitted about two expeditions per year bound for India and Malaysia, traveling around the Cape of Good Hope. Knowing the route east was necessary for participation in the spice trade, but simply being able to get there was not sufficient to guarantee a profit. Trading companies faced daunting conditions. The voyage to India lasted nine months each way, including a brief stop at Cape Town to take on fresh water, food, and other supplies. The round-trip voyage took at least two years, more if the ship had to lay over due to bad weather (Bruijn et al. 1987). Without reliable charts of reefs, winds, or currents, and because a means of calculating longitude had not yet been developed, there was a substantial risk of shipwreck. These risks of the voyage were compounded by the threat of capture by pirates operating under the protection of a rival European power. A further problem was disease due to overcrowding in accommodations, poor diet, and unsanitary conditions. Charles Fayle (1933: 178) cites a contemporary observer as stating that some Dutch seamen remained in Asia plying the regional trade because they did not like their odds of surviving the trip home.

Offsetting these risks was the fact that the potential profit on an expedition was great. Kristof Glamann's (1958: 258–259) painstaking reconstruction of revenues and expenses from records of the United East India Company suggests that the East Asian trade was substantially more lucrative on a per voyage basis than was the European trade, with profits ranging from 100 to 200 percent.[19] But mounting a voyage to East Asia required a substantial up-front investment in equipment, supplies, and wages. The costs were such that even the wealthiest of merchants could not afford to finance simultaneous trips. At the same time, it was impractical to wait two years for one ship to return and its goods to be sold before sending out another.

Of course, the investment in a trading expedition was lost entirely if the ship went down. The physical risks of the trip to the Far East were apparent from the first Dutch voyage in 1595, when only three of the four ships and 89 of the original crew of 284 returned (de Haas 1943: 165–166). Even if the ship made it back to home port, profits depended on the terms of trade found in the Indies and in Europe. Ship captains arriving in Asia and obviously in need of completing their trades were in a weak bargaining position vis-à-vis native rulers.[20] Competition not only with the English and Portuguese but also with other Dutch trading companies also led to variable prices for Asian goods once they were brought back. If two ships arrived in Amsterdam at about the same time, the market for Asian spices, tea, and cloth was glutted and prices came down. In short, East Asian trade required a large and highly speculative investment.

The Dutch States General solved all these problems in a single stroke by creating the United East India Company (*Vereenigde Oostindische Compagnie*, or VOC) in March 1602. In modern terms, the VOC would be called a quasi-governmental organization, for although privately owned and controlled it was given many of the prerogatives of a sovereign state. The Dutch government gave the VOC a legal monopoly on the eastern trade, and all Dutch companies then engaged in the Asian trade were ordered to merge their operations in exchange for partial ownership and seats on the VOC's board of directors. By consolidating the existing trading companies, the problems of coordinating activities were solved and the risks attendant on any one voyage were pooled among the much larger number of expeditions the VOC was able to mount.[21] The large capital needs of the eastern trade were met by selling stock in the VOC to the public on terms that made participation for small investors relatively easy. Shares in the VOC were traded in Amsterdam through mechanisms little different from a modern stock exchange, with prices quoted every other day.[22] The States General granted the VOC wide latitude in governing its trade relations with Asian countries. The company received blanket permission to establish trading outposts where it saw fit, to fortify those outposts with VOC-owned and controlled armies and warships, and to conclude treaties with local rulers on its own authority.[23] In exchange for its twenty-year charter, the VOC paid a flat licensing fee to the Dutch government, paid additional amounts to the state for convoy protection by the navy's warships, and agreed to provide ships to the government in the event of war.[24] So autonomous was the VOC in protecting its Asian interests that the Dutch navy never sent a single ship beyond the Cape of Good Hope until late in the eighteenth century (Bruijn 1990: 193). Malachy Postlethwayt noted in his "Universal Dictionary" (published in 1751) that the VOC was "invested with a kind of sovereignty and dominion . . . [It] makes peace and war at pleasure, and by its own authority; administers justice to all; . . . settles colonies, builds fortifications, levies troops, maintains numerous armies and garrisons, fits out fleets, and coins money."[25] It is little wonder that historians of the VOC call it "a state outside the state" (Glamann 1958: 7). "What is good for the VOC is good for the country" might have been the motto of both VOC directors and the States General.[26]

The VOC, drawing on Dutch experience in the European trade, came quickly to understand the great potential for increasing its profits by trading among Asian powers, rather than simply shuttling back and forth between Europe and Asia. The early trading voyages had acquired tea and spice primarily in exchange for gold and silver shipped from Europe. But this pattern was soon replaced with multilateral trade relations that capitalized on such price spreads as nutmeg selling in India for thirty times what it cost to buy in the "Spice Islands" of Malaysia. The Japanese, though not interested in European goods, were ready to trade copper and gold for silk from China, cotton cloth from India, and spices from

Malaysia. Pepper, cloves, nutmeg, mace, and other spices came from Malaysia; cinnamon, pearls, and areca nuts, from Ceylon; cottons, callicoes, sugar, and opium, from India; silk, porcelain, tea, and lacquerware, from China; copper and precious metals, from Japan; animal skins and exotic hardwoods, from Siam. Having come to understand each of the markets in which it was involved, the VOC developed its trade in Asia as a series of overlapping triangles. Buying and selling at each port of call, the VOC sped up its turnover and greatly increased its profits.

The Dutch trading influence in the Americas was never as extensive as it was in the East Indies. But the VOC's sister company, the West India Company (WIC), did gain access to ports and goods in the New World, and incorporated goods from the Americas into the trading network. The import of tea to Europe created a demand for sugar, which the Dutch filled by capturing sugar production areas in northeast Brazil between 1624 and 1654. African gold and American silver were shipped to Asia in exchange for spice, silk, and cotton cloth; Indian cotton prints were taken to West Africa and traded for slaves; slaves were taken to Brazil and to the Caribbean to be traded for sugar; the sugar was brought back to Holland to sweeten the coffee and tea brought by the VOC from India, China, and Java (Steensgaard 1990).

The VOC represented a substantial advance in the commercial organization of an inherently risky venture. To be sure, the profitmaking possibilities of legally granted monopolies were understood before formation of the VOC: The Portuguese trade with the East Indies had been organized as a governmental monopoly, *Estada da India*. The Dutch innovation was to put the monopoly under private ownership and control. While the Portuguese royal monopoly was always starved for cash due to the other financial commitments of the Crown, the VOC made sure that a sufficient portion of its profits went into the protection and expansion of its trade. The VOC paid for its own war fleets and fortresses, and set aside money to invest in the development of specialized ship designs. The large, slow *fluyt* continued to be used for the long-distance European-Asian trade; heavily armed ships were built to patrol the Spice Island navigational lanes and keep competitors out; and small, faster ships shuttled between the outlying islands of the Malaysian archipelago to collect spices for delivery to Siam (now Thailand), Persia (Iran), China, and Japan, as well as to the VOC trading post in India, where the spices were loaded onto *fluyt*s for delivery to Holland. The VOC shipbuilding yard turned out about 1,600 oceangoing ships in the course of the company's two-hundred-year existence (Bruijn et al. 1987).

Pressure from stockholders contributed to the efficiency of the VOC, preventing it from becoming mired in the corruption that often attended state-run enterprises. Stockholders were outspoken about company policies, particularly about policies that could affect profitability. One complaint voiced early in the VOC's history was that cargoes were frequently sold to company directors by advance contract rather than by auction. The directors then made enormous personal profits by acting as distributors and wholesalers. Stockholder pressure against this practice led the States General in 1629 to ban directors from purchasing cargoes by contract.[27]

Steady pressure from stockholders also contributed to the strategic flexibility shown by the VOC over the years. The emphasis given to particular trade routes and goods shifted with remarkable sensitivity to changed terms of trade. In the middle of the seventeenth century, pepper and spices accounted for nearly 60 percent of the trade from the east, but by 1700 this had been reduced to just under 40 percent (Glamann 1958: 14). The predominant role of spices was increasingly taken over by silk and cotton, whose share of the Asian trade increased from 17 percent in 1650 to over 40 percent in 1700. The rising European demand for tea caused the VOC to increase its intra-Asian trade, sending Malaysian spices and Japanese precious metals to India and China in exchange for their tea. To meet the burgeoning European demand for coffee, the VOC succeeded in transplanting the crop to Java (Indonesia), where it was grown on plantations controlled directly by the company. Trade in coffee and tea grew to 25 percent of the Asian trade by the early eighteenth century (Steensgaard 1990: 116).

Stockholder vigilance appears to have paid off, for the best estimates of VOC profitability suggest a return on capital of about 30 percent per year, and dividends paid to stockholders ranged from 18 to 50 percent per year.[28] Hendrik Riemens (1943: 156) estimates that the VOC paid out twenty-eight times its initial capital over the 193 years of its life. These profits were achieved despite the enormous costs of shipbuilding, creating fortifications, and providing warship escorts as dictated by the political situation and the extent of privateering. To protect their trade routes and cargoes, the VOC established settlements and fortifications at the Cape of Good Hope, on Mauritius, on the west coast of India, and in the Spice Islands themselves.[29] Where the VOC collided with the Portuguese (as in Japan), or with the English (as in Malaysia), its agents were ruthless in gaining a foothold and then pushing out all competitors.[30] VOC directors were among those most in favor of resuming the war against Spain in 1623, a war that enabled them to prey at will on Spanish and Portuguese shipping. By the middle of the seventeenth century, the VOC owned 150 trading ships and 40 warships—a combat navy larger than that of any European state. This period was, as Carla Phillips (1990: 89) describes it, the "Golden Age of Piracy," with bullion-laden Spanish and Portuguese ships available to the daring, the well armed, and the fleet.

A large portion of the domestic Dutch economy also came to center on its engagement with trade. Shipbuilding and the ancillary industries that employed sailmakers, rope makers, lumber cutters, and carpenters flourished in the coastal strip of land between Amsterdam and Rotterdam. Many goods shipped to Amsterdam were processed or refined before being shipped on to their destinations; this led to the spread of mills, sugar refineries, breweries, and distilleries. The Dutch became leaders in the dyeing and dressing of cloth, processes that accounted for nearly half the price of finished woolens (Wilson 1968: 31).

Warehousing and insurance for cargoes may have contributed as much to the Dutch economy as did the trade itself.[31] Credit banking developed for the loans needed to mount long trade voyages, and exchange banking developed to handle the many currencies and notes of obligation involved in multilateral trade. Amsterdam's private banking industry created an international market in stock and commodities futures (van der Wee 1993: 24–33). Christian Huygens and Antony van Leeuwenhoek, best known respectively for improvements to the telescope and for invention of the microscope, got their starts as lens makers helping to supply the insatiable demand for navigational tools on Dutch ships. A great deal of Dutch wealth, in short, came from the entrepôt activities connected with serving as the hub of a global trade network. VOC prosperity became Dutch prosperity, and Dutch prosperity created a large middle-class market for the goods of the VOC. The best symbol of the country's transformation may be the Amsterdam coffeehouse, from which emanated the mingled aromas of Virginia tobacco and Turkish coffee.

The innovations that made all this possible were primarily cultural rather than technical. First and foremost was the development of the VOC itself, an institution that combined trade activities with expertise in finance, ship construction, marketing, and geopolitics. The VOC was a working demonstration of the economies of scale, the efficiency of vertical integration (e.g., in building its own ships), and the flexibility of a corporation owned by private shareholders. A second cultural innovation was the mentality of the Dutch merchant, who was prepared to buy anything anywhere in the world, and to sell it anywhere else in the world, as long as the price differential justified the effort. As the seventeenth-century poet Joost van den Vondel put it, "For love of gain, the wide world's harbours we explore."[32]

The means by which this global trade network was created and maintained should not, of course, be idealized. The VOC started wars, commissioned pirates to prey on rivals, and took direct control of the island of Java in order to set up coffee plantations for its profit (Boxer 1990: 105–117). The VOC's sister company, the West India Company, traded African slaves for Caribbean sugar, and the slave trade eventually became the dominant source of its profits. The West India Company controlled two ports in West Africa at which it purchased slaves, as many as 20 percent of whom died en route to the Caribbean (Brand 1980: 257). Bernard Vlekke (1945: 261) estimates that "by the middle of the [seventeenth] century more than thirty thousand slaves were used on four hundred plantations, entirely financed by Dutch capital."[33] Despite the deeply religious nature of the company's directors and middle-class stockholders, no profitmaking activity appears to have been rejected on moral grounds.[34]

If some elements of the Dutch trade network are seen today as morally repugnant, and if other elements seem hopelessly quaint as a basis of wealth (pepper and tea), these were still elements of a recognizably modern economic activity. The Dutch, to a greater extent than the Spanish and Portuguese whom they supplanted, separated their economic activities from any demand that the local population convert to Christianity or acknowledge the rule of a distant sovereign. Dutch traders could certainly be ruthless with native populations, meddling in disputes over authority to serve their own interests and reorganizing local economies to better serve the European market. After all is said and done, though, the Dutch were not plunderers; trading was for them a bargaining relationship, and they were interested in building long-term trade relationships. Local authorities were most often left in place, even where the VOC established territorial control over trading ports (Boxer 1990: 217). The cannon and bayonet were generally reserved for European rivals.[35]

These activities brought the preindustrial world economy to its apex of possibilities. The Dutch trade network fostered regional economic specialization throughout Europe and had a profound impact on the development of an international economy. Its benefits were not confined to the Netherlands. As Rogowski (1989: 154) points out, the seventeenth century was a period of relative prosperity across the western part of the European continent:

> Cities, able to nourish themselves from afar for the first time since the collapse of Rome, grew to encompass—despite their lamentable hygiene and endemic violence—populations of hundreds of thousands. Moreover, there is little doubt that the security, if not the average standard, of living among this growing population steadily improved: diets grew richer and more varied, and regional famines yielded to improved transportation; perhaps more conclusively, the plague, which battened always on the chronically undernourished, disappeared from Europe after 1665.

Even Spain, with whom the Netherlands remained at war for most of the first half of the seventeenth century, benefited from trade with Dutch merchants and became reliant on it. Before the Dutch rebellion began, traders from the provinces Holland and Zeeland sold Baltic grain and timber to the Spanish government. After the outbreak of war in 1568, the Dutch government at first tried to ban the trade with Spain. All the government succeeded in doing was to push the trade underground, in the form of smuggling. In 1573 the States General legalized the Spanish trade, subject to payment of a license fee. Merchants could buy a license to sell anything to Spain, including arms and ships. The cost of a license was adjusted from year to year depending on the intensity of the hostilities and the progress of the war. In most years the trade flourished, but license fees were set at a prohibitive level when the war did not go well for the fledgling republic. This practice not only generated much-needed cash for the United Provinces, but also kept Spain dependent on rebel merchants for a substantial portion of its imported grain and arms. That dependency was used to Dutch advantage in 1598–1599, critical years of the war when the States General refused to issue any licenses at all.

The story of the development of Dutch-Asian trade is one of the great adventure tales of human history. It was a time of voyage and discovery for naval fleets from several leading European powers, but for none more so than the merchant fleet of the Dutch Republic. In the course of extending and refining its trade routes, explorers commissioned by the VOC discovered Australia in 1606. A few years later, the VOC's Abel Tasman came upon the islands of Tasmania and New Zealand while seeking an easterly passage to South America. The VOC sent Henry Hudson to find a western route to Asia, and it was during that voyage that Hudson founded New Amsterdam and sailed up what is today known as the Hudson River. These discoveries had to be recorded, and so the Flemish mapmaker Gerard Kremer (better known by his professional name, Mercator) developed his projection technique in response to the need for more accurate world maps. As the seventeenth-century English travelers Johnson and Marsh (1664: 66) marveled, "their Intelligence is as spreading as their Traffick, and their Traffick as large as the World; there being no Nation under heaven to the bottom of whose Counsels, Interests and concernes they have not insinuated themselves."

Although the European trade remained the backbone of the Dutch economy because of sheer volume, the development of trade with Asia vaulted the Netherlands to the forefront of world powers by positioning the country at the center of a vast trading web. The great bulk of the goods bought and sold by Dutch traders were neither made in the Netherlands nor destined for the Dutch market. Dutch prosperity came instead from the arbitrage of possibilities inherent in the development of global free trade on a scale never before seen. The seventeenth-century network set a pattern for the Dutch economy that is observed to this day. As Bob Fitch (1995: 36) points out, "Refining North Sea oil and translating American software have replaced refining Brazilian sugar and processing Virginia tobacco, but the principle is the same, and it works: If you route the goods everyone needs through your cities and add value somehow before you re-export them, you will get rich."

Dutch Colonial Policy

The Dutch did indeed become rich by routing goods through their cities and adding value to them, but along the way the Netherlands also became a colonial power. The country technically remains one to this day.

In total, the Dutch colonial empire comprised a million square miles of land strategically located so as to support the global trade network (see Figure 8.1). The colonial empire of the Netherlands was never anywhere near as extensive as that of England, and was never part of a policy of cultural extension and national aggrandizement as was the case with France. Like the colonies of those other two empires, though, the Dutch colonies were organized for maximum economic return both to the Dutch population and to the Dutch government.

For the most part, the Dutch were content to limit their relationships with other countries to trade, working through treaties with local sovereigns. However, they were quite prepared to exert direct political and military control when it was

245

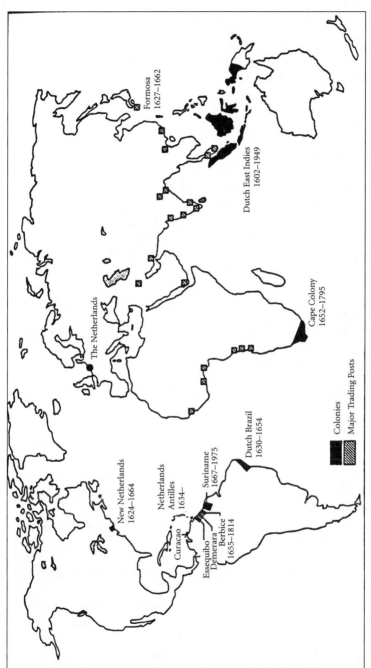

Formosa
1627–1662

Dutch East Indies
1602–1949

Cape Colony
1652–1795

The Netherlands

New Netherlands
1624–1664

Netherlands
Antilles
1634–

Curaçao

Suriname
1667–1975

Essequibo
Demerara
Berbice
1655–1814

Dutch Brazil
1630–1654

Colonies

Major Trading Posts

MAP 8.1   *The Dutch Global Empire*

convenient to do so. Thus, for example, the VOC established outposts under its control at the Cape of Good Hope in South Africa and in India. The island of Java was directly controlled by the VOC in order to further the intensive cultivation of coffee for VOC profit.[36] The West India Company also controlled ports in Africa for the embarkation of slaves, as well as New Amsterdam (later New York), which was used as a base for fur trading. Colonies were established in the West Indies for sugar cultivation on slave plantations run by the West India Company.

An example of the drive for revenue from the colonies was the introduction of the "cultivation system" for coffee in Java (Newton 1978: 158). Under this Dutch-imposed form of agriculture, local authorities were forced to set aside a certain portion of their land for the intensive cultivation of export crops (tea, coffee, tobacco, sugar, indigo), which had to be sold to the Netherlands Trading Company (NHM—a governmental enterprise) at a fixed price. The anti-competitive nature of this trade made it enormously profitable for the government. In 1849, for example, 20 million guilders of the 70-million-guilder governmental budget came from revenues originating in the East Indies, revenues that were, in the words of a contemporary, "the cork that kept the Netherlands afloat."[37] Although Dutch colonial activity is sometimes justified with reference to the modern transportation infrastructure left behind in Indonesia, the truth is that the nineteenth-century construction of railroads, bridges, canals, and dikes in the Netherlands itself was made possible by the revenues coming in each year from the East Indies (Schöffer 1973: 128). An annex to the governmental budget of 1854 declared that "save for the welfare of the natives, [the East Indies] must continue to furnish the Netherlands with those material benefits for which they were acquired."[38]

Unfortunately, "the welfare of the natives" did not play a very great role in Dutch policymaking until early in the twentieth century. A series of revolts in the East Indies resulted in an interminable sequence of wars against native populations, ranging from the Java wars (1825–1830) to the so-called Atjeh expeditions (1873–1904) (Schöffer 1973: 123–124). These revolts stemmed from the cultivation system, which was devastating to the local economy because the land reserved for subsistence crops was insufficient to feed the local population. In one district in central Java in 1849, 80,000 members of a population of 89,000 died in the wake of a famine (Newton 1978: 73).

Even after such disasters, the lucrative revenue stream made the Dutch government slow to reform the cultivation system. Eventually, after a series of investigations in 1869 and 1870, compulsory production was abolished, landownership was determined by indigenous law, and private (western) investment was limited to uninhabited territory (Vlekke 1945: 311–312). These reforms eased the extent of agricultural exploitation, but not long afterward the first large oil discoveries in Borneo, Sumatra, and Java (now all part of Indonesia) led to a new wave of Dutch investment and exploitation. The Royal Dutch Shell Oil Company got its start exploiting these finds. Rubber and tin also became major exports from the region, controlled by Dutch interests (Hyma 1942: 189–190).

By the beginning of the twentieth century, organization of the Dutch colonies was being shaped by the so-called ethical policy. As Brand (1980: 263) describes it, "From then onward the Dutch mission was perceived as a 'dual mandate,' namely the opening up of the natural resources of the country for the benefit of the world and the raising of the human wealth entrusted to it so that the population of the Indies would be able to cope with its introduction into a rapidly changing world." The civil service gradually became imbued with an ethic of assisting the economic and social development of regions under Dutch control. In 1938 about 7 percent of those with a Dutch university degree resided in the East Indies, working either as civil servants or in the private sector as lawyers, doctors, and biologists.[39] The present-day "solidarity movement" in the Netherlands is a direct descendant of this period of idealism toward the colonies. The solidarity movement is a loose coalition of organizations concerned with human rights abuses in authoritarian regimes, conditions for asylum-seekers and political refugees, racism at home and abroad, and movements for democracy and economic justice in other parts of the world. The most tangible effect of this movement may be the existence of over two hundred "world stores" in the Netherlands, which sell only goods made in Third World countries.[40]

This sense of mission to help develop the less industrialized parts of the world also continues in the Dutch commitment to international aid and development cooperation. On a per capita basis, the Netherlands contributes more than any other country to Third World development aid and to United Nations humanitarian aid missions. In his role as chair of the U.N. Research Institute for Social Development, the Dutch economist Jan Tinbergen was instrumental in setting 1.5 percent of net national income as the norm for contributions by wealthy countries to Third World development. The Netherlands became the first country to reach this level of assistance in 1976, and development aid continues to command a wide consensus in the population and among party leaders. The budgetary line for development aid has been largely spared the reductions in government expenditure carried out in the 1980s and 1990s; despite the country's relatively small size the Netherlands remains among the top five donors in total volume of aid given.[41] As Rudy Andeweg and Galen Irwin (1993: 226) point out, the only controversies in development assistance concern the criteria used for selecting recipients and the extent to which such assistance is tied to purchase of Dutch exports.[42] The Netherlands is one of the few countries about which a political scientist can write without blushing that "Development [assistance] policy is inspired to a considerable degree by sincere feeling for the lot of poor people outside our borders" (van Staden 1993: 342).

Decline of Hegemony and Rebirth as a Small Power

One lesson that statisticians have taught students of history is that the great shall be humbled. (This rule is known in statistical circles as regression to the mean.)

The Dutch period of dominance in creating the global trading economy rested on a convergence of opportunities. Taking advantage of its maritime location, Amsterdam became the port through which much of Europe traded both with itself and with the rest of the world. The fortunes of war also helped Amsterdam become the center of world trade by legalizing piracy on Spanish ships and by enabling the Dutch to close off rival port Antwerp by blockading the Schelde River. The war also brought a flood of immigrants to Amsterdam, many of whom were highly skilled workers. Half the capital initially needed to support the Bank of Amsterdam came from immigrants.

Once the Dutch trade network had been established, though, further war could only be disruptive. Paul Kennedy (1987: 51) notes that "The whole economy of the United Provinces had been built upon its role as a trader, transporter, middleman, producer of finished goods and financier, so that if its shipping was stopped its credit in the world would collapse and it would be ruined." This is almost exactly the sequence of events that transpired.

The Dutch were fully aware of the risks they faced, a fact illustrated by the ceiling mural in the chamber where the States General of what was then the Province of Holland assembled. The mural is a trompe l'œil portraying an English intruder looking in on the proceedings from the roof, dangling one leg into the chamber. On the opposite wall a French observer is painted as peering into the room (Carter 1971: 37). The Dutch were acutely and humorously conscious of being part of a three-cornered diplomatic game, but it was a game in which they were at a substantial disadvantage.

The Dutch were wealthy enough to have built a navy equal to England's. They could hire enough mercenaries to maintain an army comparable to that of France. But they could not match both the British navy and the French army at the same time. Whenever the threat from France or England appeared to reach crisis proportions—and this occurred with astonishing regularity in the eighteenth century—the States General deadlocked between the desire of the stadholder to increase the land forces and the determination of the coastal provinces (Holland and Zeeland) to augment the naval convoys for trading ships.

A series of wars with varying alliances between the Netherlands, England, and France forced the diversion of Dutch wealth from productive investment in more and better trading ships to defensive investment in armed convoys. Ultimately, the greater size of France and England enabled the former to field a more powerful army and the latter a more powerful navy. In a vain effort to keep up, taxes were raised to prohibitive levels in the United Provinces; on a per capita basis the Dutch citizen paid three times the taxes that were paid in France and England. The combination of rising taxes and rising labor costs helped send the textile and shipbuilding industries into decline.[43]

Just as the Eighty Years War had seriously damaged Spain's trade network while creating new opportunities for Dutch merchants, so did the naval wars of the seventeenth century sap the strength of the Netherlands while laying the foundation for the rise of a new hegemon. Supported by their growing naval power, the English were increasingly able to dictate the terms of trade with the United Provinces, as well as to muscle the Dutch out of markets in the New World. The Treaty of Breda in 1667, for example, reaffirmed Dutch colonies in Indonesia but handed over to the English the trading outpost at New Amsterdam, which the English promptly named New York. The Baltic was once known as "the breadbasket of the Netherlands," but by the 1770s the English were dominant and the Dutch trade share had fallen to negligible levels (van Houtte 1977: 272). Only in Indonesia did the Dutch retain their dominance, though the VOC lost its base in India to the English, along with its outposts in Ceylon (1780), Cape Colony (1798), and the Spice Islands of Malaysia (1801). In market after market, the English moved in and pushed the Dutch out, even taking over the slave trade established by the West India Company (Vlekke 1945: 212). The VOC itself was liquidated as a corporation in 1791, and its debts were taken over by the state.

As devastating as was the loss of markets and trading bases abroad, the greatest blow came overland, from the French, at the end of the eighteenth century. The Dutch spent decades preparing for this war, developing defensive alliances with England and the Austrian Hapsburgs and erecting a series of "barrier fortresses" in what is now Belgium to hinder a French advance (Carter 1971). These efforts were ultimately fruitless, and the Napoleonic conquest of the Netherlands put an end both to the government of the United Provinces and to the autonomy of the merchant class.

Although sovereignty would be restored to the Netherlands by the victorious allies, the circumstance of being rescued by England and Prussia was indicative of the country's reduced status. The Netherlands was no longer a great power player in the European mosaic; it would now become a pawn rather than a decision-maker in the series of wars that plagued the continent for the next 150 years. This demotion forced an adaptation of Dutch foreign policy and the development of a new set of foreign policy principles. Previously, the Dutch had been proactive, assisting the spread of their trade network by diplomatic and military engagement with the other great powers. Dutch prosperity continued to depend on trade in the nineteenth century, but the Dutch understood that their interests could no longer be defended by military means. A new diplomatic approach was required. The Netherlands turned to the policy of neutrality.

The Era of Neutrality

The strategic use of neutrality policy began in the middle of the eighteenth century, at a time when Dutch superiority in shipping and allied services (warehousing, finance, cargo insurance) was already on the wane. The Netherlands remained neutral between its two principal rivals, France and England, during the Seven Years War (1756–1763). Dutch banks and individual investors made loans to both governments and sold military supplies to both sides. Dutch shipping suffered some from attacks by English privateers seeking to interdict trade with France, but that effect was small compared to the growth of revenue from trade and the sale of cargo insurance to both belligerents. Alice Carter (1971: 102) summarized the matter by noting that "Dutch neutrality in the Seven Years War is best described as pro-Dutch."

The logic of neutrality was extended further in the nineteenth century, when the secession of Belgium in 1830 reduced Dutch influence on world affairs and, in the words of Joris Voorhoeve (1979: 31), "Non-alignment, non-participation in international politics, and strict political neutrality became obsessions." With German unification and industrialization in the second half of the century, Dutch security came to depend on good will from Germany as well as from France and England. Neutrality was a means of keeping the lowest possible profile between the European powers of the nineteenth century, while maintaining trade links with all of them. Even the Boer War (1899–1902), which elicited strong public feelings of support for the Dutch-descended *boers* (or farmers), did not tempt the government to abrogate the principle of neutrality (Voorhoeve 1979: 33).

Neutrality was not the same as passivity. Indeed, the Dutch took the lead in the late-nineteenth-century movement toward international law and the search for mechanisms other than war to resolve international disputes. The Dutch government organized Europe-wide conferences in The Hague in 1899 and 1907, at which participants advocated a system of international arbitration combined with an international police force that would be used to enforce agreements where necessary. One outcome of the conferences was establishment of a Permanent Court of Arbitration in The Hague, a forerunner of the World Court.

The efficacy of the neutrality policy was established during the Franco-German war of 1870, in which Dutch neutrality was honored. World War I posed a sterner test. The war was hard on the Dutch economy because it disrupted many trading patterns. To cope with the cutoff of imported food and other goods, the Dutch themselves shifted land into vegetable production and began to manufacture industrial goods that had previously been imported from Germany (Newton 1978: 114–115). This economic transformation created hardships, but paid off as the Netherlands escaped invasion between 1914 and 1917, thereby avoiding the devastation visited upon neighboring Belgium.

Subsequent studies of British and German war plans show that the Netherlands was not spared either because of scruples about Dutch neutrality or because of the 450,000 soldiers deployed on Dutch borders. Rather, the British stayed out because of the utility of a neutral Netherlands as a supply line to their troops in Belgium. Germany left the Dutch alone in order to reap the benefits of uncontested territory through which goods could be imported to their country. As Joris Voorhoeve (1979: 34) put it, "The teetering equilibrium between the utility and the risks of an invasion by one of the belligerents remained about the same for both Germany and Great Britain during the whole war. . . . [T]he Dutch policy of giving in a little to the demands of the most exacting Power, be it

Germany, Britain, or the United States, saved the Netherlands from the scourge of war."

In the late 1930s, the Dutch policy of neutralism came to a disastrous end. The first reaction to the outbreak of World War II was to reaffirm the policy that had worked so well for a century. By then the Dutch economy was so intertwined with that of Germany that the Nazi rearmament program of the late 1930s actually alleviated the employment crisis in the Netherlands.[44] But the German invasion on May 10, 1940, ended any illusions that neutrality would work again. Facing nineteenth-century artillery and a few ancient tanks, the Germans expected to conquer the country in a single day (Voorhoeve 1979: 38). The Dutch army held out long enough for Queen Wilhelmina and the government to escape to London. Even so, the defeat shattered the neutrality principles of Dutch foreign policy, just as surely as it shattered other aspects of the society and economy.

Realignment: The Netherlands in NATO

The neutrality policy ended in war and defeat. Already in 1942 the foreign minister of the Dutch government-in-exile, E. N. van Kleffens, had broadcast to the nation from London a plea for an "active" foreign policy, one of alignment rather than neutrality, so as to contain Germany in the future. In 1943 van Kleffens rejected a policy of renewed isolation and suggested instead

> a strong formulation in which America with Canada and the other British Dominions would function as arsenal, Great Britain as base (particularly for the air force) and the Western parts of the European continent—I refer to Holland, Belgium and France—as bridgehead. In this manner we would be dependent, it is true, on the Western powers; but these powers would, conversely, have a need of us. It is difficult to think of a stronger position for our country.[45]

This, of course, is almost precisely the shape that the western alliance eventually took, except that van Kleffens envisioned cooperation with Russia in an effort to contain Germany, whereas postwar developments actually led to inclusion of part of Germany in the western alliance in order to contain the Soviet Union. The failure of the neutrality policy, then, created in the Netherlands a determination to join a collective security alliance.

Recognizing that the United States was the only country sufficiently powerful and disinterested in intra-European squabbles to serve as protector, Dutch policy began even before the end of the war to emphasize the necessity of keeping the United States involved in whatever security arrangements would be created in postwar Europe. This was precisely the formula offered by NATO. Virtual unanimity among parliamentary parties on the neutrality policy in 1939 was transformed into general support for the Treaty of Brussels in 1948, which pledged joint defense efforts between Great Britain, France, and the Benelux countries. The Treaty of Brussels, in turn, was viewed by the Dutch as merely a preliminary to the NATO treaty signed one year later.[46] Successive foreign ministers referred to the Atlantic Alliance as the cornerstone of Dutch foreign policy. "The Dutch have no foreign policy; we have only NATO," according to one foreign policy official.[47]

This official support for NATO was also reflected in both elite and public opinion throughout the postwar period. A survey of Dutch political leaders in 1976, for example, found that 90 percent of members of parliament and the top civil service endorsed NATO membership. Between 75 and 80 percent of the sample agreed that NATO has been responsible for the European peace since 1945, that NATO gives the Netherlands more influence on international affairs than it would otherwise have, and that American guarantees for West European security within NATO are credible. Only 12 percent thought that NATO membership interferes with the "peace diplomacy" of the Netherlands.[48]

The general public has been as supportive of Dutch membership in NATO as the political leadership. Even during the relatively controversial years of 1967 to 1982 (a period that began with the Vietnam War and closed with controversy over deployment of nuclear-armed cruise missiles in the Netherlands), public support for membership in NATO averaged 75 percent of the population.[49] This is a more favorable response to NATO than has been found in any West European country except Germany.

During the Cold War, the Dutch were also among those countries most convinced of the need to enhance the conventional military capacity of European members of the alliance. When Charles de Gaulle withdrew France from the military command structure of NATO in the mid-1960s, the Netherlands took on extra tasks as part of the adjustment that had to be made. In the early 1970s the Dutch supported the European Defense Improvement Program, and in the late 1970s the Netherlands was a leader in meeting the commitments of the Long Term Defense Program, which required of NATO countries that they increase their defense expenditures by 3 percent above inflation per year. In the 1980s the Dutch maintained defense spending at about 3.2 percent of GNP, despite a program of drastic cuts in the government budget in virtually every other category of expenditure.[50] The Dutch commitment to NATO is also illustrated by reconfiguration of the country's military around its NATO commitments. As William Domke (1987: 276) points out, "Dutch force structure decisions are clearly delineated by their commitment to NATO."[51]

Belief that the United States must be involved in European security is so strong that it has had an effect even on the Dutch commitment to the European Union. The Dutch conception of European integration has been focused on the economic and social reforms needed to integrate markets and foster increased trade. In the Cold War era, the Netherlands consistently opposed efforts to give the European Union political tasks as well, fearing that even a discussion of security issues might detract from the importance of NATO and the strength of the American commitment to European defense. In the 1960s the Dutch were at the forefront of opposition to de Gaulle's designs for increasing European political cooperation, embodied in the Fouchet Plan of 1961–1962 (Voorhoeve 1979: 165–172). More recent proposals to create an EU-based "security council" and to establish a common European foreign and defense policy have also been resisted by the Netherlands (Honig 1994: 148). Joris Voorhoeve (1979: 115) explains that "The Netherlands, like the other small European powers, preferred the gentle hegemony of a remote Atlantic Super Power over what would be a less credible leadership, but a more immediate domination by Britain, Germany, France, or any combination of them."[52]

Peacekeeping After the Cold War

The NATO alliance enabled the Netherlands to provide for its security, particularly from the threat of attack by the Soviet Union. NATO membership represented not only a break from the neutrality policy, but also a commitment to international peacekeeping operations. In the neutrality period, the idea of Dutch involvement in international military missions of any kind was always controversial. Those who wanted the Netherlands to stay out of the League of Nations, for example, based their opposition primarily on a concern that Dutch neutrality would be compromised by the obligation to join League of Nations–sponsored international military operations.

Since World War II, though, the Netherlands has participated in a variety of UN peacekeeping operations, beginning with those in Palestine and Korea. Since 1963 the Netherlands has maintained a standing offer of troops for UN peacekeeping operations (van Staden 1993: 360–361). Dutch participation has focused on those activities that emphasize the peacekeeping nature of the mission. These include the provision of mine-clearing services (in the Red Sea in 1984; in the Persian Gulf in 1987; and in Mozambique, Cambodia, and Bosnia in 1992), of disarmament monitors (in the Golan Heights in 1948; in Angola in 1985), of human rights investigators (in Uganda and Rwanda in 1995), and of civilian police (in Namibia in 1989; in Somalia in 1994–1995). Since the end of Cold War constraints on European security, the Dutch government has also reconfigured its own defense forces in a way more suited to peacekeeping missions elsewhere. This has meant primarily the development of rapid-deployment units within the navy and air force at the expense of regular army units, whose assignment during the Cold War had been the defense of Germany from a Soviet invasion (Honig 1994: 150–151).

The war of ethnic cleansing in several republics of the former Yugoslavia has posed a stern test of UN peacekeeping capacities in general, and of Dutch participation in particular. The Dutch government responded to American statements that this was a European problem by proposing in 1991 that the European members of NATO send a peacekeeping force to Yugoslavia. The Dutch proposal was not accepted, though, and ultimately the United States did get involved in negotiating a cease-fire. The U.S.-brokered cease-fire committed the United Nations to oversight of the disengagement of combatants. The Dutch participated fully in the subsequent peacekeeping operation, contributing fighter planes to help enforce a no-fly zone as well as sending 3,000 personnel to the region, including a mobile infantry battalion of 800 men. This battalion, known as the "Dutchbat," was charged with protecting the Moslem population in the Bosnian safe haven of Srebrenica.

At first, this commitment did not appear to be a significant departure from other UN peacekeeping operations in which the Dutch had participated. But events were soon to prove otherwise. The Bosnian Serb Army, entrenched in the surrounding areas, maintained pressure on the safe haven by allowing only 60 percent of the Dutch battalion to enter Srebrenica, and by preventing the entry of spare parts and fuel. In July 1995 the Serbian troops seized UN observation posts around the safe haven, taking Dutch monitors hostage. A request for air support by the Dutchbat commander Ton Karremans was denied by the UN command, which was concerned about the effects of an air attack on negotiations then under way in Belgrade. Only after a second attack on the remaining observation posts did a NATO air strike disable several Serbian tanks. However, when Serb general Ratko Mladic threatened to kill his Dutch hostages and shell Srebrenica, the air strikes ceased. It is unclear to this day whether the air strikes were discontinued by order of the UN commander, Bernard Janvier of France, or by order of the Dutch defense minister, Joris Voorhoeve, who was following events from The Hague. It is clear, however, that neither the UN field command nor the Dutch government were willing to risk the lives of Dutch hostages.

While the Dutchbat looked vainly to the skies for NATO air support, the Bosnian Serb Army amassed 1,500 men, supported by tanks, to attack Srebrenica. Defense of the safe haven was supposed to be carried out by Dutch troops under the UN flag along with 6,000 Bosnian Moslem troops. But the Dutchbat had never been able to establish good relations with the Moslems. When the Serbian attack was mounted, the Bosnian Moslem troops did not respond, leaving the Dutchbat outnumbered by four to one and with no defense against the Serbian tanks. Rather than engage the battle, the Dutchbat retreated to the northern end of the enclave together with 15,000 Moslem refugees and sought to negotiate their removal from the area. The Moslem refugees were taken out on buses escorted by the Serbian Army. It was later learned that male refugees between the ages of 15 and 50, at least 5,000 in number, were executed rather than being delivered to the refugee camp. Of the 42,000 people living in the safe haven, as many as 10,000 were dead or missing after the Serbian takeover. The remaining 30,000 Moslems were dumped in an overcrowded and undersupplied refugee camp at Tuzla.

Although the men of the returning Dutchbat were greeted by the government as heroes, the fact remains that the worst European war crime since World War II happened in Srebrenica, on their watch. A three-month inquiry by the Dutch government into the matter concluded that the Dutch troops could not have saved the Moslems under their protection, given the lack of air support or assistance from Bosnian Moslem troops. Even so, for years questions continued to be asked in the Second Chamber and in the country as to whether the Dutchbat did everything in its power to protect the Moslem refugees, and as to whether the UN commander made the massacre possible by reaching an advance agreement with the Serbian troops that there would be no air strikes.

Memories of Srebrenica are to the Dutch public what memories of Vietnam and Somalia are to Americans. There have been parliamentary inquiries, journalistic commentaries, and books devoted to the question of whether the Dutchbat could have prevented the massacre. One controversial stage play compared the behavior of the troops to the passivity of the Dutch public in the face of Nazi deportation of Dutch Jews.[53] It is a divisive topic, but one thing on which most Dutch can agree is that the rules of engagement for UN peacekeeping troops make such tragedies possible. The Dutch learned in Bosnia the painful lessons of the vulnerability that comes from embarking on a mission with limited forces and restrictive rules of engagement.

Inevitably, the disillusion that comes with the disappointment of good intentions has resulted in a new cautiousness about participation in future peacekeeping missions. But this setback has not destroyed the continuing Dutch commitment to define the country's role in the international system proactively, embracing participation in multilateral peacekeeping missions even when the security of the Netherlands is not threatened. Indeed, shortly after the Srebrenica debacle the government approved the participation of Dutch troops under UN command in the Implementation Force (IFOR), the next phase of peacekeeping in that area. Moreover, substantial cuts in defense spending beginning in 1999 have been distributed so as to leave intact the capacity for rapid responses to international crisis.[54] This attitude hearkens back to the Dutch lawyers and politicians of the nineteenth century, who advocated an international peacekeeping police force as part of their general orientation toward international law and the arbitration of disputes.

The European Union

Despite increased involvement in peacekeeping missions, the most significant international commitment of the Netherlands in the postwar era has been its membership in the European Union. Membership in the EU poses for the Netherlands, as it does for all member states, a serious dilemma between the benefits of standardizing policy on certain issues and the costs in loss of sovereignty. For the Dutch, though, this aspect of EU membership is simply a replay of the process that created the Netherlands itself. In the seventeenth and eighteenth centuries, the Netherlands was still a federation of autonomous provinces that faced on a daily basis the issue of balancing provincial sovereignty with the central coordination of policy. Holland, the dominant province, consistently argued for local self-rule. The smaller and poorer Dutch provinces demanded a stronger central government, reasoning that this would give them the best chance of controlling the Hollanders. Ultimately, of course, the centralists won—not least because only a strong central government could deal with the security issues that constantly plagued the United Provinces.

After World War II, Dutch foreign policy makers faced a situation that was uncannily analogous to that of the smaller Dutch provinces two hundred years earlier. Germany—and to a lesser extent France—played the role of the province Holland: large, wealthy, powerful, and vital to the prosperity and security of their smaller neighbors. The response of the Dutch government was exactly the same as the response of the smaller Dutch provinces from that earlier period: to seek close ties with the large neighbors on whom they depended. The Dutch entered the postwar world determined to build regional economic and security networks, thus abandoning their earlier principles of neutrality.

The security network took form as the NATO alliance, whose central principle was, in Dutch eyes, to guarantee continued American involvement in European defense. The other leg of the regional network was economic, and although the Netherlands welcomed American aid in reconstruction through the Marshall Plan, it was nonetheless clear that a strictly European economic cooperation zone would be necessary to postwar prosperity. Consequently, the Dutch government-in-exile negotiated the Benelux customs union in 1944, even before the end of World War II (Urwin 1995: 39–40).

The Benelux customs union was intended as just a preliminary step to a wider European agreement. Dutch foreign minister J. W. Beyen was thus one of the prime forces behind the 1957 Treaty of Rome, which established the European Economic Community (EEC) (Voorhoeve 1979: 160–165). In the first years of the EEC, the Dutch were quite influential as counterweight to the French emphasis on defense and security issues, for the Dutch did not want the EEC to become a replacement for NATO and its guarantee of American involvement. At the same time, the Netherlands was a champion of the transfer of sovereignty from the member states to the EEC in policy areas related to economic integration. Dutch supranationalism (the granting of decisionmaking powers to international institutions) stood opposed to French intergovernmentalism (in which national governments retain sovereignty, and European decisions require the agreement of all member states).

The European Union has developed as a mixture of supranational powers and intergovernmental arrangements. The supranational powers of the EU are centered primarily on those measures connected to creation of an integrated internal market. This has led to the development of EU powers not only over rules governing such directly trade-related issues as tariffs and quotas, but also over rules governing taxation, product standards regulation, occupational health and safety, gender equality in the workplace, environmental protection, and social welfare and security.[55] Intergovernmentalism is still the form of rule-making in foreign and security policy, as well as in most noneconomic aspects of domestic policy.

This mixed profile of EU powers at the turn of the twenty-first century is a very close mirror of the Dutch vision as first developed in the 1950s.

Since the end of the Cold War the Netherlands has become substantially more open to movement toward political union. The Maastricht Treaty, adopted during the Dutch presidency of the European Council in 1991, pledged increasing cooperation in the areas of justice and home affairs, and foresaw as well the development of a common foreign and security policy.[56] Although the Maastricht Treaty represented a far-reaching extension of the scope of European integration, the Dutch had originally pressed for a still more ambitious treaty that would eventually merge the member states of the EU into a single governmental federation.

Although the Netherlands has become a champion of political integration, the benefits of membership in the European Union continue to be primarily in the realm of trade. The Dutch benefit particularly from open markets for agricultural products. It is no accident that Sicco Mansholt, a Dutch politician, wrote the first draft of the plan for agricultural free trade in the EEC (Urwin 1995: 59). A complementary initiative was the Common Agricultural Program (CAP), which offered guaranteed prices for agricultural products, and from which the Netherlands gains a substantial benefit. The Dutch government would later join its Danish, French, and Irish colleagues in defending the CAP in an open-ended form that would guarantee prices for all agricultural goods produced. For example, the price for dairy products is set by the CAP at a level that ranges as high as five times the world market price. In response to that stimulus, Dutch milk production doubled between 1962 and 1982 (Hommes 1990: 44). Dairy production in the EU was limited in 1984, thereby eliminating the mountains of butter and lakes of milk that had been created by artificially high guaranteed prices. Even so, the Dutch continue to benefit from the CAP, which absorbs about two-thirds of the EU budget (Urwin 1995: 189).

The European orientation of the Netherlands is not just a means of aiding Dutch farmers. As a small nation with an open economy, the Netherlands also benefits from the growth in trade brought about by membership in the EU. Over half the Dutch GDP is traded, and so it is hardly surprising that the growth of world trade accounts for half of Dutch economic growth (Molle and van Mourik 1990: 28). Any development that increases the overall level of world trade, then, is likely to be good for the Dutch economy. Between 1958 and 1972, the value of Dutch exports to other EEC countries increased by 14.8 percent per year, versus an increase in value of 7.6 percent per year for Dutch exports to the rest of the world (Griffiths 1980a: 287). For the next twenty years, between 1973 and 1992, European integration stagnated and there was no difference between the rate of growth of Dutch trade with other EU members and the rate of growth of Dutch trade with the rest of the world.[57] Since completion of the internal market by full implementation of the Single Europe Act in 1992, Dutch trade with the EU has grown at 19 percent per year, compared to a 14 percent annual growth in Dutch trade with the rest of the world.[58]

Part of this annual increase in intra-European trade was pure gain to the Dutch economy, due to the stimulating effects of lowered tariffs between the member countries. However, some of the gains in trade between EU members were the product of trade diversion (trade with fellow members that would otherwise have occurred anyway with countries outside the EU) rather than trade creation (trade that would not otherwise have occurred at all). The reason is that the common external tariffs of the EU were in many cases higher than Dutch tariffs prior to the formation of the common market. As the Dutch raised their external tariffs in conformity with EU policy, some of the trade that would have occurred with non-member countries shifted to fellow EU members instead. Although the trade diversion element of the EU tariff structure makes membership a bit less valuable than it might otherwise be, the EU's guarantee of access to the markets of neighboring economies makes it an extremely important institution for Dutch economic welfare. Sixty percent of Dutch imports and 75 percent of Dutch exports are with fellow members of the European Union.

The Dutch have benefited materially from free trade within the European Union, and particularly from EU support of farmers. The budget of the EU has shifted in recent years, however, with reduced emphasis on agricultural support and increased emphasis on assistance to the less developed regions. The Netherlands receives little direct benefit from these development funds, and has consequently become the biggest net contributor to the EU on a per capita basis. In 1998 the Dutch government joined with the other net contributors among EU members, Germany and Great Britain, to obtain a reduction of the overall EU budget and a fairer distribution of the financial burden. For some months the Netherlands took the lead in forcing the issue by vetoing all new expenditure requests until some resolution was found. In March 1999 a new budget agreement was signed that will lower agricultural support prices. The Dutch contribution to the EU budget was also lowered by 790 million guilders (US$385 million) and the Netherlands was promised 150 million guilders (US$73 million) in structural funds to fight unemployment in the north and west portions of the country.[59] The Dutch are deeply committed to the European Union, but not blindly so.

Careful calculation of the costs and benefits of membership could paralyze the EU were it not for the fact that all member states gain from some EU policies. For example, the EU has consistently adopted policies in favor of economic competition that make it easier for member states to reduce the size of their least efficient industries—indeed, the downsizing of traditional industries has in many cases been mandated. The EU's pro-competition policies have helped the high-tech sector of the Dutch economy, particularly in electronics. More traditional parts of the Dutch economy, such as shipbuilding, have been all but phased out.[60] The textile and steel sectors have also reduced their workforces substantially. Hoogovens was the first European steel concern to regain profitability with a reduced labor force under EU market-share arrangements reached in the 1980s.

The focus of activity within the European Union at the turn of the twenty-first century is on the European Monetary Union (EMU). Development of a common currency is part of the broader desire to create a single market within the European Union, because it reduces the transaction costs of trading with multiple currencies and because it makes price differences (and consequently trade possibilities) more apparent. The greatest single impact of the European Union on its member states to date may well have been the drive within each country during the 1990s to qualify for participation in the EMU. In order to be part of the EMU, member states had to meet stringent targets on public spending deficits, government debt, and rates of inflation. The scramble to meet EMU targets unleashed a wave of privatization and budget cuts across Europe. As we saw in Chapter 7, this took the form in the Netherlands of a concerted reevaluation of the social welfare state, and included the launching of the six great efficiency operations designed to reduce the size of government. The impact of the EMU on restructuring the Dutch welfare state is a vivid demonstration of the far-reaching role European unification has come to play in policymaking.[61]

The development of supranational powers in the European Union sometimes causes observers to wonder why sovereign nation-states agree to give up so much of their authority. To put the matter sharply in the Dutch context, why did political leaders allow the EMU to force the pace at which some policies of the social welfare state were abandoned? The fact that the European Union is so popular among leaders and the general public in the Netherlands increases the paradox. Van Schendelen (1992: 230–232) found that 98 percent of members of the Second Chamber in 1990 agreed that membership in the European Union was advantageous for the Netherlands. Forty percent believed that the powers of the European Union should be increased still further, and only 10 percent believed that the EU had too much authority. Although support for the EU is slightly greater among leaders of the economically conservative parties (the VVD and D66) than among leaders of the PvdA and the CDA, this support is nonetheless one of the few major issues (along with support for NATO) that enjoys a strong consensus across the spectrum of Dutch political parties. The same point can be made about the Dutch public, which is consistently among those publics most supportive of European integration.[62]

The resolution to the paradox of Dutch support for supranational authority within the European Union (and, ultimately, the reason behind any EU member's support for this authority) is that the alternative of national sovereignty is an illusion. Development of the EMU, for example, transfers authority over the Dutch currency and interest rates to the European Central Bank, located in Frankfurt. But the Dutch guilder had already been pegged to the German Mark in the early 1980s, a measure taken in order to make trade with Germany easier,[63] as well as to signal to the rest of the world that the guilder was a low-inflation currency. Interest-rate movements decided by *Bundesbank* officials were, in effect, already binding on the

Dutch central bank. The extent of Dutch monetary sovereignty under the EMU is no less than it was when the guilder was tied to the German Mark.

In fact, the transfer of formal authority from nation-states to the European Union *increases* the authority of small countries such as the Netherlands. No Dutch person sits on the board of the *Bundesbank,* but the Dutch are represented on the board of the European Central Bank.[64] The Dutch government increases its control over its own monetary policy by merging the guilder with other European currencies and ceding authority to a supranational institution. The same logic holds for other small European countries, and in the global economy all EU members have become in essence small countries. This accounts for the shift in French policy from dogged intergovernmentalism in the early 1960s to acceptance of an EU with broad supranational powers over economic policy in the 1990s. It also accounts for the fact that Germany has now become the greatest advocate of supranationalism, taking over a role that once belonged to the Netherlands.

The influence of the Netherlands on the EU is no longer what it was in the early years, when the Dutch were outspoken and influential advocates for such causes as British membership, direct elections to the European Parliament, and supranational authority over economic issues. Expansion of the EU has of course diluted the weight of the original members of the EEC, and the future membership of such large countries as Poland will further reduce the share of Dutch influence. Moreover, Britain has now become the most Atlanticist of EU members (a role once played by the Netherlands),[65] and Germany has taken up the torch of supranationalism. Although these developments reduce the direct visibility and influence of the Netherlands within the EU, it is important to keep in mind that Dutch interests continue to be well-served by the integration of markets and the free flow of trade. The institutions of the EU offer far more opportunity for Dutch prosperity and international influence than would a Europe composed solely of nation-states.

The Foreign Policy Process

Having examined the history of Dutch foreign policy and the most important foreign policy commitments of the Netherlands today, we turn now to the process by which foreign policy is made. The content of foreign policy is a function not only of constraints created by the international environment, but also of domestic factors. Basic shifts in Dutch foreign policy are of course predicated on such external influences as the German invasion in 1940 and the breakup of the Soviet Union. Despite the undeniable significance of these external conditions, though, a complete understanding of Dutch foreign policy requires that we examine the process by which it is made. This process has changed over time as a function of fluctuations in the degree of party polarization, the mobilization of public opinion on foreign affairs, and parliamentary activism.

According to the Dutch constitution, foreign policy is made by the Crown, which delegates this responsibility to the foreign minister. Formal accounts of the foreign policy establishment in the Netherlands emphasize the power and autonomy of the government over parliament, and of the foreign minister within the government.[66] The nineteenth-century assertion of the parliamentary right to participate in policymaking did not extend to foreign policy, where executive privilege lasted much longer. Only in 1917 did the Second Chamber even pass a motion opining that it would be desirable for the government to consult with the States General in making foreign policy (Bovend'Eert and Kummeling 1991: 293). At this time the Second Chamber also established a committee on Foreign Affairs, though the committee was not very active until after World War II. Philip Everts (1983: 29) comments that until the late 1960s there was a "lack of debate over issues of foreign policy and [a] relatively limited time devoted by parliament to problems of foreign policy in general." Nor was foreign policy subject to the extensive process of consultation with interest groups and advisory councils that characterizes domestic policy issues.

The fact that the international environment is almost completely beyond the control of the Dutch government reinforces the formal authority of the foreign minister. When the broad outlines of policy are seen as being externally determined, the foreign minister is viewed as an expert who fits Dutch policy to a predetermined situation, rather than as a partisan figure who enjoys latitude in policymaking. The pre–World War II policy of strict neutrality, and especially the feeling during the 1930s of being in an increasingly hostile international environment, led to a general acceptance in the Second Chamber that foreign policy should be left in the hands of the government.[67]

As a result, Dutch party leaders were for a long time disinclined to use foreign policy issues to partisan advantage. Even the painful series of decisions first to resist with force and then to acquiesce to the independence of Indonesia were taken in a climate of elite accommodation and secrecy, despite the polarization of public opinion and parliamentary parties on the issue. Commenting on this period, Bank (1984: 82) concludes that "especially during the last stages of the Indonesian crisis all important decisions had been taken under the cover of summit diplomacy." In short, foreign policy in the Netherlands long remained the province of the foreign minister, whose powers far exceeded those of counterparts in other parliamentary democracies. As long as the foreign minister retained the overall support of the cabinet, even a parliamentary majority could not challenge his position (Baehr 1980: 226).

The autonomy of the foreign ministry has significantly declined in recent decades. One reason for this is the increasing importance of regional coordination carried out through the European Union's Council of Ministers. Consultation between member-state ministers responsible for a given policy area results in diffusing responsibility for international negotiations and coordination among many departments. Dutch foreign minister E. N. van Kleffens once said that "A diplomat does not talk about cheese."[68] That may be so, but trade in cheese and other goods is now a significant part of Dutch foreign policy. Consequently, the minister of economic affairs and the minister of agriculture and fisheries have taken particularly large roles in the development of EU policies. The foreign ministry no longer has exclusive prerogative over international negotiations.[69] The foreign ministry is charged with coordinating the involvement of other ministries in various European negotiations. But, as Richard Griffiths (1980a: 286) points out, "Valuable ministerial time has been wasted in resolving blistering interdepartmental rows over both policy content and departmental competence." This politicization of foreign policy within the ministerial council has weakened the unchallenged authority of the foreign minister.

The authority of the foreign minister is further diluted by creation of the post of minister for development cooperation in 1965, effectively dividing what had been a unified domain. The minister of development cooperation inevitably represents perspectives on foreign policy distinct from those of the foreign minister. In 1997, for example, when the Gumus family was deported to Turkey because they could not demonstrate six years of legal income, Minister of Development Cooperation Jan Pronk stated that the Dutch, and his fellow ministers in particular, had lost their humanity.[70] Faced with the wrath of the rest of the cabinet, Pronk issued a halfhearted retraction, but the point had been made that cabinet decisions on immigration issues are seen as moral issues by the minister of development cooperation.

Since the 1960s, the Dutch public has become active over a series of international controversies, adding to the politicization of foreign policy issues. U.S. involvement in the Vietnam War, Dutch relations with the apartheid regime in South Africa, the NATO memberships of Greece and Portugal during their dictatorships, NATO's nuclear weapons policies, and Dutch participation in the UN's "blue helmet" peacekeeping operations have all aroused public controversy. Philip Everts (1983: 40) points out that "Groups of all kinds are today involved in the debate over foreign policy questions . . . concerned with issues such as the problems of war and peace, armament, Third World issues, human rights, or problems of particular areas or countries."[71] A study of foreign policy views held by leaders in business, unions, the media, churches, political parties, academia, and external advisory commissions (Baehr et al. 1978) shows that their advocacy of particular foreign policies substantially widens the spread of opinion on such basic issues as NATO membership and European integration.

As recently as 1977, Arie van der Hek could conclude his study of parliamentary involvement in foreign affairs with the observation that the Second Chamber chooses to remain on the sidelines of foreign policy making. But the clamor of public groups for a voice in foreign policy since that time also led to the politicization of foreign policy in parliament. Where once consensus was the hallmark of the Dutch political system, it is now common for partisan disagreement to be articulated in every policy area, including foreign policy. The Foreign Affairs

Committee of the Second Chamber now meets more often and the foreign minister is obliged to meet with the committee to discuss policy directions. Most standing committees in parliament today spend at least part of their time—sometimes
a great portion of their time—considering the consequences of European policy.[72] European summits are followed by a debate in the Second Chamber in
which the direction of European policy and its implications for the Netherlands
are explored. Parliament's international expertise and interest are also heightened
by participation in the Parliamentary Assembly of the Council of Europe, the
Assembly of the West European Union, the North Atlantic Assembly, and the
Interparliamentary Advisory Council of Benelux.

There are, in short, three reasons why the foreign policy process has become
more openly contested: changes in the policymaking process within the ministry
and the ministerial council, the mobilization of public opinion, and the politicization of foreign policy in the parliament. All three of these changes in the foreign policy process were on display during the most hotly contested international
issue faced in the country since decolonization in the early 1950s. This was the decision taken in 1979 to deploy forty-eight NATO cruise missiles in the
Netherlands.

The Cruise Missile Controversy

The NATO decision in 1979 to deploy a new generation of intermediate-range
nuclear forces (INFs) in five West European countries led in the early 1980s to a
general uprising of public opposition across the continent. The movement
against the cruise and Pershing II missiles is still today the largest cross-national
protest in West European history (Rochon 1988). And the Dutch peace movement was the largest and most influential of the peace movements within Europe.

For much of the postwar period, the Dutch commitment to NATO included
unswerving loyalty to the American nuclear arsenal as a key element in NATO's
deterrent capacity. The Dutch government was first to accept the introduction of
NATO nuclear weapons into West European nations in 1957, when they were
viewed as an alternative to the creation of nationally controlled nuclear weapons
systems in Europe (Siccama 1985: 124). The Dutch government argued in nuclear
planning councils that authority for the use of NATO's nuclear weapons should
lie solely with the president of the United States, and the Dutch remained opposed to the independent French and British nuclear arsenals.

Beginning in the 1970s, though, this consensus on NATO nuclear policy began
to erode, both among the Dutch public and in the political leadership. Already in
1975, 60 percent of the public were opposed to the nuclear missions assigned to
Dutch forces in the event of a Soviet invasion (Siccama 1985: 131). President
Carter's decision to undertake production of the neutron bomb generated a public campaign of opposition that culminated in the collection of 1.2 million signatures on a petition demanding that the decision be reversed.[73] Shortly thereafter

the parliament passed a resolution instructing the government to inform Washington of its opposition to the neutron bomb. In the 1960s, Foreign Minister Joseph Luns refused on several occasions to convey to the American government parliamentary resolutions condemning U.S. involvement in the Vietnam War. In 1978 Defense Minister Roelof Kruisinga not only passed the anti–neutron bomb resolution to his American counterpart, but also expressed his own opposition to the new weapon and resigned his post.

The campaign against the neutron bomb was only a warm-up for the movement against deployment of forty-eight cruise missiles in the Netherlands. The major impetus for the cruise missile protest came from the Interchurch Peace Council (IKV), an organization set up in 1967 in a cooperative endeavor between all major denominations to study problems of peace and to make recommendations for consideration by the churches (Everts 1983). The IKV's slogan, "Rid the world of nuclear weapons, beginning with the Netherlands," became the rallying cry for the Dutch peace movement.[74]

Although the public never shared the anti-NATO sentiments prevalent in the IKV, opinion polls in the early 1980s showed that about 40 percent of the public was unconditionally opposed to the new nuclear missiles, with another 40 percent saying that the decision was "acceptable but regrettable." Less than one-fifth of the Dutch public described it as a "good decision" (Domke 1987: 286–287). A report compiled by the USIA Office of Research on Dutch foreign policy opinions concluded that over 40 percent of the public favored unilateral nuclear disarmament. Opinions on cruise missile deployment varied depending on how the question was phrased, but as many as three-quarters of the Dutch wanted to see deployment at least deferred.

Armed with widespread support in the churches, in the labor unions, and among the public, the campaign against the cruise missiles developed into a powerful movement, with support even in the Dutch military.[75] The Netherlands was one of the few countries in which a full parliamentary debate on the INF decision was held before the December 1979 NATO meeting that finalized the decision. In that debate the parliamentary group of the CDA, to the chagrin of its own ministers, proposed that a decision on cruise missile deployment be postponed. They also suggested that Dutch acceptance of the cruise missiles be contingent on ratification of the Salt II Treaty by the U.S. Senate, as well as on reduction of the six nuclear tasks that the Netherlands performed within NATO.[76] This suggestion was adopted by the Second Chamber and became the official Dutch position at the December meeting of the NATO defense ministers. It is an extraordinary example of parliamentary activism, in effect a legislative dictation of Dutch treaty negotiations.

At that NATO meeting, the Dutch government dutifully made its proposal, which was discussed and then rejected. The government then accepted the INF decision while noting its reservations with regard to deployment in the Netherlands. The Dutch were given an additional two years to evaluate the progress of arms control talks before deciding whether or not to accept the missiles.

Even with the grant of extra time, divisions within the governing coalition and the assertiveness of the Second Chamber made it difficult for the Dutch policy process to reach any resolution. Both were responding to the mobilization of public opinion against the missiles. In September 1981, 400,000 people marched against the cruise missiles in Amsterdam, and there were over a half million demonstrators in The Hague the following year. In 1983, 3 million Dutch citizens signed a petition to reject the cruise missiles.[77] Although 87 percent of the public continued to believe that "NATO is necessary for the preservation of peace," 79 percent added that the use of nuclear weapons to maintain that peace is not acceptable (Everts 1983: 169). This opposition was concentrated on the left and center of the political spectrum, but surveys showed that one-third of Liberal Party voters also opposed deployment.

When the Labor Party joined the opposition in 1982, the parliamentary group immediately declared its opposition to cruise missile deployment under any circumstances. Even more troubling for the government was the decision of twelve members of the CDA parliamentary group also to oppose bringing new nuclear weapons into the Netherlands. When the moment for decision arrived in 1981, the coalition of Christian Democrats, Labor, and D66 was split evenly on the issue. With at least some sentiment against deployment in each of the three governing parties, the government of Andries van Agt decided to begin site preparations while deferring an actual decision on deployment. The peace movement and its political allies had effectively paralyzed the government, in sharp contrast to the conduct of foreign policy in an earlier era (1957), when the Dutch first accepted American tactical nuclear weapons without significant parliamentary or public debate.

In June 1984 the Lubbers government was finally able to announce that the Netherlands would accept cruise missiles in 1988 should the Soviet Union increase its own stock of intermediate-range nuclear weapons (SS-20s) between June 1984 and November 1985.[78] By putting the burden of the first move on the Soviet Union, the government undercut the arguments of peace-movement organizations that the Dutch should take the lead in stopping the nuclear arms race. In effect, the Dutch government permitted the Soviets to decide whether new nuclear weapons would be deployed in the Netherlands.

In the end, deployment of the cruise missiles never went forward in the Netherlands. When the November 1985 deadline arrived, the Soviet Union had indeed added to its arsenal of SS-20s. Despite a new petition campaign that generated 3.7 million signatures, a resolution to accept the forty-eight cruise missiles sailed through the Second Chamber after a debate that followed strictly partisan lines. The Christian Democratic defections that threatened the life of the government in prior years did not materialize. A date in 1988 was chosen to begin installation of the cruise missiles, but those missiles never arrived because arms control agreements reached between the United States and the Soviet Union in the interim resulted in the cancellation of the entire INF program.

The cruise missile controversy exemplifies the significant changes that have taken place in the Dutch foreign policy process over the last decades: the mobilization of public opinion, the activation of parliamentary prerogative, and reduction of the foreign minister's autonomy within the ministerial council. The cruise missile decision also illustrates the typical governmental response to these conditions: delay of the decision combined with a proliferation of compromise proposals and—more often than not—resolution of the issue by an ingenious reframing through linkage to other conditions.

Conclusion

It is a great distance for a country to travel, from being master of its own global trading empire to being a small NATO member agonizing over whether to accept decisions made by the larger members of the alliance. The Netherlands has traversed this distance in a span of three hundred years. It is a journey that accounts at least in part for the Dutch tendency to take a more active stance in the international system than that typical of other small nations.

Dutch foreign policy at times articulates positions critical of the powers that be. The Netherlands has led international protest against nuclear weapons, opposed French plans for a European Defense Force, and targeted development aid to Castro's Cuba and Sandinista Nicaragua. At other times the Dutch are among the leaders in cooperative international ventures, such as development of the European Union and deployment of UN peacekeeping missions. The common theme in these positions is neither contrariness nor submissive followership, but rather activism.

The Dutch understand that their security and prosperity depend on an active search for coexistence with other countries. This is the common thread between their deeply felt commitment to international law and organizations and their laserlike focus on the mutual benefits of trade relationships. Peace, profits, and principles (to return to Joris Voorhoeve's themes) must be found together or they will not be found at all.

The Netherlands has had three centuries to prepare for the kind of interdependent and multipolar world in which we all live today. The patterns of Dutch foreign policy are therefore instructive for those whose own period of global preeminence is more recent.

NOTES

1. Cited in Griffiths (1980a: 299, footnote 11).
2. Dutch imports from the United States are about twice as much as their exports, due primarily to the import of such raw materials as grain and vegetable oils.

3. Cited in de Haas (1943: 173).

4. Voorhoeve's (1979) slightly longer version of the three principles is that the Dutch have three foreign policy traditions: maritime commercialism, neutralist abstentionism, and international idealism.

5. The United States instituted an arms embargo against the Netherlands and threatened to suspend Marshall Plan aid until the Dutch government accepted the independence of the Republic of Indonesia. Decolonization policy is described in detail in Lijphart (1966) and Newton (1978: 160–172).

6. Cited in Heldring (1978: 310).

7. Cited in Newton (1978: 111).

8. Cited in Wilson (1957: 36).

9. Cited in Brand (1980: 252).

10. Cited in Daalder (1966: 193).

11. Hyma (1942: 136–170). Hyma further reports (page 158) that "the Dutch would go out of their way to hunt for Portuguese priests and deliver them to the Japanese officials." This, of course, helped the Dutch as traders as well as being in accord with their anti-Catholic sentiments.

12. See for example Voorhoeve (1979: 45–49).

13. Because of its use in preserving fish, salt has always been an important part of the Dutch economy. The letters in the acronym for the Dutch multinational corporation AKZO, which today produces a wide range of household products, stand for General Royal Salt Company.

14. Wallerstein (1974: 96) calls the Dutch European trade network an instance of "the classic colonial pattern."

15. Cited in Wilson (1968: 22). On Defoe's advocacy of trade as a means of increasing the wealth of a nation, see also Dharwadker (1998).

16. Timing is often overlooked as a factor helping the rapid growth of a new power. In the case of the Netherlands in the first half of the seventeenth century, timing involved the following: The German Empire was absorbed in the Thirty Years War (1618–1648), there were religious wars and regional rebellions in France, there was civil war in England, and there were a variety of revolts—including that of the Dutch—in the Spanish Hapsburg Empire ('t Hart 1993: 27). In short, potential rival superpowers were busy with internal issues.

17. Price (1974: 54) and Boxer (1990: 315). The trade with England, France, and the Baltics each surpassed in annual value the trade with the East Indies.

18. Bruijn (1990). Glamann (1958: 46) notes that use of the *fluyt* pushed the cargo value of a voyage up to 75 percent of the total cost, with wages accounting for only 10 percent of costs.

19. This calculation includes profits from trade within Asia as well as from the sale of goods brought back to Amsterdam.

20. Hyma (1942: 63) reports one instance in which three ships arrived in Malaysia from the Dutch province of Zeeland to buy pepper, only to find that a convoy from Amsterdam had already purchased the entire crop. They were obliged to wait eight months for the next harvest before returning home.

21. According to Bruijn (1990: 185–187), the VOC made almost 5,000 voyages to Asia via the Cape of Good Hope, and none of the ships or cargoes were insured. The VOC relied instead on the number of its voyages to indemnify losses when they occurred.

22. Neal (1990: 196). Hyma (1942: 66–68) notes that dividends were paid both in cash and in spices in the early years of the VOC.

23. See Glamann (1958) for details of the VOC's charter, organization, and internal operations.

24. The VOC was called upon to fulfill this agreement several times in the seventeenth century. It provided four outfitted warships for the first war with England in 1639 and twenty warships for the second war in 1665.

25. Cited in Neal (1990: 196).

26. The identity between the interests of the VOC and those of the Dutch government was so great that no one thought it odd when Grotius was sent to England in 1613 to carry out a negotiation as a representative of *both* the VOC and the States General. See Hyma (1942: 92).

27. See Glamann (1958: 27–30) for details of the distribution system developed by the VOC for its cargoes. Even with stockholder vigilance, the VOC suffered from trading on the side by "everyone from Governor-General to cabin-boy," according to Boxer (1990: 225).

28. See Glamann (1958: 259) and Boxer (1990: 51).

29. The VOC also employed 10,000 soldiers to guard its trading outposts (Murray 1967: 71).

30. See Hyma (1942) for a detailed account of the Dutch conflicts with the English and Portuguese over Asian trade rights.

31. There were one hundred insurance offices in Amsterdam by 1721, and among their patrons were English merchants who insured themselves against Dutch privateers during the Anglo-Dutch naval wars.

32. Cited in Boxer (1990: 126).

33. The VOC also used slaves in its Cape Town operations, according to Boxer (1990: 294–296).

34. Slavery was not abolished in the West Indies (Surinam) by the Dutch until 1862, and then only under pressure from the English and French, both of whom had abolished slavery in their territories decades earlier. On slavery and its abolition in the Dutch plantations of the West Indies, see Newton (1978: 173–174) and Boxer (1990: 268–272).

35. The West India Company, founded in 1621 just months after cessation of the twelve-year truce with Spain, reverted to the earlier principles of plunder and also tried to convert native populations to Calvinism. The high point of West India Company profitability was the capture of the Spanish silver fleet by Piet Heijn in 1682.

36. Even in their colonies, the Dutch generally operated by indirect rule, as seen in the fact that there were only about 175 civil servants on Java to govern a population of about 12 million.

37. Cited in Vlekke (1945: 306).

38. Cited in Brand (1980: 262).

39. Brand (1980: 264). See also Newton (1978: 159–160).

40. Kriesi (1993: 177). See also Voorhoeve (1979: chapter 9).

41. Dutch foreign aid is currently about 0.8 percent of GNP. According to Gladdish (1991: 177) this places the Netherlands behind only the United States, Japan, France, and Germany in amount of aid given. On Dutch aid policy, see Voorhoeve (1979: chapter 10).

42. Compared to development assistance in other nations, Dutch aid is relatively untied to the purchase of exports. Gladdish (1991: 177) notes that over 90 percent of Dutch bilat-

eral aid is in the form of outright grants. More than eighty countries received Dutch aid in 1998, and the question periodically rises as to whether aid should be focused on a smaller number of countries. In 1998 the government announced plans to reduce the number of aid recipients to about twenty, hoping to make a bigger impact by concentrating on countries with which the Netherlands has long-term relationships.

43. See Wallerstein (1980: 80–91) and Boxer (1990: 322–331). Mercantilism elsewhere in Europe also hurt Dutch industry, particularly the protective tariffs on textiles in England and France as those countries sought to develop their own industrial capacities.

44. Newton (1978: 122–123) estimates that German rearmament gave jobs to 40,000 Dutch people who crossed the border each day to work in German factories, "helping to build the weapons that would later be turned against their own country."

45. Cited in van Campen (1958: 14).

46. All parties in the Second Chamber except the Communists approved Dutch membership in NATO—a strikingly broad repudiation of the neutrality policy.

47. Cited in Russell (1978: 169). See also Holsti (1970), van Staden (1978), Voorhoeve (1979: 146–150), and Domke (1987).

48. These figures are from Leurdijk (1978). The same study also surveyed political party leaders, church leaders, members of advisory councils, employers, leaders in the media and in education, and members of action groups interested in foreign policy issues. Among these "informal elites," support for NATO was lower but still impressive: 76 percent endorsed NATO membership. Between 50 and 60 percent agreed that NATO has been responsible for the European peace since 1945, that the Netherlands has more influence on international affairs within NATO than it would have outside the alliance, and that American guarantees for European security within the NATO alliance are credible. Only 16 percent thought that NATO membership interferes with the "peace diplomacy" of the Netherlands.

49. Domke (1987: 276). See also Voorhoeve (1979: 137–139). Opposition to NATO membership never went above 15 percent of the population during this period.

50. See also Voorhoeve (1979: 125) for a discussion of Dutch defense expenditures within NATO. Reductions in governmental spending during the 1980s are described in Chapter 7.

51. See Domke (1987) for details of the Dutch roles within NATO during the Cold War period.

52. As we shall see later in this chapter, Dutch concerns about political unification in Europe have all but vanished in the post–Cold War era.

53. For an account of the stage play, see *The Sunday Telegraph*, May 26, 1996, page 28. Some of the more painful claims have been that the Dutchbat simply turned over the Moslem population to the Bosnian Serb Army, and that in their own haste to escape, Dutch troops in armored personnel carriers ran over fleeing civilians. Among the books published on Srebrenica are Honig and Both (1996), Westerman and Rijs (1997), and Rohde (1997). Danner (1998) places the attack on Srebrenica and the subsequent executions in the wider context of the Bosnian war.

54. *InterNetKrant*, September 5, 1998, page 1.

55. Ironically, given their commitment to supranationalism, the Dutch have often been laggards in implementing directives emanating from Brussels in these areas. When asked about this, government officials usually refer to the lengthy process of policy negotiation described in Chapter 6.

56. For example, the Amsterdam Treaty, signed during the Dutch presidency of the European Council in 1997, gives the EU supranational power over the visa and asylum policies of member states.

57. Dutch trade grew at a rate of 10 percent per year, both within the EU and outside it.

58. These figures cover the period from 1993 to 1995.

59. *InterNetKrant,* March 27, 1999, pages 1 and 2.

60. Employment in shipbuilding—a Dutch industry dating back to the seventeenth century—fell from 23,000 jobs to less than 4,000 jobs between 1975 and 1987 (Hobbelen 1990: 37). See Chapter 7 on structural reform of the Dutch economy.

61. I owe this observation to Paulette Kurzer (personal communication).

62. Dutch public support for the European Union is consistently in the range of 70 to 80 percent, according to the European Union Commission (1998).

63. Germany is the source of 25 percent of all Dutch imports and the destination of 30 percent of all exports.

64. In fact, Wim Duisenberg, former chair of the Dutch central bank, is the first board chair of the European Central Bank.

65. "Atlanticism" in this context refers to an orientation that does not allow the EU to develop in such a way that would tend to reduce American participation in security and defense issues affecting Europe. The most important Atlanticist issue has always been the extent of foreign policy and defense cooperation within the EU.

66. On the structure and operation of the foreign ministry, see Deboutte and van Staden (1978).

67. On the weakness of the Second Chamber in foreign policy, see Voorhoeve (1979: 81–84). The phenomenon is similar to that found in the United States from about 1945 to 1965, when the constraints of Soviet containment removed foreign policy from partisan politics.

68. Cited in Voorhoeve (1979: 75).

69. This fact was embarrassingly illustrated by an episode in 1964 when two delegations arrived at a conference to discuss Nigeria's association with the EEC, each claiming the right to represent the Dutch point of view. See Griffiths (1980a: 286).

70. *InterNetKrant,* September 13, 1997, page 1. See Chapter 3 for an account of the Gumus family and their deportation to Turkey.

71. On the role of new groups in foreign policy, see also Siccama (1985: 135–137).

72. A standing committee for European Affairs was created in 1986 to consult with the government on upcoming European decision areas, to follow the work of the European Parliament, and to coordinate Dutch policy in areas that cut across existing committee lines (Bovend'Eert and Kummeling 1991).

73. Everts and Walraven (1984: 49–51). Over 8 percent of the Dutch population signed this petition.

74. For accounts of the IKV and the Dutch campaign against cruise missiles, see Faber et al. (1983), Rochon (1988), and Kriesi (1989).

75. A Ministry of Defense survey of training bases showed that 8 percent of commissioned officers, 25 percent of noncommissioned officers, and 65 percent of draftees would face a difficult moral dilemma if ordered to use nuclear weapons. For details on the role of the churches in the peace movement, see Everts (1983, especially pages 135–138, 150–167) and Rochon (1988: 128–135). The support of church leaders for a mass political move-

ment can be attributed to their relatively poor direct access to political decisionmakers—in sharp contrast to the situation that obtained during the period of pillarized politics.

76. Those tasks were to serve as a site for nuclear antiaircraft weapons, land mines, short-range ground-to-ground missiles, Starfighter bombers, artillery, and Neptune aircraft carrying nuclear depth charges.

77. The petition campaign has a venerable history and strikes a deep cultural chord in the Netherlands, comparable to civil rights marches in the United States. Petition campaigns against governmental plans for rearmament in 1923 and 1930 collected 1.1 million and 1.5 million signatures respectively.

78. There was some fine print. The Netherlands would take fewer than the full complement of forty-eight missiles if negotiations between the United States and the Soviet Union produced limitations on land-based medium-range missiles.

9

▬▬▬▬▬▬

NEGOTIATING
SOVEREIGNTY IN
AN INTERDEPENDENT
WORLD

*The transition from ease and opulence to extreme poverty is remarkable on
crossing the line between the Dutch and Prussian territories. The soil and climate are the same; the governments alone differ.*
                                    —Thomas Jefferson (1788)[1]

As Thomas Jefferson passed from the Netherlands to Prussia on the way to Paris
to take up his post as American ambassador, he observed a startling and sudden
change in economic fortunes. To Jefferson's democratic mind, the cause of Dutch
prosperity and of Prussian poverty lay in the contrast between a republic and a
monarchy. And indeed, the relative freedom enjoyed by the Dutch population was
fundamental to the prosperity of merchants and farmers alike. It accounts for the
success of the VOC, the credit and exchange banks, the insurance companies, and
the world's first stock market. The limited government characteristic of the Dutch
Republic was a powerful force in creating the "ease and opulence" that was so
striking to Jefferson.

Though Jefferson was favorably disposed to the United Provinces, the young
state was a religious outcast in Catholic Europe because of its Calvinism and a political outcast in absolutist Europe because of its republicanism. Having created

the world's premier trade network with a small population inhabiting a marshy land, the Dutch were subject to much scrutiny. The idea that a country could be well governed without a strong king was so radical in the seventeenth century that many observers predicted the country's demise.[2] Some, including even those who benefited from Dutch tolerance, heaped scorn on the crass materialism of the merchants. René Descartes, living in Amsterdam because he was not free to pursue his philosophic work in France, complained about life "In this great town, where apart from myself there dwells no one who is not engaged in trade."[3] Montesquieu (1964) condemned the Dutch for their avarice and their single-minded focus on work for economic gain, calling them "ant people"[4] even while also disparaging their fondness for sugar and tea (both luxuries elsewhere in seventeenth-century Europe). Roger Coke, in a 1670 commentary on reasons for "the Growth and Increase of the Dutch Trade above the English," found it "monstrous that the Dutch Nation, who are denied these advantages [of abundance in natural resources], and are of a more dull and heavy constitution than the English, should out-wit us in that wherein God and Nature have given us all the Prerogatives we our selves can desire" (Coke [1670] 1970).[5]

If the English were confused, the French were envious. Louis XIV's minister of finance, Colbert, looked at the Netherlands with greedy eyes: "If the King were to subjugate all the United Provinces of the Netherlands, their trade would become His Majesty's trade; there would be nothing left to wish for."[6] As Sir William Templeton put it in 1673, "The United Provinces are the envy of some, the fear of others and the wonder of all their neighbors."[7]

In the end, though, the most significant sentiment inspired by Dutch success was that of imitation. Roger Coke, after fulminating about how strange it was that the "dull" Dutch could achieve more than the English, concluded that their secrets of success were low interest rates, efficient ship design, and extensive warehousing facilities that enabled merchants to buy low and sell high on international markets. Anticipating the institutionalist orientation of contemporary scholarship in political economy, Pierre-Daniel Huet attributed Dutch success in 1718 to maintenance of a republic of laws, protection of private property, and avoidance of tyrannical rule oriented to military conquest. The conclusions drawn by these and other observers of the Dutch miracle had an enormous impact on neighboring governments and on the international economy. The Dutch emphasis on pragmatic trading relationships, stripped of visions of monarchical grandeur and generally also of Christian proselytism, eventually came to be the foundation of the modern international economy.

In a large world of many states, most have concluded that attempts at conquest and extraction are nearly always futile. The VOC demonstrated that a private venture was more likely than a governmental monopoly to set aside the money needed for investment and to be nimble in response to changes in the market. The democratic peace of the last two centuries, during which democracies have avoided war with each other and prospered instead by building trade relationships, owes a great deal to the much admired, much envied, and much imitated Dutch example set in the seventeenth century.[8]

Interdependence and the Narrow Margins of Politics

Those were the lessons of the sixteenth and seventeenth centuries. Today the Netherlands no longer stands out as a uniquely wealthy country, but its experience continues to be instructive as an example of how to prosper under conditions of interdependence. Although it is a commonplace today to note the linkage of national economies within international markets, the Dutch were forerunners in the experience of interdependence with trading partners and security partners. With just 0.3 percent of the world's population and 3.4 percent of the world economic product, the country is rarely or never in a position to determine the international institutions, practices, and markets within which it must operate. Even within the European Union, the Netherlands represents just 4 percent of the population and has only 5 percent of the EU Commissioners and members of the European Parliament.

Dutch exposure to the international economic system is magnified by its lack of natural resources (other than natural gas) and by its long-established reliance on trade. Dutch multinationals such as Philips, Royal Dutch Shell, Heineken, AKZO-Nobel, and Unilever give the country a significant presence in the international economy. But as Paulette Kurzer (1993) points out, Dutch firms have always maintained a relatively large share of their investment and employment outside the country. Increased capital mobility and the integration of the European market have made it ever easier for Dutch business leaders to view their domestic operations as but one piece of an international puzzle of production and distribution. The Dutch economy is structured as a piece of a larger whole.

Politically too, interdependence has been a reality for hundreds of years. In the seventeenth and eighteenth centuries the Dutch attempted to protect their home territory and their trade routes by taking part in the major-power game of shifting alliances. Once the country dropped from the ranks of the great powers, the Dutch adopted a policy of neutralism in the hope of remaining unaffected by continuing conflicts on the European continent. Neutralism was replaced by alliance more than fifty years ago, and today the Dutch military is no longer even configured for defense of the country. Rather, the military is structured so as to carry out operations in conjunction with NATO allies and UN forces. Interdependence, then, is no less the rule in security issues than it is in the economy.

The contemporary world also presents dilemmas of cultural autonomy, which represents a third dimension of international influence less often recognized than economic and political interdependence. We live in a world of instant communication of news and ideas across borders. When the Dutch listened to the radio and read a newspaper forty years ago, the messages they received were not only in their own language but were also clothed in the worldview of their specific pillar.

The cultural isolation of the pillars has long since broken down, and the specifically Dutch content of cultural communication threatens to break down as well. When Dutch children today watch television programs, attend movies, or visit Internet sites, they do so in English or German at least as often as in Dutch. This influence has contributed to rapid cultural change, and specifically to a widespread questioning of the social, moral, and political values that had long been deeply rooted in the Dutch culture.

One example of German cultural influence in the Netherlands is the increasingly popular custom of putting up a Christmas tree and exchanging gifts on Christmas Eve, rather than following the Dutch tradition of exchanging gifts on December 5, the feast day of Saint Nicholas (also known as Santa Clause).[9] A more serious issue of cultural preservation arose at the University of Amsterdam during the 1980s when it was proposed that all university courses be taught in English. Since a good working knowledge of English is important in the academy and in international business, and since many of the texts and research articles used in Dutch universities are published in English anyway, administrators reasoned that full conversion to English-language instruction would benefit Dutch students and attract more students from other countries. Concern about the reduced status of the Dutch language caused the plan to be shelved. Even so, many courses in Dutch universities are taught in English, and a goodly share of theses and dissertations are written in English by students seeking an international audience for their work.

Interdependence, then, creates thorny issues for the Netherlands in the areas of economic policy, security arrangements, and the preservation of its own language and culture. These are realities the Dutch have long experienced and the rest of the world has recently discovered. Economic autarky is not possible, political isolation is not possible, and clinging to established customs is not possible. At the same time, no government is willing to become fatalistic by deferring policy decisions to international markets or political allies.

What, then, is the line between an unrealistic assertion of national prerogatives and a fatalistic impotence? To what extent can domestic values and priorities still matter in an era when international investors shift their capital between countries from one day to the next? With a centuries-long experience of having half their economy directly involved in trade and the other half dependent on the prosperity that comes with trade, the Dutch have had good reason and a lot of time to think about the political implications of interdependence and rapid change.

Does the need to act in concert with other nations, both for economic prosperity and for security, reduce Dutch autonomy in policymaking? Of course it does. But it has not eliminated the ability to act, as long as international and domestic constraints are accounted for. It has been common in the Netherlands for some time now to talk of "the narrow margins of politics." Joop den Uyl, leader of the Labor Party during the polarization era and minister-president of the most progressive government in Dutch history, invented the phrase as a way of reducing the exuberant expectations of his supporters.

In contrast to the hope and expectation that we can bring about radical changes, I am convinced that the densely woven fabric of our complex social system would tear if we undertake more than limited changes. But—and equally important—small changes of direction within the narrow margins of democratic politics can have large consequences. They can be decisive as to whether there is war or peace, whether we are on an upward or downward spiral, whether we feel hope or despair.[10]

Den Uyl makes it clear that political power in the Netherlands does not confer a license to implement a program of radical change. International markets and the will of other countries limit the Dutch government's room for maneuver. Domestically, any policy proposal must run the gauntlet of interest groups and advisory commissions before being finalized in the ministerial council and Second Chamber. These international and domestic constraints may be disappointing to those whose ideological élan leads them to seek enactment of a comprehensive blueprint of political change. But the art of politics under conditions of interdependence is correctly described by den Uyl as being the capacity to identify small changes of direction that can have large consequences. To govern successfully within the limits of international constraints and domestic consensus, one must achieve big results with a light touch.

Reform of the welfare state, described in Chapter 7, offers an example of working within the narrow margins of democratic politics. We have seen that the Dutch were able first to build an extensive welfare state and then to transform it into an even more ambitious social welfare state. When it became impossible to pay for the social welfare state, the Dutch created a hybrid that retains the core guarantees of material security while placing greater stress on labor force participation. The development of extensive part-time and temporary work opportunities was a small course correction with large consequences. Increased labor force participation through part-time work enabled the government to restore the linkage between social insurance benefits and wages, while at the same time enabling the society to maintain its tradition of a relatively sharp division of labor between men working full-time and women oriented more to the home than to the labor force. The overreach of the social welfare state showed the limits of state autonomy. But the response of retaining key features of the social welfare state while encouraging fuller labor force participation is a classic instance of working within the narrow margins.

In foreign policy as well, the Dutch experience shows the potential for maneuver despite relatively modest power resources. The constraints on a small country like the Netherlands require that its foreign policy be conducted in concert with others. The most recent effort to go it alone on a major international issue was the series of military actions taken in the late 1940s to retain the Indonesian colonies. Militarily and diplomatically, this policy was a disaster. Today, the Dutch conduct their foreign policy almost exclusively through international alliances and organizations.[11] This does not necessarily mean, however, that all freedom of action is lost. Under conditions of interdependence, small nations can actually increase their influence when they operate multilaterally. To go it alone is to forfeit all possibility of influence.

The decision in July 1998 to establish an international court for the prosecution of war crimes and acts of genocide is an excellent example of the potential for influence that comes from working within the narrow margins of international alliances. The United States, surely the last of the countries for whom a go-it-alone foreign policy is a plausible alternative, resisted the establishment of such a court unless it was accompanied by a guarantee that American citizens and soldiers would never be prosecuted under its auspices. With the United States unwilling to participate without this guarantee and the other 147 participating governments unwilling to make such a promise, the United States lost virtually all influence on the treaty establishing the court. The Dutch, on the other hand, embraced the concept of a war crimes court as part of their longtime support for international law. The Netherlands ended up being substantially more influential than the United States on the formation of the court, which will be located in The Hague.

The experience of the Netherlands suggests that the best way to maximize a country's influence under conditions of interdependence is to embrace multilateralism. Despite its small size, the Netherlands has taken a leadership role in the design of international organizations and is an active participant in those organizations once they are established. Although the Netherlands is the fortieth largest country in terms of population, it has the most memberships of any country in international organizations.[12] A country's influence can be increased through engagement that is not halfhearted, that does not blatantly attempt to use the organization for narrow national interests, and that is not discontinued even when a particular decision or policy is not what the country would wish.

In situations of collective decisionmaking, when no single country can either determine the outcome or block a given outcome from occurring, the option of walking away from the negotiating table can be costly. The Netherlands has more influence on European Union decisionmaking with 5 percent representation in the EU's parliament, commission, and council, than it would if it were not present at all. When a small and trade-dependent nation like the Netherlands joins the European Monetary Union, for example, control over its own monetary policy actually increases. A go-it-alone strategy brings an independence more apparent than real.

Working in the Narrow Margins

How does a government identify its room for maneuver within the narrow margins of available action? Equally important, how can a government identify those small actions that can have large consequences? These may be the two most important questions facing any political leader under conditions of interdependence.

Identification of the narrow margins of action is aided by recognition that the effects of international interdependence and domestic political constraints are not additive. Instead, constraints in one arena can be used to enlarge the realm of possible action in the other. As Robert Putnam (1988) points out, international commitments can be used to cut through logjams in the domestic policy process. At the same time, an extensive process of domestic policy consultation strengthens leaders in international negotiations because it constrains the range of agreements the leader can accept.[13] In other words, the highly consultative domestic policy process strengthens the hand of Dutch leaders in international negotiations, particularly when combined with the generally positive stance that Dutch governments take toward international agreements. Breakdowns of Dutch partnership in negotiations are much more likely to be involuntary (due to domestic political constraints) than voluntary (due to governmental unwillingness to participate). This positioning enhances Dutch influence on international negotiations.

As Putnam's work on the links between international negotiations and domestic policy makes clear, aspects of the domestic political process can affect a country's control over its international environment. Although the Netherlands has limited ability to control its international environment, due both to its small size and to the extent of its political and economic interdependence, the Dutch policy process nonetheless has traits that maximize its potential impact. For maximizing international influence, the key traits of the Dutch policy process are those that:

- Accept inaction when there are no effective choices to be made, and minimize the temptation to rail helplessly against decisions over which one has no control.
- For issues in which there is room for policy choice, consult widely before deciding upon a course of action.
- Use international commitments to break through domestic policy stalemates and to forge new coalitions for change.
- Reward political leadership for effectiveness in formulating policies that maximize common interests and that blur the distinction between policy winners and losers.

Accepting Inaction

The art of not making decisions is generally underappreciated in politics. The Dutch experience, however, shows that there can be substantial benefits from deliberately choosing *not* to have a policy on some issue, or from allowing ambiguity in policy. When the society is deeply divided on some value, for example, inaction prevents social division from turning into political divisiveness. The quintessential examples of calculated inaction in Dutch politics are the instances of tolerance policy. Tolerance policies occur when some illegal behavior is not prosecuted because of its prevalence and because many in society do not think it should be illegal.

Dutch policies on drug use, abortion, and euthanasia are examples of tolerance policies that permit discrepancies between laws and behavior. Despite the secularization of the last several decades, many Dutch people are deeply religious and have relatively conservative social values. Abortion, euthanasia, and drug use are thus sensitive and potentially conflictual topics. The Netherlands has permissive laws in each of these areas, but in every case the law began as a policy of tolerance. In the case of euthanasia, the existing policy might best be phrased as an acceptance that the current state of medical knowledge leaves some people desiring to end their lives rather than endure both their illness and the procedures used to treat it. Given that this is so, the policy seeks to channel the process by which the decision to end a life with medical means will be made. The procedure, which involves consultation with a doctor, a lawyer, and an ethicist, is designed to establish that euthanasia is the patient's informed and consistent desire. It protects the medical personnel who carry out the procedure while placing strict boundaries on the conditions under which they may do so. Regardless of what one thinks of euthanasia, this policy is eminently practical if one assumes that the alternative is to push the practice underground by making it illegal.

Much the same can be said of the tolerance policy with respect to soft drugs. Tolerance for selling and using soft drugs in Amsterdam's "coffee shops" begins with the proposition that it is not possible to eliminate the use of such drugs. The policy is then predicated on minimizing the social harms that come from an illegal soft drug trade (including rampant criminality and the marketing of impure drugs), while maintaining a stringent policy of control against such hard drugs as heroin, cocaine, and synthetically derived substances. For the Dutch, the ongoing controversy is whether or not the tolerance policy works—that is, whether it succeeds in minimizing the social costs of soft drug use and the population of hard drug addicts.[14] A debate centered on this question is likely to be more productive of decisions responsive to the real problems of drug use in society, than is a policy that results from an all-or-nothing debate over formal legalization.

Another example of a tolerance policy, though it is not often thought of as such, is the policy of delay that was adopted with respect to a final decision on accepting NATO cruise missiles in the early 1980s. The government maintained an agreement in principle to participate with other NATO allies in the deployment of intermediate-range nuclear forces, while refusing in practice to accept the missiles as long as there was a possibility of an arms control treaty that would make them unnecessary. Governmental behavior deviated from declared policy as long as no domestic consensus for action could be found.

In short, Dutch policies on euthanasia and drug use today, like the policy on abortion during the 1970s and on cruise missiles in the 1980s, are inspired by a spirit of pragmatism rather than permissiveness.[15] They involve an acceptance that government cannot impose resolution of divisive issues. The tendency of

Dutch governments is to act in the area of what is possible rather than to break apart in a fruitless effort to legislate the impossible.

Consulting Widely

As we have seen, the Dutch policy process features regularized consultation with leading interest groups and professional associations. Dutch corporatism is not limited to industrial relations and bargains struck between the peak associations of labor and employers. Nor have the institutional forms of Dutch corporatism remained stable, as witnessed by the recent disestablishment of the Socio-Economic Council and of the Social Insurance Council that administered social insurance programs. Pluralistic corporatism in the Netherlands instead incorporates a wide array of consultative and implementing bodies, and does so in all policy sectors.

When domestic policy choices are based on widespread consultation, international constraints are reduced because the political leadership can credibly claim to international partners that there is little room for compromise. Consultation also tends to generate domestic consensus by helping domestic interest groups understand both the issues and the limits on action. Consultation does not guarantee agreement, but it does help identify (sometimes surprising) avenues for potential agreement between divergent interests. Consultation also provides all interested parties with the opportunity to trade acceptance of one policy for concessions in some other area. Jelle Visser and Anton Hemerijck (1997) point out that policy consultation creates norms of reciprocity in making concessions, with the possibility of bundling issues to distribute some desired outcomes to all groups that are prepared to share responsibility for the policies decided upon.

To the extent that it generates domestic consensus, policymaking rooted in extensive domestic consultation also increases international influence. An example of how domestic consensus increases international strength is the effort of other member states of the European Union, led by France, to force the Netherlands to bring its tolerance policy for soft drugs into conformity with their stricter anti-drug laws. There is no question that the Dutch tolerance policy makes control of soft drugs more difficult in neighboring countries. Even when faced with strong international pressure, though, the Netherlands made only minor modifications to its policy.[16] The ability of the Dutch government to stand firm in the face of this pressure from EU partners was due in very large part to domestic consensus among political leaders for the tolerance policy. Christian democrats, social democrats, and liberals all accept the tolerance policy as the best means of keeping social peace while concentrating the anti-drug effort against hard drugs. As a consequence, all parties rallied behind the government's contention that Dutch policy on drugs must be made in the Netherlands. International pressures are weakened when there is no one in the domestic political arena willing (or even desiring) to use that pressure to advance their own policy claims.

Making Use of International Commitments

Extensive consultation of domestic interest groups enlarges the influence of leaders in international bodies, but it comes with a cost. Interest groups that are consulted by right are generally able to establish themselves as veto players over policy in their areas. Nothing can be accomplished without their assent. Once policies have been established, interest groups align themselves around the defense of those policies. These are the closed circuits of policymaking.

International interdependence helps cut through these constraints. Overhaul of the Dutch social insurance system in the 1980s and 1990s is an example of a fundamental shift in policy that could only be made outside the corporatist consultation process rather than through it. The 1982 Wassenaar Accord between employers and union leaders, under which wage moderation was traded for reduced working hours, made the labor market more flexible and helped increase employment in the 1990s. This series of agreements between unions and employers associations did not extend, however, to reform of the social insurance system. On the contrary, unions and employers associations administered the existing system and both had much to gain from its structure of easy access and high income-replacement rates. The Socio-Economic Council, consulted by law on all legislation related to the social insurance system, deadlocked on every reform proposal placed before it. It was obvious that the government could not indefinitely foot the bill for a social insurance system that rewarded exit from the labor force to such a great degree. But arguments that reform was needed were not accepted until the eligibility criteria for membership in the EMU came into play. With its stringent targets on government deficits, public debt, and inflation for EMU eligibility, the European Union gave the Dutch government a mandate for action. As we saw in Chapter 7, this mandate was used not only to reduce social insurance payments but also to reform the systems of administration and implementation by reducing the direct role of the unions and employers associations. Even the Socio-Economic Council was disestablished from its previously sacrosanct role as policy adviser. International constraints in the form of the EMU, then, were used to carry out a domestic agenda of structural reform.

Recruiting Leaders Who Can Find Compromises

For most of the last fifty years, the Netherlands has been led by individuals gifted in the art of compromise. The three minister-presidents of longest tenure in that period were Willem Drees, Ruud Lubbers, and Wim Kok, two social democrats and a Christian democrat. Biographies of these three leaders stress the same leadership traits in each case. Politically, each was highly knowledgeable in the details of a wide range of policies, and each was inclined to seek technical solutions to policy problems rather than to phrase policy in terms of party ideologies. All three were skilled in using control of the ministerial council's agenda to avoid conflicts. And all three were gifted in their ability to formulate compromise solutions to policy issues, focusing on the elements of an issue that unite the governing coalition rather than those that divide it. Drees, Lubbers, and Kok even resemble one another in their public personas, for each of the three was seen by the general public more as "grandfather to the nation" than as a partisan leader.[17]

There is no rule of democratic politics that says leaders with these traits will rise to the top. American and French presidents, and British and German prime ministers, are far more likely to be seen as party leaders for whom public assessments depend chiefly on their ability to lead the country by impressing upon it their own visions of the future.[18] Dutch minister-presidents, by contrast, are most popular when they are seen as shepherds of the policy process. Policy emerges from the process, not from the mind of a leader or the program of a governing coalition. The role of political leadership in the Netherlands is to push the process along by directing attention to important issues and searching for ideas and avenues that will overcome the tendency to stalemate. Persistence is a more important trait in a Dutch leader than is vision.[19]

Participants in a consultative policy process must be comfortable with the idea that policy will reflect a wide range of perspectives, rather than reflecting the vision either of a leader or of a simple majority coalition. Policy is instead the result of continual adjustment to experience based on the perspectives of participating groups. Even a grand experiment such as the launch of the social welfare state was neither an ideological crusade nor a technocratic blueprint, but rather emerged piecemeal as a result of convergence between the perspectives of Christian democracy and social democracy. These origins made it easier to modify key elements of the social welfare state as experience showed that they were untenable. It did not take anything like the Reagan revolution in the United States or the Thatcher revolution in Great Britain to bring about these changes. In the Netherlands, the same political forces that launched the social welfare state were also instrumental to the retrenchment programs that profoundly modified it.

Despite all the changes in the Dutch political system over the last 150 years, this element of governance by negotiation has been a constant. When J. R. Thorbecke launched the Netherlands on the path to parliamentary democracy with his mid-nineteenth-century constitutional reform, he was asked how the novel idea of collective ministerial responsibility to the parliament would work in practice. *"Wacht op onze daden,"* was his reply: "Wait to see our deeds." The words reflected Thorbecke's view that only time and experience would show how the new constitution could actually work. "Wait to see our deeds" summarizes the pragmatism and the flexibility of the Dutch system of governance by negotiation.

Conclusion

The tradition of governance by negotiation was begun under the Dutch Republic, when any policy decision required the consent of each of the sovereign provinces.

The negotiating polity of the Netherlands has since then been expanded to incorporate the parties and interest groups that come with representative democracy based on universal suffrage. What was once a search for consensus among the regents of the various provinces later became the politics of accommodation between the pillar elites, and is today the system of pluralistic corporatism. These eras all have in common a general acceptance that negotiation is at the heart of the political process. The range of actors admitted to the process has changed over the centuries, as have the self-identified interests of those who are present at the table. But the Dutch policy process has always allowed all relevant parties (stakeholders) to voice their perspective on an issue, has always expected of each stakeholder that they will articulate their interests in a way that is open to compromise, and has always accepted that the decision ultimately made will give each participant at least part of what they are looking for. If it cannot, then postponement of a decision becomes a likely outcome.

These policy requirements create narrow—but real—room for domestic policy choice. The wide consultation that characterizes the Dutch policy process enables the identification of narrow margins for action within the boundaries of domestic consent and international constraint. The Netherlands has social democratic, Christian democratic, and liberal ideological traditions that offer competing visions of society, government, and the future. Finding a way to make these visions mesh in a context of international constraints on action is the peculiar genius of the Dutch system of government.

The Dutch policymaking process plays international commitments against the demands of domestic consensus-building to maximize its room for maneuver in both arenas. A multilateral approach to international issues and a highly consultative domestic policy process thus enable the government to identify the narrow margins of political choice, and to act on them. This is the lesson that the Dutch experience offers to countries that are only now becoming aware of their loss of autonomy in an era of interdependence and rapid change.

NOTES

1. Jefferson (1984: 634).

2. England's Queen Elizabeth was not among the skeptics, and observed that the republic was "so full of good order and policy so to surpass by far in its wisdom the intelligence of all kings and potentates. We kings require—all of us—to go to school to the States General." Cited in Wilson (1968: 21).

3. Cited in Boxer (1990: 206).

4. Montesquieu refers here to the legend told by Ovid (in *Metamorphoses*) of Jupiter's intervention in turning people into ants in order to repopulate the island of Aegina after a disastrous plague. The ant people were known for their thrift, endurance, and willingness to work hard for economic gain.

5. Quoted from unnumbered preface.

6. Cited in Murat (1984: 150).

7. Cited in Parker (1977: 267).

8. The potential power of trade relationships to motivate peacekeeping is illustrated by the intervention of the Dutch naval fleet in 1645 to impose peace between Sweden and Denmark. Their periodic wars were disruptive of Dutch interests in the Baltic trade.

9. The mingling of the Dutch tradition of *Sinterklaas* with the German celebration of Christmas has been the cause of cultural backlash in the Netherlands, according to *The Week in Germany,* December 15, 1995.

10. Den Uyl (1986: 52). I am grateful to André Mommen for finding this citation.

11. The only significant exception is the policy of Third World development assistance, though even in this instance much Dutch aid is channeled through multilateral organizations.

12. The Netherlands belongs to about one hundred international organizations, according to van Staden (1993: 344).

13. The range of domestically acceptable international agreements, which Putnam (1988) calls the win-set, depends on the preferences of leading domestic political forces as well as the complexity of the domestic policy process. With the importance of free trade to Dutch prosperity, the preferences of leading economic interests are generally in favor of agreements that maintain an open and stable international system.

14. Piryns (1982). This calculation of the costs and benefits of the tolerance policy is more characteristic of the political and civil service elite than of the public. As much as two-thirds of the public has agreed in surveys conducted between 1970 and 1991 that "Smoking marijuana and hashish should be severely punished" (Sociaal en Cultureel Planbureau 1993: 332). This attitude has softened slightly in more recent surveys, but it is clear that the tolerance policy in the area of drug use is more responsive to elite preferences than to public desires.

15. Noise reduction at Schiphol airport is yet another recent example of a tolerance policy. Airport expansion was approved in the mid-1990s in exchange for a reduction in the number of homes affected by the noise of takeoffs and landings to just 10,000. Failure to meet that target was to result in restrictions on the number of flights in and out of the airport, a move that would have serious consequences both for the airport and for the wider economy. The number of homes actually affected remains above 12,000, but any change in the regulation would prompt a strong reaction both from affected residents and from environmental groups. The result, as of 1999, has been a series of one-year exemptions from the rule, creating in effect a policy of tolerance for formally illegal noise levels.

16. For example, the amount of marijuana one can purchase for personal use without the threat of prosecution was substantially reduced.

17. This is true despite the great disparities in their ages; Drees was perhaps naturally seen as grandfatherly, but both Lubbers and Kok were much younger men during their terms as minister-president.

18. Dwight Eisenhower, whose public image and style of leadership more closely conform to the Dutch pattern described here, would be an exception to this rule. Other American leaders of the last fifty years who fit this Dutch leadership profile include Lyndon Johnson as majority party leader in the Senate (but not as president) and Wilbur Mills, longtime chair of the House Ways and Means Committee.

19. This is true even of the most ideological and activist of recent Dutch governments, that of Joop den Uyl (1973–1977). Although his government ultimately split apart over divisions on a policy to curb real estate speculation, the end came only after ten compromise proposals had been proposed and rejected.

Reference List

Aalders, Marius, Peter Korrel, and Rosa Uylenburg. 1987. *Handhaving van milieurecht.* Meppel: Boom.

Aberbach, Joel, Robert Putnam, and Bert Rockman. 1981. *Bureaucrats and Politicians in Western Democracies.* Cambridge: Harvard University Press.

Albeda, W. 1988. "Overheid en sociaal belied in de onderneming," pages 169–176 in E.D.J. de Jongh and A. Walravens, eds. *Sociaal Belied in Perspectief.* Kampen: J. H. Kok.

Albeda, W., and M. D. ten Hove. 1986. *Neocorporatisme: Evolutie van een gedachte, verandering van een patroon.* Kampen: J. H. Kok.

Andeweg, Rudy. 1975. "Om de kleur van de burgemeester," *Acta Politica* 10 (October): 421–454.

_____. 1982. *Dutch Voters Adrift: On Explanations of Electoral Change, 1963–1977.* Rijksuniversiteit te Leiden: Ph.D. dissertation.

_____. 1985. "The Netherlands: Cabinet Committees in a Coalition Cabinet," pages 138–154 in Thomas Mackie and Brian Hogwood, eds. *Unlocking the Cabinet: Cabinet Structures in Comparative Perspective.* London: Sage.

_____. 1988. "Centrifugal Forces and Collective Decision-Making: The Case of the Dutch Cabinet," *European Journal of Political Research* 16 (March): 125–151.

_____. 1989. "Institutional Conservatism in the Netherlands: Proposals for and Resistance to Change," pages 42–60 in Hans Daalder and Galen Irwin, eds. *Politics in the Netherlands: How Much Change?* London: Frank Cass.

_____. 1990. "Tweeërlei Ministerraad," pages 17–41 in R. B. Andeweg, ed. *Ministers en Ministerraad.* The Hague: SDU Uitgeverij.

_____. 1991a. "Volksvertegenwoordiging en regering," pages 231–250 in J.J.A. Thomassen, ed. *Hedendaagse democratie.* Alphen aan den Rijn: Samsom H. D. Tjeenk Willink.

_____. 1991b. "The Dutch Prime Minister: Not Just Chairman, Not Yet Chief?" *West European Politics* 14 (April): 116–132.

_____. 1992. "De Eerste Kamer: Tussen doublure en dwarsdrijverij," pages 129–157 in J.J.A. Thomassen, M.P.C.M. van Schendelen, and M. L. Zielonka-Goei, eds. *De geachte afgevaardigde: Hoe kamerleden denken over het Nederlandse parlement.* Muiderberg: Dick Coutinho.

_____. 1993. "De burger in de Nederlandse politiek," pages 77–100 in R. B. Andeweg, A. Hoogerwerf, and J.J.A. Thomassen, eds. *Politiek in Nederland.* 4th ed. Alphen aan den Rijn: Samsom H. D. Tjeenk Willink.

_____. 1994. "De formatie van de paarse coalitie," pages 149–171 in *Jaarboek 1994.* Groningen: Documentatiecentrum Nederlandse Politieke Partijen, Rijksuniversiteit Groningen.

_____. 1995a. "Afscheid van de verzuiling?" pages 111–125 in J.J.M. van Holsteyn and B. Niemöller, eds. *De Nederlandse kiezer 1994.* Leiden: DSWO Press, Rijksuniversiteit Leiden.

_____. 1995b. "The Reshaping of the National Party System," *West European Politics* 18 (July): 58–78.

_____. 1997. "Role Specialisation or Role Switching? Dutch MPs Between Electorate and Executive," pages 110–127 in Wolfgang Miller and Thomas Saalfeld, eds. *Members of Parliament in Western Europe: Roles and Behavior.* London: Frank Cass.

Andeweg, Rudy, and Wim Derksen. 1978. "The Appointed Burgomaster: Appointments and Careers of Burgomasters in the Netherlands," *The Netherlands Journal of Sociology* 14 (July): 41–57.

Andeweg, Rudy, Karl Dittrich, and Theo van der Tak. 1978. *Kabinetsformatie 1977.* Leiden: Published by the authors.

Andeweg, Rudy, and Galen Irwin. 1993. *Dutch Government and Politics.* New York: St. Martin's Press.

Andeweg, R. B., and H. W. Nijzink. 1992. "De verhouding tussen parlement en regering," pages 158–194 in J.J.A. Thomassen, M.P.C.M. van Schendelen, and M. L. Zielonka-Goei, eds. *De geachte afgevaardigde: Hoe kamerleden denken over het Nederlandse parlement.* Muiderberg: Dick Coutinho.

Anker, Hans. 1992. *Normal Vote Analysis.* Amsterdam: Het Spinhuis.

Baakman, Nico, Jan van der Made, and Ingrid Mur-Veeman. 1989. "Controlling Dutch Health Care," pages 99–115 in Giorgio Freddi and James Warner Björkman, eds. *Controlling Medical Professionals: The Comparative Politics of Health Governance.* Newbury Park, CA: Sage.

Baehr, Peter R. 1980. "The Dutch Foreign Policy Elite," *International Studies Quarterly* 24 (June): 223–261.

Baehr, P. R., Philip Everts, J. H. Leurdijk, Frans Roschar, Arie van Staden, C. P. van den Tempel, W. H. Vermeulen, and R. M. de Vree, eds. 1978. *Elite en buitenlandse politiek in Nederland.* The Hague: Staatsuitgeverij.

Bagehot, Walter. 1914. *The English Constitution.* New York and London: D. Appleton and Co.

Bagley, Christopher. 1973. *The Dutch Plural Society: A Comparative Study in Race Relations.* London: Oxford University Press.

Bakema, Wilma, and Ineke Secker. 1988. "Ministerial Expertise and the Dutch Case," *European Journal of Political Research* 16 (March): 153–170.

_____. 1990. "Vakbekwame Ministers," pages 71–96 in R. B. Andeweg, ed. *Ministers en Ministerraad.* The Hague: SDU Uitgeverij.

Bakker, B.F.M. 1986. "Social Background Theory and Culture Consumption," *The Netherlands' Journal of Social Sciences* 22 (October): 162–174.

Bakvis, Herman. 1981. *Catholic Power in the Netherlands.* Kingston, Ontario, Canada: McGill–Queen's University Press.

Bank, J. 1984. "Lijphart *malgré lui:* The Politics of Accommodation in the 'Indonesian Question,'" *Acta Politica* 19 (January): 73–83.

Barnes, Samuel, Max Kaase, et al. 1979. *Political Action: Mass Participation in Five Western Democracies.* Beverly Hills, CA: Sage.

Barnouw, Adriaan Jacob. 1943. "The Seventeenth Century: The Golden Age," pages 39–59 in Bartholomew Landheer, ed. *The Netherlands.* Berkeley: University of California Press.

_____. 1948. *The Making of Modern Holland: A Short History.* London: George Allen and Unwin.

Baumgartner, Frank, and Bryan Jones. 1993. *Agendas and Instability in American Politics.* Chicago: University of Chicago Press.

Bax, Erik. 1990. *Modernization and Cleavage in Dutch Society: A Study of Long Term Economic and Social Change.* Brookfield, VT: Gower Publishing.

Baylis, Thomas. 1989. *Governing by Committee.* Albany, NY: SUNY Press.

Becker, Uwe, and Mirham van Tiel. 1990. "Seksverhoudingen, patriarchaat, feminisme," pages 41–64 in Uwe Becker, ed. *Maatschappij, Macht, Nederlandse Politiek.* Amsterdam: Het Spinhuis.

Bellquist, Eric. 1948. "Political and Economic Conditions in the Low Countries," *Foreign Policy Reports* 24 (May 1): 42–47.

Bennett, Graham. 1986. *Netherlands' Water and Waste: A Study of the Implementation of the EEC Directives.* London: Graham and Trotman.

_____. 1991. "The Netherlands' National Environmental Policy Plan," *Environment* 33 (September): 7–9, 31–33.

Betlem, Gerrit. 1993. *Civil Liability for Transfrontier Pollution.* London: Graham and Trotman; Dordrecht: Martinus Nijhoff.

Blakely, Allison. 1993. *Blacks in the Dutch World: The Evolution of Racial Imagery in a Modern Society.* Bloomington: Indiana University Press.

Blits, Arnold. 1989. "The Great Lubricator," pages 11–20 in *Het succes van Lubbers.* Amsterdam: GW Boeken.

Boot, J. M., and M.H.J.M. Knapen. 1986. *De Nederlandse gezondheidszorg.* Amsterdam: Spectrum.

Bosch, Mineke, with Annemarie Kloosterman, eds. 1990. *Politics and Friendship: Letters from the International Women's Suffrage Alliance, 1902–1942.* Columbus: Ohio State University Press.

Bosscher, D.F.J. 1987. "Na het overlijden van J. M. den Uyl," pages 58–65 in *Jaarboek 1987.* Groningen: Documentatiecentrum Nederlandse Politieke Partijen, Rijksuniversiteit Groningen.

Bovend'Eert, P.P.T. 1990. "De Ministerraad en de betekenis van het regeringsprogramma," pages 43–70 in R. B. Andeweg, ed. *Ministers en Ministerraad.* The Hague: SDU Uitgeverij.

Bovend'Eert, P.P.T., and H.R.B.M. Kummeling. 1991. *Het Nederlandse parlement.* The Hague: SDU Uitgeverij.

Boxer, C. R. 1990. *The Dutch Seaborne Empire, 1600–1800.* London: Penguin Books.

Brand, W. 1980. "The Legacy of Empire," pages 251–275 in Richard Griffiths, ed. *The Economy and Politics of the Netherlands Since 1945.* The Hague: Martinus Nijhoff.

Brants, Kees. 1985. "Broadcasting and Politics in the Netherlands: From Pillar to Post," *West European Politics* 18 (April): 104–121.

Brants, Kees, and Walther Kok. 1978. "The Netherlands: An End to Openness?" *Journal of Communication* 28 (Summer): 90–95.

Briët, Martien, Bert Klandermans, and Frederike Kroon. 1987. "How Women Become Involved in the Women's Movement of the Netherlands," pages 44–63 in Mary Katzenstein and Carol Mueller, eds. *The Women's Movements of the United States and Western Europe.* Philadelphia: Temple University Press.

Briggs, David, and Barry Wyatt. 1988. "Rural Land-Use Change in Europe," pages 7–25 in Martin Whitby and John Ollerenshaw, eds. *Land-Use and the European Environment.* London: Pinter.

Bruijn, Jaap. 1990. "Productivity, Profitability, and Costs of Private and Corporate Dutch Ship Owning in the Seventeenth and Eighteenth Centuries," pages 174–194 in James Tracy, ed. *The Rise of Merchant Empires: Long-Distance Trade in the Early Modern World, 1350–1750.* New York: Cambridge University Press.

Bruijn, J. R., F. S. Gaastra, and I. Schöffer. 1987. *Dutch-Asiatic Shipping in the 17th and 18th Centuries.* Vol. 1. The Hague: Martinus Nijhoff.

Bryant, Christopher. 1981. "Depillarisation in the Netherlands," *British Journal of Sociology* 32 (March): 56–74.

Buikhuisen, W. 1966. "Provo en provo," pages 86–107 in F. E. Frenkel, ed. *Provo: Kanttekeningen bij een deelverschijnsel.* Amsterdam: Polak and van Gennep.

Cameron, David. 1978. "The Expansion of the Public Economy," *American Political Science Review* 72 (December): 1243–1261.

Carmiggelt, Simon. 1966. *A Dutchman's Slight Adventures.* Amsterdam: De Arbeiderspers.

Carter, Alice. 1971. *The Dutch Republic in Europe in the Seven Years War.* Coral Gables, FL: University of Miami Press.

Cawson, Alan. 1985. "Introduction: Varieties of Corporatism," pages 1–21 in Alan Cawson, ed. *Organized Interests and the State: Studies in Meso-Corporatism.* Beverly Hills, CA: Sage.

Centraal Bureau voor de Statistiek (CBS). 1966. *Vrijetijdsbesteding in Nederland, 1962–1963; Deel 8: Een samenvattend overzicht: Karakteristieke patronen.* Hilversum: Centraal Bureau voor de Statistiek.

_____. 1996. *Statistisch Jaarboek 1996.* The Hague: SDU.

Cohen, M. J., A.P.M. Coomans, and C. Flinterman. 1993. "Rechter en politiek," pages 299–317 in R. B. Andeweg, A. Hoogerwerf, and J.J.A. Thomassen, eds. *Politiek in Nederland.* 4th ed. Alphen aan den Rijn: Samsom H. D. Tjeenk Willink.

Coke, Roger. [1670] 1970. *A Discourse on Trade.* Reprint, Yorkshire: SR Publishers Limited; New York: Johnson Reprint Corporation.

Coleman, John. 1978. *The Evolution of Dutch Catholicism, 1958–1974.* Berkeley: University of California Press.

Cox, Robert. 1990. "Alternative Patterns of Welfare State Development: The Case of Public Assistance in the Netherlands," *West European Politics* 13 (October): 85–102.

_____. 1992. "After Corporatism: A Comparison of the Role of Medical Professionals and Social Workers in the Dutch Welfare State," *Comparative Political Studies* 24 (January): 532–552.

_____. 1993. *The Development of the Dutch Welfare State: From Workers' Insurance to Universal Entitlement.* Pittsburgh: University of Pittsburgh Press.

_____. 1994. "Changing Conceptions of Social Entitlement: The Moral Dimension of Retrenchment Efforts in Denmark and the Netherlands." Paper presented at the meetings of the American Political Science Association, New York, September 1–4.

_____. 1995. "Willem Drees," pages 111–117 in David Wilsford, ed. *Political Leaders of Europe: A Biographical Dictionary.* Westport, CT: Greenwood Press.

_____. 1998. "From Safety Net to Trampoline: Labor Market Activation in the Netherlands and Denmark," *Governance* 11 (October): 397–414.

Cramer, Jacqueline. 1989. "The Rise and Fall of New Knowledge Interests in the Dutch Environmental Movement," *The Environmentalist* 9 (number 2): 101–120.

Daalder, Hans. 1955. "Parties and Politics in the Netherlands," *Political Studies* 3 (February): 1–16.

_____. 1966. "The Netherlands: Opposition in a Segmented Society," pages 188–236 in Robert Dahl, ed. *Political Oppositions in Western Democracies.* New Haven: Yale University Press.

_____. 1974. *Politisering en lijdelijkheid in de Nederlandse politiek.* Assen: van Gorcum.

_____.1975. "Parlementaire taken, machtsmiddelen, invloeden: Meningen van kamerleden en kiezers," pages 67–114 in Hans Daalder, ed. *Parlement en politieke besluitvorming in Nederland.* Alphen aan den Rijn: Samsom.

_____. 1978. "The Netherlands and the World, 1940–1945," pages 49–87 in J. H. Leurdijk, ed. *The Foreign Policy of the Netherlands.* Alphen aan den Rijn: Sijthoff en Noordhoff.

_____. 1979. "The Netherlands," pages 175–208 in Stanley Henig, ed. *Political Parties in the EC.* London: Allen and Unwin.

_____. 1984. "On the Origins of the Consociational Democracy Model," *Acta Politica* 19 (January): 97–116.

_____. 1991. "De ontwikkeling van de parlementaire democratie in Nederland," pages 52–83 in J.J.A. Thomassen, ed. *Hedendaagse democratie.* Alphen aan den Rijn: Samsom H. D. Tjeenk Willink.

_____. 1992. "De kamerleden in 1990: Herkomst, ervaring en toekomstperspectief," pages 18–52 in J.J.A. Thomassen, M.P.C.M. van Schendelen, and M. L. Zielonka-Goei, eds. *De geachte afgevaardigde: Hoe kamerleden denken over het Nederlandse parlement.* Muiderberg: Dick Coutinho.

Daalder, Hans, and Ruud Koole. 1988. "Liberal Parties in the Netherlands," pages 151–177 in Emil Kirchner, ed. *Liberal Parties in Western Europe.* New York: Cambridge University Press.

Dalton, Russell. 1994. *The Green Rainbow: Environmental Groups in Western Europe.* New Haven: Yale University Press.

Danner, Mark. 1998. "Bosnia: The Great Betrayal," *The New York Review* (March 26): 42–52.

Daudt, Hans. 1972. "Constante kiezers, wisselaars en thuisblijvers," *De Nederlandse kiezer, '71.* Meppel: Boom.

Davies, D. W. 1961. *A Primer of Dutch Seventeenth Century Overseas Trade.* The Hague: Martinus Nijhoff.

de Beus, Jos, and Kees van Kersbergen. 1994. "Employment Policy Legacy and Political Party Strategy in the Netherlands." Paper presented at the Conference of Europeanists, Chicago, March 31–April 2.

de Graaf, Nan Dirk, and Paul de Graaf. 1988. "Family Background, Postmaterialism and Life Style," *The Netherlands Journal of Sociology* 24 (April): 50–64.

de Groot-van Leeuwen, Leny. 1992. "The Equilibrium Elite: Composition and Position of the Dutch Judiciary," *The Netherlands' Journal of Social Sciences* 28 (November): 141–154.

de Haas, J. Anton. 1943. "Holland's Role in World Trade," pages 164–175 in Bartholomew Landheer, ed. *The Netherlands.* Berkeley: University of California Press.

de Jong, H. M. 1992. "De gedecentraliseerde eenheidsstaat," pages 111–126 in J. W. van Deth and P. A. Schuszler, eds. *Nederlandse Staatkunde.* 2nd ed. Muiderberg: Dick Coutinho.

de Jong, J. J. 1959. "Het Opereren der Verbanden in het Politiek Proces," pages 11–24 in J. J. de Jong, M. J. Brouwer, J.A.A. van Doorn, and J. Pen, eds. *Pressiegroepen: De invloed der georganiserde groepen op het maatschappelijk en politiek leven.* Utrecht: Het Spectrum.

de Jong, Mart-Jan. 1988. "Ethnic Origin and Educational Careers in Holland," *The Netherlands Journal of Sociology* 24 (April): 65–75.

de Jong, Rudolf. n.d. *Provos and Kabouters.* Buffalo, NY: Friends of Malatesta.

de Jong Gierfeld, Jenny, and Aart Liefbroer. 1995. "The Netherlands," pages 102–125 in Hans-Peter Blossfeld, ed. *The New Role of Women: Family Formation in Modern Societies.* Boulder: Westview Press.

de Jongh, Aad. 1966. *Provo: Een jaar Provo-activiteiten.* Rotterdam: Kerco.

de Kam, C. A., and J. de Haan. 1991. *Terugtredende overheid: Realiteit of retoriek?* Schoonhoven: Academic Service.

de Roos, W.A.A.M., G. J. Wijers, and C.W.A.M. van Paridon. 1980. *Economie en samenleving.* Assen: van Gorcum.

de Swaan, Abram. 1982. "The Netherlands: Coalitions in a Segmented Polity," pages 217–236 in Eric Browne and John Dreijmanis, eds. *Government Coalitions in Western Democracies.* New York: Longman.

de Vries, Bernhard. 1966. "Provo van binnenuit," pages 18–31 in F. E. Frenkel, ed. *Provo: Kanttekeningen bij een deelverschijnsel.* Amsterdam: Polak and van Gennep.

de Vries, Jan. 1984. *European Urbanization, 1500–1800.* Cambridge: Harvard University Press.

de Vries, Johan. 1978. *The Netherlands Economy in the Twentieth Century.* Assen: van Gorcum.

de Winter, Reiner. 1991. *De overheid.* The Hague: SDU Uitgeverij.

de Wolff, P., and W. Driehuis. 1980. "A Description of Post War Economic Developments and Economic Policy in the Netherlands," pages 13–60 in Richard T. Griffiths, ed. *The Economy and Politics of the Netherlands.* The Hague: Martinus Nijhoff.

Deboutte, Jan, and Alfred van Staden. 1978. "High Politics in the Low Countries," pages 56–82 in William Wallace and William Paterson, eds. *Foreign Policy Making in Western Europe.* Westmead, England: Saxon House.

Dekker, Paul. 1993. "Xenophobie en nationaal populisme in de vergelijking van publieke opinie," pages 227–256 in Uwe Becker, ed. *Nederlandse politiek in historisch en vergelijkend perspectief.* Amsterdam: Het Spinhuis.

Dekker, Paul, and Peter Ester. 1990. "Ideological Identification and (De)Pillarisation in the Netherlands," *The Netherlands' Journal of Social Sciences* 26 (October): 168–185.

den Uyl, J. M. 1986. *De toekomst onder ogen: Beschouwingen over socialisme, economie en economische politiek.* Amsterdam: Bert Bakker.

Dendermonde, Max. 1945. *Groningen Bevrijd.* De Waal: De Vuurslag.

Denters, S.A.H. 1992. "De parlementaire democratie," pages 80–97 in J. W. van Deth and P. A. Schuszler, eds. *Nederlandse Staatkunde.* 2nd ed. Muiderberg: Dick Coutinho.

———. 1993. "Gemeentelijke politiek," pages 318–340 in R. B. Andeweg, A. Hoogerwerf, and J.J.A. Thomassen, eds. *Politiek in Nederland.* 4th ed. Alphen aan den Rijn: Samsom H. D. Tjeenk Willink.

Dharwadker, Aparna. 1998. "Nation, Race, and the Ideology of Commerce in Defoe," *The Eighteenth Century* 39 (Spring): 63–84.

Dittrich, Karl. 1987. "The Netherlands, 1946–1981," pages 207–229 in Ian Budge, David Robertson, and Derek Hearl, eds. *Ideology, Strategy and Party Change: Spatial Analyses of*

Post-War Election Programmes in 19 Democracies. Cambridge: Cambridge University Press.

Dogan, Mattei. 1975. *The Mandarins of Western Europe: The Political Role of Top Civil Servants.* Beverly Hills, CA: Sage.

Domke, William. 1987. "The Netherlands: Strategy, Options and Change," pages 273–293 in Catherine Kelleher and Gale Mattix, eds. *Evolving European Defense Policies.* Lexington, MA: D. C. Heath.

Dörr, Silvia, and Thomas Faist. 1997. "Institutional Conditions for the Integration of Immigrants in Welfare States," *European Journal of Political Research* 31 (June): 401–426.

Downs, Anthony. 1957. *An Economic Theory of Democracy.* New York: Harper and Row.

_____. 1972. "Up and Down with Ecology: The Issue Attention Cycle," *Public Interest* 28 (Summer): 38–50.

Drees, Willem, Sr. 1983. *Herinneringen en opvattingen.* Naarden: Strengholt.

Drummond, Steven, and Lynn Nelson. 1994. *The Western Frontiers of Imperial Rome.* Armonk, NY: M. E. Sharpe.

Dutt, Ashok, and Frank Costa. 1985. *Public Planning in the Netherlands: Perspectives and Change Since the Second World War.* New York: Oxford University Press.

Easton, David. 1971. *The Political System.* New York: Alfred Knopf.

Eckert, Roland, and Helmut Willems. 1986. "Youth Protest in Western Europe: Four Case Studies," pages 127–153 in *Research in Social Movements, Conflicts and Change.* Vol. 9. Greenwich, CT: JAI Press.

Eldersveld, Samuel. 1947. "Government and Politics in the Netherlands During Reconstruction," pages 121–134 in James K. Pollock, ed. *Change and Crisis in European Government.* New York: Rhinehart.

_____. 1980. "Political Elite Linkages in the Dutch Consociational System," pages 157–182 in Kay Lawson, ed. *Political Parties and Linkage.* New Haven: Yale University Press.

_____. 1998. "Party Change and Continuity in Amsterdam," *Party Politics* 4 (number 3): 319–346.

Eldersveld, Samuel, Jan Kooiman, and Theo van der Tak. 1981. *Elite Images of Dutch Politics.* Ann Arbor: University of Michigan Press.

Eldersveld, Samuel, Lars Strömberg, and Wim Derksen. 1995. *Local Elites in Western Democracies: A Comparative Analysis of Urban Political Leaders in the U.S., Sweden, and the Netherlands.* Boulder: Westview Press.

Ellemers, Jo. 1984. "Pillarization as a Process of Modernization," *Acta Politica* 19 (January): 129–144.

Ellman, Michael. 1984. "The Crisis of the Welfare State—The Dutch Experience," pages 191–211 in Kenneth Boulding, ed. *The Economics of Human Betterment.* Albany: SUNY Press.

Elzinga, D. J., and G. Voerman. 1992. *Om de stembus . . . : verkiezingsaffiches 1918–1989.* The Hague: SDU Uitgeverij.

Engels, J.W.M. 1990. "De Minister zonder portefeuille," pages 147–174 in R. B. Andeweg, ed. *Ministers en Ministerraad.* The Hague: SDU Uitgeverij.

Entzinger, Han. 1994. "A Future for the Dutch 'Ethnic Minorities' Model?" pages 18–38 in Bernard Lewis and Dominique Schnapper, eds. *Muslims in Europe.* New York: Pinter.

Esping-Andersen, Gøsta. 1990. *The Three Worlds of Welfare Capitalism.* Princeton: Princeton University Press.

Ester, P., and A.P.N. Nauta. 1986. "A Decade of Social and Cultural Reports in the Netherlands," *The Netherlands Journal of Sociology* 22 (April): 72–86.

European Union Commission. 1998. *Eurobarometer 48: Public Opinion in the European Union.* Luxembourg: Office for Official Publications of the European Communities.

Everts, Philip. 1983. *Public Opinion, the Churches and Foreign Policy.* Leiden: Institute for International Studies, University of Leiden.

Everts, Philip, and Guido Walraven. 1984. *Vredesbeweging.* Utrecht: Spectrum.

Faber, Mient Jan, Laurens Hogebrink, Jan ter Laak, and Ben ter Veer. 1983. *Zes jaar IKV campagne.* Amersfoort: De Horstink.

Faber, Sytze. 1974. *Burgemeester en democratie.* Alphen aan den Rijn: Samsom.

Farah, Barbara, Samuel Barnes, and Felix Heunks. 1979. "Political Dissatisfaction," pages 409–447 in Samuel Barnes, Max Kaase, et al. *Political Action.* Beverly Hills, CA: Sage.

Fayle, Charles Ernest. 1933. *A Short History of the World's Shipping Industry.* London: Allen and Unwin.

Felling, A., and J. Peters. 1986. "Conservatism: A Multidimensional Concept," *The Netherlands Journal of Sociology* 22 (April): 36–60.

Fitch, Bob. 1995. "The Dutch Masters," *World Business* (November/December): 35–39.

Franssen, H. M. 1982. *Tweede Kamer en Binnenlandse Zaken.* Assen: van Gorcum.

Gadourek, Ivan. 1961. *A Dutch Community: Social and Cultural Structure and Process in a Bulb-Growing Region in the Netherlands.* 2nd ed. Groningen: Wolters.

Gaebe, Wolf, and Eiki Schamp. 1994. *Gateways to the European Market: Case Studies from the Netherlands and Germany.* Münster: LIT Verlag.

Gallhofer, Irmtraud, Willem Saris, and Robert Voogt. 1994. "From Individual Preferences to Group Decisions in Foreign Policy Decision Making: The Dutch Council of Ministers," *European Journal of Political Research* 25 (February): 151–170.

Gielen, J. J. 1965. "Verzuiling en politiek: Zuilvorming—verzuiling—ontzuiling," pages 98–138 in J. J. Gielen et al. *Pacificatie en de zuilen.* Meppel: J. A. Boom en Zoon.

Gladdish, Ken. 1983. "Coalition Government and Policy Outputs in the Netherlands," pages 169–186 in Vernon Bogdanor, ed. *Coalition Government in Europe.* London: Heinemann.

_____. 1991. *Governing from the Center: Politics and Policy-Making in the Netherlands.* DeKalb: Northern Illinois University Press.

Glamann, Kristof. 1958. *Dutch-Asiatic Trade, 1620–1740.* Danish Science Press: Copenhagen and The Hague: Martinus Nijhoff.

Goddijn, Walter. 1957. *Katholieke minderheid en protestantse dominant.* Assen: van Gorcum.

Gomes, Carlos. 1991. *Regulating Death: Euthanasia and the Case of the Netherlands.* New York: Free Press.

Gouda, Frances. 1995. *Poverty and Political Culture: The Rhetoric of Social Welfare in the Netherlands and France, 1815–1854.* Lanham, MD: Rowman and Littlefield.

Goudsblom, Johan. 1959. *De nieuwe volwassenen; een enquête onder jongeren van 18 tot 30 jaar.* Amsterdam: Querido.

_____. 1967. *Dutch Society.* New York: Random House.

Goverde, H.J.M. 1993. "Verschuivingen in het milieubeleid: Van milieuhygiëne naar omgevings-management," pages 49–87 in A.J.A. Godfroij and N.J.M. Nelissen, eds. *Verschuivingen in de besturing van de samenleving.* Bussum: Dick Coutinho.

Griffiths, John, Alex Bood, and Heleen Wyers. 1998. *Euthanasia and Law in the Netherlands.* Amsterdam: Amsterdam University Press.

Griffiths, Richard. 1980a. "The Netherlands and the EEC," pages 277–303 in Richard Griffiths, ed. *The Economy and Politics of the Netherlands Since 1945.* The Hague: Martinus Nijhoff.

_____. 1980b. "The Netherlands Central Planning Bureau," pages 135–161 in Richard Griffiths, ed. *The Economy and Politics of the Netherlands Since 1945.* The Hague: Martinus Nijhoff.

Grofman, Bernard, and Peter van Roozendaal. 1994. "Toward a Theoretical Explanation of Premature Cabinet Termination," *European Journal of Political Research* 26 (September): 155–170.

Haley, K.H.D. 1972. *The Dutch in the Seventeenth Century.* London: Harcourt Brace Jovanovich.

Hanf, Kenneth. 1989. "Deregulation as Regulatory Reform: The Case of Environmental Policy in the Netherlands," *European Journal of Political Research* 17 (March): 193–207.

't Hart, H., and W. Kok. 1993. "Publieke opinie, communicatiemedia en politiek," pages 121–144 in R. B. Andeweg, A. Hoogerwerf, and J.J.A. Thomassen, eds. *Politiek in Nederland.* 4th ed. Alphen aan den Rijn: Samsom H. D. Tjeenk Willink.

't Hart, Marjolein. 1993. *The Making of a Bourgeois State: War, Politics and Finance During the Dutch Revolt.* New York: Manchester University Press.

Hayashi, Chikio, Ichiro Miyake, Tatsuzo Suzuki, Masamichi Sasaki, and Fumi Hayashi. 1992. *Cultural Link Analysis for Comparative Social Research.* Tokyo: Institute of Statistical Mathematics.

Heeroma, Klaas Hanzen. 1943. *Margrieten.* Oegstgeest: Published by the author.

Heidenheimer, Arnold, Hugh Heclo, and Carolyn Teich Adams. 1990. *Comparative Public Policy.* 3rd ed. New York: St. Martin's Press.

Helder, E. 1992. "Rechtspraak," pages 127–145 in J. W. van Deth and P. A. Schuszler, eds. *Nederlandse Staatkunde.* 2nd ed. Muiderberg: Dick Coutinho.

Heldring, J. L. 1978. "Between Dreams and Reality," pages 307–322 in J. H. Leurdijk, ed. *The Foreign Policy of the Netherlands.* Alphen aan den Rijn: Sijthoff and Noordhoff.

Hermsen, Joke, and Alkeline van Lenning. 1991. *Sharing the Difference: Feminist Debates in Holland.* New York: Routledge.

Hexham, Irving. 1981. *The Irony of Apartheid.* New York: Edwin Mellen Press.

Hippe, Joop, Paul Lucardie, and Gerrit Voerman. 1994. "Kroniek 1994: Overzicht van de partijpolitieke gebeurtenissen van het jaar 1994," pages 14–91 in *Jaarboek 1994.* Groningen: Documentatiecentrum Nederlandse Politieke Partijen, Rijksuniversiteit Groningen.

Hobbelen, Wouter. 1990. "Industrial Policy," pages 33–40 in Menno Wolters and Peter Coffey, eds. *The Netherlands and EC Membership Evaluated.* London: Pinter.

Holsti, K. J. 1970. "National Role Conceptions in the Study of Foreign Politics," *International Studies Quarterly* 14 (September): 233–309.

Hommes, Peter. 1990. "The Common Agricultural Policy," pages 41–47 in Menno Wolters and Peter Coffey, eds. *The Netherlands and EC Membership Evaluated.* London: Pinter.

Honig, Jan Willem. 1994. "The Netherlands and Military Intervention," pages 142–153 in Lawrence Friedman, ed. *Military Intervention in European Conflicts.* Oxford: Blackwell Publishers.

Honig, Jan Willem, and Norbert Both. 1996. *Srebrenica: Record of a War Crime.* London: Penguin.

Hoogerwerf, Andries. 1993. "Het politieke systeem van Nederland," pages 19–37 in R. B. Andeweg, A. Hoogerwerf, and J.J.A. Thomassen, eds. *Politiek in Nederland.* 4th ed. Alphen aan den Rijn: Samsom H. D. Tjeenk Willink.

Houska, Joseph. 1985. *Influencing Mass Political Behavior: Elites and Political Subcultures in the Netherlands and Austria.* Berkeley: University of California Institute of International Studies, number 60.

Huet, Pierre-Daniel. 1718. *Mémoires sur le commerce des Hollandois.* Amsterdam: du Villard & Changuion.

Hueting, Roefie, and Peter Bosch. 1991. "Note on the Correction of National Income for Environmental Losses," pages 29–38 in Onno Kuik and Harmen Verbruggen, eds. *In Search of Indicators of Sustainable Development.* Dordrecht: Kluwer Academic Press.

Huggett, Frank. 1971. *The Modern Netherlands.* New York: Praeger.

Huppes, Gjalt, and Robert Kagan. 1989. "Market-Oriented Regulation of Environmental Problems in the Netherlands," *Law and Policy* 11 (April): 215–239.

Hyma, Albert. 1942. *The Dutch in the Far East.* Ann Arbor, MI: George Wahr Publishers.

Idenburg, Ph. 1985. "The Dutch Paradox in Social Welfare," pages 123–143 in Catherine Jones and Maria Brenton, eds. *Yearbook of Social Policy in Britain, 1984–85.* New York: Routledge.

Inglehart, Ronald. 1990. *Culture Shift in Advanced Industrial Society.* Princeton: Princeton University Press.

Inglehart, Ronald, and Rudy Andeweg. 1993. "Change in Dutch Political Culture: A Silent or a Silenced Revolution?" *West European Politics* 16 (July): 345–361.

International Social Science Program. 1989. *Work Orientations.* Ann Arbor, MI: Inter-University Consortium for Political and Social Research.

Irwin, Galen. 1974. "Compulsory Voting Legislation: Impact on Voter Turnout in the Netherlands," *Comparative Political Studies* 7 (October): 292–315.

Irwin, Galen, and Karl Dittrich. 1984. "And the Walls Came Tumbling Down: Dealignment and Realignment in the Netherlands," in Russell Dalton, Scott Flanagan, and Paul Allen Beck, eds. *Electoral Change in Advanced Industrial Democracies.* Princeton: Princeton University Press.

Irwin, G. A., and J.J.M. van Holsteyn. 1989a. "Towards a More Open Model of Competition," pages 112–138 in Hans Daalder and Galen Irwin, eds. *Politics in the Netherlands: How Much Change?* London: Frank Cass.

_____. 1989b. "Decline of the Structured Model of Electoral Competition," pages 21–41 in Hans Daalder and Galen Irwin, eds. *Politics in the Netherlands: How Much Change?* London: Frank Cass.

_____. 1997. "Where to Go from Here? Revamping Electoral Politics in the Netherlands," *West European Politics* 20 (April): 93–118.

Jamison, Andrew, Ron Eyerman, Jacqueline Cramer, and Jeppe Laessøe. 1990. *The Making of the New Environmental Consciousness: A Comparative Study of the Environmental Movements in Sweden, Denmark and the Netherlands.* Edinburgh, Scotland: Edinburgh University Press.

Jefferson, Thomas. 1984. *Writings.* New York: Library of America.

Jennings, M. Kent. 1972. "Partisan Commitment and Electoral Behavior in the Netherlands," *Acta Politica* 7 (October): 445–470.

Johnson, Th., and H. Marsh. 1664. *The Dutch Drawn to Life: A Description of Holland and the Dutch Provinces*. London: N.P.

Joustra, Arendo, and Erik van Venetië. 1993. *De Geheimen van het Torentje: Praktische gids voor het premierschap*. Amsterdam: Prometheus.

Juffermans, Paul. 1982. *Staat en gezondheidszorg in Nederland*. Nijmegen: Socialistiese Uitgeverij.

Katzenstein, Peter. 1985. *Small States in World Markets*. Ithaca: Cornell University Press.

Kennedy, Paul. 1987. *The Rise and Fall of British Naval Mastery*. London: Ashfield Press.

Key, V. O., Jr. 1955. "A Theory of Critical Elections," *Journal of Politics* 17 (February): 3–18.

Kieve, Ronald. 1981. "Pillars of Sand: A Marxist Critique of Consociational Democracy in the Netherlands," *Comparative Politics* 13 (April): 313–337.

Kitschelt, Herbert. 1994. *The Transformation of European Social Democracy*. New York: Cambridge University Press.

Klein, P. W. 1980. "The Foundations of Dutch Prosperity," pages 1–12 in Richard Griffiths, ed. *The Economy and Politics of the Netherlands Since 1945*. The Hague: Martinus Nijhoff.

Kleinnijenhuis, Jan, and Paul Pennings. 1995. "Campagnes en berichtgeving," pages 27–43 in J.J.M. van Holsteyn and B. Niemöller, eds. *De Nederlandse kiezer 1994*. Leiden: DSWO Press, Rijksuniversiteit Leiden.

Kleinnijenhuis, Jan, and Jan de Ridder. 1998. "Issue News and Electoral Volatility: A Comparative Analysis of Media Effects During the 1994 Election Campaigns in Germany and the Netherlands," *European Journal of Political Research* 33 (April): 413–437.

Kloosterman, Robert. 1994. "Three Worlds of Welfare Capitalism? The Welfare State and the Post-Industrial Trajectory in the Netherlands After 1980," *West European Politics* 17 (October): 166–189.

Koole, Ruud. 1992. *De opkomst van de moderne kaderpartij*. Amsterdam: Uitgeverij Het Spectrum.

_____. 1993. "The Specifics of Dutch Political Parties," *The Netherlands' Journal of Social Sciences* 29 (December): 164–182.

_____. 1994. "The Vulnerability of the Modern Cadre Party in the Netherlands," pages 278–303 in Richard Katz and Peter Mair, eds. *How Parties Organize*. Thousand Oaks, CA: Sage.

Koopmans, Ruud. 1996. "New Social Movements and Changes in Political Participation in Western Europe," *West European Politics* 19 (January): 28–50.

Koppenjan, J.F.M., A. B. Ringeling, and R.H.A. te Velde. 1987. *Beliedsvorming in Nederland: Een vergelijkende studie naar de totstandkoming van wetten*. The Hague: VUGA.

Korrel, Peter. 1987. *In actie voor het milieu: Een handleiding*. Meppel: Boom.

Kramer, Ralph. 1993. *Privatization in Four European Countries*. Armonk, NY: M. E. Sharpe.

Kraus, Franz. 1987. "The Historical Development of Income Inequality in Western Europe and the United States," pages 187–236 in Peter Flora and Arnold Heidenheimer, eds. *The Development of Welfare States in Europe and America*. New Brunswick, NJ: Transaction Books.

Kriesi, Hanspeter. 1989. "The Political Opportunity Structure of the Dutch Peace Movement," *West European Politics* 12 (July): 295–312.

_____. 1993. *Political Mobilization and Social Change: The Dutch Case in Comparative Perspective*. Aldershot, U.K.: Avebury.

Kriesi, Hanspeter, and Philip van Praag. 1987. "Old and New Politics: The Dutch Peace Movement and the Traditional Political Organizations," *European Journal of Political Research* 15 (May): 319–346.

Kruijt, J. P. 1948. "Rooms Katholieken en Protestanten in Nederland," *Sociologisch Bulletin* 1 (number 1): 3–29.

————. 1957. "Sociologische beschouwingen over zuilen en verzuiling," *Socialisme en Democratie* 14 (number 1): 1–29.

————. 1959. *Verzuiling.* Zaandijk: Heijnis.

Kruijt, Jacob P., and Walter Goddijn. 1972. "Verzuiling en ontzuiling als sociologisch proces," pages 227–263 in A.N.J. den Hollander et al., eds. *Drift en koers: Een halve eeuw sociale verandering in Nederland.* Assen: van Gorcum.

Kuik, Onno, Huib Jansen, and Johannes Opschoor. 1991. "The Netherlands," pages 106–140 in Jean-Philippe Barde and David Pearce, eds. *Valuing the Environment.* London: Earthscan Publications.

Kurzer, Paulette. 1993. *Business and Banking: Political Change and Economic Integration in Western Europe.* Ithaca: Cornell University Press.

————. 1995. "Assessing the Impact of the New Europe and the New Germany on Money, Welfare, and Policing in Small Countries." Paper presented at the annual meeting of the American Political Science Association, Chicago, August 31–September 3.

Lambert, Audrey. 1971. *The Making of the Dutch Landscape: An Historical Geography of the Netherlands.* New York: Seminar Press.

Landman, Nico. 1997. "The Islamic Broadcasting Foundation in the Netherlands: Platform or Arena?" pages 224–244 in Steven Vertovec and Ceri Peach, eds. *Islam in Europe: The Politics of Religion and Community.* New York: St. Martin's Press.

Laqueur, Walter. 1981. "Hollanditis: A New Stage in European Neutralism," *Commentary* 72 (August): 19–26.

Leijenaar, Monique. 1993. "A Battle for Power: Selecting Candidates in the Netherlands," pages 205–230 in Joni Lovenduski and Pippa Norris, eds. *Gender and Party Politics.* Thousand Oaks, CA: Sage.

Leijenaar, Monique, and Kees Niemöller. 1997. "The Netherlands," pages 114–136 in Pippa Norris, ed. *Passages to Power: Legislative Recruitment in Advanced Democracies.* Cambridge: Cambridge University Press.

Leurdijk, J. H. 1978. "De buitenlandse-politieke elite en het veiligsheidsbeleid van Nederland," in P. R. Baehr, Philip Everts, J. H. Leurdijk, Frans Roschar, Arie van Staden, C. P. van den Tempel, W. H. Vermeulen, and R. M. de Vree, eds. *Elite en buitenlandse politiek in Nederland.* The Hague: Staatsuitgeverij.

Lijphart, Arend. 1966. *The Trauma of Decolonization: The Dutch and West New Guinea.* New Haven: Yale University Press.

————. 1969. "Kentering in de Nederlandse politiek," *Acta Politica* 4 (April): 231–247.

————. 1974. "The Netherlands: Continuity and Change in Voting Behavior," pages 227–268 in Richard Rose, ed. *Electoral Behavior: A Comparative Handbook.* New York: Free Press.

————. 1975. *The Politics of Accommodation.* 2nd ed. Berkeley: University of California Press.

————. 1977. *Democracy in Plural Societies.* New Haven: Yale University Press.

————. 1984a. *Democracies: Patterns of Majoritarian and Consensus Government in Twenty-One Countries.* New Haven: Yale University Press.

_____. 1984b. "The Politics of Accommodation: Reflections—Fifteen Years Later," *Acta Politica* 19 (January): 9–18.

_____. 1989. "From the Politics of Accommodation to Adversarial Politics in the Netherlands: A Reassessment," pages 139–153 in Hans Daalder and Galen Irwin, eds. *Politics in the Netherlands: How Much Change?* London: Frank Cass.

Lipschits, Ivan. 1977. *Politieke stromingen in Nederland.* Deventer: Kluwer.

Lorwin, Val. 1971. "Segmented Pluralism: Ideological Cleavages and Political Cohesion in the Smaller European Democracies," *Comparative Politics* 3 (January): 141–175.

Lovenduski, Joni. 1986. *Women and European Politics.* Amherst: University of Massachusetts Press.

Lubbers, R.F.M. 1991. "Reactie van de minister-president," pages 138–142 in C. A. de Kam and J. de Haan, eds. *Terugtredende overheid: Realiteit of retoriek?* Schoonhoven: Academic Service.

Lubbers, R.F.M., and C. Lemckert. 1980. "The Influence of Natural Gas on the Dutch Economy," in Richard T. Griffiths, ed. *The Economy and Politics of the Netherlands.* The Hague: Martinus Nijhoff.

Lucardie, A.P.M. 1982. "Waar blijft Nieuw Rechts in Nederland?" pages 138–157 in *Jaarboek 1981.* Groningen: Documentatiecentrum Nederlandse Politieke Partijen, Rijksuniversiteit Groningen.

_____. 1988. "Conservatism in the Netherlands: Fragments and Fringe Groups," pages 78–97 in Brian Girvin, ed. *The Transformation of Contemporary Conservatism.* London: Sage.

_____. 1993. "Politieke partijen," pages 59–76 in R. B. Andeweg, A. Hoogerwerf, and J.J.A. Thomassen, eds. *Politiek in Nederland.* 4th ed. Alphen aan den Rijn: Samsom H. D. Tjeenk Willink.

Lucardie, A.P.M., and W. H. van Schuur. 1994. "GroenLinks," pages 261–269 in *Jaarboek 1994.* Groningen: Documentatiecentrum Nederlandse Politieke Partijen, Rijksuniversiteit Groningen.

Lucas, Henry. 1929. *The Low Countries and the Hundred Years' War, 1326–1347.* Ann Arbor: University of Michigan Press.

Luther, Martin. 1941. *Sendbrief an die Christen im Niederland.* Heerenveen: H. N. Werkman and De Blauwe Schuit.

Maas, P. F. 1986. "Coalition Negotiations in the Dutch Multi-Party System," *Parliamentary Affairs* 39 (April): 214–229.

Mair, Peter. 1994. "The Correlates of Consensus Democracy and the Puzzle of Dutch Politics," *West European Politics* 17 (October): 97–123.

Marshall, T. H. [1950] 1992. *Citizenship and Social Class.* Reprint, Concord, MA: Pluto Press.

Matreyek, Dee. 1998. *The Birth of Democracy in South Africa: The Churches Respond.* Claremont Graduate University: Ph.D. dissertation.

Maynard, Alan. 1975. *Health Care in the European Community.* London: Croom Helm.

Middendorp, C. P. 1977. *Progressiveness and Conservatism.* The Hague: Mouton.

_____. 1991. *Ideology in Dutch Politics: The Democratic System Reconsidered, 1970–1985.* Assen/Maastricht: van Gorcum.

Middendorp, C. P., and P. R. Kolkhuis Tanke. 1990. "Economic Voting in the Netherlands," *European Journal of Political Research* 18 (September): 535–555.

Mijnhardt, Wijnand. 1998. "The Dutch Republic as a Town," *Eighteenth Century Studies* 31 (Spring): 345–348.

Miller, Warren, and Philip Stouthard. 1975. "Confessional Attachment and Electoral Behavior in the Netherlands," *European Journal of Political Research* 3 (September): 219–258.

Mokken, Robert, and Frans Stokman. 1972. "Strijdpunten en electorale tegenstellingen (woningnood en milieuvervuiling)," *Acta Politica: De Nederlandse Kiezer, '71* 7 (January): 78–98.

Molenaar, Bert. 1990. *Rechters: De opkomst van de zwarte macht.* Bloemendaal: Aramith.

Molle, Willem, and Aad van Mourik. 1990. "Internal Market Policy," pages 25–32 in Menno Wolters and Peter Coffey, eds. *The Netherlands and EC Membership Evaluated.* London: Pinter.

Mommen, André. 1986. "Recept voor en heilstaat?" *Intermediair* 22 (March 13–28): 31–35.

———. 1990. "Politieke partijen en politieke stromingen: Een vergelijkend en historisch onderzoek," pages 181–204 in Uwe Becker, ed. *Maatschappij, Macht, Nederlandse Politiek.* Amsterdam: Het Spinhuis.

Montesquieu, Charles de Secondat, Baron de. 1964. "Hollande," pages 326–331 in *Oeuvres complètes.* Paris: Macmillan Co./Editions de Seuil.

Moree, Marjolein. 1994. "A Quiet Revolution: Working Mothers in the Netherlands, 1950–1990," *The Netherlands' Journal of Social Sciences* 30 (August): 25–42.

Morlan, Robert. 1974. *Gemeentepolitiek in debat.* Alphen aan den Rijn: Samsom.

Mulisch, Harry. [1973] 1989. *Last Call.* New York: Viking/Penguin. Translated by Adrienne Dixon.

Münchau, Wolfgang, and Gordon Cramb. 1997. "Debunking the Dutch Myth," *Financial Times,* September 18, page 13.

Murat, Ines. 1984. *Colbert.* Charlottesville: University Press of Virginia.

Murray, John. 1967. *Amsterdam in the Age of Rembrandt.* Norman: University of Oklahoma Press.

Neal, Larry. 1990. "The Dutch and English East India Companies Compared: Evidence from the Stock and Foreign Exchange Markets," pages 195–223 in James Tracy, ed. *The Rise of Merchant Empires: Long-Distance Trade in the Early Modern World, 1350–1750.* New York: Cambridge University Press.

Nederlandse Instituut voor Publieke Opinie (NIPO). 1956. *De Nederlandse kiezer: Een onderzoek naar zijn gedragingen en opvattingen.* The Hague: Staatsuitdrukkerij-en Uitgeverijbedrijf.

Need, Ariana, and Nan Dirk de Graaf. 1996. "The Changing Electorate of the Confessional Parties: Effects of Socialization and Intergenerational Religious Mobility in the 1956–1994 Elections," *The Netherlands' Journal of Social Sciences* 32 (November): 51–70.

Newton, Gerald. 1978. *The Netherlands: A Historical and Cultural Survey, 1795–1977.* Boulder: Westview Press.

Nooteboom, Cees. 1983. *Rituals.* Baton Rouge: Louisiana State University Press. Translated by Adrienne Dixon.

Olson, Mancur. 1969. "The Relationship Between Economics and the Other Social Sciences," pages 137–162 in Seymour Martin Lipset, ed. *Politics and the Social Sciences.* New York: Oxford University Press.

Olson, Susan. 1995. "Comparing Women's Rights Litigation in the Netherlands and the United States," *Polity* 28 (Winter): 189–216.

Oppenhuis, Erik. 1996. "The Netherlands: Small Party Evolution," pages 209–226 in Cees van der Eijk and Mark Franklin, eds. *Choosing Europe? The European Electorate and National Politics in the Face of Union.* Ann Arbor: University of Michigan Press.

Organisation for Economic Co-operation and Development. 1990. *Health Care Systems in Transition: The Search for Efficiency.* Paris: OECD.

_____. 1996. *Historical Statistics, 1994.* Paris: OECD.

Outshoorn, Joyce. 1986. "The Feminist Movement and Abortion Policy in the Netherlands," pages 64–84 in Drude Dahlerup, ed. *The New Women's Movement: Feminism and Political Power in Europe and the USA.* Beverly Hills, CA: Sage.

_____. 1992. "Women and Politics in the Netherlands," *European Journal of Political Research* 21 (June): 453–467.

_____. 1994. "State Feminism and 'Femocrats' in the Netherlands." Paper presented at the annual meeting of the American Political Science Association, New York, September 1–4.

Parker, Geoffrey. 1977. *The Dutch Revolt.* Ithaca: Cornell University Press.

Peters, B. Guy. 1991a. *The Politics of Taxation: A Comparative Perspective.* Cambridge, MA: Blackwell.

_____. 1991b. *European Politics Reconsidered.* New York: Holmes and Meier.

Phillips, Carla Rahn. 1990. "The Growth and Composition of Trade in the Iberian Empires, 1450–1750," pages 34–101 in James Tracy, ed. *The Rise of Merchant Empires: Long-Distance Trade in the Early Modern World, 1350–1750.* New York: Cambridge University Press.

Pinder, David. 1976. *The Netherlands.* Boulder: Westview Press.

Piryns, Piet. 1982. *Verslaafd in Nederland: Over drugs, dealers en gebruikers.* Amsterdam: van Gennep.

Post, Harry. 1989. *Pillarization: An Analysis of Dutch and Belgian Society.* Aldershot, England: Avebury.

Price, J. L. 1974. *Culture and Society in the Dutch Republic During the Seventeenth Century.* London: B. T. Batsford Ltd.

_____. 1994. *Holland and the Dutch Republic in the Seventeenth Century: The Politics of Particularism.* New York: Oxford University Press.

PSP (Pacifistisch Socialistische Partij). 1982. *Ontwapend: Geschiedenis van 25 jaar PSP.* Amsterdam: PSP.

Putnam, Robert. 1988. "Diplomacy and Domestic Politics: The Logic of Two-Level Games," *International Organization* 42 (Summer): 427–460.

Rath, Jan. 1988. "Political Action of Immigrants in the Netherlands: Class or Ethnicity?" *European Journal of Political Research* 16 (November): 623–644.

Riemen, Gerard. 1992. "Van aalmoes tot aan basisinkomen: Ontwikkelingen in de Nederlandse sociale zekerheid," pages 9–31 in Gerard Riemen, Thomas Rochon, Frans Verboekend, and Patrice Visser, eds. *Sociale Zekerheid: Achtergronden en perspectief.* Culemborg, NL: Phaedon.

Riemens, Hendrik. 1943. "The Growth of the Netherlands Economy," pages 151–163 in Bartholomew Landheer, ed. *The Netherlands.* Berkeley: University of California Press.

Rijkswaterstaat. 1956. *The Dutch and Their Dikes.* Amsterdam: De Bezige Bij.

Rochon, Thomas. 1982a. "Direct Democracy or Organized Futility? Action Groups in the Netherlands," *Comparative Political Studies* 15 (April): 3–28.

_____. 1982b. "Patterns and Consequences of Subcultural Integration of the Dutch Elite," pages 243–264 in Moshe Czudnowski, ed. *Does Who Governs Matter? Elite Circulation in Contemporary Societies.* DeKalb: Northern Illinois University Press.

_____. 1984. "The Creation of Political Institutions: Two Cases from the Netherlands," *International Journal of Comparative Sociology* 25 (September-December): 173–188.

_____. 1985. "Mobilizers and Challengers: Toward a Theory of New Party Success," *International Political Science Review* 6 (October): 419–439.

_____. 1987. "Beyond Perfection," *The Wilson Quarterly* 11 (Spring): 53–69.

_____. 1988. *Mobilizing for Peace: The Antinuclear Movements in Western Europe.* Princeton: Princeton University Press.

_____. 1991. "The Communist Party of the Netherlands," pages 615–617 in Richard Staar, ed. *1991 Yearbook on International Communist Affairs.* Stanford: Hoover Institution Press.

_____. 1992. "Sociale zekerheid in een internationaal perspectief," pages 73–87 in Gerard Riemen, Thomas Rochon, Frans Verboekend, and Patrice Visser, eds. *Sociale Zekerheid: Achtergronden en perspectief.* Culemborg, NL: Phaedon.

Rochon, Thomas, and John Strate. 1981. "Attachment to Political Parties in Industrial Democracies: An Aggregate Analysis." Paper presented at the annual meetings of the Midwest Political Science Association, Cincinnati, April 16–18.

Rogier, L. J. 1956. *Katholieke Herleving.* The Hague: Pax.

Rogowski, Ronald. 1989. *Commerce and Coalitions: How Trade Affects Domestic Political Alignments.* Princeton: Princeton University Press.

Rohde, David. 1997. *Endgame: The Betrayal and Fall of Srebrenica, Europe's Worst Massacre Since World War II.* New York: Farrar, Straus and Giroux.

Rood, Niels. 1989. "Voorwoord," pages 8–9 in *Het succes van Lubbers.* Amsterdam: GW Boeken.

Rose, Richard, and Derek Urwin. 1970. "Persistence and Change in Western Party Systems Since 1945," *Political Studies* 18 (September): 287–319.

Rosenthal, U. 1986. "Crisis Decision-Making in the Netherlands," *The Netherlands Journal of Sociology* 22 (October): 103–129.

_____. 1993. "De departementen," pages 236–262 in R. B. Andeweg, A. Hoogerwerf, and J.J.A. Thomassen, eds. *Politiek in Nederland.* 4th ed. Alphen aan den Rijn: Samsom H. D. Tjeenk Willink.

Rowen, Herbert. 1986. *John de Witt: Statesman of the "True Freedom."* New York: Cambridge University Press.

_____. 1988. *The Princes of Orange: The Stadholders in the Dutch Republic.* New York: Cambridge University Press.

Rozemond, S. 1983. "Buitenlandse politiek en Nederlands belang," *Acta Politica* 18 (January): 3–35.

Russell, Robert. 1978. "The Atlantic Alliance in Dutch Foreign Policy," pages 169–185 in J. H. Leurdijk, ed. *The Foreign Policy of the Netherlands.* Alphen aan den Rijn: Sijthoff and Noordhoff.

Schama, Simon. 1988. *The Embarrassment of Riches: An Interpretation of Dutch Culture in the Golden Age.* Berkeley: University of California Press.

Schmitter, Phillipe. 1979. "Still the Century of Corporatism?" pages 7–52 in Phillipe Schmitter and Gerhard Lehmbruch, eds. *Trends Toward Corporatist Intermediation.* Beverly Hills, CA: Sage.

Schöffer, Ivo. 1973. *A Short History of the Netherlands.* 2nd rev. ed. Amsterdam: Allert de Lange.

Scholten, G. H. 1968. *De sociaal-economische raad en de ministeriële verantwoordelijkheid.* Meppel: Boom.

Scholten, Ilja. 1980. "Does Consociationalism Exist? A Critique of the Dutch Experience," pages 329–354 in Richard Rose, ed. *Electoral Participation.* Beverly Hills, CA: Sage.

_____. 1987. "Corporatism and the Neo-Liberal Backlash in the Netherlands," pages 120–152 in Ilja Scholten, ed. *Political Stability and Neo-Corporatism.* Beverly Hills, CA: Sage.

Siccama, Jan. 1985. "The Netherlands Depillarized: Security Policy in a New Domestic Context," pages 113–170 in Gregory Flynn, ed. *NATO's Northern Allies.* London: Rowman and Allanheld.

Singh, Wazir. 1972. *Policy Development: A Study of the Social and Economic Council of the Netherlands.* Rotterdam: Rotterdam University Press.

Sinner, Louis. 1973. *De wortels van de Nederlandse politiek.* Amsterdam: Wetenschappelijke Uitgeverij.

Smeets, Ingrid. 1995. "Opkomst bij de verkiezingen voor de Tweede Kamer," pages 56–70 in J.J.M. van Holsteyn and B. Niemöller, eds. *De Nederlandse kiezer 1994.* Leiden: DSWO Press, Rijksuniversiteit Leiden.

Smits, José. 1996. "Privatisering van de sociale zekerheid is een heel slecht idee," *De Volkskrant,* January 13, page 43.

Sociaal en Cultureel Planbureau. 1993. *Social and Cultural Report 1992.* Rijswijk: Sociaal en Cultureel Planbureau.

Sociaal-Wetenschappelijk Instituut van de Vrije Universiteit Amsterdam. 1967. *De Nederlandse kiezers in 1967.* Amsterdam: Agon Elsevier.

Steensgaard, Niels. 1990. "The Growth and Composition of the Long-Distance Trade of England and the Dutch Republic Before 1750," pages 102–152 in James Tracy, ed. *The Rise of Merchant Empires: Long-Distance Trade in the Early Modern World, 1350–1750.* New York: Cambridge University Press.

Stråth, Bo. 1987. *The Politics of De-Industrialization: The Contraction of the West European Shipbuilding Industry.* New York: Croom Helm.

Szirmai, Adam. 1984. "How Do We Really Feel About Income Equalization?" *The Netherlands Journal of Sociology* 20 (October): 115–133.

_____. 1988. *Inequality Observed: A Study of Attitudes Towards Income Inequality.* Brookfield, VT: Avebury/Gower Publishing Company.

te Grotenhuis, H., and J. Dronkers. 1989. "Unequal Opportunities in a West-European Welfare State," *The Netherlands' Journal of Social Sciences* 25 (April): 18–29.

Thomassen, Jacques. 1976a. "Party Identification as a Cross-National Concept: Its Meaning in the Netherlands," pages 63–79 in Ian Budge, Ivor Crewe, and Dennis Farlie, eds. *Party Identification and Beyond.* New York: John Wiley and Sons.

_____. 1976b. *Kiezers en gekozenen in een representatieve democratie.* Alphen aan den Rijn: Samsom.

Thomassen, Jacques, and Jan van Deth. 1989. "How New Is Dutch Politics?" pages 61–78 in Hans Daalder and Galen Irwin, eds. *Politics in the Netherlands: How Much Change?* London: Frank Cass.

Thomassen, J.J.A., and M. L. Zielonka-Goei. 1992. "Het parlement als volksvertegenwoordiging," pages 195–224 in J.J.A. Thomassen, M.P.C.M. van Schendelen, and M. L. Zielonka-Goei, eds. *De geachte afgevaardigde: Hoe kamerleden denken over het Nederlandse parlement.* Muiderberg: Dick Coutinho.

Thurlings, J.M.G. 1971. "The Case of Dutch Catholicism: A Contribution to the Theory of Pluralistic Society," *Sociologia Neerlandica* 7 (number 2): 118–136.

———. 1978. *De Wankele Zuil: Nederlandse Katholieken tussen assimilatie en pluralisme.* 2nd ed. Deventer: van Loghum Slaterus.

———. 1979. "Pluralism and Assimilation in the Netherlands, with Special Reference to Dutch Catholicism," *International Journal of Comparative Sociology* 20 (March-June): 82–100.

Timmermans, A., and W. E. Bakema. 1990. "Conflicten in Nederlandse kabinetten," pages 175–192 in R. B. Andeweg, ed. *Ministers en Ministerraad.* The Hague: SDU Uitgeverij.

Timmermans, J. M., and J. W. Becker. 1985. "Social Planning in the Netherlands: Organization and Practice," pages 87–106 in Ashok Dutt and Frank Costa, eds. *Public Planning in the Netherlands: Perspectives and Change Since the Second World War.* Oxford: Oxford University Press.

Tömmel, Ingeborg. 1992. "Decentralisation of Regional Development Policies in the Netherlands—A New Type of State Intervention?" *West European Politics* 15 (April): 107–125.

Toonen, Theo. 1987. "The Netherlands: A Decentralized Unitary State in a Welfare Society," *West European Politics* 10 (October): 108–129.

———. 1996. "On the Administrative Condition of Politics: Administrative Transformation in the Netherlands," *West European Politics* 19 (July): 609–632.

Traag, Annemieke. 1990. "Equal Treatment of Women," pages 182–190 in Menno Wolters and Peter Coffey, eds. *The Netherlands and EC Membership Evaluated.* London: Pinter.

Tracy, James. 1990. *Holland Under Habsburg Rule, 1506–1566: The Formation of a Body Politic.* Berkeley: University of California Press.

Urwin, Derek. 1995. *The Community of Europe.* 2nd ed. New York: Longman.

Valkman, Otto. 1982. *De BKR en de krisis van de verzorgingsstaat.* Amsterdam: Boekmanstichting.

van Amersfoort, Hans, and Rinus Penninx. 1994. "Regulating Migration in Europe: The Dutch Experience, 1960–1992," *Annals of the American Academy of Political and Social Science* 534 (July): 133–146.

van Campen, S.I.P. 1958. *The Quest for Security: Some Aspects of Netherlands Foreign Policy, 1945–1950.* The Hague: Martinus Nijhoff.

van Delden, A. Th. 1993. "Externe adviesorganen van de centrale overheid," pages 145–165 in R. B. Andeweg, A. Hoogerwerf, and J.J.A. Thomassen, eds. *Politiek in Nederland.* 4th ed. Alphen aan den Rijn: Samsom H. D. Tjeenk Willink.

van de Velde, Hella. 1994. *Vrouwen van de Partij: De integratie van vrouwen in politieke partijen in Nederland, 1919–1990.* Leiden: DSWO Press, University of Leiden.

van den Berg, H. 1980. "Inleiding: Ontwikkelingen in het welzijnswerk," pages 11–46 in H. van den Berg, ed. *Welzijnswerk en samenleving.* Assen: van Gorcum.

van den Berg, J.Th.J. 1981. "Parlement tussen partijen en actiegroepen," *Acta Politica* 16 (number 4): 490–499.

———. 1990. "De Minister-President: 'Aanjager van noodzakelijk beleid,'" pages 97–125 in R. B. Andeweg, ed. *Ministers en Ministerraad.* The Hague: SDU Uitgeverij.

———. 1993. "De regering," pages 209–235 in R. B. Andeweg, A. Hoogerwerf, and J.J.A. Thomassen, eds. *Politiek in Nederland.* 4th ed. Alphen aan den Rijn: Samsom H. D. Tjeenk Willink.

van den Berg, J.Th.J., and H.A.A. Molleman. 1974. *Crisis in de Nederlandse politiek.* Alphen aan den Rijn: Samsom.

van den Brink, J.R.M. 1984. *Zoeken naar een Heilstaat.* Amsterdam: Elsevier.

van der Eijk, Cees, Mark Franklin, and Tom Mackie. 1996. "The Dog That Did Not Bark," pages 268–282 in Cees van der Eijk and Mark Franklin, eds. *Choosing Europe? The European Electorate and National Politics in the Face of Union.* Ann Arbor: University of Michigan Press.

van der Eijk, Cees, and Kees Niemöller. 1983. *Electoral Change in the Netherlands: Empirical Results and Methods of Measurement.* Amsterdam: CT Press.

_____. 1992. "The Netherlands," pages 255–283 in Mark Franklin, Thomas Mackie, and Henry Valen, eds. *Electoral Change: Responses to Evolving Social and Attitudinal Structures in Western Countries.* New York: Cambridge University Press.

_____. 1994. "Election Studies in the Netherlands: Pluralism and Accommodation," *European Journal of Political Research* 25 (April): 323–342.

van der Hek, Arie. 1977. "De parlementaire bemoeienis met het buitenlands beleid," pages 9–20 in W. F. van Eekelen et al., eds. *Parlement, partijen en buitenlands politiek.* Baarn: Uitgeverij In Den Toren.

van der Lippe, Tanja. 1994. "Spouses and Their Division of Labour," *The Netherlands' Journal of Social Sciences* 30 (August): 43–62.

van der Meer, F. M., and Roborgh, L. J. 1993. *Ambtenaren in Nederland: Omvang, bureaucratisering en representativiteit van het ambtelijk apparaat.* Alphen aan den Rijn: Samsom H. D. Tjeenk Willink.

van der Staay, A. J. 1966. "Kanttekeningen bij een deelverschijnsel," pages 108–127 in F. E. Frenkel, ed. *Provo: Kanttekeningen bij een deelverschijnsel.* Amsterdam: Polak and van Gennep.

van der Veen, Romke, and Willem Trommel. 1997. "Managed Liberalization of the Dutch Welfare State." Paper presented at the conference on Rethinking the Welfare State, Montreal, July 5–7.

van der Wee, Herman. 1993. *The Low Countries in the Early Modern World.* Aldershot, U.K.: Variorum.

van Deth, Jan. 1992. "Het constitutionele en politieke bestel," pages 17–36 in J. van Deth and P. Schuszler, eds. *Nederlandse staatkunde.* Muiderberg: Dick Coutinho.

van Deth, Jan, and Peter Geurts. 1989. "Value Orientation, Left-Right Placement and Voting," *European Journal of Political Research* 17 (January): 17–34.

van Deursen, A. T. 1991. *Plain Lives in a Golden Age: Popular Culture, Religion and Society in Seventeenth-Century Holland.* New York: Cambridge University Press.

van Donselaar, Jaap. 1993. "The Extreme Right and Racist Violence in the Netherlands," pages 46–61 in Tore Björgo and Rob Witte, eds. *Racist Violence in Europe.* New York: St. Martin's Press.

van Gelderen, Martin. 1992. *The Political Thought of the Dutch Revolt, 1555–1590.* New York: Cambridge University Press.

_____. 1993. *The Dutch Revolt.* New York: Cambridge University Press.

van Geleuken, B. P. 1990. *Mestbeleid en milieu: Wet van behoud van ellende?* Zeist: Kerckebosch.

van Goor, H. 1993. "Politieke participatie van collectiviteiten: Pressiegroepen," pages 101–120 in R. B. Andeweg, A. Hoogerwerf, and J.J.A. Thomassen, eds. *Politiek in Nederland.* 4th ed. Alphen aan den Rijn: Samsom H. D. Tjeenk Willink.

van Houtte, Jan. 1977. *An Economic History of the Low Countries, 800–1800.* London: Weidenfeld and Nicolson.

van Kemenade, J. A. 1968. *De Katholieken en hun Onderwijs, een sociologisch onderzoek naar de betekenis van Katholiek onderwijs onder ouders en docenten.* Meppel: J. A. Boom en Zoon.

van Kersbergen, Kees. 1991. "De Nederlandse verzorgingsstaat in vergelijkend perspectief," pages 265–293 in Uwe Becker, ed. *Maatschappij, Macht, Nederlandse Politiek.* Amsterdam: Het Spinhuis.

———. 1995. *Social Capitalism: A Study of Christian Democracy and the Welfare State.* New York: Routledge.

van Koppen, Peter. 1992. "Judicial Policy-Making in the Netherlands: The Case-by-Case Method," *West European Politics* 15 (July): 80–92.

van Lier, Hubert. 1988. "Land-Use Planning on Its Way to Environmental Planning," pages 89–107 in Martin Whitby and John Ollerenshaw, eds. *Land-Use and the European Environment.* London: Pinter.

van Mierlo, Hans. 1986. "Depillarisation and the Decline of Consociationalism in the Netherlands, 1970–1985," *West European Politics* 9 (January): 97–119.

van Mierlo, J.G.A., and L. G. Gerrichhauzen. 1988. *Het particulier initiatief in de nederlandse verzorgingsmaatschappij.* Lochem: De Tijdstroom.

van Noort, W. 1988. *Bevlogen Beweging: Een vergelijking van de anti-kernenergie-, kraak- en milieubeweging.* Amsterdam: Sua.

van Praag, Philip, Jr. 1991. "The Netherlands: Action and Protest in a Depillarized Society," pages 295–320 in Dieter Rucht, ed. *Research on Social Movements.* Boulder: Westview Press; Frankfurt: Campus Verlag.

———. 1993. "Hoe uniek is de Nederlandse consensusdemokratie?" pages 151–178 in Uwe Becker, ed. *Nederlandse politiek in historisch en vergelijkend perspectief.* Amsterdam: Het Spinhuis.

van Putten, Jan. 1980. *Haagse Machten: Verslag van een politicologisch onderzoek naar de totstandkoming van acht regeringsmaatregelen.* The Hague: Staatsuitgeverij.

———. 1982. "Policy Styles in the Netherlands: Negotiation and Conflict," pages 168–196 in Jeremy Richardson, ed. *Policy Styles in Western Europe.* London: Allen and Unwin.

van Rhijn, A. A. 1944. "De sociale politiek," pages 225–262 in A. A. van Rhijn, ed. *Nieuw Nederland.* New York: Querido.

van Roozendaal, Peter. 1993. "Cabinets in the Netherlands (1918–1990): The Importance of 'Dominant' and 'Central' Parties," *European Journal of Political Research* 23 (January): 35–54.

van Schendelen, M.P.C.M. 1992. "Parlement, pressiegroepen en lobby's," pages 225–248 in J.J.A. Thomassen, M.P.C.M. van Schendelen, and M. L. Zielonka-Goei, eds. *De geachte afgevaardigde: Hoe kamerleden denken over het Nederlandse parlement.* Muiderberg: Dick Coutinho.

———. 1993. "Het parlement," pages 187–208 in R. B. Andeweg, A. Hoogerwerf, and J.J.A. Thomassen, eds. *Politiek in Nederland.* 4th ed. Alphen aan den Rijn: Samsom H. D. Tjeenk Willink.

van Staden, Alfred. 1978. "Role Conceptions in the Post-War Foreign Policy of the Netherlands," pages 119–135 in J. H. Leurdijk, ed. *The Foreign Policy of the Netherlands.* Alphen aan den Rijn: Sijthoff and Noordhoff.

———. 1993. "Nederland in internationale organisaties," pages 341–366 in R. B. Andeweg, A. Hoogerwerf, and J.J.A. Thomassen, eds. *Politiek in Nederland.* 4th ed. Alphen aan den Rijn: Samsom H. D. Tjeenk Willink.

van Vree, Wilbert. 1994. *Nederland als vergaderland: Opkomst en verbreiding van een vergaderregime.* Groningen: Wolters-Noordhoff.

van Vught, F. A. 1993. "Nationale overheidsplanning," pages 166–186 in R. B. Andeweg, A. Hoogerwerf, and J.J.A. Thomassen, eds. *Politiek in Nederland.* 4th ed. Alphen aan den Rijn: Samsom H. D. Tjeenk Willink.

van Wijnen, H. A. 1984. *Willem Drees, Democrat.* Weesp: van Holkema and Warendorf.

van Zijst, Hans. 1993. "A Change in the Culture," *The Environmental Forum* 10 (May-June): 12–17.

Veenstra, W. 1976. "Openbare hoorzittingen in het parlement," *Acta Politica* 11 (July): 383–405.

Verba, Sidney, Norman Nie, and Jae-on Kim. 1978. *Participation and Political Equality: A Seven-Nation Comparison.* New York: Cambridge University Press.

Verboekend, Frans. 1992. "Politieke en sociale achtergronden," pages 33–57 in Gerard Riemen, Thomas Rochon, Frans Verboekend, and Patrice Visser, eds. *Sociale Zekerheid: Achtergronden en perspectief.* Culemborg, NL: Phaedon.

Verrips, K. 1987. "Noblemen, Farmers and Labourers: A Civilizing Offensive in a Dutch Village," *The Netherlands' Journal of Social Sciences* 23 (April): 3–16.

Vis, Jan. 1983. "Coalition Government in a Constitutional Monarchy: The Dutch Experience," pages 153–168 in Vernon Bogdanor, ed. *Coalition Government in Western Europe.* London: Heineman Educational Books.

Visscher, G. 1976. "Wijziging van de enquêtewet," *Acta Politica* 11 (October): 525–533.

Visser, Jelle. 1990. "Continuity and Change in Dutch Industrial Relations," pages 199–242 in Guido Baglioni and Colin Crouch, eds. *European Industrial Relations: The Challenge of Flexibility.* London: Sage.

_____. 1993. "Work Councils and Trade Unions: Rivals or Allies," *The Netherlands' Journal of Social Sciences* 29 (June): 64–92.

Visser, Jelle, and Anton Hemerijck. 1997. *A Dutch Miracle: Job Growth, Welfare Reform and Corporatism in the Netherlands.* Amsterdam: University of Amsterdam Press.

Visser, Patrice. 1989. *Overlegeconomie.* Assen: van Gorcum.

_____. 1992. "Economische aspecten van de sociale zekerheid," pages 59–72 in Gerard Riemen, Thomas Rochon, Frans Verboekend, and Patrice Visser, eds. *Sociale Zekerheid: Achtergronden en perspectief.* Culemborg, NL: Phaedon.

Vlekke, Bernard. 1943. "The Dutch Before 1581," pages 17–38 in Bartholomew Landheer, ed. *The Netherlands.* Berkeley: University of California Press.

_____. 1945. *Evolution of the Dutch Nation.* New York: Roy Publishers.

Voerman, Gerrit. 1995. "The Netherlands: Losing Colours, Turning Green," pages 109–127 in Dick Richardson and Chris Rootes, eds. *The Green Challenge: The Development of Green Parties in Europe.* New York: Routledge.

Voerman, Gerrit, and Paul Lucardie. 1992. "The Extreme Right in the Netherlands," *European Journal of Political Research* 22 (July): 35–54.

Voorhoeve, Joris. 1979. *Peace, Profits and Principles: A Study of Dutch Foreign Policy.* The Hague: Martinus Nijhoff.

Vossen, Hélène. 1991. "Production of Sexual Differences in Catholic 'Life Schools,' 1947–1968," pages 82–103 in Joke Hermsen and Alkeline van Lenning, eds. *Sharing the Difference: Feminist Debates in Holland.* New York: Routledge.

Wallerstein, Immanuel. 1974. *The Modern World System: Capitalist Agriculture and the Origins of the European World-Economy in the Sixteenth Century.* New York: Academic Press.

———. 1980. *The Modern World System II: Mercantilism and the Consolidation of the European World-Economy, 1600–1750.* New York: Academic Press.

Weil, Gordon. 1970. *The Benelux Nations: The Politics of Small-Country Democracies.* New York: Holt, Rinehart and Winston.

Werkgroep Afdeling Politicologie van de Vrije Universiteit te Amsterdam. 1971. "Invloed van demonstranten op de standpunten van Tweede-Kamerleden," *Acta Politica* 6 (October): 417–440.

Westerman, Frank, and Bart Rijs. 1997. *Srebrenica: The Darkest Scenario.* Amsterdam: Contact.

Wilensky, Harold. 1975. *The Welfare State and Equality.* Berkeley: University of California Press.

Wilson, Charles. 1957. *Profit and Power: A Study of England and the Dutch Wars.* London: Longmans, Green and Co.

———. 1968. *The Dutch Republic and the Civilisation of the Seventeenth Century.* New York: McGraw-Hill.

Wilterdink, Nico. 1990. "The Monarchy Contested: Anti-Monarchism in the Netherlands," *The Netherlands' Journal of Social Sciences* 26 (April): 3–16.

Windmuller, John. 1969. *Labor Relations in the Netherlands.* Ithaca: Cornell University Press.

Witte, Rob. 1996. *Racist Violence and the State.* New York: Longman.

Wolinetz, Steven. 1988. "The Netherlands: Continuity and Change in a Fragmented Party System," pages 130–158 in Steven Wolinetz, ed. *Parties and Party Systems in Liberal Democracies.* New York: Routledge.

———. 1989. "Socio-Economic Bargaining in the Netherlands: Redefining the Post-War Policy Coalition," pages 79–98 in Hans Daalder and Galen Irwin, eds. *Politics in the Netherlands: How Much Change?* London: Frank Cass.

———. 1993. "Reconstructing Dutch Social Democracy," *West European Politics* 16 (January): 97–111.

———. 1995. "J. M. (Joop) den Uyl," pages 105–111 in David Wilsford, ed. *Political Leaders of Europe: A Biographical Dictionary.* Westport, CT: Greenwood Press.

WRR (Wetenschappelijke Raad voor het Regeringsbeleid). 1989. *Allochtonenbelied.* Report no. 36. The Hague: SDU Uitgeverij.

Zeegers, L.H.L., G. Dekker, and J.W.M. Peeters. 1967. *God in Nederland.* Amsterdam: van Ditmar.

Zielonka-Goei, Mei Lan. 1992. "Members Marginalising Themselves? Intra-Party Participation in the Netherlands," *West European Politics* 15 (April): 93–106.

Index

["